STEPHEN DAVIES
BRUCE LYONS
with
HUW DIXON
PAUL GEROSKI

Economics of industrial organisation

SURVEYS IN ECONOMICS

LONGMAN
London and New York

LONGMAN GROUP UK LIMITED
Longman House, Burnt Mill, Harlow
Essex CM20 2JE, England
and Associated Companies throughout the world

Published in the United States of America
by Longman Inc., New York

First published 1988

600 340 8870

BRITISH LIBRARY CATALOGUING IN PUBLICATION DATA
Economics of industrial organisation.——
    (Surveys in economics).
    1. Industrial organization (Economic
    theory)
    I. Davies, Stephen, *1948*
    II. Series
    338.7   HD38

ISBN 0-582-29567-X

LIBRARY OF CONGRESS CATALOGING IN PUBLICATION DATA
Economics of industrial organisation/Stephen Davies . . . [et al.].
        p.   cm. ——(Surveys in economics)
    Includes bibliographies and indexes.
    ISBN 0-582-29567-X
    1. Industrial organisation (Economic theory)   I. Davies, Stephen,
    1948–   . II. Series.
    HD2326.E237 1988
    338.7——dc19

87–30261
CIP

Set in 10/12 Comp/Edit Times Roman

Produced by Longman Singapore Publishers (Pte) Ltd.
Printed in Singapore

340887

Contents

Editors' preface

The aim of this series is to survey the primary literature on selected economic topics at a level designed for intermediate and advanced undergraduate students. Few textbooks contain an adequate perspective on the development of their subject, and still fewer portray the focus of current research; but it has become progressively more difficult to supplement textbooks by selecting journal articles which provide a satisfactory, comprehensive, coherent and self-contained treatment of a topic, at a length and level of technique within the capacity of a student. The widening gap between the pedagogic and the professional literature stems partly from the increasing volume of the latter, the consequent pressure to abbreviate manuscripts, and the dissemination of research in a growing number of more specialised journals. It also reflects the increasing technical sophistication of the subject in all spheres of application, and particularly the integration of theoretical and empirical analysis which characterises much recent research, in marked contrast to the teaching of economics and econometrics in separate compartments of most undergraduate courses.

The surveys have been written for those who are studying or have completed intermediate courses in economic theory and quantitative methods. They aim to guide the reader through the professional literature, paying particular attention to the introduction of empirical work and to synthesising relevant contributions from different areas of specialisation. The major issues are explained and attention is directed towards the most useful sources for further study. By providing a comprehensive overview of its subject, each survey enables users to pursue particular aspects of the topic in greater depth through the medium of primary sources, within a frame of reference which enables the significance of those individual contributions to be assessed in their broader context.

The subjects of the surveys have been selected for their economic importance and for the extent and inaccessibility of the literature in journals and monographs devoted to them. Each is complete and self-contained, and can be read without reference to the surveys of related topics which appear in the same volume. The volumes themselves are not intended to replace textbooks by providing comprehensive coverage of their area, but to supplement textbooks by conveying the current flavour of the state of the art.

The series as a whole has been designed for second- and third-year undergraduate students at universities and polytechnics, but individual surveys will also appeal to postgraduate students and to practising economists in government, nationalised industries and the private sector who wish to update their knowledge of the subject. Economics has developed rapidly in the last two decades, and even active members of the profession have experienced difficulty in keeping pace with progress outside their own field of specialisation. It is hoped that the series will prove useful to this wider readership of continuing students as well as those beginning their education in economics.

Robert Millward
Michael T. Sumner
George Zis

SURVEYS IN ECONOMICS
Series editors: Robert Millward, Michael T. Sumner and George Zis

Economics of industrial organisation
International economics
Labour economics
Macroeconomics
Public sector economics

Forthcoming:
Monetary economics

CHAPTER ONE

Introduction[1]

Stephen Davies and Bruce Lyons

As a prelude to the detailed and specialised surveys which are to follow, we intend in this introductory survey to establish an overall perspective: how is industrial organisation to be defined? What are its roots in economic theory? What are the prevailing methodologies of analysis? What are the implications for public policy? To answer these questions, we offer a short history of thought in industrial organisation, which is presented in the following two sections. The first traces what might be called the mainstream over the last thirty years; this comprises the neo-classical (broadly defined) approach which has dominated industrial organisation, at least as measured by its share of practitioners in the subject. But our second section acknowledges that there are other ways of looking at the subject, and we describe three: Austrian, Schumpeterian and Marxist. Since these schools of thought appear only infrequently in the following surveys, this part of our Introduction is, in some ways, the most important. It may be particularly useful to reread this section following the surveys. The third section introduces the five main surveys of the book.

We should acknowledge at the outset an important omission in this Introduction, and indeed the volume as a whole. As explained presently, we interpret industrial organisation as the study of the organisation of industries rather than the firms therein. In terms of the producer side of micro-economics, this places the emphasis on oligopoly theory and its applications rather than the theory of the firm. This delineation is not totally arbitrary – different traditions can be discerned in the literature – but, to be honest, our main motive for so limiting this volume is the simple and obvious one of space constraints. However, an unfortunate consequence is that we largely ignore the important contributions over the last two decades of O. E. Williamson. Building on the earlier insights of Coase (1937), Williamson's transactions costs approach has revolutionised parts of the subject, in particular the explanation of why firms exist in terms of their efficiency relative to the market; the motives for vertical integration; and explanations of the evolution of internal organisational form (the U and M forms).[2]

1. Mainstream industrial organisation theory

We identify the dawn of the modern economics of industrial organisation (I.O.) with the work of Joe Bain in the 1950s. This is not to deny the importance of earlier writers. Bain's ideas owe much to the writings of Mason (1949) and Clark (1940), and we argue below that contemporary theoretical analysis flows more directly from the contributions of Chamberlin, Hotelling and the nineteenth-century economists, Cournot and Bertrand. Nor is it true that his approach to the subject has attracted universal approval even among neo-classicists (an appellation to be defined in due course); even from the early days, Bain and others belonging to what is sometimes loosely referred to as the Harvard School, have been the subject of persistent criticism from other notable economists, especially those such as Stigler, Director, Friedman and Demsetz emanating from Chicago. Moreover, we shall not argue that Bain is one of the theoretical giants of the subject; apart from highlighting the role of entry barriers and the notion of limit pricing, his impact on the analytical armoury of I.O. theory is modest. Rather, his historical role was to popularise a framework or paradigm within which to approach the subject. This structure–conduct–performance (S–C–P) paradigm provided a definition of the subject matter of I.O. which has prevailed with only minor modification up to the present time. Perhaps more important, it established an analytical and empirical methodology which was to dominate the subject for at least twenty years. This entailed theoretical analysis of one or more of the causal links in the S–C–P trilogy which was typically subjected to empirical testing against large scale inter-industry data, increasingly with the use of econometric techniques. There is a loose analogy which may be made with the impact of large-scale econometric models on the development of macro-economics over roughly the same period.

The preface to Bain's (1959) textbook delineates quite clearly his own interests:

> I am concerned with the environmental setting within which enterprises operate and in how they behave in these settings as producers, sellers' and buyers. By contrast, I do not take an internal approach, more appropriate to the field of management science, such as would inquire how enterprises do and should behave in ordering their internal operations and would attempt to instruct them accordingly.
>
> Being concerned in the main with the market behaviour of enterprises, I have given major emphasis to the relative incidence of competitive and monopolistic tendencies in various industries or markets. Correspondingly, my primary unit for analysis is the industry or competing group of firms, rather than the individual firm or the economywide aggregate of enterprises.   (ibid.: vii–viii)

This is a fairly exclusive vision of the subject which abstracts from what is usually termed 'managerial economics' and also 'the theory of the firm'. Nevertheless it is a definition which survives today under the title of 'industrial organisation' and one which we follow in this volume.[3]

It is fashionable among modern scholars in this field to suggest that most of the early work in I.O. was devoid of formal theoretical content, preferring instead a more *ad hoc*, even cavalier, approach to theory. A reading of Bain's work and that of his immediate followers tends to confirm that this particular fashion is not without foundations. To be fair, Bain never claimed to be anything other than an avowed empiricist.[4] He suggests the theoretical foundations of the subject reside in 'modern Price Theory',[5] by which we take him to mean the work of Clark and Mason coupled with more traditional price theory. In particular he identifies two 'levels of assumptions', the first concerning the demand and cost setting and the motivation of firms, and the second the influence of market structure. The world is one of downward-sloping demand curves, L-shaped cost curves and profit-maximising firms, and against this backcloth 'market structure may logically be expected (and is observed) to influence the conduct of firms in maximising profits, the interaction of the conduct of competing firms in the same market, and the end performance emerging from the industry' (ibid.: 27). This quote captures the essence of the paradigm. Bain identifies three elements of structure from received theory:

1. The *concentration of sellers*. This is associated closely in his view with the scope for collusive restraint.
2. The degree of *product differentiation*. Differentiated products entail downward-sloping demand curves at the firm level and thus at least 'a little bit of monopoly power' in even large number industries. Equally important, differentiation is typically associated with advertising, and this means an additional policy variable (or element of conduct) in the oligopoly arena.
3. The *condition of entry*, by which is meant 'the degree to which established firms can persistently elevate their prices above minimal average or competitive costs before making it attractive for new firms to enter' (ibid.: 33). This is expected to influence conduct and performance by placing limits on the price obtaining, either because incumbent firms deliberately limit price or because the supply of new entrants depresses price if incumbents do not.

Looking back a quarter of a century later, his explanations of how these elements of structure determine the behaviour or conduct of firms do appear *ad hoc* and imprecise. To be fair, however, he was well aware that the theory of product differentiation was underdeveloped and he himself, along with Sylos-Labini (1956), was responsible for some advances in the theory of limit pricing. But on the central issue of concentration and collusion, we are left with vague assertions that the likelihood of the latter increases, the higher is the former.

Whatever his theoretical limitations, Bain can certainly claim to have been highly influential with respect to empirical methodology:

> I have abandoned, in the main, the common approach of studying all these things together in a series of separate industry studies. Although the industry-study approach has a demonstrated entertainment value, it is seriously deficient in that it encourages a casuistic process of 'generalising from a single instance'; correspondingly is prone to engender confusion between accidental associations and fundamental tendencies toward association; nearly always deals with too many parameters and variables for effective analytical handling; and provides no straight or passable road toward scientific generalisations. (ibid.: viii)

This signalled a major break in the prevailing methodology of the subject – case studies were out, to be replaced by large-scale comparative studies of inter-industry differences. To those economists schooled in the last twenty years, Bain's comments will sound familiarly like a call for the econometric methodology. His own work largely pre-dated the econometric revolution and if we suggest that it now appears a little crude technically this is hardly a criticism. Neither do we wish to underplay his painstaking efforts in data collection in a period when official Census data was far less comprehensive than today. The 1960s represent a period of rapid diffusion of structure–conduct–performance and the econometric approach, especially in the US. The research output of this period is brilliantly surveyed in Scherer's (1970) textbook. This summarises the developments made in the subject with an awe-inspiring knowledge and command of the literature, skilfully intertwining and interpreting other case study and cross-section evidence. The strength of this text does not lie in any great originality; but as a summary of the work of a generation of economists working in a specific field, it is an invaluable bible. Figure 1.1, reproduced from Scherer, illustrates two important features of the post-Bain literature. Firstly, the various elements of S–C–P had been noticeably widened. Especially significant, the determinants of two elements of conduct, advertising and research and development, had generated substantial bodies of literature. Secondly, upward pointing arrows indicate a realisation of reverse causalities: not only does structure affect conduct, but also conduct, say advertising, may influence structure. The system had become simultaneous, reinforcing our analogy with the macro model.

This, then, was the heyday of S–C–P, but with a notable change in emphasis from Bain's original conception. Scherer expresses it as follows:

> Bain stresses the formulation of direct empirical links between market structure and economic performance, deemphasising intermediate conduct. Only one chapter out of fifteen in his text is devoted explicitly to the analysis of conduct. In this volume, by contrast, much of the analysis in Chapters 5 through 16 attacks the question of structure-performance associations by focusing intensely on the business conduct which spans those phenomena. If the difference in approaches had to be characterised by means of labels, it could be said that Bain is predominantly a structuralist, while the author of the present volume is a behaviorist.
> (Scherer: 1970)

This comment on Bain is undoubtedly justified; moreover Scherer's greater attention to conduct reflects a general trend within the literature of his time. It is noticeable, however, that most of the exciting developments during the 1960s were of an essentially empirical nature. There remained a distinctive shortage of what might be called custom-made theory; the analytical backbone of Scherer's survey resided in simple models of price leadership, some developments of limit price theory, and informal (but perceptive) discussions of the conditions facilitating or militating against collusion. While Scherer does include an intuitive discussion of game theory, this is relatively primitive in the light of what was to come.

Both Bain and Scherer were anxious to relate their subject to policy issues

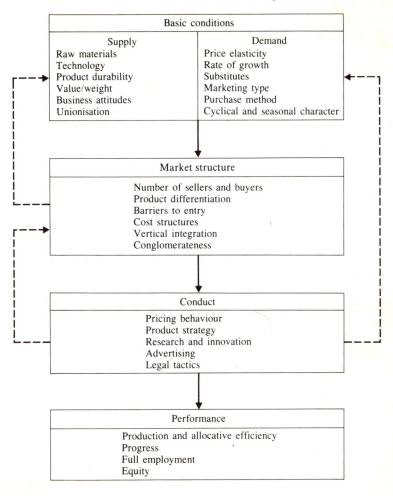

FIG. 1.1
Source: Scherer 1970, p. 5

and given the underlying assumption of the paradigm, that collusion and concentration are closely connected, it carries the undeniable presumption against monopoly power and big business. Nevertheless, Scherer in particular was anxious to signal an open mind:

> Readers seeking a precise, certain guide to public policy are bound to be disappointed by this survey, for we have found none. The competitive norm does seem to serve as a good first approximation, but it is difficult to state a priori how much competition is needed to achieve desirable economic performance, nor can we formulate hard and fast rules for, identifying cases in which a departure from competition is desirable.
>
> (ibid.: 38)

In the introduction to this section we briefly mentioned dissenting voices from Chicago. Indeed, one can identify a Chicago School in this subject, as in others. At the heart of many of their criticisms is an unmistakable call for I.O. to return to what might be termed the basics of neo-classical price theory. For example, throughout the 1960s a debate unfolded concerning the value, or otherwise, of Chamberlin's model of monopolistic competition (associated with the Harvard School). The gist of the Chicago critique was that this model offered little if nothing in predictive ability beyond the traditional model of perfect competition. In such circumstances, they argued, it is better to adopt the simple theory rather than the one with apparently more realistic assumptions.[6] However, there was also an obvious dislike of empirics without theory. For example, Stigler, in his famous explanation of why I.O. had evolved as a subject separate from price theory, suggests that 'much of its literature has been so nontheoretical, or even antitheoretical, that few economic theorists were attracted to it' (1968: 1). Another characteristic of the Chicago School is its more benign view of market outcomes, even if they involve monopoly and concentration; Demsetz, for example, argues that concentration is more often than not the result of efficiency.[7] But a sweeping identification of Chicago with the defence of Big Business is probably unjustified: for instance, Stigler's (1968: Ch.5) elegant formalisation of the reasons for expecting collusion to be facilitated by concentration has become an influential part of the anti-trust case.

Academic research in the early and middle 1970s continued very much in the tradition of the work summarised by Scherer, though there was a growing unease at what some would call catholic and others call *ad hoc* theorising behind the new empirical work. This gave rise to an approach which is perhaps most appropriately described as 'empirically driven theory'. By this we mean research with an ultimate empirical objective, but based on explicit theoretical model-building designed to establish a formal relationship between the variables concerned; the theoretical model is then used to guide the specification of estimating equations. The most obvious example of this approach concerns the relationship between price–cost margins and concentration which is described in section 1 of Chapter 3. This movement towards empirically motivated theory was joined in the late 1970s by a growing number of mathematically trained economists who were interested in the theoretical problems of I.O., but not necessarily in the specification of econometric work. The latter movement has become known, somewhat controversially, as the 'New I.O.' Such was the confidence generated, that by 1984 Waterson was able to write an I.O. textbook entitled *The Economic Theory of Industry* which included only one 'afterthought' chapter on empirical work.[8] Such is the speed with which this literature is expanding, that Waterson is already out of date!

We have suggested that the term 'New I.O.' is controversial. This is largely because those who have worked in the subject for many years sometimes find little new in the analytical results, and they probably find the claims for originality hard to take. This may be understandable, but it is our view that the rigour of the new I.O. compared with the catholicism of earlier years is sufficiently different in emphasis to warrant some sort of distinctive label, even if some would wish for an alternative adjective.

Rather than Clark, Mason and Bain, the roots of the new I.O. lie in the work of Cournot (1838), Hotelling (1929), Chamberlin (1933), von Stackelberg (1938), and Schelling (1960). Characteristic features are that the mode of analysis is mathematical and often couched in game-theoretic terms, and the treatment of economic welfare is usually explicit. Furthermore, and probably most importantly, the lines of causality outlined in Fig. 1.1 are explicitly replaced by a methodology which specifies the conduct of firms in terms of an *equilibrium concept*. An example of an equilibrium concept is that used by Cournot: the output rates chosen by firms constitute an equilibrium if, given the outputs chosen by rivals, no firm can improve its own profits by altering its output. Alternatively, if price is the decision variable, then price should replace output in the last sentence; this is often called a Bertrand equilibrium. More generally, output or price may be replaced by any other decision variable and the same basic idea of each firm optimising given the strategy of rivals is known as a Nash equilibrium.[9] Other more cooperative equilibrium concepts do exist, but the non-cooperative Nash equilibrium is central to most of the new I.O. to date. This choice may, regrettably, have as much to do with ease of modelling as with any fundamental belief in non-cooperative behaviour. Nevertheless, Nash equilibria have provided some particularly fruitful results. A typical methodology in the new I.O. is to specify the initial conditions and equilibrium concept as exogenous, then investigate: (i) the social optimum in a planned economy (where policy makers have access to the same information as industrialists); this is then used as a yardstick to compare with (ii) the market equilibrium (price, output, investment, or whatever is endogenous) when firm numbers are fixed; and (iii) the long-run equilibrium structure and performance when firm numbers are variable. The basic idea is illustrated in Fig. 1.2. Compared with Scherer's Fig. 1.1, both the initial conditions and mode of conduct are exogenous and there is no feedback. Market structure is also treated as more centrally endogenous. Four examples, each of which is developed more fully in later chapters, provide a more concrete introduction to the new I.O.

    1. *Product differentiation* as a concept has run through the literature since before Bain's time, yet its exact meaning has often been left implicit and very vague. Explicit modelling has revealed a sharp distinction between vertical and horizontal differentiation. Vertical differences between products are those which we normally

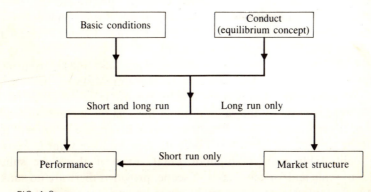

FIG. 1.2

associate with quality. Thus, most consumers will agree that, *ceteris paribus*, a computer with more memory is better than one with less, and will be willing to pay more for the former. Other, horizontal, product differences are not uniquely ranked by all consumers. For instance, farmers with differing types of soil will prefer different types of fertiliser; alternatively, young consumers may value the variety of sweets available at the local shop while being unable to claim that any one is best for their tastes. It turns out that these two types of horizontal differentiation, as well as pure vertical differentiation, can be used to specify different sets of initial conditions and, using the same Bertrand–Nash equilibrium concept, generate very different market equilibria and implications for social welfare. For instance, Shaked and Sutton (1987) show that markets in which firms can differentiate their products vertically by incurring increased fixed costs are likely to exhibit a greater concentration of sellers than are those in which horizontal differentiation is prevalent. Furthermore, the long-standing idea that monopolistic competition leads to too many products being produced at too high a cost is shown to rest on very shaky foundations (Spence 1976; Dixit and Stiglitz 1977; Lancaster 1979; Salop 1979).

2. Cournot's duopoly model and the associated analytical tool of *reaction functions* can be applied to investigate entry barriers simply by labelling one duopolist as the potential entrant and the other as the incumbent firm. This approach is followed by Dixit (1979, 1980), who is able to elucidate a number of issues within a unified framework. For instance, under what conditions will the incumbent prefer to passively accept entry rather than adjust this behaviour to keep the entrant out? Does product differentiation leave potential entrants at a disadvantage or does it aid entry by opening up market niches? And under what conditions can the incumbent credibly threaten retaliation against an entrant? It is the last of these questions that has gained most attention in the literature and two important concepts have emerged as crucial to an understanding of strategic behaviour by firms. First, the advantage obtainable by incumbents depends on their ability to make commitments to the market, and these depend crucially on *sunk costs*, that is costs which cannot be recovered once they have been spent (for instance, advertising but not office space which can easily be re-sold for alternative uses). Second, a great deal of important information on the competitiveness of the market is summarised in the slope of the reaction curves, and this provides a unifying framework for investigating many apparently diverse oligopoly problems (Bulow, Geanakoplos and Klemperer 1985; Fudenberg and Tirole 1985; Dixit 1986; see also Lyons 1987 for a simple introduction).

3. Recent work on *contestable markets* has sought to provide an alternative benchmark market structure to the unrealistic notion of perfect competition. If there are no sunk costs, if there exists at least one potential entrant who could produce exactly the same product lines as the incumbent, and if the equilibrium concept is such that the entrant can undercut the incumbent for long enough to be able to sell her desired output, then we have what is known as a perfectly contestable market (Baumol 1982). Even if there are substantial economies of scale and/or economies of scope, provided there are no sunk costs, there can be no exploitation of monopoly power, as a price in excess of average cost

would result in undercutting entry. This essential insight, which Baumol curiously believes to be the source of 'an uprising in the theory of industrial structure',[10] can be used to argue that competition policy should address the problem of exit as well as entry barriers. For instance, industries in which capital goods are non-specific and can be leased, re-sold or transferred to other uses with no loss of value should present no monopoly problem (even if they are highly concentrated) because anyone could enter if there were a profitable opportunity and, importantly, could get out quickly if competition hotted up. It is the ability to withdraw costlessly that encourages entry and so ensures that incumbents act competitively in the first place.

    4. Some types of *uncertainty* have been explicitly analysed within the framework of the new I.O.. Much economic modelling characterises the world as a place in which firms and consumers know all the relevant information on costs and demand. Very often, this provides a useful abstraction from reality, but sometimes uncertainty can become the cornerstone on which a genuine understanding of the world must be based. This theme is taken up in some detail in section 2, but here we note the way in which a category of uncertainty can be explicitly modelled.[11] Dasgupta and Stiglitz (1980) investigate competition between firms which are competing to try to discover a specific, patentable invention. The value of the invention is known, but the cost of discovering it is not. What *is* known about the discovery procedure is that the probability of any one firm being the one to win this patent race increases with the amount it is willing to spend. One extreme case is when all firms follow exactly the same research plan: if they were to spend the same money, they would make the same mistakes and eventually come to the same answer at the same time. In fact, this extreme is equivalent to the analysis of certainty and with free entry into the patent race, only one firm will carry out R & D.[12] That firm will carry out so much R & D that it will not make any excess profits. Despite the fact that only one firm actually enters the industry, the monopoly is the result of great competition to enter the market. It is as if there is perfect contestability in the 'R & D industry'. In contrast to Baumol's world of given production costs, however, there need be nothing socially optimal about this level of R & D; it may be too much or too little. A more interesting specification of uncertainty (also modelled by Dasgupta and Stiglitz) is if firms can pursue different lines of enquiry and the probability of success by any one firm is not perfectly correlated with the success of others spending similar amounts of money. In such circumstances, more than one firm will find it attractive to do R & D, even though there will be only one winner of the patent race. This sort of analysis can be pursued to investigate changes in the economic environment (e.g. the comparative static effects of increases in risk) as well as various institutional options open to the government (e.g. social planning, the optimal life of a patent, statutory monopoly).

    Such theoretical developments of the new I.O. have as yet inspired relatively little formal empirical testing, though there are recent signs of that changing. Some of the earlier I.O. literature has been exploited to generate 'stylised facts' against which to judge some of the main theoretical predictions, but the main empirical legacy of the new I.O. will probably be felt in a new emphasis on case study research. Since small differences in the specification of the basic conditions or even in the solution concept, can lead to significantly different results, it may be that cross-section regression analysis is too blunt a tool to tease out the important influences in industrial markets. If there is a resurgence in case study work, it will be against a much more rigorous theoretical background than was earlier work along similar lines (e.g. Schmalensee 1978; Shaw 1982). Some good examples of the new emphasis in empirical research can be found in a recent special issue of the *Journal of Industrial Economics*, confidently titled as 'The empirical renaissance in industrial economics'.

2. Radical approaches to industrial organisation

Notwithstanding the distinctions we have drawn concerning the relative prominence of theory and empirics, the mathematical formalism or otherwise, and the policy implications of I.O. as it has evolved in the last quarter-century, the subject has been dominated by neo-classical economics. As always, we must be careful with this term as it has no undisputed definition. However, we offer the following as a working definition of 'neo-classical' in the present context. Firstly, economic agents are assumed to be optimisers and in particular firms are invariably assumed to be profit maximisers. Secondly, most theoretical analysis (and its empirical counterpart of cross-industry regression analysis) focuses on equilibrium solutions. The effects of changes in underlying demand, cost and other conditions are developed using comparative statics. The inevitable consequence is that the equilibrium positions are emphasised and little is said about the process by which they are attained.[13] Thirdly, uncertainty is either ignored as, for example, in simple limit pricing models where cost and demand parameters, both actual and potential, are assumed to be known; or uncertainty is incorporated in the standard neo-classical manner by subjective probability distributions (as in Dasgupta and Stiglitz) which may or may not be revised systematically in the light of subsequent experience or information. As far as we are concerned here, these three analytical characteristics of optimisation, equilibrium, and uncertainty represented only by a subjective probability distribution, are shared by all the authors cited in section 1 and, more generally, by the vast majority of researchers in I.O.; and this unifies them under the 'neo-classical' label.

A fourth characteristic relates to welfare judgements and is central to the formation of policy recommendations by neo-classical economists. The first fundamental theorem of welfare economics rigorously demonstrates the conditions under which a perfectly competitive market system will give an efficient allocation of resources. It is in this sense that perfect competition (or perfect contestability) represents an 'ideal' or benchmark market structure. The second fundamental theorem of welfare economics states the conditions under which any desired distribution of income can be attained by a competitive market combined with a suitable initial distribution of resources. And it is in this sense that ethical or political beliefs in the egalitarian (or otherwise) distribution of income can be separated from a belief in the virtues of a competitive market system, *provided* action is taken to get the initial distribution of resources right.

The neo-classical approach is overwhelmingly dominant in the specialist I.O. literature. Nevertheless, there are dissenting voices, some of whom are exerting a major influence on current British and American economic policy. Most prominent among the dissenters are those who derive their inspiration from the Austrian economists Menger, Mises, Schumpeter and Hayek. In fact, it is possible to discern two distinct traditions. We begin with the group following on from Mises and known as the neo-Austrians, including Hayek and more recently Kirzner, before discussing Schumpeter (Mises' contemporary) and his followers. Finally, we discuss the Marxian view of competition and how it relates to the modern I.O. literature. Apart from providing an implicit critique of the neo-classical view, it is hoped that this fairly concise scan of different approaches will help to put the subject matter of I.O. in its broader context. These authors have much wider economic and political interests than the conduct of monopoly and merger policy alone. The subject turns out to play a crucial role in debates as important as the justification for freedom in a libertarian society, as envisaged by Hayek, and the essence of exploitation, as envisaged by neo-Marxists.

Hayek identifies a central concern that neo-classical I.O. has yet to address:

> the economic problem of society is ... not merely a problem of how to allocate 'given' resources – if 'given' is taken to mean given to a single mind which deliberately solves the problem set by these 'data'. It is rather a problem of how to secure the best use of resources known to any of the members of society, for ends whose relative importance only these individuals know. Or, to put it briefly, it is a problem of the utilization of knowledge which is not given to anyone in its totality ... The solution to the economic problem of society is ... always a voyage of exploration into the unknown, an attempt to discover new ways of doing things better than they have been done before.
>
> (Hayek 1949: 77–8, 101)

In our terms then, the problem is not so much with what firms do with the initial cost and demand conditions, but in how to discover those conditions in the first place. The central question posed by the Austrians is how best to facilitate this discovery procedure, and the answer they unanimously provide is 'competition'.

The Austrian view of competition is quite different from the neo-classical view which, for our purposes, can be thought of as the degree to which actual and potential oligopolistic rivalry reduce price towards marginal cost in equilibrium.[14] Austrian competition, on the other hand, ignores the oligopoly problem and emphasises the dynamic process through which facts about unused opportunities and the plans of others are discovered. The exploitation of such opportunities in itself spreads information and so changes awareness of the 'basic data', the Austrian term equivalent to what we have called the initial conditions.

> The overambitious plans of one period will be replaced by more realistic ones; market opportunities overlooked in one period will be exploited in the next. In other words, even without changes in the basic data of the

> market (i.e. in consumer tastes, technological possibilities, and resource
> availabilities), the decisions made in one period of time generate
> systematic alterations in the corresponding decisions for the
> succeeding period. Taken over time, this series of systematic changes in
> the interconnected network of market decisions constitutes the market
> process.
> (Kirzner 1973: 10)

The competitive process does not generate equilibrium (the basic data change too rapidly for that) but it does tend to bring about 'order' in that: 'the systematic alteration in decisions between each period and the succeeding one renders each opportunity offered to the market more competitive than that offered in the preceding period – that is, it is offered with fuller awareness of the other opportunities being made available, against which it is necessary to compete.' (ibid.: 12) Although Hayek identifies this central concept of 'order' equally with Adam Smith's 'invisible hand' and the 'negative feedback' of modern cybernetics, it is *not* the same as equilibrium. Equilibrium is a description of an end point at which competition and uncertainty have ceased to exist, where all firms have got it right and information is perfect. Order is the tendency of the economy to move towards such an equilibrium.

The Austrian view of competition clashes head on with the neo-classical view in analysing the role of profits. To the neo-classical economist, super-normal profits are typically evidence of the exploitation of monopoly power. To the Austrians, they indicate scope for more complete coordination of individual plans.

> The essence of the 'profit incentive' (and in particular its significance for
> normative economics) is ... not to be seen as motivation to work harder
> or to allocate resources more efficiently. The profit incentive (including,
> of course, the disincentive of loss) operates most significantly by
> encouraging the alertness of entrepreneurs – by encouraging them to
> keep their eyes open for new information that will lead to new plans.
> And its powerful effect in this regard acquires normative significance
> because of the market's prior failure to coordinate sets of decisions.
> (ibid.: 223)

Thus, entrepreneurs have the crucial role of being alert to new profit (coordination or arbitrage) opportunities, a role that is missing in neo-classical economics where, at best, entrepreneurship is equated with the ability to compute complicated optimisation problems.

The idea of competition as a discovery process has more in common with the theory of scientific method than it has with, say, the Newtonian physics with which neo-classical economics might wish to be compared. Scientific facts have an enduring value, but economic facts discovered are only of subsidiary interest to the Austrian theorist because they are essentially transient, depending on time and place. What is important is the best way to *discover* economic facts. We return to this theme below, but first digress to discuss the implications for empirical work.

> The necessary consequence of the reason why we use competition is
> that, *in those cases in which it is interesting*, the validity of the theory
> can never be tested empirically. We can test it on conceptual models,

and we might conceivably test it in artificially created real situations, where the facts which competition is intended to discover are already known to the observer. But in such cases it is of no practical value, so that to carry out the experiment would hardly be worth the expense. If we do not know the facts we hope to discover by means of competition, we can never ascertain how effective it has been in discovering those facts that might be discovered. All we can hope to find out is that, on the whole, societies which rely for this purpose on competition have achieved their aims more successfully than others. This is a conclusion which the history of civilisation seems eminently to have confirmed.

(Hayek 1984: 255)

Thus, the empirical foundations for the Austrian belief in the benefits of competition rest entirely on casual observation of the relative success of capitalist, socialist and other systems of government.[15]

It is time for a brief summary of the distinctive features of Austrian economics. In comparing the neo-classical and Austrian schools of thought, we find that optimisation is replaced by entrepreneurial alertness; equilibrium is replaced as the focus of attention by 'order' in the competitive process; and basic conditions which are known (at least in the form of a probability distribution of possible outcomes) are replaced by ignorance of all but a few privately known opportunities.

Thus far, we find ourselves in broad agreement with the Austrian economists in that process competition is an important concept which is too often overlooked in the formal neo-classical tradition (though much less so in verbal discussions). Unfortunately, those readers who may so far have felt an empathy with the Austrian view will now have to assent to a fundamental act of faith if they are to accept the Austrian policy recommendations. Clearly, the fundamental theorems of welfare economics cannot provide a guideline for government policy in an Austrian world where: 'competition is valuable *only* because, and so far as, its results are unpredictable and on the whole different from those which anyone [including politicians and civil servants] has, or could have, deliberately aimed at.' (Hayek 1984: 255).[16] But Hayek's alternative is simply to state that: 'the grounds of [sic] which the achievement of competition ought to be judged ... ought to be the situation as it would exist if competition were prevented from operating.' (1949: 100)

Consequently, the best that a government can do is to create the institutional setting in which 'unknown people' can best discover profitable opportunities. The most appropriate system, in the Austrian view, is one of maximum individual freedom and minimal government intervention. Note that in the Austrian theory competition is good *by definition*, whereas in the neo-classical theory competition is proved good by deduction (recall the fundamental welfare theorems). Furthermore, given that empirical confirmation of the virtues of competition has been ruled out, the belief in the benefits of competition must be given the status of an article of faith in the Austrian creed. This is, no doubt, why the Austrians have had so little effect on most academic economists, and why they have had so much effect on some politicians.[17]

Two examples should demonstrate why we believe the Austrian creed to be at odds with a more dispassionate and balanced view of government policy. Austrians do not revile monopoly as long as it has been created without government assistance. Neo-classical worries concerning restricted output and the social harm of lost consumer surplus associated with high profits, are replaced by the argument that higher profits represent greater benefits arising from the monopolist satisfying a particularly highly valued need. Anti-monopoly legislation would have the undesirable consequence of reducing the incentive for entrepreneurial alertness and so slowing down the introduction of new products and services, or even leading to some not being provided at all. The second example relates to the legal protection of trademarks and patents.

> A mechanical extension of the simplified conception of private property has produced undesirable results ... in the field of trade-marks and proprietory names ... [where] exclusive stress on the description of the producer and the neglect of similar provisions concerning the character and quality of the commodity has to some extent helped to create monopolistic conditions because trade-marks have come to be used as a description of the kind of commodity, which then of course only the owner of the trade-mark could produce (e.g. 'Kodak', 'Coca-Cola'). This difficulty might be solved, for example, if the use of trade-marks were protected only in connection with descriptive names which would be free for all to use.   (Hayek 1949: 114–5).

Littlechild (1986) makes a similar case against patents. Thus, monopoly is okay if it is not the result of government legislation, but it is bad if it is![18]

In many ways, Schumpeter is part of the Austrian tradition in that he emphasised change and the competitive process. Using a broad definition of technical progress, one that includes organisational change as well as product development, the dynamics of the capitalist system are at the core of his analysis. However, his theoretical and empirical methodologies, and his welfare and policy conclusions, are a good deal more pragmatic than Hayek's and such characteristics go a long way towards explaining his greater popularity with modern I.O. economists.

If the appropriate analogy from the natural sciences is Newtonian physics for the neo-classical school, and scientific method for the Austrians, then Schumpeter's theme corresponds with evolutionary biology:

> The opening up of new markets ... and the organizational development from the craft shop and factory to such concerns as US Steel illustrate the same process of industrial mutation ... that incessantly revolutionizes the economic structure *from within*, incessantly destroying the old one, incessantly creating a new one. This process of Creative Destruction is the essential fact about capitalism ... in capitalist reality ... it is not [neo-classical] competition which counts but the competition from the new commodity, the new technology, the new source of supply, the new type of organization (the largest scale unit of control for instance) – competition which commands a decisive cost or quality advantage and which strikes not at the margins of the profits and the outputs of the existing forms but at their foundations and

their very lives. This kind of competition is as much more effective than the other as a bombardment is in comparison with forcing a door, and so much more important that it becomes a matter of comparative indifference whether competition in the ordinary [neo-classical] sense functions more or less promptly; the powerful lever that in the long run expands output and brings down prices is in any case made of other stuff ... [Such competition] acts not only when in being but also when it is merely an ever-present threat. It disciplines before it attacks.

(Schumpeter 1943: 83–5)

In effect, creative destruction shifts the economy from one equilibrium towards another, entrepreneurs being driven on by the fear of others innovating first. The neo-classical emphasis on each equilibrium is largely dismissed as being of relatively little social importance compared with the qualitative leaps forward generated by creative destruction. For Schumpeter, the path between equilibria depends on liquidity constraints and the diffusion and imitation of new ideas. This path is interesting in its own right, particularly since it can generate business cycles, but it is not the root source of all progress. Schumpeter's entrepreneur is an innovator, and not the neo-Austrian alert arbitrageur.

Because economic welfare depends more on creative destruction than on any temporary equilibrium, Schumpeter was unworried by the conventional welfare costs of output restriction. But this does not mean that he viewed market structure with equanimity. Although he fully recognised the danger that monopolists might be tempted to rest on their laurels, he argued that the institutional setting which most encourages creative destruction may still involve all sorts of monopolistic, restrictive practices. For instance, the risks attached to very large-scale investments may be so great that they will only be undertaken in the knowledge that entry barriers, collusive agreements or government intervention will ensure that competition is actually discouraged. The view that government intervention may be necessary for the market to work efficiently is clearly anathema to the neo-Austrians.

Another point of implicit disagreement relates to empirical work, the value of which we have already seen is dismissed by Hayek. Schumpeter bases his argument on a detailed knowledge of economic history but there is nothing inherent in his argument that prevents the application of, for instance, the inter-industry comparisons of cross-section regression analysis.[19] In fact, many of his less careful followers have undertaken a very crude version of such studies, and these are discussed elsewhere in this book (Chapter 6), but one important methodological point can be made here. Monopolistic restrictions may give the profits, financial reserves and stability to induce the investments necessary for progress, but creative destruction also implies monopolisation as the result of success. Market structure and performance are simultaneously determined and this fact should be incorporated in any econometric analysis.

Many economists, including some of the neo-classical writers mentioned in section 1, have claimed to be followers of Schumpeter. Were he alive today, however, he would probably be disappointed with the neo-classical 'straitjacket' into which his ideas have been strapped. The joint work of Nelson and Winter does attempt to place Schumpeter's ideas into an alternative formal framework. Although they are no more successful than anyone else at fully capturing the process of creative destruction, it is because they provide a link with the behavioural school led by Herbert Simon that they warrant a mention in this chapter. Simon argues that because our ability to solve problems is imperfect (that is, we suffer from bounded rationality), we often have to use rules of thumb as an aid to decision making (for instance, in pricing or investment). Nelson and Winter develop the idea that although these rules may initially be fairly arbitrary, evolutionary pressures tend to result in relative success for better rules; and furthermore, if a rule of thumb is demonstrably inefficient, then there will be pressure for a better 'mutation' to appear: 'Through the joint action of search and selection, the firms evolve over time, with the condition of the industry in each period bearing the seeds of its condition in the following period.' (Nelson and Winter 1982: 19). It might be expected that the profit-maximising optimum rule would eventually be discovered. However, many rules are not tested sufficiently frequently for any underlying 'optimal' rule to emerge. Although a long-run equilibrium (in the neo-classical sense) may theoretically exist, the world (i.e. the 'basic conditions') changes so rapidly relative to adjustments towards equilibrium that only the process of getting there, so Nelson and Winter argue, is of any real interest.[20] Although this sounds fairly neo-Austrian, the result of their formal modelling turns out to be a much more mechanistic form of evolution.

The final major approach which we review is that of Marx and the neo-Marxians. Marx followed in the tradition of the great classical economists, notably Smith and Ricardo, in basing his analysis on the social and political institutions of capitalism. His emphasis on the dynamics of the capitalist system was to be a direct influence on Schumpeter. However, it is the interpretation of the consequences of competition, rather than a deep analysis of the 'what is competition?' question (which has largely concerned us so far), that constitutes Marx's greatest contribution to the I.O. literature. This is because Marx was less interested in how a given price is formed, than in how the income generated by the sale of goods is distributed between labour, landowners and capital. This emphasis encouraged him to leave aside the monopoly problem as a relatively unimportant side-issue. In particular, he assumes that real wages are fixed (by subsistence, class relations or social convention), so that if consumer prices rise due to monopoly in one industry then in order to preserve the real wage the nominal wage must rise and so reduce profits elsewhere in the economy (Marx 1894: 861). The distributionally important magnitudes remain unchanged. It is the monopoly that capitalists *as a class* have over the means of production, rather than any monopoly held by a sub-set of capitalists, that is relevant to Marx's central interest in income distribution. Nevertheless, Marx is fairly explicit as to what he means by competition and it is interesting to bring this out, particularly as one line of modern Marxism *does* put monopoly at the heart of exploitation theory.

It is possible to distinguish both a neo-classical and a more dynamic process competition in Marx's work. We begin with the former, which is essentially rooted in what is, by modern standards, conventional supply and demand theory. Competition within an industry (or 'sphere' to use Marx's terminology) ensures a similar price for similar goods and then: 'it is competition of capitals in different spheres, which first brings out the price of production equalising the rates of profit in the different spheres' (1894: 180). The speed and effectiveness with which capital flows between industries to equalise the profit rate depends on the mobility of both labour and capital, and these improve with the degree of capitalist development. More specifically, labour is more mobile if *inter alia* it is less skilled, more dependent on capital to supply the means of production, and the larger is the reserve army of unemployed (1894: 196, and 1867: Ch. XXV, sect. 3). Capital mobility depends on the sophistication of credit markets, the degree to which production is controlled by capitalists, and 'the removal of all monopolies with the exception of the natural ones, those, that is, which naturally arise out of the capitalist mode of production' (1894: 196). It is this last comment that comes close to the heart of I.O. theory. Interestingly, Marx claims that natural monopolies, presumably the result of substantial economies of scale, do not prevent the equalisation of profits between industries. It appears that Marx deserves credit as an early contestability theorist!

It is important to understand the context in which Marx interpreted this neo-classical strand to his analysis of competition. First, although competition tends to equalise profit rates, it does not determine the average rate of profit. It is the latter, of course, which is crucial to an understanding of income distribution: 'In short, competition has to shoulder the responsibility of explaining all the meaningless ideas of the economists' (1894: 866). Second, there is nothing welfare optimal about free competition. Adam Smith's benevolent invisible hand in the presence of free competition, which modern neo-classical economists have formalised as the first fundamental welfare theorem, is not the ultimate development of human freedom. It may be in the capitalist system, but this would be to assume 'that middle-class rule is the culmination of world history – certainly an agreeable thought for the parvenus of the day before yesterday' (1939: 652). Capitalism may be an improvement on feudalism, but it is still based on one class exploiting another. Thus, Marx rejects neo-classical reasons, such as the reward for risk taking and the return to waiting, as not providing an ethical justification for receiving profit. Such payments, and this point lies at the heart of Marxist welfare judgements, reflect only the exploitation of workers. He argues that socialism, particularly communism, could provide a more attractive distribution of income.

The second type of competition discussed by Marx is far more important to his historical analysis. This is because it is at the heart of his vision of the dynamics of the capitalist system: 'The battle of competition is fought by cheapening of commodities. The cheapness of commodities depends, *ceteris paribus*, on the productiveness of labour, and this again on the scale of production. Therefore, the larger capitals beat the smaller.' (1867: 626). Possible reasons for the increasing scale of production are the division of labour, economies due to the introduction of new machines and new materials, learning-by-doing, and also economies of scope.[21] Early innovators may be able to increase their profits as a result of their lower costs,[22] but 'a coercive law of competition forces his competitors to adopt the new method' (1867: 319) so profit rates do not diverge for long. Soon, however, further innovation reduces costs and raises economies of scale to begin the process over again. The inevitable consequence is a greater concentration of industry. Two factors encourage this tendency. First, the banking, credit and joint-stock company system and second, the predatory instincts of capitalists:

> a capitalist disposing of a large capital will receive a larger mass of profit than a small capitalist … [and so] when the greater capitalist wishes to make room for himself on the market, and to crowd out the smaller ones, as happens in times of crisis, he makes practical use of this, i.e., he deliberately lowers his rate of profit in order to drive the smaller ones to the wall.   (1894: 225)

This dynamic competition is driven by the impulsive desire on the part of capitalists to accumulate[23] and leads to rising capital intensity and consequently declining rate of average profit. It is in this dynamic sense, and not in the neo-classical dimension, that competition can be said to affect the distribution of income, which is obviously dependent on capital intensity and the rate of profit. Thus, the capitalist system gets progressively more concentrated over time yet, recalling Marx's earlier description of 'neo-classical' competition, does not become any less intensely competitive. In essence, capitalists find themselves in a prisoners' dilemma. They must invest in large-scale capital-intensive plant themselves, or else rivals will do so and thereby undercut them. Capitalists are not inherently nasty people, but the oppressive competitiveness of the system requires that they exploit their workers. Thus, for Marx, dynamic competition is a central cause of capitalist exploitation.

The early followers of Marx, such as Hilferding and Lenin, laid greater stress on monopoly mainly because of the concentration of industry that they could observe in the late nineteenth and early twentieth centuries. Nevertheless, they maintained Marx's essentially competitive view of capitalism. However, more recent neo-Marxist thought has shifted positions sharply and put monopoly power centre stage. The most important inspiration for this change is to be found in the work of Kalecki (1938, 1939), who argued that the distribution of income depends crucially on the 'degree of monopoly'. If this is true, then the theory of industrial organisation moves centre stage in understanding the key Marxist issue of capitalist exploitation. Put very simply, and ignoring his careful treatment of materials costs, economic cycles, etc., Kalecki argued as follows. Wages constitute the variable cost of production, and firms price according to a fixed mark-up on such costs. The size of the mark-up increases with the degree of monopoly. Define units of output such that one unit of labour is needed to manufacture one unit of output; and let w be the wage rate, m be the mark-up, and $L=Q$ be the number of workers employed and amount produced. The price of output is $p=(1+m)w$, so $pQ=(1+m)wL$, and $wL/pQ=1/(1+m)$. The share of labour in national income is, therefore, inversely related to the degree of monopoly as represented by m. Thus, in Kalecki's view, the more competitive is the capitalist system, the greater is the share of labour.

This conclusion is clearly at odds with Marx's own view of exploitation, in which monopoly is not relevant to the distribution of income, and in fact, intense dynamic competition is a prime cause of exploitation. The competitiveness of capitalism is largely an empirical issue and is a continuing source of debate, but the theoretical role of monopoly in distribution theory is more easily clarified. Marx, as we said earlier, believed that *real* wages were fixed in the short run, determined by subsistence, class struggle or social convention, so monopoly in one industry inevitably leads to a squeeze on profits in another and so competition does not matter. Implicit in the Kaleckian view is that real wages are endogenous in the sense that they *are* determined by competition. Workers may have some influence in setting nominal wages, but as long as firms can set the mark-up it is the bosses who have the whip hand in determining real wages and so income distribution. This view of monopoly capitalism with its greater emphasis on exploitation by big business rather than by the owners of capital *per se* was taken up by Steindl (1952), and Baran and Sweezy (1968). The latter are quite clear on modern monopoly capitalism. Firms collude to maximise joint profits, so:

> the appropriate general price theory . . . is the traditional monopoly price theory of classical and neo-classical economics. What economists have hitherto treated as a special case turns out to be under conditions of monopoly capitalism, the general case. [But] the abandonment of price competition does not mean the end of all competition: it takes new forms and rages on with ever-increasing intensity. Most of these new forms of competition come under the heading of what we call the sales effort.   (Baran and Sweezy 1968: 69, and 76)[24]

Thus, owners of capital are not necessarily the major beneficiaries of the system because of the expensive trappings of capitalism such as advertising, and also the bureaucratic costs such as accountants, solicitors, civil servants and military expenditures which are necessary to prop up the system. Recent books by Semmler (1984) and Cowling (1982) both make extensive use of the traditional and modern I.O. literature surveyed in this book in order to try to support the respective cases for a traditional Marxist and a 'neo-Marxist monopoly capitalism' interpretation of the modern world.

3. Layout of the book

The five surveys which follow cover those areas of I.O. in which we believe the literature has advanced most rapidly in recent years, and which most merit up-to-date surveys to complement existing textbooks. We have attempted to make each survey self-standing, and to that extent the order in which they are read should not be particularly important. Nevertheless, we follow tradition in opening with 'structure' in the entry barriers and concentration surveys, and closing with two 'performance' surveys, on profitability and technical change. The middle survey discusses recent developments in oligopoly theory, i.e. market conduct. The newcomer to the subject may therefore feel most comfortable in following our ordering.

Ever since Bain's early work, over thirty years ago, barriers to entry have been recognised as lying at the heart of I.O. In their absence, there can be no monopoly power because either actual entry or the threat of entry would ensure competitive markets. However, only in the last decade have Bain's fairly vague hypotheses been formulated more rigorously so as to bring out the fundamental sources of entry barriers. Particular advances have been made in identifying their welfare consequences and in examining the ways in which firms can deliberately create and exploit barriers. For instance, it is now recognised that not all impediments to entry need be socially disadvantageous; and following a long history of debate, we now have a clearer idea of the roles of economies of scale and of product differentiation. The first survey provides a comprehensive summary of these developments. It begins with a discussion of the problems of defining a barrier to entry, and goes on to provide a detailed theoretical analysis of individual barriers. Inasmuch as this material is covered in the conventional textbooks (and much of it is not), it is usually spread over many different chapters. For instance, advertising is often discussed in a different chapter to capital requirements, and its exact role as an entry barrier can be lost. This part of the survey therefore has an additional use as a compendium of barriers. The final section reviews some empirical evidence, and also attempts to quantify the relative significance of different barriers.

The concentration of sellers in a market is the other cornerstone of the S–C–P paradigm; it is the element of structure which is apparently the most amenable to public policy, through such institutions as the Monopolies and Mergers Commission, and since it is also fairly easy to measure, it is unsurprising that concentration has figured so centrally in econometric analysis of profitability and other elements of industry performance. But until fairly recently the literature on concentration was very unbalanced. While there had been a seemingly endless debate on the merits of various measurement indices, and some excellent descriptive statistical studies establishing the facts on historical trends and inter-industry differences in concentration, the empirical and theoretical explanation of concentration was rather patchy. Things have recently changed for the better, and a more interesting picture is starting to emerge on the causes of concentration. Our second survey reflects this change: while we do summarise the debate on the merits of alternative indices and report some recent evidence for the UK, the main emphasis is placed on explanations of concentration. The theoretical picture is still rather confused, with suggestive pointers from each of traditional price theory, the S–C–P literature, and the new I.O. Our survey attempts to impose an order on this divergent literature and also brings the alternative stochastic explanations closer to the centre of the stage. In addition, there is a short treatment of aggregate concentration, i.e. concentration of the manufacturing sector as a whole. This is a subject largely ignored in the S–C–P tradition, but one which is increasingly more relevant to a world dominated by large conglomerate firms.

The third survey, by Huw Dixon, is on new developments in oligopoly theory, and is the exception within the book in that it is concerned exclusively with theory. It has a dual purpose: it provides a useful background for the newcomer on the basic concepts and definitions of neo-classical oligopoly and game theory, and therefore offers a reference point for the other surveys where they discuss that theory; but also it represents the growing importance within the subject of the mathematical theorist, and is a consequence of the advent of the new I.O. In the early part of the survey, basic concepts are explained and Cournot and Bertrand behaviour are contrasted within a simple linear framework. It turns out that the nature of oligopoly game has a strong influence on the relationship between structure and performance, as does the distinction between homogeneous and differentiated products. The notion of precommitment is essential to strategic behaviour and Dixon discusses the recent literature on two aspects of this, prior investment in physical capital and choice of managerial objectives. Later parts of the survey explore the implications of recent developments in game theory, notably the repeated game. Because this part of I.O. is still developing rapidly, it would be premature to assess its long-term implications for the subject, but the survey serves to underline how charges of an 'antitheoretical' literature are no longer applicable to I.O.

The following survey, by Paul Geroski, returns to a central policy issue: competition policy. The starting point is the ubiquitous correlation between concentration and profitability on which so much of the attention of early empirical practitioners was focused. Geroski surveys a critical literature which is both theoretical and econometric. He points to a growing realisation that structure is not the dominant influence on conduct, and to the ambiguity in the interpretation of a positive correlation across industries between concentration and profits. There is an increasing tendency in more recent research towards examination of data on intra-industry differences on the one hand, and a persistence of profits over time on the other. This switch in empirical emphasis underlines our earlier remark that cross-industry econometrics can be a blunt tool, especially in a world where conduct is not uniform, and in which competition is seen more as a process. It would be wrong to interpret this last remark as a conversion of neo-classical empirics to an Austrian perspective, but it probably does reflect a rather more catholic theoretical perspective extending beyond merely simplistic static models.

The final survey reviews the theory and evidence on another aspect of performance: technical change and productivity. We suggested earlier that the relationship between structure and research and innovation formed an important part of the second wave of S–C–P in the 1960s. The bulk of this work was empirical tests of so-called Schumpeterian hypotheses which, if validated, might help to redress the balance of policy prescription in favour of concentration and large scale. Our survey of this literature suggests that on balance the Schumpeterian hypotheses are not confirmed: there does not seem to be a beneficial (or detrimental) influence of concentration, nor of large firm size beyond some threshold. Rather surprisingly, the empirical work on innovation developed almost independently of economic theory. Once again, however, in recent years the rate of theoretical advance seems to have quickened noticeably. Modelling of research activity in general, and the race for patents in particular, have attracted some outstanding contributions under the umbrella of the new I.O., with the familiar characteristics of a game-theoretic setting and highly formalised mathematical deduction. Our survey departs from normal practice by including a final section on productivity, efficiency and market structure. This reflects our opinion that evidence on the impact of structure on productivity provides an overlooked, if indirect, test of the effects of innovation. Given the present preoccupation of the British with low productivity, the effects of industrial organisation on this may be a subject which will attract increasing attention in the near future, at least on this side of the Atlantic.

Notes

1. All of the surveys in this volume have benefited from the useful comments of friends and colleagues and this is especially so for this introductory survey. A preliminary draft was widely circulated and we were inundated by helpful criticisms. Most gratifying was the response of those holding views which we question in the text. They will forgive us if the narrative stance remains overtly neo-classical in spite of their comments. This probably reflects as much on our stubbornness as on the strength of their arguments! The reader should be warned that we know of a score of other practising industrial economists who disagree with at least part of our potted history and views on Austrian and Marxist economics, as well as our failure to mention important English economists – we have the correspondence to prove it. More seriously, the interested reader will wish to consult the seminal papers and books we refer to in order to make up his/her own mind on the relative merits of the different schools.

    The helpful friends include: Mark Casson, Keith Cowling, Peter Hart, Donald Hay, Geoff Harcourt, Shaun Hargreaves-Heap, Steve Littlechild, Brian Loasby, Tony McGuinness, John Sutton, Mike Waterson and Basil Yamey. Bob Millward and Mike Sumner are also owed thanks more generally for their comments and tolerance on all chapters.

2. Williamson's contribution is recognised and discussed in detail in a recent text/survey on the theory of the firm (Clarke and McGuinness 1987), to which we have both contributed. This also includes a full list of Williamson's numerous articles and books.

3. Hence the title to the book rather than the more general alternative, historically preferred by the British, 'industrial economics', which may or may not include managerial economics and the theory of the firm.

4. For example, see his equation of theory to a priori speculation and hypothesising (ibid.: 19).

5. He also points to general equilibrium analysis. But this appears to be little more than the proverbial 'touch of the cap', with the suggestion that normative appraisal of industrial performance necessarily requires yardsticks and value judgements, and that these should derive from general equilibrium analysis (ibid.: 24–5).

6. Rowley (1972) includes most of the interesting contributions to this debate in his collection of readings.

7. More specifically, Demsetz argues that concentration–profits correlations are explicable in terms of the greater efficiency of larger firms, rather than the tendency to collusion where concentration is higher. Another example of Demsetz championing the cause of monopoly is his well known critique of Arrow's proof that competition is more favourable to invention than is monopoly. Both instances are discussed in more detail elsewhere in this volume (Chapters 5 and 6 respectively), as is Stigler's model of collusion mentioned in the following sentence in the text (discussed in Ch. 3).

8. It is not that the literature covered by Waterson is all post-1975: on the contrary, much of it is much older in origin, but we wish to stress the change in emphasis of the subject.

9. The differences between Cournot–Nash and Bertrand–Nash equilibria are treated in some detail in Chapter 4.

10. He also implies that only modesty prevents him from using the term 'revolution' instead of 'uprising' or 'revolt'! It has also been pointed out to us by economists of an

earlier generation that the relevance of asset specificity (sunk costs) in the study of monopoly was 'drummed into' them by their teachers. Even if there is little new in contestability theory, the formalisation does highlight some consequences of the extreme (and implausible?) case of no sunk costs.

11. This is not to claim that the incorporation of uncertainty is absent from the earlier I.O. tradition; merely to illustrate how it can be formally handled. In fact, in Knight's (1933) classification, the new I.O. tackles only 'calculable' risk and not true uncertainty which Knight reserves for events to which probabilities cannot be attached. However regrettably, modern usage no longer makes this clear distinction, and typically uses uncertainty in cases of Knightian risk. In the text, we follow the slovenly modern usage.

12. It can be shown that a Nash equilibrium does not exist in this model, so Dasgupta and Stiglitz employ a Stackelberg equilibrium which does exist! This is what is discussed in the text. The Stackelberg leader is the firm which actually carries out the R & D. Note the implication that the choice of equilibrium concept is not as exogenous as our earlier discussion suggests.

13. This last comment should be mildly qualified. It is true that the examination of stability conditions implies the description of the system as it moves towards or away from equilibrium; moreover, not all equilibrium analysis need be static. For instance, in I.O. we might appeal to mathematical investigations of the stability of Cournot equilibrium or the application of optimal control theory to limit pricing when entry is slow. However, the former tend to be highly stylised and free of a real time dimension, and the latter merely emphasise the belief in equilibrium, insisting that temporary equilibria exist at all points in time.

14. Of course, neo-classical competition can also be in advertising, R & D, new products, etc., but the point to emphasise is that it always results in an equilibrium.

15. The interesting possibility of experimental evidence has received only limited testing (e.g. Smith 1982).

16. The fundamental theorems can only be strictly applied in a world in which equilibrium is actually attained. Furthermore, the vast literature on Second Best policies suggests problems in identifying welfare improvements even in equilibrium.

17. For instance, one leading member of Mrs Thatcher's first Cabinet, Sir Keith Joseph, insisted that his senior civil servants read Littlechild (1978); which is a very accessible introduction to the application of neo-Austrian ideas to economic policy.

18. This idea is further examined in Chapter 2.

19. In fact, Schumpeter was a founder of the Econometric Society. But this does not mean that he would have approved of crude econometric tests of his ideas. For instance, some cartels may facilitate progress while others hinder it, so there may be no clear relationship between cartelisation and technical progress. A critique based on such complexities would be similar to the view we have attributed to the new I.O.

20. This view leads Nelson and Winter to use a fairly novel methodology. The main theoretical tools of neo-classical equilibrium and optimisation theory are replaced by the Markov processes of stochastic theory, and varying transition probabilities replace comparative statics as the means for deriving theoretical results. Empirical work is eschewed in favour of simulation studies, and their welfare analysis is pragmatic.

21. Especially in the use of by-products and waste materials – what Marx, in a rare moment of humour, enjoys calling the 'excretions of production' (Marx 1894, Ch. V).

22. This is not to deny 'that the trail-blazers generally go bankrupt, and only those who

later buy the buildings, machinery, etc., at a cheaper price, make money out of it. It is, therefore, generally the most worthless and miserable sort of money-capitalists who draw the greatest profit out of all new developments of the universal labour of the human spirit and their social application through combined labour' (Marx 1894: 104).

23. 'Accumulate, accumulate! That is Moses and the prophets!' (Marx 1867: 595)

24. Incidentally, they argue that collusive behaviour also applies to technical progress so big corporations do not strive to undermine each other by competitive innovation. Neither can small innovators cause any major upsets because they get taken over by the giants. Thus 'Schumpeter's perennial gale of creative destruction has subsided into an occasional mild breeze' (Baran and Sweezy 1968: 82).

References

Bain, J. S. (1959) *Industrial Organisation*, John Wiley & Sons: New York.

Baran, P. A. and Sweezy, P. M. (1968) *Monopoly Capital*, Penguin: Harmondsworth.

Baumol, W. J. (1982) Contestable markets: an uprising in the theory of industrial structure, *American Economic Review*, **72**, 1–15.

Bulow, J. I., Geanakoplos, J. D. and Klemperer, P. D. (1985) Multimarket oligopoly: strategic substitutes and complements, *Journal of Political Economy*, **93**, 488–511.

Chamberlin, E. H. (1933) *The Theory of Monopolistic Competition*, Harvard University Press: Cambridge, Mass.

Clark, J. M. (1940) Toward a concept of workable competition, *American Economic Review*, **30**, 241–56.

Clarke, R. and McGuinness, A. J. (eds.) (1987) *Economics of the Firm*, Blackwell: Oxford.

Coase, R. H. (1937) The nature of the firm, *Economica*, IV, 386–405.

Cournot, A. A. (1838) reprinted as *Researches into the Mathematical Principles of the Theory of Wealth* (1927), Macmillan: New York.

Cowling, K. (1982) *Monopoly Capitalism*, Macmillan: London.

Dasgupta, P. and Stiglitz, J. (1980) Uncertainty, industrial structure and the speed of R & D, *Bell Journal of Economics*, **11**, 1–28.

Dixit, A. K. (1979) A model of duopoly suggesting a theory of entry barriers, *Bell Journal of Economics*, **10**, 20–32.

Dixit, A. K. (1980) The role of investment in entry deterrence, *Economic Journal*, **91**, 95–106.

Dixit, A. K. (1986) Comparative statics for oligopoly, *International Economic Review*, **27**, 107–22.

Dixit, A. K. and Stiglitz, J. E. (1977) Monopolistic competition and optimum product diversity, *American Economic Review*, **67**, 297–308.

Fudenberg, D. and Tirole, J. (1984) The fat-cat effect, the puppy-dog ploy and the lean and hungry look, *American Economic Review, Papers and Proceedings*, **74**, 361–6.

Hayek, F. A. (1949) *Individualism and Economic Order*, Routledge & Kegan Paul: London.

Hayek, F. A. (1984) collected readings in Nishiyama, C. N. and Leube, K. R., *The Essence of Hayek*, Hoover Institution Press: Stanford.

Hotelling, H. (1929) Stability in competition, *Economic Journal*, **39**, 41–57.

Kalecki, M. (1938) Distribution of national income, *Econometrica*, **6**.

Kalecki, M. (1939) *Essays in the Theory of Economic Fluctuations*, Allen and Unwin: London.

Kirzner, I. M. (1973) *Competition and Entrepreneurship*, University of Chicago Press: Chicago.

Knight, F. H. (1933) *Risk, Uncertainty and Profit*, Houghton Mifflin: Boston.

Lancaster, K. (1979) *Variety, Equity and Efficiency*, Columbia University Press: New York.

Littlechild, S. C. (1978) *The Fallacy of the Mixed Economy*, Institute of Economic Affairs, Hobart Paper 80: London.

Littlechild, S. C. (1986) Three types of market process, in Langlois, R. N., *Economics as a Process*, Cambridge University Press: Cambridge.

Lyons, B. R. (1987) Strategic Behaviour, in Clarke R., and McGuinness A., (eds), *The Theory of the Firm*, Blackwell: Oxford.

Marx, K. (1867) *Das Kapital*, vol. I, reprinted in 1974, Lawrence & Wishart: London.

Marx, K. (1894) *Das Kapital*, vol. III, reprinted in 1974, Lawrence & Wishart: London.

Marx, K. (1939) *Grundrisse*, Penguin: Harmondsworth.

Mason, E. S. (1949) The current state of the monopoly problem in the United States, *Harvard Law Review*, **62**, 1265–85.

Nelson, R. R. and **Winter, S. G.** (1982) *An Evolutionary Theory of Economic Change*, Harvard University Press: Cambridge, Mass.

Rowley, C. K. (1972) *Readings in Industrial Economics*, vol. 1, Macmillan: London.

Salop, S. C. (1979) Strategic entry deterrence, *American Economic Review Papers and Proceedings*, **69**, 335–8.

Schelling, T. C. (1960) *The Strategy of Conflict*, Harvard University Press: Harvard.

Scherer, F. M. (1970) *Industrial Market Structure and Economic Performance*, Rand McNally: Chicago.

Schumpeter, J. A. (1943) *Capitalism, Socialism and Democracy*, Unwin: London.

Schmalensee, R. (1978) Entry deterrence in the ready-to-eat breakfast cereal industry, *Bell Journal of Economics*, **9**, 305–27.

Semmler, W. (1984) *Competition, Monopoly and Differential Profit Rates*, Columbia University Press: New York.

Shaked, A. and **Sutton, J.** (1987) Product differentiation and industrial structure, *Journal of Industrial Economics*, **36**, 131–46.

Shaw, R. W. (1982) Product proliferation with in characteristics space: the U.K. fertiliser industry, *Journal of Industrial Economics*, **31**, 69–92.

Smith, V. L. (1982) Markets as economisers of information: experimental examination of the 'Hayek Hypothesis', *Economic Enquiry*, **20**, 2.

Spence, A. M. (1976) Product differentiation and welfare, *American Economic Review*, **66**, 407–14.

von Stackleberg, H. (1938) *The Theory of the Market Economy*, (1952 edition) Oxford University Press: Oxford.

Steindl, J. (1952) *Maturity and Stagnation in American Capitalism*, Oxford University Press: Oxford.

Stigler, G. J. (1968) *The Organisation of Industry*, Irwin: Homewood

Sylos-Labini, P. (1962) *Oligopoly and Technical Progress*, Harvard University Press: Cambridge, Mass.

Waterson, M. (1984) *Economic Theory of Industry*, Cambridge University Press: Cambridge.

CHAPTER TWO

Barriers to entry

Bruce Lyons

Barriers to entry are essential to the existence of non-competitive behaviour. In their absence, most of monopoly and oligopoly theory becomes vacuous as free entry ensures competitive pricing. Furthermore, if barriers are insufficient to permit monopoly pricing without encouraging entry, a monopolist can no longer employ the simple calculus of setting marginal revenue equal to marginal cost in order to maximise profits. He must explicitly take entry barriers into account whenever pricing and investment decisions are made.[1] Yet despite their crucial importance, they were not seriously investigated until just thirty years ago (Bain 1956; Sylos-Labini 1962). Further empirical work took place through the 1960s but only after the mid-1970s did a serious reappraisal of the theory of entry barriers take place.

This reassessment has led to a considerable new literature which is still developing and has yet to be properly reviewed[2] or assimilated into the standard textbooks. Consequently, many students, policy makers, and even professional economists, have little more understanding of entry barriers than they first learned from Bain's important, pioneering, but by modern standards non-rigorous, theoretical work. In view of the central role that the theory of entry barriers should play in our understanding of the industrial world, this is obviously an undesirable state of affairs.

As the following survey shows, Bain's original work still provides the foundations for our understanding, but formal modelling has unearthed many complexities and at least one major new theme – the importance of commitment to the industry through sunk (non-recoverable) costs. One of the significant implications of sunk costs is that current competition depends on what has happened in the past. Thus, firms A and B may be identical in every way *before* either enters an industry; but once A has actually entered, he becomes committed in such a way that B can find herself relatively disadvantaged. Had B been the firm to enter first then A would have been the disadvantaged firm. In a nutshell, *history matters*.

There are several questions that the economic theorist must ask about entry barriers:

Q1:   Under what conditions can actual or potential entry discipline the industry to act competitively?

Q2:   What are the causes of long-run deviations in price from the competitive level?

Q3:   Do entry barriers result in lower social welfare than would be the outcome in their absence?

Applied economists and policy makers are also interested in:

Q4:   Which barriers are empirically most significant and in which industries?

The basic framework and definitions necessary for tackling these questions are set out in section 1 of this survey and an answer is given to Q1. Section 2 sets about answering Q2 in detail and introduces some problems associated with Q3. Section 3 reviews the empirical work and attempts an answer to Q4. Some of the theoretical issues in sections 1 and 2 are, at first sight, technically quite difficult. No formal mathematical techniques are employed, but the approach of modern game theory is quite rigorous. The reader is urged not to get bogged down on first reading, but a more detailed second reading should reap handsome rewards in understanding how contemporary economic theorists set about analysing business behaviour. Section 3 should be immediately accessible. Each of the three sections is largely self-contained. Finally, for clarity, potential entrants are referred to as female and incumbent firms as male throughout this survey.

1. Basic concepts

(a) DEFINITIONS OF THE TERM 'BARRIER TO ENTRY'

The distinctive features of new entry into an industry are that both (i) a new legal entity is established in that industry and (ii) new productive capacity is set up. To analyse situations where only one of these conditions is met would be to discuss the related but quite distinct phenomena of takeover and fixed capital formation (new investment). Having defined 'entry', it might appear straightforward to define the term 'barrier to entry' simply as anything that prevents new firms from actually entering an industry. Such a simplistic definition, however, would suggest nonsensically that there are entry barriers even in long-run perfectly competitive equilibrium since no new firm then has any incentive to enter. Clearly, any meaningful definition of an entry barrier must have a more substantive content. Which definition is chosen, however, will depend crucially on what use we wish to make of the term. We consider just three possible definitions, which are labelled D1–D3.

Bain, in his classic work on the subject, was troubled 'that most analyses of how business competition works and what makes it work have given little emphasis to the force of the potential or threatened competition of possible competitors, placing a disproportionate emphasis on competition among firms already in any industry' (1956: 1). His motivation was therefore to answer Q1, Q2 and Q4, and this leads naturally to his definition of the height of entry barriers (or the *condition of entry*, as he terms it).

D1: 'the advantage of established sellers in an industry over potential entrant sellers, these advantages being reflected in the extent to which established sellers can persistently raise their prices above a competitive level without attracting new firms to enter the industry'. (Bain 1956: 3)

Thus, Bain's definition is quite general with an entry barrier being, by implication, *anything* that permits high prices in the long run. Several aspects require elaboration.

1. Entry barriers may or may not be reflected in current industry prices. Even if incumbent firms are able to collude perfectly to exploit them, either entry barriers may be so high that even monopoly pricing does not trigger entry (entry is 'blockaded'), or so low that it is better to take high profits now even if entry occurs and future profits are lower ('ineffectively impeded entry'). Only if there is 'effectively impeded' entry might prices directly reflect the height of entry barriers and even here, informational problems may prevent their full exploitation. Bain completes this taxonomy of entry categories with 'easy' entry, which is when price can only exceed 'the minimum attainable average cost of production, distribution and selling' in short-run disequilibrium.

2. Bain lays considerable stress on the fact that there is usually a heterogeneous queue of potential entrants and both the barriers facing the least disadvantaged potential entrant (the 'immediate condition of entry') and those facing potential entrants further down the queue (the 'general condition of entry') may be significant in determining industrial behaviour. This aspect has been largely ignored in the last thirty years and, while acknowledging its potential importance, the theoretical section of this survey follows the trend and is almost entirely concerned with two polar cases: either there is only one potential entrant, or there is a very large number of identical potential entrants.

3. Bain has been criticised for failing to discuss the identity of potential entrants. In particular, it may be of great significance if a firm which is already producing in another, possibly related, industry is willing to diversify (see e.g. Brunner, 1961). The importance of diversifying entry will be seen in the empirical work of section 3.

4. Caves and Porter (1977) suggest that the concept of entry barriers should not be restricted only to entry into 'an industry'. Most industries divide into segmented groups between which there is some interdependence, but within which it is substantially greater. Groups may be due to heterogeneous products, product range, vertical integration, ownership, branding, or mode of distribution. New firms enter into the groups rather than 'the industry' and there will be barriers to mobility between groups, of a similar nature to those barriers which are usually discussed in relation to the industry. For instance, specialist firms may prefer to initially enter a low-barrier group and only tackle the more profitable high-barrier sector once they have become well established, or not at all. Of course, this discussion raises the question of how an industry should be defined in the first place, but that is not an issue we have space to tackle here.

Stigler has attempted a more direct definition of what constitutes an entry barrier.

D2: a barrier to entry is 'a cost of producing (at some or every rate of output) which must be borne by a firm which seeks to enter an industry but is not borne by firms already in the industry'.   (Stigler 1968: 67)

Two features of this definition stand out. Firstly, it rules out anything that does not raise the potential entrant's cost curve above that of incumbents. Secondly, it is designed to answer a different question to those which interested Bain. Stigler asks simply: 'on what does firm size depend – economies of scale, barriers to entry, or something else?' (ibid.: 67). His answer is 'that demand and cost (economies of scale) conditions govern the size of firms. The barriers to entry would then be restricted to differentially higher costs of new firms which act as one force – others are location and advertising and product characteristics – which affect the demands of individual firms' (ibid.: 69). Stigler is thus concerned with firm size, and unlike Bain he is not attempting to directly answer Q1. Consequently, Stigler's semantics require that economies of scale cannot be counted as an entry barrier, for if he included them as such, this would be double counting! However, if Stigler were asked Q1 or Q2, he would not be able to deny without further argument that economies of scale, together with demand conditions, *might* contrive to permit prices to persist above the competitive level. For our purposes, D1 is clearly the more interesting. This detailed analysis of Stigler's motivation is only necessary because D2 is often used out of context.

　　More recently, several authors have expressed concern at both of these definitions. This is primarily because they wish, with some justification, to change the question. Behind the intrinsic interest economists have in business behaviour and its determinants, there lies a deeper concern about the ability of market economies to provide the best possible allocation of resources. Does Adam Smith's 'invisible hand' actually work? Under what conditions should governments intervene? And, in this particular case, are all impediments to free entry bad (i.e. Q3)? From this point of view, it can be worrying if 'barriers to entry', as defined by Bain or Stigler, is used as an unquestioned pejorative term. It would be quite untrue to state that entry barriers always lead to inefficiencies greater than any other feasible outcome. A classic example is given by the Schumpeterian mechanism for technical progress whereby the lure of monopoly profits is necessary for the initial development of the product. Without the protection of some form of entry barrier (for example, a patent), there would be no incentive to invent. We should not compare a Schumpeterian world with one in which new products fall as manna from heaven, but with some other feasible alternative.[3]

　　Such trade-offs between the positive externalities generated by some restraint (e.g. invention generated by patents) and monopolistic distortions (e.g. the consequent output restriction) may be quite common. This leads von Weizsacker (1980a: 400) to 'distinguish between two opposing causes of a distortion. Entry into an activity may be socially suboptimal because the activity is not sufficiently protected. This is the case of positive externalities. Or it is suboptimal because incumbent firms are protected from entry i.e. incumbent firms are overly protected. This is the case of barriers to entry'.[4] His welfare-based definition of entry barriers naturally follows.

D3: 'they thus can be defined to be socially undesirable limitations of
entry, which are attributable to the protection of resource owners
already in the industry.   (von Weizsacker 1980a: 400)

Demsetz develops a related argument based on the appropriate allocation
of property rights: 'the problem of defining ownership is precisely that of creating
properly scaled legal barriers to entry' (1982: 49). It would be possible to draw such
legal rights at any number of places: the right not to have your factory burned down
by a rival, the right not to have your trademark copied, the right not to have your
technology copied, the right not to have your price undercut, and so on. The policy
question for Demsetz is whether the evolving legal system has drawn the line in the
right place.

While it is clearly important to understand the welfare implications, it can
confuse the arguments to rush straight in. We therefore prefer a two-stage
approach. We first consider the conditions that permit price to exceed cost in the
long run. Only then do we ask whether or not the allocation of resources could be
improved upon if such barriers were removed by some feasible policy intervention.

(b) CONTESTABLE MARKET THEORY

Neither D1 nor D3 give any direct idea of what actually constitutes a barrier to
entry. One constructive way to approach this question (Q2) is to first find a set of
conditions under which established sellers would have *no* advantage relative to
potential entrants (i.e. answer Q1). Barriers are then found in the absence of such
conditions.

Bain suggests that the following are necessary:

'(1) established firms have no absolute cost advantages over potential
entrant firms;
(2) established firms have no product differentiation advantages . . .; and
(3) economies of large-scale firm [relative to total output] are negligible'
(1956: 12).

Although many of Bain's arguments have stood the test of time, it took a
quarter of a century before a group of economists, figure-headed by Baumol,[5]
provided a rigorous set of sufficient conditions for entry barriers not to exist when
scale economies are present. A market which satisfies these conditions is said to be
perfectly contestable. 'A perfectly contestable market can be defined as one where
(1) all producers have access to the same technology; (2) the technology may have
scale economies such as fixed costs, but must not have sunk [non-recoverable] costs;
and (3) incumbents cannot change prices instantly [yet] consumers respond
instantly to price differences' (Dixit 1982). The important implication is that
because 'entry is absolutely free *and exit is absolutely costless*, potential entrants find
it appropriate to evaluate the profitability of entry in terms of the incumbent firms'
pre-entry prices' (Baumol 1982: 3–4).
Imagine a firm producing any number of products and which is making
positive pure profits. If each market is perfectly contestable, then whatever the

economies of scale or cost complementarities, another firm can simply duplicate the incumbent's output pattern but shave prices fractionally to grab all existing customers and still make a profit. If the original incumbent later retaliates with even lower prices, the entrant can costlessly leave the market. This threat of 'hit-and-run' entry is sufficient to deter the incumbent from pricing above average costs. By the same reasoning, if the incumbent makes zero profits but is technologically inefficient he is similarly vulnerable to profitable hit-and-run entry.

The implication is that such markets can have no entry barriers as defined by Bain and it is in the absence of the three characteristics summarised by Dixit that we should find examples of potential barriers. The first condition is the same as Bain's 'no absolute cost advantages' (and Stigler's definition of an entry barrier), but the next two have a significantly different focus, particularly in the emphasis on sunk costs rather than economies of scale and also on expected price responses and response lags. This new emphasis will be applied extensively in the search for entry barriers in section 2.

Before leaving contestability, however, we demonstrate that perfectly contestable markets also satisfy the welfare-based definition of zero entry barriers. Consider a firm producing in several markets, one of which is being cross-subsidised (price is set at less than marginal cost). Once more, an entrant could duplicate the incumbent's output except for producing less in the subsidised market (thus earning higher overall profits), and price shaving would ensure that she could snatch all existing customers (except a few in the costly, subsidised market) and force the incumbent out. Consequently, neither cross-subsidisation nor predatory pricing can be sustainable practices and price cannot be set at less than marginal cost.

It is less straightforward to show that price cannot exceed marginal cost. Indeed, if the incumbent is a monopolist, this need not be so. A simple example is given by a single-product monopolist who has fixed overheads and constant marginal costs, and who is selling at a price that equals average cost. Although price exceeds marginal cost, there is no output that an entrant would wish to sell at any lower price. Moving away from monopoly, however, if there are at least two incumbent firms charging a price greater than marginal cost, an entrant can always undercut them both and sell some output, greater than that of either incumbent but less than the previous combined industry output, to make a profit. Thus, as long as at least two firms exist in a contestable market, price cannot exceed marginal cost. Combined with the earlier result that cross-subsidisation is not possible, such markets must have price equal to marginal cost. This means that, with the possible exception of pure monopoly,[6] contestable markets provide the same optimality properties as perfectly competitive markets, but with much less restrictive assumptions regarding the size of firm relative to the market.

(c) 'INNOCENT' AND 'STRATEGIC' ENTRY DETERRENCE[7]

It is often useful to distinguish between entry barriers which are in some sense natural, exogenous, structural or, the term we shall follow Salop (1979) in using, *innocent*; and those which have been manipulated by incumbents and are endogenous, behavioural or, the term we use, *strategic*. This distinction is developed below for the case where there is one incumbent monopolist, IM, and one potential entrant, PE. This simplification of only two firms is very helpful for the purpose of clarification, but we return to the more general cases of more than one potential entrant and an incumbent oligopoly at the end of this section.

Innocent entry barriers arise simply as the side-effect of profit-maximising decisions taken without regard to their implications for potential entrants. Such barriers may be divided into *post-entry absolute advantages*, such as superior product design or lower cost (see e.g. section 2a); and *pre-entry asymmetry advantages*, because even when IM and PE are each equally efficient, IM has usually committed some capital resources to the industry while PE has yet to do so (see e.g. section 2b). In terms of contestability theory, the difference between post- and pre-entry advantages is the difference between violating Dixit's conditions (1) and (2) given on page 30. Note that the third contestability condition gives a (fairly implausible) post-entry asymmetric advantage to the *entrant* in that she can undercut the incumbent without fear of immediate retaliation.

The first-mover advantage that results from pre-entry asymmetries provides a foundation for the theory of *strategic* entry barriers. Broadly speaking, there are three ways in which the pre-entry asymmetries may be strategically exploited; that is to say, developed and exploited by incumbents so as to deter entry.

(i) Independent commitment

Certain types of strategic commitment, while leaving a potential entrant's costs unchanged, will leave her in little doubt that entry would not be profitable. The basic, and rather subtle, idea is that IM acts so as to influence PE by altering PE's expectations of how IM will behave (Schelling 1960). Consider an industry which has two possible technologies, A and B. A has relatively high marginal costs, but B has higher overheads. Following entry, the original incumbent would have to choose between two levels of output, q_1 or q_2, with $q_2 > q_1$. Assume that if q_1 is chosen, the entrant will make positive profits, but if q_2 is chosen, both the entrant and the original incumbent make losses. Suppose the lower overhead cost technology A is more profitable pre-entry and, furthermore, that if entry occurs the incumbent makes post-entry profits of $\pi_1^A > 0$ if he produces q_1 but only $\pi_2^A < \pi_1^A$ if q_2 is produced. Then innocent profit maximisation would lead to technology A being chosen with the result that PE, who believes that IM will set output rationally post-entry, will enter (because she expects q_1 to be chosen which, in turn, makes entry profitable).

However, commitment to the apparently inefficient technology B may reverse IM's payoffs to his post-entry output choice. Lower marginal costs encourage higher output rates so it is quite possible that $\pi_2^B > \pi_1^B$ (with the possibility that profits are negative at both output levels). In this case, the entrant must expect IM to choose high output q_2, so entry would not be profitable. As long as the monopoly profits with technology B exceed duopoly profits with technology A, IM will adopt technology B in order to commit himself to high output levels and so deter entry. An example of this sort of strategic behaviour may be found in the choice made by a multinational enterprise (MNE) between supplying a foreign market by exporting or by direct investment producing abroad. Overseas production has the advantage of avoiding (marginal) tariff and transport costs, but the disadvantage of incurring extra (overhead) search, administrative and set-up costs. In the absence of any threat of entry into the foreign market, the MNE may prefer to supply it by exporting. But if competitive entry is a genuine possibility, then strategic considerations may dictate the overseas production option.

(ii) Joint cost raising

Another class of strategic commitment raises PE's costs as well as IM's. A case where PE's costs rise even more than IM's is discussed in section 2b, but here we investigate the simple abstract case where IM chooses the cost structure which must then be matched by PE. As an example, it might be the case that the incumbent can choose to advertise, in which case advertising becomes necessary for marketing in the industry. Alternative cost commitments could relate to research and development, product range, etc.[8]

If he does not advertise, and there is no entry, IM earns π_0; but if there is entry he gets only $\pi_1 < \pi_0$. If PE is at no post-entry disadvantage, then by symmetry, she too can expect π_1 so entry will occur whenever $\pi_1 > 0$. Next consider IM's payoff if he spends α on advertising, a cost that he knows PE would have to match but which is assumed to have no other discernible benefit such as raising revenue. If $\pi_1 - \alpha < 0$, neither firm would make a profit post-entry, so entry will not occur (as long as PE believes that IM will continue advertising post-entry).[9] Thus this advertising strategy both prevents entry and gives IM profits of $\pi_0 - \alpha$; and choosing $\alpha = \pi_1$, which is the minimum level of advertising necessary to deter entry, he will decide to advertise if the profit resulting from advertising, $\pi_0 - \pi_1 > \pi_1$, which is what is expected without advertising and with consequent entry. But it has already been argued that unless there is perfect collusion monopoly profits exceed joint duopoly profits, $\pi_0 > 2\pi_1$, so the advertising option is always worth while. Clearly, as long as the post-entry market is sufficiently competitive it remains possible to deter entry even when advertising need not be matched pound for pound by PE.

(iii) Crude threat

This leads on to the third class of entry-deterring strategies which involves the threat of possibly irrational post-entry behaviour by IM. In particular, IM may threaten a price war if PE dares to enter. This would be mutually destructive and it may appear not to be in IM's interest to actually carry out such threats, but as long as there is some doubt in PE's mind as to IM's reaction, crude threat may still deter entry. For instance, if $\pi_1 > 0$ is the profit that results for each firm if IM passively shares the market post-entry, $\pi_2 < 0$ is the loss each firm expects from an aggressive price war, and x is the probability PE attaches to such a price war, PE can expect a payoff to entry of $(1 - x) \pi_1 + x \pi_2$. This is negative as long as $x > \pi_1/(\pi_1 - \pi_2)$. Thus, it is in IM's interest to try to convey that a price war would be both likely (x is large) and expensive ($-\pi_2$ is large); while PE is likely to defy the threats if accommodating duopoly profits, π_1, are high enough.

For each of these three categories to be totally effective there must be some irrecoverable commitment by IM to the industry (Schelling 1960). Without such sunk costs, PE may reasonably expect IM for instance, to revert to technology A or cut back on advertising post-entry. It is because it is so difficult to commit *ex ante* to a price war *ex post* that some economists argue they will never take place, and entrants should rationally set $x = 0$ in the 'crude threat' example. However, this ignores the important fact that there are usually many potential entrants and not just one. In such cases, a price war with one can be seen as a commitment to defend IM's position and so discourage the others (Yamey 1972). On this alternative logic, x may be rated as higher the more potential entrants there are, and entry will be easier when IM does not view it as the thin end of the wedge.[10] In Bain's terminology, therefore, we need to consider both the immediate and the general conditions of entry when assessing the likelihood of a price war. Influential theoretical papers by Kreps and Wilson (1982) and Milgrom and Roberts (1982) demonstrate that even a very small probability that IM is genuinely committed to a price war, a probability much smaller than the critical x in the above example, can be sufficient to deter entry if IM is threatened in more than one market and so wishes to build a reputation for aggressively responding to entrants.

Finally, Caves and Porter (1977) point out the problems that arise once we move away from the world of monopoly. If the industry is oligopolistic, there are two opposing forces at work. Firstly, strategic entry barriers are a collective capital good, that is a public good as far as the oligopolists are concerned, and as such their appropriate provision and exploitation would have to be settled by collusive agreement. This introduces all the usual coordination and free-riding problems and there may be under-provision of entry barriers. However, against this is the fact that much oligopolistic rivalry is via non-price competition, such as advertising and product development, and entry barriers may be the (relatively) innocent by-product of such behaviour. On balance, therefore, oligopolistic barrier-building activities may be either more or less than those designed for joint profit maximisation. In section 2 of this survey, the polar case of an incumbent pure monopolist is maintained in order to clarify the issues, though the oligopoly problem is discussed once more in section 3, since it cannot be divorced from actual industrial behaviour. A recent theoretical treatment by Gilbert and Vives (1986) suggests that free-riding will not be a problem for oligopolists wishing to deter entry, even when they act non-cooperatively.

2. Sources of entry barriers

The discussion so far has been somewhat abstract in order to clarify some fundamental concepts behind the theory of entry barriers. In this section, one step is taken towards the application of these concepts to problems that may be faced by, for example, the Monopolies Commission or industrialists. We analyse four types of phenomena which are widely observed in the world at large, and focus on two central questions. In what circumstances do they result in long-run deviations in price from the competitive level? Do such entry barriers result in lower social welfare than would be the outcome in their absence?

(a) ABSOLUTE COST ADVANTAGES

Bain (1956) isolates four main sources of absolute cost advantage:

1. Patents or secrecy may restrict access to the most efficient production techniques.
2. Incumbents may control the most efficient (cheapest or highest quality) sources of supply of an important factor of production (e.g. natural resources or management expertise).
3. If a factor is in very limited supply, even a small increase in demand following entry may raise price significantly to both entrant and incumbents.
4. Incumbents may have access to lower-cost funds than are available to potential entrants; this advantage is magnified if production techniques are capital intensive and subject to large economies of scale.

Such cost advantages may be either innocent or strategically manipulated. Three examples are suggestive of how the higher cost of capital faced by entrants can be strategically exploited. We continue with the simplifying assumption of one incumbent monopolist, IM, and one potential entrant, PE.

1. Forward vertical integration by IM reduces the size of PE's potential market, so PE must either face a restricted number of potential buyers or borrow more heavily to set up a parallel integrated enterprise. Exclusive dealing contracts with retailers perform the same function of squeezing PE's options. Backward vertical integration causes a similar loss of choice and increased uncertainty with respect to sources of supply. An entrant once more has to enter at two stages of production in order to compete on equal terms. Not only does this raise her capital requirement, but she must also produce at one stage where she may not be technically competent.[11]

2. 'Full line forcing' is a practice whereby IM requires dealers to carry either a whole range of his products or none at all. If dealers do not have the space or money to carry more than one range, then PE must enter right across the product range if she is to be able to sell anything. The consequent capital cost and possible technological disadvantages are similar to those incurred by strategic vertical integration.

3. Advertising and R & D are inherently risky activities with little or no resale value in the event of bankruptcy. Even if the cost of raising finance for a mortgageable property like a factory may not be particularly high, borrowing for advertising and R & D can be prohibitively expensive if it can be obtained at all. This can clearly be exploited by IM as long as PE's required expenditure is positively related to IM's. Advertising and R & D are further discussed in section 2d, but note here that the entry problems may be much less acute for large diversifying firms.

Whether innocent or strategic, absolute cost advantages permit IM to maintain price above his own long-run average cost without attracting new entry. However, is this always socially undesirable? It is convenient to look at each of Bain's sources of cost advantage in turn.

1. The social benefits of patents (or, equivalently, secrecy) have already been discussed. Without the prospect of monopoly profits the incentive to invent would be very much reduced. A similar argument applies to any organisational change that raises efficiency. This is not to argue that the present patent system is optimal, but it is almost certainly better than no protection at all for new ideas.[12]

2. The ownership of scarce resources constitutes an entry barrier, but only into the 'scarce resource industry' and not the downstream manufacturing process. If a vertically integrated aluminium manufacturer owns a bauxite mine that can produce at low cost, the accounts may show that he has a lower aluminium cost curve than any potential entrant could hope for, and he is making super-normal profits. Were the bauxite mines auctioned to potential entrants, however, they would command a price that leaves PE no better off than if she were to purchase more marginal mines. On resource ownership grounds, there is no barrier into the aluminium smelting industry. Of course, this does not mean that we should not be worried about monopoly in the scarce resource industry but this is where attention should be focused. If the scarce resource is skilled labour or management, the same basic principle applies. Either they will earn scarcity rents themselves or the firm will record paper profits. If an entrant can only tempt such personnel away by paying their true opportunity cost, PE cannot earn a positive profit. The only welfare implication of such a barrier is that shareholders are earning profits at the expense of the owners of scarce talents. There is no loss of consumer surplus unless the scarce talents deliberately restrict their own supply in order to raise their rewards.

3. If factor prices would rise equally to IM and PE post-entry, the problem is formally identical to industry price falling as supply increases. The analysis of such situations is postponed until the discussion of economies of scale in the next section.

4. The reason why PE has to pay a higher rate of interest than IM is often put down to 'capital market imperfections'. If capital markets are imperfect, then this is a problem that is best tackled, if possible, directly and not in the capital-using industry. However, a probably more important reason for the interest premium paid by PE is the risk involved in penetrating a new market. Such risk premiums will naturally be demanded by even the most perfect capital market. It is useful to distinguish between the risk associated with entry (e.g. how will IM react?) and the inherent riskiness of an industry (e.g. if demand is volatile). Strategic threatening postures by IM may be designed to exploit the former to the general social detriment. However, were the regulatory authorities to attempt to reduce the rate of return in inherently risky industries, this would reduce the incentive to enter and might actually worsen the allocation of resources. Finally, capital cost disadvantages may be much less severe to a diversifying entrant, who is backed by large financial reserves, than to a specialist entrant with only the banks and private investors behind her.

Thus, although absolute cost advantages are clearly a barrier to entry on definitions D1 and D2, the welfare consequences of each such barrier require careful thought before appropriate policy recommendations can be proposed.

(b) ECONOMIES OF SCALE AND EXCESS CAPACITY

(i) Natural monopoly

We begin by investigating a very strong form of economies of scale, natural monopoly, before going on to develop the argument with more limited scale economies.[13] Natural monopoly provides a useful benchmark as well as being of particular interest in the analysis of public utilities and other industries which are often regulated or nationalised because supply by more than one firm would lead to high costs (for example telephones, gas and electricity distribution, some air routes).

A formal definition of a natural monopoly is that the total cost, $C(q)$, of producing any output, q, is less than that of two or more firms producing the same total output, i.e., $C(q) < C(y) + C(q-y)$ where $0 < y < q$. This must hold for all y in this range and for all $q \leqslant q^*$, where q^* is the socially desirable output. This definition is illustrated in Fig. 2.1 for an L-shaped single-product firm's average cost curve, AC. There exists a natural monopoly as long as $M > \frac{1}{2} q^*$. Only if $M \leqslant \frac{1}{2} q^*$ could two firms both produce at minimum average cost, c.

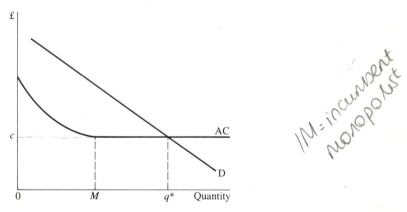

FIG. 2.1 Natural monopoly if $M > \frac{1}{2} q^*$

It has already been argued that as long as the preconditions for a perfectly contestable market hold, no entry barriers exist even when there is a natural monopoly. The first precondition is the absence of absolute cost advantages. These have already been discussed and we here consider only firms which have access to identical cost curves. Secondly, contestable markets require that there be no sunk costs. Sunk costs destroy the feasibility of profit snatching hit-and-run entry and consequently IM may be safe from entry even when price exceeds marginal cost. The 'sunkness' of costs is clearly central to the issue of economies of scale as an entry barrier, so can we expect to observe industries in which there are economies of scale but no sunk costs? Weitzman (1983) argues no – economies of scale *must* imply sunk costs. Essentially, his argument is as follows. Consider the production of steel in the absence of sunk costs. PE can buy the most efficient blast furnace on the market (say 2 million tons annual capacity), produce 30 tons of steel in just 8 minutes, then immediately resell the furnace at cost less normal depreciation. This is quite feasible if there are no sunk costs. Alternative institutional arrangements might permit hiring the furnace at competitive interest costs plus depreciation. PE can now sell one ton a day before starting up production again the following month. The ability to produce 365 tons of steel per annum for exactly the same unit cost as a firm producing 2 million tons, means that the absence of sunk costs destroys the concept of economies of scale.[14] Clearly, this is an absurd example, but only if one can find a case where such an argument does not sound absurd, can one find an example of nil sunk costs.[15]

Whenever there exist any sunk costs, PE must necessarily consider the response of IM to her entry, and the ground is set for an entry barrier. The longer PE is able to undercut IM post-entry (the third, and rather implausible, precondition for contestability), the less troubled she will be about sinking costs. At one extreme, if IM is *never* able to respond to PE's low price, he must price at average cost or else lose his market forever. Only in this case are sunk costs not crucial to contestability. On the other hand, if, as is far more probable, IM can respond immediately, PE must give careful thought to the degree of competition that is likely to develop. At the other extreme, where cut-throat Bertrand price competition is expected, even the tiniest sunk cost is sufficient to deter entry because price is driven down to marginal cost, and average cost exceeds marginal cost if there are economies of scale. A loss must therefore be expected by PE. In general, it may be possible to argue that the greater the proportion of costs that is non-recoverable on exit, and the quicker and more aggressively IM is willing and able to respond, then the greater is the premium over cost that IM can earn before PE is willing to risk entry. Such a proposition, however, has not yet been proved in formal theoretical models (the Appendix in Vickers and Yarrow 1985 makes an accessible start) though it is supported by some interesting experimental work (Coursey *et al.* 1984) which is discussed in section 3b(ii).

There is one tactic whereby PE might be able to reduce IM's ability to respond to cut-price entry. Prior to entry, PE could contact potential customers and sign a contract to supply at a price less than IM is currently charging. Although this would not be possible when there were many small buyers, it may be feasible when purchasers are more concentrated, such as large retail chains or major construction projects (Demsetz 1968). Two further major problems must, however, also be surmounted if PE is to make advance contracts. First, she has no reputation for high-quality production. Buyer uncertainty may be less if PE is an established firm diversifying from a related industry but it cannot be eliminated.[16] Second, it is usually open to IM to insert a 'meeting the competition' clause in his contracts, for example committing to match or even undercut by 5 per cent any rival tender. Although such contracts should alert customers to excessive prices, in practice they may be able to do little about it. On balance, in most industrial markets, there is little reason to believe that IM can respond to price cuts other than almost immediately and this is the stylised assumption adopted in the rest of this section.[17]

Overall, then, it is likely that natural monopoly *is* a barrier to entry except in some rather unusual circumstances. But if a natural monopoly confers an entry barrier, does it matter in the practical sense that there is an alternative, better institutional arrangement? In an ideal world, of course, it does. We would wish to have marginal cost pricing everywhere with a subsidy whenever that is necessary in order for there to be no losses and so assure production. This is rarely a real-world option. The second best might be to impose average cost pricing, but even this is often difficult to enforce in the public sector, let alone in the private sector. One possible policy option, however, may be to encourage (e.g. by subsidy or a guiding governmental hand) the setting up of one or more rival firms to compete with IM. If p_i is the price when there are i firms in the industry, with $p_i < p_j$ *for all* $i > j$, due to greater competition, and AC_i is the average cost when there are i firms charging p_i with $AC_i > AC_j$ for all $i > j$, due to unreaped scale economies, then there is a trade-off between lower prices (i.e. greater consumer surplus) when the number of firms increases, and higher costs (i.e. lower profits). The argument is illustrated in Fig. 2.2. Marginal costs are constant, c, but each firm has overheads of F. A second firm reduces price from p_1 to p_2 leading to social gains of the shaded area G. However, this gain is bought at the cost of additional overheads. Only if $F < G$ is it worth encouraging actual entry into the industry.[18]

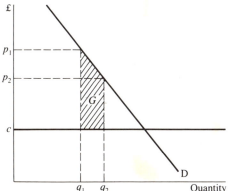

FIG. 2.2 Welfare trade-off with natural monopoly

(ii) The general case

Having concluded that, except in exceptional circumstances, economies of scale do confer an entry barrier on natural monopolists, we next examine whether or not the arguments can be generalised to other situations. The discussion is limited, for simplicity, to L-shaped cost curves as in Figure 2.1, but we now develop the case where $M < \frac{1}{2} q$. Modigliani (1958), based on the work of Bain (1956) and Sylos-Labini (1962), provides a famous formulation of one strategy IM may use, known as *limit pricing*. The crucial assumption is that PE reads current output by IM as a signal for his future output. This belief, known as *Sylos' postulate*, can be exploited by IM acting as a Stackelberg leader to the follower PE. IM chooses output q_L such that for any output $y > 0$ produced by PE, the total industry output $(q_L + y)$ generates a price that does not quite cover PE's average costs.

This limit-pricing strategy is illustrated in Fig. 2.3. Given that IM will be producing q_L, PE must expect her output to push down price along the residual demand curve to the right of the vertical dash-dot line. Her cost of production is therefore given by horizontal displacement of the AC curve to a new origin at q_L. The expected demand curve is everywhere below her cost curve so entry would not be profitable. The height of the entry barrier $(p_L - c)$ increases with minimum efficient size (M), the slope of the cost curve before M, and the slope of the demand curve. Note that IM may be able to strategically raise costs in order to exploit these conditions. For instance, if small-scale production is relatively labour intensive and trades unions ensure that the same wage rates apply right across the industry, IM may be able to concede unduly high wages in order to steepen the cost curve and so raise the limit price more than his own costs (Williamson 1968). More generally, if IM can succeed in raising the degree of economies of scale by any means, this may be profitable. For instance, if the technology originally involves constant costs so no entry barrier exists, but IM can devise a fixed cost to be faced by all firms (e.g. advertising), this will enable an economies-of-scale entry barrier to be created. There may also be a bias in directing R & D in favour of new large-scale technologies.

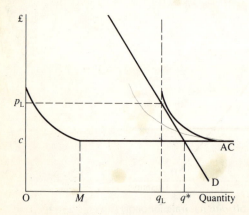

FIG. 2.3 Limit pricing with economies of scale

The theory of limit pricing as a means of converting economies of scale into a strategic entry barrier has been subject to a barrage of criticisms.[19] We focus on just three. First, if entry is slow, IM can usually maximise present value by initially raising price to nearer the monopoly level. Higher current profits are earned at the expense of lower but discounted future profits once entry has taken place.[20] Although this is a criticism of the static theory, it leaves intact the basic idea of a limit price to slow down entry. Second, even if entry is instantaneous when it occurs, it may not be profitable for IM to limit price. In particular, if scale economies are relatively small, the limit price maybe very close to average cost. As long as IM can rely on PE not to act too competitively, it may then be more profitable to reduce output, raise industry price and permit limited entry, rather than earn very low profits while deterring entry.[21] The feasibility of such an option requires that there be only a very limited number of potential entrants or else IM's market share would be rapidly eroded.

The above two points do not dispute the basic belief by the entrant that IM's output will be unaltered by entry. A third, more fundamental criticism has been the attack on Sylos' postulate. Why should PE expect IM to maintain his output post-entry? The assumption is equivalent to the belief that were PE to enter, IM would engage in a costly price war. Surely, the argument goes, it would be better to collude post-entry to avoid mutual ruination. PE, expecting IM to act rationally rather than obstreperously, would therefore not be deterred. IM, realising this, will not attempt to deter entry. However, we have met this argument and its rebuttal before (towards the end of section 1c). Once more the 'rationality of collusion' ignores the possibility that there is more than one potential entrant. In that case, accommodation of one into the collusive group would only encourage the others. An expensive price war with the first entrant may then look like a worthwhile investment to IM if it serves to act as a warning to others (see section 1c(iii)). Once we accept the possibility of an aggressive post-entry response by IM, however, pre-entry limit pricing comes under another source of attack. Why should IM waste valuable profits by pricing at p_L prior to entry? Why should he not charge the higher, monopoly price pre-entry, but be prepared to aggressively slash his price when entry is seriously threatened? Far from over-predicting the ability of IM to exploit market power, Sylos' postulate begins to look very conservative. But how can IM signal to PE that he is willing and able to fight a price war?

(iii) Strategic investment in excess capacity

As long ago as 1940, Stigler suggested that a simple telephone call might do the trick of effectively signalling a price war. The attraction of a verbal threat is that it is cheap and simple, and it is not entirely without appeal.[22] It could certainly be effective if aimed at a diversifying PE who could be reminded that her own key markets might be vulnerable to IM's diversification plans. In general, however, such a threat is empty unless it can be backed up by some form of commitment. If IM is producing the monopoly output at full capacity when PE signs a contract to build a rival factory, IM has two options. He can either accept PE's entry as a *fait accompli*, or he can suicidally sign up to increase his own capacity at the same time.

If, on the other hand, IM is currently producing the monopoly output but already has the capacity to carry out his threat to expand production, PE must think twice before she too commits.[23] IM has the ability to rapidly signal his aggression by cutting price to p_L or even to marginal costs prior to PE's capacity coming on stream. PE may be inclined to regard such excess capacity with disdain, preferring the logic of post-entry cooperation, were it not for two additional characteristics associated with excess capacity.[24] First, if capacity is in the nature of a sunk cost which would be a millstone round IM's neck post-entry, PE will be more circumspect before concluding that IM is bluffing. Second, if, as must nearly always be the case, PE is not fully aware of the exact shape and position of the industry demand curve, or her own cost curve, she may read the signal of excess capacity to mean that industry output is already near its competitive level. IM's apparent profitability (the textbook signal for entry to occur) could then be put down to exceptional efficiency, very inelastic demand, or 'creative' accounting.

On a dissenting note, Dixit (1980) cautions against the power of excess capacity to create an entry barrier. Excess capacity is futile (except as a means of confounding the profits signal) if PE believes that IM's output will fall from the monopoly level, not rise, post-entry.[25] This would usually be the case if, say, the post-entry pricing game is Cournot duopoly. The real importance of Dixit's point is that it draws attention once more to the critical role of expected post-entry competition in deciding the extent to which economies of scale and excess capacity create a barrier to entry. Ironically, the more competitive the market is *expected* to be, the greater the entry barrier.

It is time to summarise the basic issues discussed in this section. In natural monopolies, the existence of sunk costs and the ability of IM to respond to price cuts, if only by matching them, means that IM can price in excess of average cost without attracting entry. The same logic can be applied to any industry in which production involves scale economies as long as potential entrants do not expect to be fully accommodated post-entry by IM. It is clearly in IM's interest to try to convey to PE that far from welcoming her with open arms, he will come out kicking and fighting. Rather than threaten to go into battle with his trousers down, IM will usually do better to gird his loins, perhaps by holding excess capacity, in order to signal that he is ready and willing for aggressive action. Finally, strategic investments such as excess capacity are socially wasteful in that they raise costs without raising output. Such entry barriers therefore involve both allocative and technical inefficiency. In fact, it is even possible that the threat of entry actually reduces social welfare below that achieved by a simple monopolist who does not fear entry and so does not make strategic investments. This issue is further explored in Lyons (1986).

(c) PRODUCT DIFFERENTIATION

Ever since Bain first wrote on the subject, discussions of product differentiation and advertising have been casually thrown together with often confusing results. This survey recognises that the two are often empirically inter-twined, but attempts to clarify their respective roles. Product differentiation is a situation where two or more products are perceived by consumers to be close but imperfect substitutes. Such differentiation may be supported by the laws of trademark, copyright, patent, etc. Advertising, along with other promotional and R & D expenditures, is an investment by firms designed to improve their market position. Thus, in this section, although we sometimes permit firms to choose their product types from an existing menu of specifications, they are not allowed to manipulate demand other than by pricing decisions. Advertising and R & D decisions are discussed in the next section.

The definition of product differentiation is broad enough to warrant division into at least two categories:

1. Quality or vertical differentiation: products may be generally ranked according to quality such that if each is the same price everyone prefers the best.
2. Product range or horizontal differentiation: either different customers perfer different products or each consumer prefers a wider to a narrower variety of products; either way similarly priced products can each find their own niche in the market.

These two categories of product differentiation require separate treatment in the theory of entry barriers.

(i) Quality differentiation

If the quality of each product is known and all consumers agree on their preferred quality, the market is essentially similar to the homogeneous case already studied.[26] However, if the quality of a new firm's product is uncertain, an entry barrier can arise even in the absence of absolute cost advantages and scale economies.

Consider the simple, stylised example of an emerging market for Bytes. There are several potential producers and each is capable of producing Bytes at the same cost. Although each firm would produce a meticulously standard product which each consumer would value at $\bar{v}$, the public does not know this for sure. Consequently, they value an untried product at $v_e < \bar{v}$.[27] The first product to enter the market can sell positive output as long as it prices at $p^* < v_e$. Once the public has sampled the first firm's product and realises its quality, the same amount could be sold at the higher price of $\bar{v}$. The demand for Bytes of known and unknown qualities is represented in Fig. 2.4 as D and D_e respectively. q_m is the maximum size of the market.

What demand can the second firm expect? In order to focus most sharply on the problem at hand, assume the potential entrant believes that the incumbent

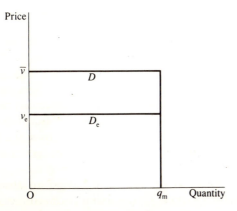

FIG. 2.4 The demand for Bytes

will not change his price, $\hat{p}_1$, post-entry. Thus, the market is contestable in every way except that the incumbent's product quality is known but the entrant's is not. Consumers will switch from the incumbent to the entrant only if they expect to gain a greater consumer surplus, that is only if $v_e - p_2 > \bar{v} - p_1$ or $p_2 < p_1 - (\bar{v} - v_e)$, where p_2 is the entrant's price. In other words, the pioneer brand is able to earn a premium of $(\bar{v} - v_e)$ over and above what a potential entrant can expect. Clearly the first firm can prevent entry by pricing at a little less than the entrant's average cost plus this premium. This entry barrier results simply from a first-mover advantage: it is easier to attract customers for non-branded products than from the pioneer's customers who are already satisfied with what they are using. Schmalensee (1982) develops this basic idea to show that the barrier to entry increases with scale economies, and when the product is purchased less frequently (frequent purchase means that it is more worth while experimenting with a possibly unsatisfactory new brand).

This analysis raises the questions: would it be beneficial to abandon the legal protection given by trademarks, etc? Would it not be better to permit firms to make good copies of Kelloggs Cornflakes even down to the cockerel on the packet? If, as in the above Bytes example, quality is exogenously given, affirmative answers may have some force.[28] However, the argument is much less clear if quality is variable *ex post* and firms can *choose* whether to produce high- or low-quality products. If firms are unable to distinguish themselves in order to build a reputation for high-quality products, they will all be tarred with the same brush and the market may move into a low-quality equilibrium trap.[29] For instance, assume there are only two possible qualities: high, H, which consumers value at v_H and which cost c_H to produce, and low, L, which is valued at v_L and costs only c_L to produce. $v_H > v_L$ and $c_H > c_L$. Furthermore, assume the consumer surplus plus profit margin is greater for H, i.e. $v_H - c_H > v_L - c_L$. Clearly the market would be better served by product H than by L. Suppose the first firm enters the market producing H. If that firm is unable to differentiate his product, an entrant can set up and provide the indistinguishable (at the time of purchase) L at lower cost and greater profitability than the first firm. However, consumers will no longer be willing to pay v_H for the first firm's product as average quality has fallen. Consequently, the first firm no longer has an incentive to maintain his quality, so only L will be provided by the market. Only if the first firm is allowed to establish a reputation for quality (protected by, e.g., trademarks) can he expect his expenditure on quality control to be rewarded.[30]

(ii) Product range

We now turn attention to products for which there is no clear quality ranking. In order to keep the essential issues clear, the assumption of identical costs is maintained throughout. Consider two firms, 1 and 2, which have the following inverse demand curves: $p_1 = f(q_1, q_2)$ and $p_2 = g(q_2, q_1)$ with price decreasing in both own and rival's output. If, when $q_1 = q_2$, $p_1 > p_2$, product 1 clearly has an advantage over product 2. This case is similar to the first firm having an absolute cost advantage and there is little to add to our earlier discussion. For instance, it is quite possible that firm 1 will choose a price $\bar{p}_1 = f(\bar{q}_1, 0)$ such that firm 2's demand curve

$p_2 = g\,(q_2, \bar{q}_1)$ always lies below her cost curve, so entry is deterred while 1 makes positive profits.[31]

More interesting in the present context is the case where the demand functions $f\,(\cdot)$ and $g(\cdot)$ are identical so no one firm has a clear advantage. Does a lower cross-elasticity of demand (greater product differentiation) raise entry barriers? Dixit (1979) asks this question and returns a negative answer. The logic is really rather simple and is best seen by considering the extreme cases. If the products are so different that the cross-elasticity is zero, there is nothing that the firm 1 can do (nor that he would want to do) to deter entry by firm 2. The two products are not in competition with each other. On the other hand, if the products are perfect substitutes, firm 1 may be able to exploit economies of scale as an entry barrier along the lines discussed in section 2b above. As Dixit puts it, 'Entry is more easily prevented if your product can be claimed to be a good substitute for any prospective entrant's product. It is when entry has occurred that you can better exploit monopoly power by claiming a special niche for your product, and thus a lower cross-price elasticity between products.' (1979: 29).

The above analysis is fine as long as each firm (actual or potential) can produce one and only one product, but this is not usually true. How does Dixit's conclusion change if firms are able to choose not only price, but also the number of products in their range? Can product range be used strategically to deter entry? The answer proves to be in the affirmative subject to a number of qualifying conditions, the most important of which again turns out to be that there are sunk costs. The remainder of this section illustrates the issues by developing a simplified model based on Hay (1976), Prescott and Visscher (1977) and Eaton and Lipsey (1978). The model has its roots firmly in the literature on spatial competition.[32]

Once more, we make simplifying assumptions in order to focus on the problem at hand. Assume there are Q consumers who wish to fly from London to New York on any given day, but each has a different optimal time of departure. The distribution of tastes is such that $Q/1{,}440$ customers would ideally wish to fly at any given minute of the day. If their ideal flight is not available, they will choose the flight which is scheduled to depart at the time nearest to their ideal (either earlier or later). Each passenger is willing to pay v for the flight regardless of when it leaves. All airlines can produce flights according to the same total cost function $C = F + cq$, where F and c are positive constants representing overheads and unit variable costs. No cost savings arise from the provision of more than one flight per day.[33]

Suppose there is only one airline providing n flights per day at equal intervals. Products (flights) are thus differentiated by the time of departure. By charging the maximum that people are willing to pay, revenue per flight is vQ/n and profit per flight is $\pi = [v - c]Q/n - F$. The possibility of an entry barrier developing now depends on the entrant's expectation as to how the incumbent will react both in pricing and flight scheduling.

As usual, there are many possible price conjectures. At one extreme the entrant might expect to be able to undercut the incumbent without his having a chance to respond.[34] The opposite extreme would be where a price war is anticipated. Such conjectures have already been discussed in the context of scale economies and homogeneous products. However, the role of product range is made clearer by adopting the intermediate expectation that there will be full collusion and the price will remain unchanged at v. As far as the entrant is concerned, this is a much more favourable conjecture than can typically be expected.

The incumbent airline's second decision variable is flight scheduling. Two product specification conjectures will be analysed. First, that the potential entrant expects the incumbent to completely re-schedule his present number of flights following entry (of one new flight) such that demand for each flight becomes $Q/(n+1)$. Since entry is deterred only if potential entrants do not expect positive profits, the entry barrier turns out to be slight. If $\bar{n}$ is the smallest n for which $\pi_{\bar{n}+1} = [v-c] Q/(\bar{n}+1) - F < 0$, only by providing $\bar{n}$ products is the monopolist able to deter entry. A little rearrangement gives $[v-c] Q < (\bar{n}+1) F$, so the monopolist's profits per product are $\pi_{\bar{n}} = [v-c] Q/\bar{n} - F < (\bar{n}+1) F/\bar{n} - F = F/\bar{n}$. Total industry profits are $\bar{n}\pi_{\bar{n}} < F$ so unless overheads per product are very high (or the market can only support a few flights), profits cannot be very large without attracting entry.

Now change the scheduling conjecture so that potential entrants believe the incumbent will under no circumstances alter his existing flight schedule following entry. This belief can be much more profitably exploited by the monopolist. If demand is such that $2n^*$ flights a day would lead to the airline just breaking even, we have $\pi_{2n^*} = [v-c] Q/2n^* - F = 0$. Then, if the airline were to schedule half as many flights, it could make profits per flight of $\pi_{n^*} = [v-c] Q/n^* - F = \pi_{2n^*} + [v-c] Q/2n^* = F$. In other words, each flight can make profits of F and total profits are n^*F.[35] Thus, fixed product specifications considerably enhance the profitability of entry deterrence.

That this multi-product monopolist is immune from entry can be demonstrated by means of an example. Suppose $n^* = 12$, then if existing flights are scheduled for the even hours, an entrant intending to fly at 3.00 can expect to attract customers whose optimal departure is between 2.30 and 3.30. Thus, she expects demand of $Q/24$. However, we know that this will not lead to entry because $\pi_{2n^*} = 0$ and the potential entrant requires strictly positive profits if she is to be induced to enter. n^* is therefore the optimum number of products for the monopolist who wants to deter entry. What has happened is that by strategically filling product space, the monopolist leaves gaps in the market which are not sufficient to support a new product, but which are large enough to give a generous market to each of his own.

The existence of economies of scale is essential to this barrier or else flights would leave each minute of the day. Product differentiation permits a magnification of their impact making even small scale economies much more significant than for homogeneous products. Also essential for this entry barrier is the expectation that product specifications will not be altered post-entry. This expectation, which raises industry profits from less than F (when product specifications are flexible) to n^*F, is much more credible if there are sunk costs (see e.g. Lyons 1984). For instance, suppose F consists entirely of sunk costs, perhaps advertising of the departure time, then there would never be an incentive for the incumbent to alter an existing specification which can *ex post* be produced at constant marginal cost, c. In the absence of sunk costs, however, the incumbent has no way of committing himself to any given specifications. Thus, sunk costs once more play a major role in creating an entry barrier; though note that this argument rests on the *incumbent's* sunk costs, while hit-and-run entry in contestability theory emphasises the potential losses of the *entrant*.

An important reservation restricting the generality of this example is that it rests on the monopolist being able to crowd an existing product space (i.e. the timing of flights). Genuinely novel products which the monopolist had not anticipated (e.g. flights from Manchester or a new level of service accompanying the flight) are excluded by assumption, but they will often provide an opportunity to find a new niche in the market.

Finally in this specific example, although consumers have preferences with respect to the timing of flights, this is not reflected in their willingness to pay (v does not depend on the number of flights). Because of these very weak preferences, the market tends to provide too many products which just add more to overheads without increasing consumer surplus. Inasmuch as strategic product proliferation reduces the total number of varieties on the market, therefore, this is socially beneficial. More generally, however, we can expect there to be a trade-off between the benefits of greater variety and the costs of unexploited scale economies, and it is not clear that the market tends to always produce too much variety. Thus, in the more general case, we cannot say whether or not the type of entry barrier just discussed will be socially beneficial.[36]

There remains at least one further means by which product differentiation might be exploited to deter entry. The following 'random buyer' model has been little discussed in the literature[37] but may be appropriate to certain products, such as detergent, cosmetics and toiletries, which are not differentiated by well defined characteristics yet over which consumers do have definite preferences. Assume that a homogeneous 'base' product can be produced subject to economies of scale. The base product can then be packaged (or modified slightly) by a second process which also displays increasing returns. For instance, there may be large set-up costs for a detergent factory, and further promotional overheads associated with the marketing of each brand of detergent. On the demand side, consumers buy randomly such that if there are n brands on the market, each product captures $1/n$ of the total market. The total market size is assumed to be fixed.

Without the threat of entry, the incumbent monopolist need provide only one brand since this minimises his costs. However, such a policy would permit an entrant to capture a half of the total market of random buyers by providing just one new brand. By marketing n brands, however, the incumbent can narrow the single-brand entrant's share of the market down to $1/(n+1)$. The effect is once more to magnify the effect of scale economies and, inasmuch as the entrant would do better to enter with more than one brand, to raise her initial capital requirement. Either way, a strategic entry barrier can be created by brand profileration. Brand loyalty to existing brands would serve to exacerbate the entry deterrent effect.

Dobe do you get your notes from 'ere ??

(d) ADVERTISING AND OTHER DISCRETIONARY EXPENDITURES

In this section we interpret advertising very broadly as a generic term for all selling expenses, running from television advertisements through promotional giveaways to full distributional networks. The characteristic of each such expenditure is that it is an investment designed to increase demand for a firm's product range. We concentrate here exclusively on the ways in which advertising can create an innocent or strategic entry barrier; unfortunately there is no space to discuss the broader welfare issues.[38] Advertising affects both costs and demand, and it is around these two aspects that the argument is couched.

(i) Advertising as a cost

Advertising is an extremely intangible asset and a genuinely sunk cost. As such it may be particularly difficult to raise capital in order to fund a campaign designed to enter a new industry. A bank which finances a new factory can ask for the deeds as security against the failure of the new enterprise. Advertising capital has no such salvage value – who wants to buy a second-hand, failed advertising campaign? Thus, finance for advertising is either expensive, to cover the higher lender risks associated with bankruptcy, or not available at all.[39] Although diversifying entrants may be able to get around this problem, advertising is certainly likely to raise the absolute cost disadvantage of specialist entrants.

Whereas advertising may increase demand, an increase in output does not require an increase in advertising. As far as output decisions are concerned, therefore, advertising is a fixed cost and so introduces an additional source of economies of scale. For instance, if new entrants have to match the advertising of incumbent firms in order to get a toehold in the market, or even if they only have to match a positive proportion of incumbent advertising, this can create an entry barrier along the lines already discussed in section 2b. Such a barrier may be the innocent by-product of profit-maximising behaviour, or it may be strategically exploited possibly introducing an economies of scale barrier into a market where production costs are constant.[40]

The above point relates to a given amount of advertising raising fixed costs and leading to economies of scale in relation to output. However, there may also be economies of scale in both the psychology and technology of advertising itself. At the psychological level, it is often the case that individual consumers need to receive several adverts before they fully realise that a product exists, register its name and become tempted to try it. Such a threshold means that a firm cannot advertise just once and hope to attract as many as one-seventh of the customers claimed by a firm which advertises every day for a week. Of course, eventually diminishing returns must set in as the advertising begins preaching to the converted or else has to be aimed at less promising market sectors or media, but this might happen only at very high levels of expenditure. On the technological front, there may be economies of scale in the production of advertising. Pecuniary economies include bulk discounts for the purchase of whole pages of newspaper advertising (or 60-second as opposed to 10-second TV slots), and discounts for regular repeat adverts. Non-pecuniary economies include the overhead costs of researching, planning and filming the advertising material. Finally, higher scale permits a switch from low-audience to high-audience media (e.g. billboards to television) and it is possible that the latter involves a lower cost per customer reached.

Apart from these cost-based aspects, advertising is distinctive in that it also affects the demand conditions facing firms.[41] It is to these that we now turn.

(ii) Advertising and demand

Bain (1956) and Comanor and Wilson (1967) have argued that advertising creates a stock of goodwill that potential entrants find hard to overcome. Thus, advertising is seen as a capital asset, accumulated in the past and reaping rewards as an entry barrier in the present. Schmalensee (1974) has tried to counter this argument by showing that in the absence of any asymmetries, such advertising cannot generate a super-competitive return. Just as a government bond purchased 10 years ago can be expected to give the same return as one purchased today unless bonds were particularly cheap at the earlier time, advertising should give the same return to a firm now unless it was cheaper to buy goodwill in the past. The trouble with this counter-argument is that there *is* likely to be a strong asymmetry between the incumbent's original position and that of a potential entrant (see e.g. Cubbin 1981). The asymmetry is easily formalised. Write the inverse demand curve faced by each firm as $p_i = f(q_i, q_j, x_i, x_j)$ where p = price, q = output, x = the stock of advertising goodwill, $i = 1, 2, i \neq j$, firm 1 is the incumbent and 2 is the potential entrant. *Ex ante*, therefore, firms 1 and 2 face identical demand conditions. However, when firm 1 entered, he faced $p_1 = f(q_1, 0, x_1, 0)$. This is clearly more favourable than the expected demand for the entrant $p_2 = f(q_2, \hat{q}_1, x_2, \hat{x}_1)$, where hats (^) denote the expected post-entry values. Even on the most optimistic assumption that the incumbent will cease advertising immediately, x_1 will not fall to zero until customers have completely forgotten about the first product and its advertising.

Even when products are completely homogeneous, there may still be a role for advertising in informing potential customers about alternative sources of supply. It might be thought that a monopolist faced with the threat of entry would be tempted to advertise excessively (i.e. more than a monopolist who has no fear of entry) in order to inform more potential customers that he exists and so reduce the potential market for an entrant. However, Schmalensee (1983) shows that, at least in the model he analyses, this is not a profitable strategy. The underlying problem for the incumbent is that the more he is committed to the market, the more costly it is for him to cut price post-entry, so the potential entrant can expect a less hostile welcome should she choose to enter. The flip side of this argument is that restraint in advertising leaves the incumbent 'lean and hungry' for a price war, and this can more effectively deter entry. It should be stressed that although Schmalensee has shown that it is not possible for the monopolist to advertise strategically in this case, this does not mean that the market will be competitive. The monopolist remains in a dominant position, but it is imperfect consumer information on sources of supply, and not advertising, that is to blame for any monopoly power in this instance. In fact, advertising helps in that it tends to reduce the entrant's informational problem.

Moving away from this world of homogeneous products, advertising may be used either informationally or persuasively to reinforce the product differentiation barriers discussed in section 2c; for example, it can be used to reinforce trademark protection of an existing brand. On the other hand, there are circumstances when advertising may be used to actually break down an entry barrier; for example, to separate a distinctive niche in the market into which an entrant may establish herself. As was discussed earlier, the appropriate response to the threat of such differentiated entry would be for the incumbent to project his product as having a very wide-ranging appeal. Alternatively, he can seek to fill all potential niches in the market with his own products. Advertising might aid such a product proliferation strategy in three ways: (a) it informs consumers of all the available specifications; (b) there may be economies of scope in providing an overall trade name to complement the individual brands; and (c) perhaps most importantly, it is a sunk cost and sunk costs are critical to the success of brand proliferation as an entry barrier.

(iii) R & D and pre-emptive patenting

Research and development expenditure has many of the same characteristics as advertising in the creation of entry barriers. For instance, R & D is an overhead as far as output decisions are concerned and there may also be economies of scale in translating R & D into useful innovations (see Ch. 6). R & D which leads to improved product quality similarly raises demand. However, it is the fact that R & D can shift the cost curve downwards that opens up some interesting new possibilities, most notably the idea of pre-emptive patenting.[42] Dasgupta and Stiglitz (1980) and Gilbert and Newbery (1980) have argued that a monopolist has an incentive to invest in R & D in order to keep ahead of the field and prevent competitive entry. In doing so he may be able to continue to make super-normal profits even when there is a large number of competitive potential entrants who each have access to the same R & D technology.

   Assume that there is just one potential, profit-enhancing invention that can be discovered more quickly if R & D expenditures are raised. If the monopolist is the first to invent, he gains the patent and a profit stream with a present value of $\pi_m -R>0$, where R is the cost of his R & D. On the other hand, if an entrant were to win the patent race she would earn $\pi^d - R$, where the superscript d refers to the fact that the entrant would be in duopolistic competition with the incumbent. Competition between potential entrants ensures that such a patent would earn zero pure profits; so the potential entrant most likely to win the patent race would be willing to spend R^*, where $\pi_d - R^* = 0$. Thus, if any potential entrant considered spending only $R <R^*$, another could win the race by spending a little more, and so on, unless the equilibrium R^* (or nothing) is spent.

   Next we introduce a crucial, but by now familiar, assumption. If an entrant wins the patent race, a duopoly will be established and, because collusion is less than perfect, joint industry profits will be less than when the monopolist is the first to invent; that is $\pi_e^d - R^* + \pi_m^d < \pi_m - R^*$, where π_m^d is the profit still earned by the original monopolist in the new duopoly. Because $\pi_e^d - R^* = 0$, this implies that $\pi_m^d < \pi_m - R^*$, so at the same level of industry R & D spending the monopolist prefers to undertake R^* himself. Now if the monopolist spends just a little more than R^* he can both prevent entry (because he will win the patent race) and earn positive monopoly rents (because $\pi_m - R^* > \pi_e^d - R^* + \pi_m^d > \pi_e^d - R^* = 0$). Pre-emptive patenting is therefore both feasible and profitable.

What are the welfare consequences of pre-emptive patenting? It is well known that a monopolist who does not fear entry is likely, from the social point of view, to underinvest in R & D (see Ch. 6, and Arrow 1962). The threat of entry in the above model induces him to step up his rate of inventive activity and this might be thought to be socially beneficial. Indeed this might be true. However, it is also quite possible that excessive resources will be spent on an unnecessarily fast patent race (or rat race) simply to gain monopoly rents. Potential entry may or may not, therefore, raise social welfare. Somewhat perversely in this model, a beneficial policy intervention would be to actually prevent the incumbent from engaging in R & D. The rate of technical progress would be unaltered, with R^* being spent by an entrant instead of the monopolist, but the duopoly that ensues leads to gains in allocative efficiency. However, it would be dangerous to generalise from such a simple model. Overall, the patent race literature suggests one important reason why established firms which engage in R & D may remain dominant and profitable even when the threat of competitive entry is very real, namely that the profitability of any given innovation is greater to a monopolist than to a duopolist. While the welfare implications are once again complex, the positive theory does contribute to our understanding of why, for instance, IBM continues to dominate the world computer industry.

3. Empirical evidence

It would be an impossible task to summarise all the empirical evidence relating to the existence of entry barriers. The more modest aim of this section is, where possible, to provide some examples of the barriers discussed in section 2 and to attempt a limited quantification of their importance. We begin by looking at the case study evidence then go on to review the cross-section studies.

(a) ABSOLUTE COST ADVANTAGES

Technical know-how and capital requirements appear to be the greatest sources of absolute cost advantage. Bain (1956) found that in his sample of 20 US industries, steel, automobiles, petroleum refining, tractors, cigarettes and rayon required the largest amounts of capital in order to establish one plant of minimum efficient size, whereas meat packing, shoes and flour represented industries with very low requirements. More recent evidence is surprisingly scant but petroleum products, chemicals and steel appear to remain among the most capital-intensive industries with clothing, furniture and some light engineering industries being of relatively low capital intensity. The wider evidence on economies of scale, which interact with capital intensity to generate an entrant's minimum capital requirement, is given in the next section.[43]

Patent protection is an important source of technological entry barriers and there are several outstanding examples where patents have conferred huge profits on the inventors (e.g. Polaroid cameras, tetracyclines, float glass and xerography. See Scherer 1970: Ch. 16). An example of patents being manipulated to reinforce the entry barrier is given by Du Pont, which invented nylon then 'systematically investigated the whole array of molecular variations with properties potentially similar to nylon, blanketing their findings with hundreds of patent applications to prevent other firms from developing an effective substitute' (Scherer 1970: 391). Scherer demonstrates that this is a far from isolated example. Taylor and Silberston (1973) provide UK evidence that, especially in the pharmaceutical, agri-chemical and synthetic fibre industries, major patents are rarely licensed and so may prevent new firms from getting a foothold in the industry. They also find that unpatented expertise is the more crucial barrier to imitation for sophisticated machinery and equipment, mass-produced components, and bulk chemical processes.

Moving away from technological barriers, there have been numerous cases in the UK where some form of restrictive practice has been used by manufacturers: tying the hands of the retail sector with the effect of either raising the capital asset or marketing expertise requirements of potential entrants; narrowing the size of their potential markets; or exploiting a potential legal barrier to entry (such as local government planning agreements). Restrictive practices such as exclusive dealing, tie-in sales or full-line forcing have been found in almost half of the 32 Monopolies Commission reports which have investigated monopoly and oligopoly[44] (HMSO 1978: Annex B). Two familiar cases of tied sales are: in brewing, where about two-thirds of public houses are owned by breweries and tenants may obtain supplies only through the parent brewery; and in petrol distribution, where 'sales' agreements tie service stations to a single supplier. In both cases, even the 'free' retailers often become effectively tied through systems of conditional loans and price or supply guarantees. Furthermore, licensing laws and town and country planning regulations serve to restrict the possibility of entry into the retail sector and so compound the problem for new firms which might wish to enter as vertically integrated enterprises.

It would be quite wrong, however, to argue that all such restrictive practices are against the public interest. For instance, the Monopolies Commission found 'that it was justifiable for Rank Xerox to control the provision of those materials and parts where the use of unauthorised supplies could materially affect the performance of machines rented, but that it was against the public interest for it to insist on the use of its own toner' (HMSO 1978: 39). Some restrictions were therefore deemed necessary for the good functioning of the machine, while others were mischievous. Nevertheless, whatever the justification, the implied necessity for an entrant to provide a vertical or horizontal range of goods or services clearly raises the costs of entry. This should not be understood to imply that such entry barriers as can be created by restrictive practices are always effective. In 1959, Shell/BP and Esso shared 79 per cent of the UK retail petrol market but 10 years later this had fallen to 66 per cent as new entrants (e.g. Jet) took about 20 per cent (Shaw 1974). A major reason for this was that while American supplies of oil were closely controlled by the leading multinationals, the opening up of the Middle East and African oilfields provided a means whereby untied service stations could obtain cheap supplies.[45] Even the most powerful monopolists or duopolists are not immune to a change in market conditions. Evidence relating to the use of advertising and R & D as sources of absolute cost advantage is postponed until section 3d.

 (b) ECONOMIES OF SCALE, SUNK COSTS AND EXCESS CAPACITY

It was argued in section 2 that economies of scale represent an entry barrier only to the extent that sunk costs are also involved. In practice, the two nearly always go hand in hand, though some possible exceptions are given at the end of this section. Empirical estimates of scale economies are fairly well covered in the standard textbooks so the review here will be brief, particularly in the criticism of the various methods of estimation.[46]

(i) Economies of scale

Engineering estimates obtained by questioning engineers and technologists provide an *ex ante* prediction of economies of scale. They offer a hypothetical 'best-practice' in idealised, static conditions, abstracting from uncertainty, and with little consideration for distribution costs, the elasticity of skilled labour supply, or demand conditions. Thus, they provide interesting information on the costs that may possibly be attained by the most efficient firms, but do not necessarily reflect the problems of an entrant going into a speciality sector of the market. Bain's (1956) original investigation of 20 US manufacturing industries found that only typewriters and tractors enjoyed scale economies such that over 10 per cent of the US market would be supplied by just one plant of minimum efficient size (MES). The later study by Scherer *et al.* (1975) of 17 industries added only refrigerators to this list. The US market is, of course, huge compared to the UK and the Scherer *et al.* estimates of MES relative to the UK market exceed 10 per cent for cigarettes, steel, storage batteries, petroleum refining and paints as well as refrigerators. Of these, only cigarettes (30%) and refrigerators (83%) exceed 16 per cent. It might be noted that many British 'manufacturers' in the 1960s and 1970s imported Italian refrigerators in order to supplement their product ranges – in other words, the size of the domestic market is often no longer the relevant constraint on production decisions. Pratten's (1971) study of 27 manufacturing industries suggests a much more pervasive influence of economies of scale in the UK. In only beer, bread, bricks, iron castings and footwear was MES less than 10 per cent of the market, while dyes, aircraft (one type), individual machine tools, turbo generators, electronic capital goods and single plastic products each required output of at least 100 per cent of the UK market in order to minimise average cost. However, only in dyes, aircraft and plastic products did the cost disadvantage of production at half MES raise costs by as much as 10 per cent. This result, that cost curves may be relatively shallow for outputs much less than the engineering estimates of MES, is supported by the work of Bain and of Scherer *et al.*, and this provides one possible explanation for the typically lower estimates of MES obtained by the alternative, *ex post* techniques discussed below. Finally, HMSO (1978: Annex C) provides a useful summary of individual engineering-type case studies covering 50 industries (including those discussed above). Largest MES's among those not already mentioned are electronic calculators and television tubes (both > 100% of the UK market).

Engineering studies require a substantial research effort, so we have comparable estimates for only a small range of industries. The alternative measures of MES have employed information in the distribution of plant sizes contained in Census of Production data in various attempts to provide a wider and less selective impression of the extent of scale economies. Two such methods are discussed here. The survivor technique attempts to identify the size class of plant which is seen to be expanding relative to others over a period of time, and argues that the lower bound (or average size) of this class represents MES. It is thus a measure which reflects the survival of the fittest in the market place. Unfortunately, the size distribution often shows no clear trend so estimation is not always possible. In his study of the USA, Saving (1961) was able to obtain 89 estimates out of an original sample of 200 four-digit industries[47] and only in piano parts and pens did MES exceed 10 per cent of the market. In nearly 90 per cent of cases, MES was less than 2 per cent. Applying the technique to the UK at the more aggregated three-digit (minimum list heading industry) level, Rees (1973) was able to estimate for only 30 industries and found a similar proportion with MES less than 2 per cent of the market, and none having MES greater than 5 per cent of the market.

The second method (Lyons 1980) based on size distribution tables argues that firms which operate more than one plant in the same industry must have achieved output rates of at least MES. On the basis of a few reasonable assumptions, it can be argued that if half of a group of firms of similar size operate just one plant, while the other half operate two, that size of firm will be roughly twice MES. This method focuses much more closely on the smaller end of the size spectrum than do the engineering or survivor estimates, since firms which operate many plants (which is typical of most leading firms in most industries) do not enter the calculations. It may, therefore, provide estimates that are particularly relevant to single-plant entrants. In only 9 of the 118 UK three-digit industries for which estimation was possible did MES exceed 2 per cent of the market, and none exceeded 5 per cent. Ordnance and small arms, tractors, watches and clocks, and motorcyles provided the largest estimates in relation to market size. Estimates could not be made for margarine, because the 15 plants in the industry were operated by 14 firms, nor for man-made fibres, where only five firms existed in 1968. Within the logic of the Lyons method, these two industries appear to enjoy the largest scale economies. Finally, it should be emphasised that the three-digit industry level is probably too aggregated for very reliable estimates of MES to be made by *any* method or technique, and caution should be exercised in interpreting estimates made at this level of aggregation.[48]

The overall impression that comes out of this discussion is that although economies of scale pervade manufacturing industry, particularly in the capital goods and process sectors, many relatively small firms are able to exist in the market place, often operating with just one plant. The extent to which economies of scale might act as an entry barrier will therefore depend on barriers to mobility and the legree of product differentiation *within* the fairly broad industries considered so far see section 3c).

(ii) Sunk costs

Ve next consider the possibility that sunk costs are independent of scale economies. n many industries, capital equipment is fairly specific to the task for which it was esigned – a blast furnace is of little use except for the manufacture of iron and steel. Iowever, there is often a considerable amount of flexibility between product lines see Berry 1967, on US engineering), and new-technology flexible engineering ystems and robotics may well be enhancing the versatility of some manufacturers. 'or the UK, Reddaway (1961) argued that individual base chemical products could e produced by firms currently producing other lines and that this constrained ricing behaviour. Bailey and Panzar (1981) provide an interesting study of the US iternal airline industry in this context. Many routes between pairs of cities are atural monopolies, but important distinctions must be drawn between local and runk airlines as well as long- and short-haul traffic. Trunk airlines have large fleets f long-haul aircraft which can be easily switched to alternative long-haul routes. he evidence shows that since deregulation in late 1978, long-haul routes have been onstrained to price competitively even when they are natural monopolies. Iowever, short-haul routes require more specialist aircraft which are in shorter ipply, and prices set by local airlines for such routes which are natural monopolies xceed prices on short-haul routes which can sustain actual competition. The vailability and flexibility of capital equipment (in this case aircraft) is clearly an nportant parameter in the assessment of scale economies as a barrier to entry.

A novel approach to the assessment of sunk costs as a barrier to entry is emonstrated in two papers by Coursey *et al.* (1984, 1986). Rather than study ctual industrial outcomes, they adopt an experimental approach which is more miliar to natural scientists and psychologists. Under well specified cost and emand conditions, which involved substantial economies of scale, volunteers were ked to play the parts of incumbent, entrant and buyers. Each participant earned a ish reward directly reflecting his resultant profit or consumer surplus. The major ndings were: (a) without the threat of entry (infinite sunk costs for the potential itrant), prices close to those of a textbook monopolist were consistently reached;) with zero sunk costs, price was consistently close to the competitive level (as redicted by contestability theory); and (c) with relatively small sunk costs, pricing nded to be competitive, but often there were bouts of tacit collusion which raised ice to near the monopoly level. Unfortunately, this form of experimental research expensive, requiring significant cash rewards if meaningful results are to be vealed, so no experiments involving high, but not prohibitive, sunk costs were nducted. Nevertheless, the relative importance of sunk costs over straightforward onomies of scale (when the two can be separated) seems to be confirmed.

(iii) Excess capacity

ttle work of any real significance can be reported on excess capacity as a barrier to try. Bain (1956) was able to make estimates for only 9 of his sample of 20

industries. He found no evidence of excess capacity in six, five of which wer
protected by other substantial or very great barriers to entry. Interestingly, the thre
industries with 'definite evidence of substantial chronic excess capacity' ($> 20\%$
excess at times of peak demand) were characterised by moderate to low barriers an
so might have wished to strategically deter entrants. Of these three, however, onl
cement was concentrated and profitable enough to suggest that excess capacit
could have actually served as a barrier.[49]

(c) PRODUCT DIFFERENTIATION

Product differentiation is ubiquitous. Only in the large process industries, such a
steel and base chemicals, are almost indistinguishable products sold by differer
firms. It even appears to be true that some products which *objectively* appear to b
the most homogeneous are bought by consumers with a brand loyalty that suggest
extreme heterogeneity (witness cigarettes and detergents). In this section w
concentrate on three case studies which have a bearing on the ability of incumber
firms to use product proliferation as an entry barrier.

Schmalensee (1978) notes that much marketing analysis in the US ready
to-eat breakfast cereal industry is carried out in explicitly spatial terms 'wit
discussions of clusters of brands, open spaces, and of close and distant competitors
The dimensions of this product space may include sweetness, crunchiness, shap
grain base and/or protein and vitamin content. Schmalensee argues that all th
preconditions for the strategic use of this product space, in particular, sca
economies and fixed product specifications, were satisfied and quite probab
exploited by the leading six firms who shared 80 brands and 95 per cent of the U
market in 1972. One result was that they were able to earn an average rate of retur
on capital of about 20 per cent compared with a 9 per cent average fc
manufacturing (Scherer 1979).

Shaw (1980, 1982) documents the development of the UK compour
fertiliser industry. These fertilisers have three main constituents (nitroge
phosphoric acid and potash) which may be mixed in differing blends an
concentrations. In the 1950s the market was dominated by Fisons with a 40–45 p
cent share and several blends; ICI had 20 per cent with just one brand, and no oth
firm had a significant market share. In 1960, ICI began to extend its range and Sh
Chemicals entered the market, importing at first before setting up a domest
manufacturing capability in 1969. In 1962/3 Fisons marketed 22 brands, ICI had
and Shell had just 2, but by 1977/8 the product ranges had extended to 43, 13 and
respectively, with the three firms having a combined market share of 80 per cent
Shaw interprets these events as the outcome of non-price competition in a triopol
but three further interpretations are possible. Firstly, whatever the initial impet
for product-proliferating behaviour, its outcome must have been to make furth
entry by new firms extremely difficult. Secondly, the entry by Shell, initially
importing, shows how, at least to some extent, scale economies can be overcor
while market share is being developed. Thirdly, entry was backed by a massi
multinational which had the credibility to take on the established duopoly.

The final example, due to Menge (1962), suggests that regular and rap changes in car styling served to keep small firms out of the US industry at little cost to large incumbents. The basic idea is that existing, large-scale producers use dies and special tools intensively so they need frequent replacement. At this point a new style may be cheaply adopted. However, small-scale manufacturers would have to either scrap their expensive dies (which have been less intensively used and so are not worn out) or lose market share due to old-fashioned styles. Menge argues that style changes were not used as an explicit strategy but were the innocent by-product of a national fashion. That may or may not be true. What is clear is that such fashion changes were far from costless to the American motorist who, according to one estimate, paid over 25 per cent of the price of her new car in advertising, over-powerful engines and re-tooling costs (Fisher *et al.* 1962).

(d) ADVERTISING AND R & D

Advertising is associated with products which are sold to consumers as opposed to firms (Buxton *et al.* 1984), and within the ranks of consumer goods, it is heavily concentrated in a few markets. According to the 1968 UK Census of Production, regrettably the last for which such data were collected, 15 per cent of the sales revenue of the toilet preparations industry was spent on advertising and related costs, 10 per cent for soaps and detergents,[51] and 8 per cent for pharmaceutical chemicals and preparations. Apart from these and certain food, confectionery, and drinks markets, cigarettes and domestic appliances, few other industries spend much more than 1 per cent of sales revenue on advertising. Within the high-spending industries, certain products are even more intensively advertised; for instance, the Price Commission (1978) reports advertising plus other marketing costs relative to sales exceeding 25 per cent for some proprietary non-ethical medicines. The size and distribution of these figures do not appear to be restricted to the UK.[52] It is also interesting to note that Scherer (1979) estimated the initial advertising costs just for launching a new US breakfast cereal in the 1960s as about $3.5 m. Although, for the reasons given in section 2d, advertising may create an entry barrier in consumer goods industries, there appears to be a significant difference when it comes to retailing (Kaldor 1950). Benham's (1972) famous study of eyeglasses showed that in areas where advertising was permitted, retail prices were lower than where advertising was legally constrained. In other words, advertising can improve the flow of price information and so make the market more contestable.

Mueller and Tilton (1969) review the case study evidence relating to R & D, and distinguish four stages of technological growth in a typical product's development. At the 'innovation stage', there is little evidence to support the view that large established firms are favoured. Although the potential rewards to success may be huge, the uncertainty concerning the payoff to R & D is a significant deterrent to entry. The next, 'imitation stage' is most conducive to entry as growth potential remains large but technological and demand uncertainty begins to fall rapidly. Apart from a few examples where no entry follows a major innovation (e.g. Polaroid), either invention around a patent (e.g. pharmaceuticals) or licensing (e.g. semiconductors) usually permits entry. Even with strong patent protection, Xerox was unable to exclude photocopier rivals at this stage. The period of highest entry barriers is the 'technological competition stage'. There are few niches left in the market and learning-by-doing gives incumbents a significant advantage. The technological developments taking place at this sophisticated stage also require the support of large-scale R & D expenditures. Finally, in the 'standardisation stage', patents expire and textbook technology emerges. Competition shifts from technology to price, and entry is now deterred by falling expected profits as sales growth tapers off and even becomes negative. Although these four stages are clearly stylised, they do provide a useful framework for analysing technologically progressive industries. For instance, the home computer and business micro industries appear to have moved into the technological competition stage so we should expect further new entry to be extremely limited.

(e) DIVERSIFYING ENTRY

A case study of the UK potato crisps industry, based on Bevan (1974), provides an interesting example of successful entry which ties up some of the threads on what makes entry difficult and how such hurdles can be overcome. In the 1950s, Smiths dominated the potato crisps market with apparently little to fear from a competitive fringe of many small, local manufacturers. There was little advertising and market growth was moderate. In 1960, a large conglomerate, Imperial Tobacco, acquired a small Scottish crisps producer called Golden Wonder. They introduced a new process of continuous (as opposed to batch) frying which improved quality control, introduced plastic (as opposed to waxed paper) packaging which extended shelf life from 3 days to 6 months, began advertising heavily (particularly on TV) and marketed intensively in non-licensed outlets (until then, most crisps had been sold in pubs). Industry advertising intensity rose from 0.11 per cent (1959) to 2.18 per cent (1966) against a backdrop of a rapidly growing total market; and Golden Wonder's market share rose from almost nothing to 45 per cent (1966) while Smiths' fell from 65 per cent (1961) to 34 per cent (1966).

 Before it be judged that entry was easy, it should be emphasised that Golden Wonder had everything going for them. In particular, Smiths was a lazy incumbent lulled into a false sense of security by a rapidly growing market in the 1960s. Golden Wonder was also able to introduce both production and marketing innovations, and was backed by the massive resources of Imperial Tobacco which spent some £10 m. establishing Golden Wonder on the national market and had to endure annual losses in each year up to 1965. As in the case of fertilisers discussed above, diversifying entry can prove far more effective than entry attempts by new, specialised firms, but it still may not be profitable. This anecdotal evidence is backed up by a cross-section study by Berry (1974) who finds that specialised entry does not affect the market shares of the leading firms; but diversifying entry, when it occurs, is on average much more disruptive. Significant specialist entry must be supported by outstanding entrepreneurial talent. Alas, such talent, without the backing of a large established firm, litters the corridors of the bankruptcy courts (witness Rolls Razor washing machines, Laker Airways and, almost, Acorn Computers which had to be rescued by the giant Olivetti).

(f) CROSS-SECTION STATISTICAL STUDIES

It is difficult to gain a clear impression of the overall effect of individual entry barriers by looking only at case study evidence. In order to stand back and attempt a general assessment, economists have turned to cross-section regression analysis relating empirical proxies for the major potential barriers in a large number of industries to such dependent variables as profit rates, the rate of actual entry, and concentration.[53]

(i) Barriers to entry and profitability

The accumulated number of profitability and price–cost margin studies is vast[54] (see for instance Weiss 1974) and the following review is necessarily highly selective. The standard approach has been to estimate an equation of the following form:

$$P = a_0 + a_1 C + a_2 \text{ MES} + a_3 \text{ MKR} + a_4 \text{ AS} + a_5 Z \qquad [1]$$

where P is a measure of rate of return on capital or the price-cost margin,

   C is a measure of industrial concentration, usually the concentration ratio or Herfindahl index,

 MES is a measure of the minimum efficient plant size relative to the market,

 MKR is a measure of minimum capital requirement for entry, usually measured by MES times the industry capital intensity,

  AS is the advertising-to-sales ratio

   Z is a vector of other variables, perhaps including the industry growth rate or a measure of import competition.

The observations are usually drawn from as wide a cross-section of manufacturing industries as data availability allows. All the a_i's are expected to be positive. Few studies have used the measures of MES discussed in section 3a, mainly because this would severely restrict the number of observations in their sample. Instead, a widely available proxy such as the median plant size has been employed.[55] The severe problems with such a measure are discussed in Chapter 3 but suffice it to say here that it may be identically, as well as behaviourally, related to C. One consequence is often a severe statistical problem known as multicollinearity which can lead to statistically insignificant results even though an economically significant relationship does, in truth, exist. By its construction, MKR faces similar problems to the MES variable. Additionally, disaggregated capital stock data are rare, so further approximation is necessary. AS is also a very imperfect proxy for the whole range of advertising effects from capital requirements and scale economies through to enhanced product differentiation and brand loyalty. Nevertheless, few investigators have been able to improve on this simple specification. Furthermore, entry barriers may be exploited by management taking either an easy life or a luxurious one such that measured profits do not reflect the true effect of such barriers. These empirical problems should be borne in mind in interpreting the following studies.

Early work on the US by Bain (1956), extended by Mann (1966), showed that profit rates were 50 per cent higher in industries judged to have very high barriers to entry, particularly when these were due to product differentiation (e.g. cars and ethical drugs). Little difference was detected between low and moderate barriers industries, and concentration appeared to have relatively little independent effect. Comanor and Wilson (1967) were the first to introduce the methodology of eqn [1]. They found AS and MKR to be significant barriers whereas MES and C did not contribute to the explanation of US profit rates. More recent work has tended to give a more positive role to C (see the survey by Weiss 1974; also Chappell *et al.*, 1983) and the insignificance of MES has also been challenged. Caves *et al.* (1975) adjust their MES proxy to take account of the cost disadvantage incurred by plants of size less than MES. They find that MES becomes significant, but only when the cost disadvantage of small firms is relatively large. The AS result has come under more fundamental attack on the grounds that advertising is a capital asset yet accounting procedures neither add such capital to total assets nor allow for depreciation. Weiss (1969), Bloch (1974) and Ayanian (1975) have tried to account for this but their results are highly sensitive to the chosen rate of depreciation. However, on most reasonable estimates, AS remains significant though its contribution to high rates of return is reduced. The main thrust of these results relating to the empirically measurable barriers of MES, MKR and particularly AS has been supported for countries as diverse as the UK,[56] Canada,[57] India,[58] and Malaysia,[59] though not for France,[60] or Japan (except for significant AS).[61]

Five further profitability studies deserve mention as providing particular insight into the effects of entry barriers. Firstly, there have been few attempts to directly measure product differentiation (other than implicity via a correlation with AS). For West Germany, however, Neumann *et al.*, (1979) find that the number of trademarks held by a firm (relative to its equity value) has a significantly positive, though quantitatively small, impact on rate of return. Secondly, the case study evidence suggested that the strongest entry threat may come from diversifying firms. Rhoades (1973) argues that such a threat is more potent if an industry's output is already being produced as a side-line in factories which primarily manufacture another product; and he finds that such industries do have lower price–cost margins. It is also possible that industries with diversified incumbent firms may have the back-up profits to implicitly threaten an aggressive response to an entrant. Rhoades finds weak support for this view that incumbent diversification may act as a barrier.[62] Thirdly, Porter (1974) distinguishes between convenience goods, which are of low unit price and are purchased frequently, and non-convenience goods, which are of high unit price and for which quality and style are important. Consumers are much more inclined to shop around and compare products in the latter category, perhaps with the aid of specialist retailers, than they are for convenience goods which they buy from a regular shop or supermarket. Consequently, manufacturers should direct their selling efforts towards retailers for non-convenience goods but use advertising to affect the consumption of convenience goods. Porter finds some empirical support for this view. Only for convenience goods does AS increase profitability, though a measure of advertising per firm was significant in the non-convenience regression. In a later piece of work,

Porter (1976) goes further to show that it is only television advertising that generates excessive returns. Thus, the role of advertising as an entry barrier appears to be concentrated on a relatively narrow group of convenience goods which use television as the main medium (i.e. food, drink, detergents, pharmaceuticals and toiletries).

Fourthly, surprisingly few studies have investigated R & D as one of the Z variables in eqn [1]. A notable exception is Grabowski and Mueller (1978), who argue that there is a fundamental difference between competition in technologically progressive industries (e.g. pharmaceuticals, chemicals, machinery) and that in non-progressive industries (e.g. paper, metals, petrol refining). They find that only in progressive industries does R & D earn a significantly above average rate of return. Within this group, high concentration tends to reduce profitability, which they claim is consistent with the view that although price competition is stifled, technological competition is taken to the point of diminishing returns. Non-progressive industries do not appear to earn excess returns on their R & D though higher concentration within this group does raise profitability as expected. Grabowski and Mueller find that progressive industries earn a post-tax rate of return on a properly capitalised measure of R & D of 15–20 per cent compared with an average return of 7.1 per cent on all capital in their sample of US firms. Although part of this may be an allowance for the riskiness of R & D, they were unable to find any association between profitability and financial risk. The conclusion must be that R & D does create a barrier to entry in progressive industries.

Finally, Stonebraker (1976) provides an interesting analysis of the role of entry risk. He argues that potential entrants are directly influenced by the risks of negative returns and eventual failure. These may be proxied by a measure of negative profits made by small firms in the industry, SR (on the argument that most entry is initially small scale); as well as dummy variable for industries with high failure rates, F. He finds that alongside a measure of the industry growth rate, SR and F can explain a large proportion of the variance in large-firm profit rates for 33 US industries. Furthermore, various measures of large-firm risks do *not* affect their own profitability so these findings do not reflect conventional risk premia. As Stonebraker puts it, 'General Motors maintains excess profits, not because its own risk level is high, but because the enormous risk faced by American Motors and the demise of such competitors as Studebaker, Packard and Kaiser effectively prohibit any new competitive threat.' Stonebraker goes on to attempt a statistical explanation of entry risk (a composite measure of SR and F) and concludes 'that the "behavioural" barriers of advertising and R & D are far more important than are the "structural" barriers of production scale economies and absolute size'.

(ii) Barriers to entry and entry rates

Moving away from the profitability studies, a number of investigators have looked at actual entry rates. Although high barriers permit high profits, if firms try to raise price too high relative to such barriers, the result will be to attract entry. Thus, eqn [1] is replaced by

$$P^* = b_0 + b_1 C + b_2 \text{ MES} + b_3 \text{ MKR} + b_4 \text{ AS} + b_5 \text{ RDS} + b_6 Z \qquad [2]$$

where P^* is the profit rate that entry barriers permit the industry to attain in the long run, and RDS is the R & D to sales ratio. This is supplemented by an entry-triggering equation:

$$E = c_0 + c_1 (P_p - P^*) + c_2 G_p \qquad [3]$$

where E is a measure of the entry rate, P_p is past profitability and G_p is the past growth rate. Substituting [2] into [3] gives an estimating equation of the form

$$E = d_0 - d_1 C - d_2 \text{MES} - d_3 \text{MKR} - d_4 \text{AS} - d_5 \text{RDS} - d_6 Z + c_1 P_p + c_2 G_p \qquad [4]$$

where $d_i = c_1 b_i$ for $i = 1, \ldots, 5$ and $d_0 = c_0 - c_1 b_0$. We note in passing that the partial adjustment eqn [2] looks more than usually *ad hoc* in this context and this might lead to econometric problems (e.g. if c_i varies across industries and is correlated with entry barriers).

Orr (1974) was the first to develop this methodology and he applied it to a cross-section of 71 Canadian industries. The standard deviation of past industry profits was included as a measure of risk but multicollinearity led to the exclusion of MES from the regression. He concluded that 'capital requirements, advertising intensity, and high concentration are significant barriers to entry ... research and development intensity and risk are modest barriers to entry, while past profit rates and past industry growth rate had a positive weak [insignificant] impact on entry'. One possible explanation for the weak showing of past profits may be that measured profits are a poor indicator of underlying profitability due to managerial appropriation of monopoly rents or changing market conditions. In a later paper, Orr (1976) employs the estimated coefficients from eqn [4] to construct a composite measure of entry barriers. In descending order, and with the major relevant barrier in brackets, the industries with the highest barriers were found to be smelting and refining (MKR), aircraft and parts (RDS), brewing (AS), petroleum refining (MKR) and toilet preparations (AS). Dividing his sample into three equal groups according to this barriers index, Orr found that only the highest barrier group earned a significantly higher rate of return (about 20% higher) than the others. This supports with Canadian data the early Bain–Mann results for the US that only very high barriers matter.

Orr's data has been reworked by Gorecki (1976) to see whether the nationality of the entrant makes any difference. Orr's entry results were confirmed for domestic entrants only, with foreign (mainly US) subsidiaries being quite undaunted by any entry barrier – they even displayed a perverse penchant for entry into slower growing industries! Gorecki (1975) has also investigated this theme, that the identity of the potential entrant is crucial, on a UK data set. This time diversifying and specialised entrants were separated. Diversifying entrants were found to be attracted by market growth but quite insensitive to the standard barriers of MES, MKR and AS. Specialised firms were also attracted by faster growth and (perversely?) by high AS, but MKR acted as a barrier; MES had no effect. Unfortunately, there were grave data problems (e.g. the dependent variable was the simple change in firm numbers so was net of exit) and these results must be taken as indicative only.

For the USA, an early study by Mansfield (1962), using a data base of just four industries over several time periods, found that profits attracted new entry while capital requirements were a barrier. Peltzman (1965) also found that past profits attracted entry, into US commercial banking and that government regulation debarred entry. More recently, Deutsch (1975) has made a cross-section study of 134 industries to find that entry is encouraged by demand growth and discouraged by the diversification of existing firms. This reaffirms Rhoades' hypothesis that diversification either masks profitable opportunities or else leads to fears of an aggressive response to entry. Entry is less likely in consumer goods industries and more prevalent in more concentrated industries. Alternative regressions suggest that the former result is at least partially due to higher advertising and the latter incorporates the incentive of higher profits. In a later paper, Deutsch finds that multi-plant operation also acts to deter entry. Masson and Shanaan (1982), also using US data, estimate both eqns [1] and [4]. Their entry equation includes growth, profits and barriers (but not concentration) and their profitability regression includes growth, barriers and concentration. Profits and, to a lesser extent, growth act as incentives to entry, MES is a significant barrier, AS slightly less so and MKR is insignificant. In the profitability equation, only concentration, growth and AS are significant.

(g) EMPIRICAL CONCLUSIONS

It is time to attempt to draw some conclusions out of this large array of results. Firstly, among the inherent structural barriers, capital requirements appear to be the greatest obstacle to entry. There is also evidence that vertical integration and various restrictive practices serve to heighten this barrier, though this does not necessarily mean that either is necessarily used as part of a deliberate entry-deterring strategy.

Scale economies are an important barrier in some industries, but their impact depends crucially on the extent to which they are compounded by product differentiation and the degree to which capital equipment can be switched between product lines (i.e. sunk costs). Although little of the empirical work surveyed here has directly looked at international trade, imports are another way in which the scale barrier has been hurdled. Very often, however, scale economies and concentration are so closely related that the individual contribution of each cannot be distinguished. Little evidence is available to either support or deny the excess capacity hypothesis.

Economists have yet to find an adequate empirical measure of product differentiation and this is a severe restriction in assessing its impact as a barrier to entry. However, case studies of breakfast cereals, fertilisers and cars are suggestive of the problems faced by firms attempting entry into industries characterised by product differentiation, and of the consequent profits for incumbents.

Advertising, particularly on television, creates the largest barrier to entry into a range of frequently purchased consumer goods. It is very difficult to believe that the levels of expenditure involved can be justified on the simple grounds of information provision. Whether advertising is so high because of strategic, entry-deterring behaviour by incumbents, or whether its effect is the by-product of non-price competition between oligopolists, the outcome is the same — high profits and low rates of entry.

Patenting behaviour, supported by R & D activity, can undoubtedly create a very significant barrier, particularly when firms engage in pyramid patenting around the main innovation. On the benefits side, this may be a necessary condition for invention to take place when genuinely new products are developed. R & D is at its most potent as a barrier, however, in technologically progressive industries once the first flush of innovation and imitation has passed, but before standardisation has set in. In these circumstances the social desirability of patents and secrecy is much more questionable.

Finally, the evidence suggests that most entry barriers can be overcome by a sufficiently determined diversifying entrant who is backed by large financial resources. This does not mean to say, however, that such entry is a common occurrence. Firstly, it can be extremely expensive to take on well established incumbents (e.g. potato crisps, breakfast cereals). Secondly, the possibility of retaliatory entry into a diversifier's own prime markets leads to a more cautious assessment of the risks of entry.

Notes

1. Wenders (1967) argues convincingly that this will be the empirically prevalent case.
2. An early review is given by Caves and Porter (1977).
3. Examples might be a world in which the state pays potential inventors a salary rather than giving actual inventors a patent (the latter being a legal barrier to entry), or one where cash prizes are given to inventors.
4. In a similar vein, Bork (1978) is not worried by restrictive business practices if they are more 'efficiency enhancing' than they are 'predatory'.
5. See Baumol et al., (1982) for a comprehensive treatment, and Baumol (1982) for a very useful summary.
6. Even in the monopoly case, Ramsey optimal prices result from contestability. In this context, Ramsey optimal prices are those which maximise social welfare subject to the constraint that firms earn non-negative profits; for instance, in the simple single-product case just mentioned, average cost pricing is Ramsey optimal.
7. This section largely follows Salop (1979) and Dixit (1982). It is difficult in places and may be skipped on first reading.
8. Another possibility is that IM creates a public taste for fashion, so raising costly overheads associated with the tooling-up and launching of new products.
9. Given that advertising has long-lasting effects (it is a capital good), even though *current* advertising may be cut, PE would still have to match IM's accumulated goodwill.
10. Note that actual price wars, as opposed to the threat of them, may still be quite rare because they only occur when PE misjudges IM's commitment to entry deterrence.
11. Williamson (1975) gives a good discussion of the issues involved, including more beneficial motives for integration. It is interesting to observe that the strategy of vertical integration as an entry barrier has recently been 'legitimised' in the *Harvard Business Review* (the organ of the Harvard Business School), where entry

deterrence is given as one of several reasons why firms should consider integration.

12. For an interesting discussion of the optimal length of patent protection, see Nordhaus (1969).

13. Sharkey (1982) provides a good summary of the theory of natural monopoly. The following definition is based on what is known as a strictly subadditive cost function.

14. Those readers worried about storage and interest costs can reduce the production period to one minute or less!

15. Baumol *et al.* (1982) argue that some goods, particularly services, cannot be stored and others require a finite time for batch production, e.g. airline flights. In such cases, Weitzman's argument cannot be used. Nevertheless, this severely restricts the value of contestability theory. Note that the necessity to warm up the blast furnace for several days prior to production (and cool it down at the end) is a sunk cost and not a consequence of batch production once the process is under way.

16. Would you agree to buy a car that has not yet been designed or manufactured, even if it is to be built by General Motors, let alone by GEC or Acme Cars (1990) PLC? This problem is further developed in section 2c(i).

17. A recent example (late 1984) where this was *not* the case was when the major airlines wished to respond to cut-price trans-atlantic flights by People Express and Virgin Airways. Fear of anti-trust action in the USA, following the collapse of Laker Airways, prevented UK government approval of lower fares by the majors. Note, however, that the majors were only prevented from responding by government intervention and strong US legislation, and not by their natural inclination.

18. The basic idea is identical to Williamson's (1968) analysis of mergers. A similar argument applies outside natural monopoly if there are too many firms for each to produce at minimum average cost (see von Weizsacker 1980a).

19. See Stigler (1968: 19–22) for a neat, early summary.

20. Wenders (1971a), Gaskins (1971) and Kamien and Schwartz (1971) each provide formal models. The same basic idea is implicit in Bain's (1956) category of ineffectively impeded entry.

21. See Dixit (1979). Osborne (1973) makes a similar point for entry barriers in general. Dixit also shows that even when IM permits entry, he can still strategically sink marginal costs in order to commit to a higher output than PE will choose and so retain leadership in the industry. (See note 25).

22. Although Stigler was not at the University of Chicago at the time, it seems appropriate that he now lives in Al Capone's home town!

23. This idea was first formalised in Wenders (1971b). His analysis does not require economies of scale and this can cause problems. If there are constant costs, it is always open to PE to produce a tiny output at no disadvantage. It is hardly worth IM sacrificing his entire profits simply to discipline such a negligible entrant who has almost nothing to lose (even when his costs are sunk). But if one such entrant is allowed, what is to stop her or other entrants expanding? The market must be competitive.

24. See Spence (1977).

25. This does not mean that even on these assumptions IM cannot use capacity investment to his own advantage. By sinking costs pre-entry he has lower *ex post* marginal costs than PE does. It is a feature of Cournot (and many other oligopolistic) equilibria, that lower marginal costs are associated with higher market shares. IM can exploit this limited form of leadership to his own advantage. See Dixit (1980).

Schmalensee (1981), however, suggests that the size of such an advantage may be quite small, particularly in terms of the welfare loss involved.

26. Only the most preferred quality of product–price combination will survive. On the other hand, if consumers differ in their willingness to pay for quality, perhaps because of differences in their wealth, several different qualities may survive. See the introduction to Shaked and Sutton (1984) for a discussion of what can happen.

27. This lower valuation may be due either to a positive subjective probability of the product breaking down or failing altogether, or to product quality being an *ex ante* random variable with mean $\bar{v}$ but being ascribed a lower utility value due to risk aversion.

28. Apart from the standard Schumpeterian point of the reduced incentive to invent cornflakes in the first place.

29. The main elements of the following example can be traced to the seminal 'lemons' paper by Akerlof (1970).

30. A detailed model of equilibrium in such markets is given in von Weizsacker (1980b). Be warned that such formal models of incomplete information soon become rather complex. Demsetz (1982) makes the point in a property rights framework.

31. Alternatively, it may be more profitable for 1 to permit some limited entry. See Dixit (1979).

32. Lancaster (1979) demonstrates how products which embody blends of any two characteristics can be subsumed within this type of approach to product differentiation. See also Bernheim (1984) for some policy implications.

33. Such cost savings due to the marketing or production of more than one product are termed economies of scope. They would serve to reinforce the incumbent's position in the argument that follows.

34. In the absence of sunk costs, of course, the market would then be contestable.

35. The result that profits per product exactly equal F is specific to this example. Inasmuch as entrants expect greater than half the demand of an existing product (e.g. because consumer demand increases when more flights are available), the monopolist must provide more flights to deter entry and this reduces his profits. However, inasmuch as any price competition is expected post-entry, the entrant's profit expectations are lowered, fewer flights need be provided, and profits rise due to the saving of overheads.

36. In a slightly more general model, Salop (1979) once more finds that the market tends to produce too much variety even when pricing is more competitive than in our example.

37. But see George and Joll (1981: 184), and Lyons (1989) for a full development of this model.

38. Such as the wastes of repetitive, competitive advertising between existing rivals, or the implications of advertising being either informative or persuasive.

39. The lender must bear in mind that the higher the interest rate he charges, the greater is the risk of bankruptcy. Thus, there may be no price at which funds for a high-risk project may be borrowed (see Stiglitz and Weiss 1981).

40. Williamson (1963) discusses how incumbent firms can choose the level of advertising so as to maximise profits given the trade-off between high advertising costs and the higher limit price they permit.

41. The interaction between cost and demand features is emphasised in Spence (1980), but the separation is preserved here in the belief that it clarifies matters.

42. Also, Levin (1978) suggests that R & D may be aimed at developing technologies which raise the degree of scale economies with a view to maximising monopoly rents.

43. Sullivan (1978, 1982) gives some rather limited evidence that more concentrated industries can obtain capital at lower cost. Such a relationship would reinforce the advantage of incumbents.

44. Of course, the Monopolies Commission tends to invetigate those industries where there are a priori grounds for believing that market power is being abused, so this is a heavily biased sample.

45. Thus, there had also been an entry barrier due to backward integration (or long-term contracts) into the supply of crude oil for refining. Another example of such an advantage is the monopoly control that the London Brick Company exercises over the clay necessary for fletton brick making (Davies 1871).

46. Also, statistical cost curves are not covered (see Johnston 1960).

47. See Chapter 3, section 3a, for a discussion of the Standard Industrial Classification, including examples of three and four-digit industries.

48. A glaring example for the UK is MLH 381, 'motor vehicle manufacturing', which included trailers, caravans, and components as well as mass assembly in the 1968 Census on which the above results were calculated.

49. Esposito and Esposito (1974) were able to obtain data on excess capacity for 35 US industries. Unfortunately, their measure is not very useful from our point of view since it is based on each firm's own judgement of its preferred and actual operating rates. Thus, a strategic monopolist would 'prefer' to be operating at less than full capacity so such spare capacity will not show up in the figures. They found that excess capacity was lower in fast growing and capital-intensive industries (as is to be expected), and higher in upper to middling (as opposed to low or very high) concentration industries. This is consistent with strategic behaviour by oligopolists.

50. Shell sold out to a Dutch firm, UKF, in 1973.

51. The equivalent figure for 1963 was 14 per cent. This drop was because the 1966 Monopolies Commission investigation recommended a 40 per cent reduction in selling expenses.

52. See e.g. Backman (1967) for the USA. Scherer (1979) reports an advertising intensity of 20 per cent for US breakfast cereals.

53. Concentration studies are reviewed in Chapter 3.

54. Due to space constraints, no distinction between profitability and price–cost margins is made in the following review.

55. More frequently, the median of the first moment distribution has been used. This is simply the size of plant such that half of the industry output is produced in larger and half in smaller plants. Another popular proxy is the average size of the largest plants accounting for half of the industry output.

56. See Sawyer (1981: table 6.2); or George and Joll (1981: table 9.1); or Devine et al. (1979: table 2.18) for neat summaries.

57. See Caves et al. (1980) and the studies cited therein.

58. Walgreen (1971) on scale economies only.

59. Gan and Tham (1977).

60. Jenny and Weber (1976) on MES and MKR.

61. Caves and Uekusa (1976): MES and MKR had no effect.

62. Although there is little well documented evidence for actual predatory pricing (Yamey 1972), the fear of a price war may remain real enough.

References

Akerlof, G. (1970) The market for lemons: qualitative uncertainty and the market mechanism, *Quarterly Journal of Economics*. **84**, 488–500.

Arrow, K. J. (1962) Economic welfare and the allocation of resources for invention, in National Bureau of Economic Research, *The Rate and Direction of Inventive Activity: Economic and Social Factors*, Princeton University Press: Princeton, N.J.

Ayanian, R. (1975) Advertising and the rate of return, *Journal of Law and Economics*, **18**, 479–506.

Backman, J. (1967) *Advertising and Competition*, New York University Press: New York.

Bailey, E. E. and Panzar, J. C. (1981) The contestability of airline markets during the transition to deregulation, *Law and Contemporary Problems*, **44**, 125–45.

Bain, J. S. (1956) *Barriers to New Competition*, Harvard University Press: Cambridge, Mass.

Baumol, W. J. (1982) Contestable markets: an uprising in the theory of industrial structure, *American Economic Review*, **72**, 1–15.

Baumol, W. J., Panzar, J. C. and Willig, R. D. (1982) *Contestable Markets and the Theory of Industry Structure*, Harcourt Brace Jovanovich: New York.

Benham, L. (1972) The effect of advertising on the price of eyeglasses, *Journal of Law and Economics*, **15**, 337–52.

Bernheim, B. D. (1984) Strategic deterrence of sequential entry into an industry, *Rand Journal of Economics*, **15**, 1–11.

Berry, C. H. (1967) Flexibility of capital stock, *Ohio State Law Journal*, **28**, 402–26.

Berry, C. H. (1974) Corporate diversification and market structure, *Bell Journal of Economics*, **5**, 196–204.

Bevan, A. (1974) The UK potato crisp industry 1960–72: a study of new entry competition, *Journal of Industrial Economics*, **22**, 281–97.

Bloch, H. (1974) Advertising and profitability: a reappraisal, *Journal of Political Economy*, **82**, 267–86.

Bork, R. H. (1978) *The Antitrust Paradox*, Wiley.

Brunner, E. (1961) A note on potential competition, *Journal of Industrial Economics*, **9**, 248–50.

Buxton, A. J., Davies, S. W. and Lyons, B. R. (1984) Concentration and advertising in consumer and producer markets, *Journal of Industrial Economics*, **32**, 451–64.

Caves, R. E. and Porter, M. E. (1977) From entry barriers to mobility barriers: conjectural decisions and contrived deterrence to new competition, *Quarterly Journal of Economics*, **91**, 241–61.

Caves, R. E. and Uekusa, M. (1976) *Industrial Organisation in Japan*, The Brookings Institution: Washington D.C.

Caves, R. E., Khalilzadeh-Shirazi, J. and Porter, M. (1975) Scale economies in statistical analyses of market power, *Review of Economics and Statistics*, **57**, 133–40.

Caves, R. E., Porter, M. and Spence, A. M. (1980) *Competition in the Open Economy: a model applied to Canada*, Harvard University Press: Harvard.

Chappell, H., Marks, W. and Park, I. (1983) Measuring entry barriers using a switching model of industrial profitability, *Southern Economic Journal*, **49**, 991–1001.

Comanor, W. S. and Wilson, T. A. (1967) Advertising, market structure and performance, *Review of Economics and Statistics*, **49**, 423–58.

Coursey, D., Isaac, R. M., Luke, M. and Smith, V. L. (1984) Market contestability in the presence of sunk (entry) costs, *Rand Journal of Economics*, **15**, 69–84.

Coursey, D., Isaac, R. M. and Smith, V. L. (1986) Natural monopoly and contested markets: some experimental results, *Journal of Law and Economics*, **27**, 91–114.

Cubbin, J. (1981) Advertising and the theory of entry barriers *Economica*, **48**, 289–98.

Dasgupta, P. and **Stiglitz, J.** (1980) Industrial structure and the nature of innovative activity, *Economic Journal*, **90**, 266–93.

Davies, S. W. (1871) The clay brick industry and the tunnel kiln, *National Institute Economic Review*, **58**, 54–71.

Demsetz, H. (1968) Why regulate utilities? *Journal of Law and Economics*, **11**, 55–65.

Demsetz, H. (1982) Barriers to entry, *American Economic Review*, **72**, 47–57.

Deutsch, L. L. (1975) Structure, performance and the net rate of entry, *Southern Economic Journal*, **41**, 450–6.

Devine, P. J., Lee, N., Jones, R. M., and **Tyson, W. J.** (1979) *An Introduction to Industrial Economics*, George Allen and Unwin: London.

Dixit, A. K. (1979) A model of duopoly suggesting a theory of entry barriers, *Bell Journal of Economics*, **10**, 20–32.

Dixit, A. K. (1980) The role of investment in entry deterrence, *Economic Journal*, **90**, 95–106.

Dixit, A. K. (1982) Recent developments in oligopoly theory, *American Economic Review Papers and Proceedings*, **72**, 12–17.

Eaton, B. C. and **Lipsey, R. G.** (1978) Freedom of entry and the existence of pure profit, *Economic Journal*, **88**, 488–510.

Esposito, F. F. and **Esposito, L.** (1974) Excess capacity and market structure, *Review of Economics and Statistics*, **56**, 188–200.

Fisher, F. M., Griliches, Z. and **Kaysen, C.** (1962) The costs of automobile model changes since 1949, *Journal of Political Economy*, **70**, 433–51.

Gan, W. and **Tham, S.** (1977) Market structure and price-cost margins in Malaysian manufacturing industries, *The Developing Economies*, **15**, 280–92.

Gaskins, D. W. (1971) Dynamic limit pricing: optimal pricing under threat of entry, *Journal of Economic Theory*, **3**, 306–22.

George, K. D. and **Joll, C.** (1981) *Industrial Organisation: competition, growth and structural change*, George Allen and Unwin: London.

Gilbert, R. J. and **Newbery, D. M. G.** (1980) Pre-emptive patenting and the persistence of monopoly, *American Economic Review*, **72**, 514–26.

Gilbert, R. J. and **Vives, X.** (1986) Entry deterrence and the free rider problem, *Review of Economic Studies*, **103**, 71–83.

Gorecki, P. K. (1975) An inter-industry analysis of diversification in the UK manufacturing sector, *Journal of Industrial Economics*, **24**, 131–46.

Gorecki, P. K. (1976) The determinants of entry by domestic and foreign enterprises in Canadian manufacturing industries: some comments and empirical results, *Review of Economics and Statistics*, **58**, 485–8.

Grabowski, H. G. and **Mueller, D. C.** (1978) Industrial research and development, intangible capital stocks, and firm profit rates, *Bell Journal of Economics,* **9**, 328–43.

HMSO (1978) *A Review of Monopolies and Mergers Policy*, Cmnd 7198, HMSO: London.

Hay, D. A. (1976) Sequential entry and entry-deterring strategies in spatial competition, *Oxford Economic Papers*, **28**, 240–57.

Hilke, J. C. (1984) Excess capacity and entry: some empirical evidence, *Journal of Industrial Economics,* **33**, 233–40.

Jenny, F. and **Weber, A.** (1976) Profit rates and structural variables in French manufacturing industries, *European Economic Review*, **7**, 187–206.

Johnston, J. (1960) *Statistical Cost Analysis*, McGraw-Hill, New York.

Kaldor, N. (1935) Market imperfections and excess capacity, *Economica*, **2**, 35–50.

Kaldor, N. (1950) Economic aspects of advertising, *Review of Economic Studies*, **58**, 1–27.

Kamien, M. K. and Schwartz, N. L. (1971) Limit pricing and uncertain entry *Econometrica*, **39**, 441–54.

Kreps, D. and Wilson, R. (1982) Reputation and imperfect information, *Journal of Economic Theory*, **27**, 253–79.

Lancaster, K. (1979) *Variety, Equity and Efficiency*, Basil Blackwell: Oxford.

Levin, R. C. (1978) Technical change, barriers to entry and market structure, *Economica*, **45**, 347–61.

Lyons, B. R. (1980) A new measure of minimum efficient plant size in UK manufacturing industry, *Economica*, **47**, 19–34.

Lyons, B. R. (1984) The pattern of international trade in differentiated products: an incentive for the existence of multinational firms, in Kierzkowski, H. (ed.) *Monopolistic Competition and International Trade*, Clarendon Press: Oxford.

Lyons, B. R. (1986) The welfare loss due to strategic investment in excess capacity, *International Journal of Industrial Organisation*, **4**, 109–19.

Lyons, B. R. (1989) Brand proliferation as a barrier to entry, *Journal of Industrial Economics* (forthcoming).

Mann, H. M. (1966) Seller concentration, barriers to entry and rates of return in thirty industries, 1950–60, *Review of Economics and Statistics*, **48**, 296–327.

Mansfield, E. (1962) Entry, Gibrat's law, innovation and the growth of firms, *American Economic Review*, **52**, 1023–51.

Masson, R. T. and Shanaan, J. (1982) Stochastic dynamic limit pricing: an empirical test, *Review of Economics and Statistics*, **64**, 413–22.

Menge, J. A. (1962) Style change costs as a market weapon, *Quarterly Journal of Economics*, **76**, 632–47.

Milgrom, P. and Roberts, J. (1982) Predation, reputation and entry deterrence, *Journal of Economic Theory*, **27**, 280–312.

Modigliani, F. (1958) New developments on the oligopoly front, *Journal of Political Economy*, **66**, 215–32.

Mueller, D. C. and Tilton, J. E. (1969) Research and development costs as a barrier to entry, *Canadian Journal of Economics*, **2**, 570–9.

Needham, D. (1976) Entry barriers and non-price aspects of firms' behaviour, *Journal of Industrial Economics* **25**, 29–43.

Neumann, M., Bobel, I. and Haid, A. (1979) Profitability, risk and market structure in West Germany, *Journal of Industrial Economics*, **27**, 227–42.

Nordhaus, W. D. (1969) *Invention, Growth and Welfare*, MIT Press: Cambridge, Mass.

Orr, D. (1974) The determinants of entry: a study of Canadian manufacturing industries, *Review of Economics and Statistics*, **56**, 58–74.

Orr, D. (1976) An index of entry barriers and its application to the market structure performance relationship, *Journal of Industrial Economics*, **23**, 39–49.

Osborne, D. K. (1973) On the rationality of limit pricing, *Journal of Industrial Economics*, **22**, 71–80.

Peltzman, S. (1965) Entry in commercial banking, *Journal of Law and Economics*, **6**, 11–50.

Porter, M. E. (1974) Consumer behaviour, retailer power and market performance in consumer goods industries, *Review of Economics and Statistics*, **56**, 419–49.

Porter, M. E. (1976) Interbrand choice, media mix and market performance, *American Economic Review: Papers and Proceedings*, 398–406.

Pratten, C. F. (1971) *Economies of Scale in Manufacturing Industry*, Cambridge University Press: Cambridge.

Prescott, E. C. and Visscher, M. (1977) Sequential location among firms with perfect foresight, *Bell Journal of Economics*, **8**, 378–93.

Price Commission (1978) *Prices, Costs and Margins in the Production and Distribution of Proprietary Non-ethical Medicines*, HMSO: London.

Reddaway, W. B. (1961) The Chemical Industry, in Burn, D. (ed.), *The Structure of British Industry*, Cambridge University Press.

Rees, R. D. (1973) Optimal plant size in UK industries: some survivor estimates, *Economica*, **40**, 394–401.

Rhoades, S. A. (1973) The effect of diversification on industry profit performance in 241 manufacturing industries: 1963, *Review of Economics and Statistics*, **55**, 146–65.

Salop, S. C. (1979) Monopolistic competition with outside goods, *Bell Journal of Economics*, **10**, 141–56.

Saving, T. R. (1961) Estimation of optimum size of plant by the survivor technique, *Quarterly Journal of Economics*, **75**, 569–607.

Sawyer, M. C. (1981) *The Economics of Firms and Markets: theories, evidence and policy*, Croom Helm: London.

Schelling, T. C. (1960) *The Strategy of Conflict*, Harvard University Press: Cambridge, Mass.

Scherer, F. M. (1970) *Industrial Market Structure and Economic Performance*, Rand McNally: Chicago.

Scherer, F. M. (1979) The welfare economics of product variety: an application to the ready-to-eat cereals industry, *Journal of Industrial Economics*, **28**, 113–34.

Scherer, F. M., Beckstein, A., Kaufer, E. and **Murphy, R. D.** (1975) *The Economics of Multiplant Operation*, Harvard University Press: London.

Schmalensee, R. (1974) Brand loyalty and barriers to entry, *Southern Economic Journal*, **40**, 579–88.

Schmalensee, R. (1978) Entry deterrence in the ready-to-eat breakfast cereal industry, *Bell Journal of Economics*, **9**, 305–27.

Schmalensee, R. (1981) Economies of scale and barriers to entry, *Journal of Political Economy*, **89**, 1228–38.

Schmalensee, R. (1982) Product differentiation advantages of pioneering brands, *American Economic Review*, **72**, 349–65.

Schmalensee, R. (1983) Advertising and entry deterrence: an exploratory model, *Journal of Political Economy*, **91**, 636–53.

Shaked, A. and **Sutton, J.** (1984) Natural oligopolies and international trade, in Kierzkowski, H. (ed.), *Monopolistic Competition and International Trade*, Clarendon Press: Oxford.

Sharkey, W. W. (1982) *The Theory of Natural Monopoly*, Cambridge University Press: Cambridge.

Shaw, R. W. (1974) Price leadership and the effect of new entry on the UK retail petrol supply market, *Journal of Industrial Economics*, **23**, 65–79.

Shaw, R. W. (1980) New entry and the competitive process in the UK fertilizer industry, *Scottish Journal of Political Economy*, **27**, 1–16.

Shaw, R. W. (1982) Product proliferation in characteristics space: the UK fertiliser industry, *Journal of Industrial Economics*, **31**, 69–92.

Spence, A. M. (1977) Entry, capacity, investment and oligopolistic pricing, *Bell Journal of Economics*, **8**, 534–44.

Spence, A. M. (1980) Notes on advertising, economies of scale and entry barriers, *Quarterly Journal of Economics*, **95**, 493–507.

Stigler, G. J. (1968) *The Organisation of Industry*, Irwin: Homewood, Ill.

Stiglitz, J. E. and **Weiss, A.** (1981) Credit rationing in markets with imperfect information, *American Economic Review*, **71**, 393–410.

Stonebraker, R. J. (1976) Corporate profits and the risk of entry, *Review of Economics and Statistics*, **58**, 33–46.

Sullivan, T. G. (1978) The cost of capital and the market power of firms, *Review of Economics and Statistics*, **60**, 209–17.

Sullivan, T. G. (1982) The cost of capital and the market power of firms, *Review of Economics and Statistics*, **64**, 523–5.

Stylos-Labini, P. (1962) *Oligopoly and Technical Progress*, Harvard University Press: Cambridge, Mass.

Taylor, C. T. and Silberston, Z. A. (1973) *The Economic Impact of the Patent System: a study of the British experience*, Cambridge University Press: Cambridge.

Vickers, J. and Yarrow, G. (1985) *Privatisation and the Natural Monopolies,* Public Policy Centre: London.

von Weizsacker, C. C. (1980a) A welfare analysis of barriers to entry, *Bell Journal of Economics*, **11**, 399–420.

von Weizsacker, C. C. (1980b) *Barriers to Entry: a Theoretical Treatment*, Springer-Verlag: Berlin.

Walgreen, T. A. (1971) Cost functions, concentration and barriers to entry in 29 manufacturing industries of India: a comment and reinterpretation, *Journal of Industrial Economics*, **20**, 90–5.

Weiss, L. W. (1969) Advertising, profits and corporate taxes, *Review of Economics and Statistics*, **51**, 421–30.

Weiss, L. W. (1974) The concentration–profits relationship and antitrust, in Goldschmid H. D., Mann H. M., and Weston J. F. (eds), *Industrial Concentration: the new learning*, Little Brown: Boston.

Weitzman, M. L. (1983) Contestable markets: comment, *American Economic Review*, **73**, 486–7.

Wenders, J. T. (1967) Entry and monopoly pricing, *Journal of Political Economy*, **75**, 755–60.

Wenders, J. T. (1971a) Collusion and entry, *Journal of Political Economy*, **79**, 1258–77.

Wenders, J. T., (1971b) Excess capacity as a barrier to entry, *Journal of Industrial Economics*, **20**, 14–19.

Williamson, O. E. (1963) Selling expense as a barrier to entry, *Quarterly Journal of Economics*, **77**, 112–28.

Williamson, O. E. (1968) Wage rates as a barrier to entry: the Pennington case in perspective, *Quarterly Journal of Economics*, **82**, 85–116.

Williamson, O. E. (1975) *Markets and Hierarchies: Analysis and Antitrust Implications,* Free Press: New York.

Yamey, B. S. (1972) Predatory price cutting: notes and comments, *Journal of Law and Economics*, **15**, 129–42.

CHAPTER THREE

Concentration

Stephen Davies

It is tempting to attribute the central role attached to seller concentration within much of contemporary industrial organisation to the pervasive influence of the 'structure–conduct–performance' (S–C–P) paradigm. Certainly, of the various dimensions of industry structure identified by Bain, it is the most widely documented statistically, and many empirical studies use the terms 'structure' and 'concentration' almost synonymously. But an interest in concentration is not confined to S–C–P economists: the theoretical pedigree of the subject plainly derives from the earlier tradition of neo-classical price theory, and the level of concentration in any particular market is easily identifiable with the degree of oligopoly. Whatever one's view of the S–C–P approach, the concept of concentration must be a central dimension of the organisation of industries and one which merits a significant research effort. As will be seen from this survey, quite often the study of the causes and consequences of concentration has emanated from economists with little sympathy for the S–C–P paradigm.

These comments relate to what is usually termed 'market concentration', that is, the extent to which the individual market is dominated by its largest sellers. For example, we can point to industries such as sugar, cigarettes, petrol, cars, tractors, man-made fibres and many others, in which the leading half-dozen or so firms account for at least 90 per cent of the market. The reasons for this and the consequences, are naturally the concern of the micro-economist. But at a more macro level the subject is also of interest, if for different reasons. Current estimates suggest that the largest 100 British manufacturing firms account for about 40 per cent of total manufacturing output. This relatively high level of overall, or 'aggregate concentration' is central to wider discussions such as the long-run evolution of the capitalist economy. The Marxist concern with the long-run tendency for power to be concentrated in the hands of a small and declining number of giant conglomerate firms is only the most obvious example. Other writers, of widely differing political persuasions, associate an economy dominated by a few large corporations with potentially anti-democratic decision-making, and impersonality, leading to the alienation of both workers and consumers, and increasing governmental impotence. From this standpoint, it is the dominance of the economy as a whole, rather than particular industries, which is the cause for concern.

To emphasise the distinction between market and aggregate concentration, this survey is presented in two distinct parts. This is not at all forced, but merely reflects the fact that two generally separate research traditions are involved. Nevertheless, the two concepts are connected, as we shall illustrate later. In Part I of the survey we examine market concentration. Section 1 establishes the neo-classical case for associating concentration with the degree of oligopoly. Section 2 surveys the range of alternative indices which abound in the literature, and section 3 summarises the evidence on the degree of concentration within UK industry using the most commonly applied of these indices, the concentration ratio. This section also includes a brief description of the Census of Production which provides so much of the data in this connection and in other areas of empirical research in industrial organisation. Section 4 is the core of the first part: it surveys the theoretical literature on the determinants of concentration in any market. Section 5 is its empirical counterpart and summarises the, mainly econometric, tradition of explaining inter-industry differences in concentration. Section 6 summarises this part of the survey, speculates on future research, and briefly explores two contemporary threats to the central role attributed to concentration: contestable market theory on the one hand, and Austrian pressure for a more dynamic view of competition on the other. Given the title and broad aims of this volume, our treatment of aggregate concentration in Part II is very truncated with only brief discussions of the evidence and some implications for market concentration. A more thorough survey would lead us too far beyond the scope of this study. The interested reader will find Prais (1976) and parts of Hannah and Kay (1977) useful entrees.

I MARKET CONCENTRATION

1. The theoretical justification

At an intuitive level the identification of seller concentration with the theoretical concept of 'the degree of oligopoly' is fairly obvious. A highly concentrated market is one which is dominated by a few large sellers. It is therefore unlikely that any one seller can make a change in major policy variables, price, advertising, research effort, etc., without seriously disturbing the environment of competitors and thereby risking their retaliation. This obvious interdependence and the importance of conjectures about rivals' behaviour is, of course, one of the cornerstones of most oligopoly theory.

Intuition is fine, but no substitute for formal theory, and we begin the survey with a prelude which establishes a theoretical connection between concentration and the degree of oligopoly. For these purposes, we shall follow the time-honoured convention of equating the degree of oligopoly with the price–cost margin[1] in the industry concerned. Under a variety of different oligopoly models this can be shown to be related in a simple way to the level of concentration.

(a) COURNOT–NASH EQUILIBRIUM

In the jargon of game theory, we start with a non-cooperative solution to the oligopoly game, i.e. one in which each firm selects a strategy which is optimal given the strategies of the other firms. In more traditional terms, one such case corresponds to equilibrium in an industry of output-setting firms, each making Cournot conjectures. Following Cowling and Waterson (1976) this is formalised as follows. Suppose an industry of N firms producing a homogeneous good for which price is determined by aggregate[2] industry output, $X = \Sigma X_i$. Thus $P = P(X)$ where the elasticity of demand is $e = -(dX/dP)(P/X)$.

In the Cournot model each firm sets its output on the supposition that the outputs of all other firms will remain unchanged; algebraically this conjecture implies that $dX/dX_i = 1$ (industry output will change by only the change in i's output.) In equilibrium this conjecture is correct and the outcome is solved easily as follows.

Given fixed costs F_i and constant marginal costs c_i, i's profits are:

$$\pi_i = PX_i - c_i X_i - F_i \tag{1}$$

and optimal output is derived from the first-order condition for a maximum:

$$\frac{d\pi_i}{dX_i} = \frac{dP}{dX_i} \cdot X_i + P - c_i = 0 \tag{2}$$

From the Cournot conjecture, $dP/dX_i = dP/dX$ and the price–cost margin can be derived from rearrangement as follows:

$$\frac{P - c_i}{P} = \frac{-dP}{dX} \cdot \frac{X}{P} \cdot \frac{X_i}{X} = \frac{S_i}{e} \qquad \text{where } s_i = \frac{X_i}{X} \tag{3}$$

Turning now to the industry as a whole, the average margin follows from summing [3] over all N firms weighting each firm's margin by its share of the market.[3] Thus

$$\Sigma \frac{(P - c_i)X_i}{P \quad X} = \Sigma \frac{s_i^2}{e} = \frac{H}{e} \tag{4}$$

The aggregate margin in Cournot or Nash quantity-setting equilibrium is therefore greater, the less elastic is demand, and the larger is the sum of squared market shares. As we shall see presently, the latter (denoted by H) is one of the most widely advocated measures of concentration, and is known as the Herfindahl index. Its properties will be examined in more detail below, but note here that its value must lie between 0 and 1 with the lower bound approached in industries comprising very many extremely small firms, and the upper bound applying in the monopoly case. Since the price–cost margin is proportionately related to this index, [4] illustrates that even in this most simple of oligopoly models, there exists a direct proportionate relationship between concentration and the degree of oligopoly.

In some ways this conclusion is rather puzzling: our intuition for expecting such a relationship derived from the supposition that high concentration implies obvious interdependence and, implicitly, the likelihood of collusion or cooperation. The above result suggests a connection between margins and concentration even when firms do not cooperate.[4] However, as a number of writers have stressed (see section 4 below), this model does not establish a *causal* relation; both the margin and concentration are jointly determined in equilibrium by the cost and demand parameters and the nature of behaviour.

(b) COOPERATIVE SOLUTIONS

Cowling and Waterson (1976), Dixit and Stern (1982) and Clarke and Davies (1982) all generalise this model to allow for non-Cournot behaviour, i.e. non-zero conjectures. Clarke and Davies, for example, substitute for the Cournot conjecture the following:

$$\frac{\mathrm{d}X_j}{X_j} = \alpha \, \frac{\mathrm{d}X_i}{X_i} \qquad \text{for all } j, \text{ where } \alpha \leq 1 \tag{5}$$

In other words, firm i expects each of its rivals to proportionally match a change in output either fully ($\alpha = 1$) or partially ($\alpha < 1$). It is easily shown that this generates the following industry average mark-up:

$$\frac{\Sigma \, (P - c_i) \, X_i}{PX} = \frac{\Sigma \, s_i^2 (1 - \alpha)}{e} + \frac{\alpha}{e} = \frac{H \, (1 - \alpha)}{e} + \frac{\alpha}{e} \tag{6}$$

Two special cases are immediately obvious: $\alpha = 1$ implies perfect collusion with fixed market shares, that is the monopoly result[5] with the margin equal to $1/e$; $\alpha = 0$, for which [6] collapses to the original Cournot result. More generally, the margin is the weighted average of the perfectly collusive and Cournot solution, with the former weighted more heavily the closer is α to unity. (See also Cowling 1982: 33–4).[6] For present purposes the significance of this result is a confirmation that the relation between the degree of oligopoly and concentration is not confined merely to the Cournot model: it applies to a whole spectrum of alternative conducts if modelled in this way.

An alternative approach to a partially collusive solution is provided by Saving (1970). This too yields a monotonic relation between the degree of oligopoly and concentration, although this time the concentration ratio replaces H as the appropriate index. Again the relationship is without implications of causality. Suppose there are two groups of firms in the industry: K large firms collude so as to maximise their own joint profits, the remaining $N - K$ smaller firms behave passively as price takers by producing where their marginal costs equal price. These followers are sometimes referred to as the 'competitive fringe', and are assumed to have rising marginal costs. In effect this is a standard price leadership model with the modification that the leader is a group rather than a single firm. In this case the equilibrium solution is most easily derived graphically as in Fig. 3.1.

DD' is the market demand curve and SS' the supply curve of the fringe. The latter is able to supply more the higher the price, and the leading group, realising this, identifies its net demand curve to be the horizontal distance between DD' and SS'. As drawn, this is the curve ABD. Assuming the leaders' set price to

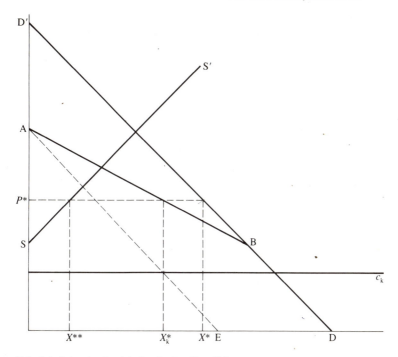

FIG. 3.1 Price leadership by the leading K firms

maximise their joint profits, they equate net marginal revenue AE to their own joint marginal cost, c_k, which is assumed horizontal for graphical clarity only. This involves an output for the leaders of X_k^*; price follows from the net demand curve as P^*, the fringe's supply, from its supply curve, is X^{**}, and total industry supply, from the market demand curve, is X^*. The reader can confirm, digrammatically, that as conditions within the industry change, the price–cost margin will move in the same direction as the leaders' market share, X_k^*/X^*. Consider, for example, an upward shift in the SS' curve, which is equivalent to a deterioration in the followers' competitiveness relative to the leaders.

Saving's own exposition of this model is algebraic and he shows that the average price–cost margin is

$$\frac{s_k^2}{e + E(1-s_k)} \qquad [7]$$

where $s_k = X_k^*/X^*$, the leaders' share, e is the price elasticity of market demand, and E is the elasticity of the SS' curve. In this model then, the degree of oligopoly is related positively (although non-linearly) to an alternative measure of concentration: the joint market share of the leading K firms. This is known as the 'K-firm concentration ratio' (and will be denoted by CR_K) and reflects the dominance of the leading firms in an obvious way; this too is examined in more detail presently.

(c) CONCENTRATION AS A DETERMINANT OF THE DEGREE OF COLLUSION

In none of these three models does the relation between concentration and the degree of oligopoly reflect causal mechanisms. Of course, one might argue that price leadership is more likely in concentrated industries, and in the Clarke–Davies model we might suppose that more concentrated industries exhibit larger values of α. In both cases this would reinforce the connection between concentration and the mark-up. But, as they stand, these models take the prevailing nature of conduct as exogenous.

The supposition that conduct is endogenous, and in particular that high concentration will increase the likelihood of collusion, dates back to at least Chamberlin (1933). His 'small numbers case' describes a market of few sellers who will inevitably recognise the interdependence of their actions; if this is the case the incentive to cut price or raise output is much reduced since firms will anticipate reactions from rivals. This will tend to lead to restriction of output, and higher prices, even in the absence of explicit collusion. Thus tacit, or implicit, collusion is the likely outcome in a market of only few sellers. Turning to more deliberately collusive behaviour, it is commonly asserted that high concentration also makes the logistics of arranging a cartel more manageable. This argument derives from the likelihood that, where sellers are few, it is easier to detect and punish any member of the group who cheats by cutting price below the agreed level. In an otherwise rather dull and descriptive literature on this subject, the outstanding theoretical contribution is provided by Stigler (1964) with a clever formulation of the detection issue. He posits a market in which there is a random element to buyer behaviour: even if all members of the collusive selling group stick to the agreed price, some buyers will switch their allegiance between sellers. The market is also such that price is not directly observable;[7] because of this the most likely way of detecting cheating is by observing the net flows of customers to the suspected cheater. The problem is, however, in deciding whether a positive flow of custom to the suspect is the result of his secret price cutting or just a random event. Stigler shows formally that the collusive group is better able to make this distinction when the industry is highly concentrated.[8] Interestingly, the model suggests quite explicitly that the appropriate measure of concentration in this context is the sum of squared market shares — once again the Herfindahl index. There has been a recent reawakening of interest in this model (see, especially, Rees 1985) and occasional relatively minor criticisms (McKinnon 1966), but the central insight, that collusive behaviour is more likely in concentrated industries, remains uncontested.[9]

We conclude from this prelude that there is a theoretically respectable case for identifying measures of concentration as the empirical counterpart to the degree of oligopoly. This short survey has also provided an important insight. The identity of the appropriate index of concentration depends on the behavioural assumptions concerning the nature of the oligopoly game. This point is pursued in more detail by Dansby and Willig (1979) and Geroski (1983) and is of some interest to the empirical issue, discussed next, of how to measure concentration. On the face of it, the Herfindahl index appears to be a strong candidate on this count.[10] We should end the section with an important qualification, however. The prevailing theme has been that higher concentration is associated with higher prices (without necessarily establishing causality.) This is by no means universally accepted; in a later section we discuss the assertion of contestable market theory that concentration may well be irrelevant to conduct and performance.

2. Concentration indices

The empirical question of how best to measure concentration has attracted considerable debate; in addition to the concentration ratio (CR) and the Herfindahl index (*H*) already mentioned, literally scores of alternative indices have been advocated and compared using statistical, theoretical and practical criteria. Indeed one might argue that rather too much research effort has been devoted to this part of the subject.

(a) THE TWO STATISTICAL COMPONENTS OF CONCENTRATION

Conceptually, two dimensions to concentration can be identified: firm numbers and size inequalities. Historically each can be associated with a different approach to concentration. If one views oligopoly as a spectrum of market structures lying between the two extremes of perfect competition and monopoly, an obvious measure is the number of sellers (*N*) in the market concerned. Indeed, in much of formal oligopoly theory we contemplate industries populated by identical (or 'representative') firms and in such cases, *N* is an obvious (inverse) measure of concentration. A good example of this is the Cournot model already discussed: in the special case in which all firms are equal, $s_i = 1/N$ for all i and $\Sigma s_i^2 = 1/N$, thus from eqn [4], the mark-up is simply $1/Ne$. Equally, it is not uncommon to find in recent theoretical work on oligopoly the notion of the symmetric equilibrium, i.e. where all firms are equal sized, and again the theoretician can quite properly employ *N* as an inverse measure.[11] However, the simplifying analytical convenience of the symmetric equilibrium should not blind us to the fact that real-world industries are never composed of identical firms. Because of this it is easy to invent plausible examples in which the ranking of industries by their values of *N* would give quite misleading rankings of concentration. Consider, for example, two industries each with 100 firms; in A each firm supplies 1 per cent of the market, while in B the two largest firms between them produce 90 per cent with the remaining 98 accounting for the other 10 per cent. In both cases $N = 100$, but A looks not dissimilar to perfect competition while B is virtually a duopoly.

Plainly the essential weakness of *N* as a concentration measure is that it ignores size inequalities between firms. It is precisely this element of business concentration which leads many to draw a parallel with the study of personal income. Consider the two following statements: 'the distribution of income is extremely unequal since the richest 5 per cent of the population receive 50 per cent of national income', and 'this industry is oligopolistic since the largest 5 per cent of firms supply 50 per cent of the market'. In both cases significance is attached to inequalities within the population; thus the rich are relatively richer, and the large firms are relatively more dominant, the more unequal are the size distributions concerned. This conceptual similarity between the two fields of study has been used to the advantage of industrial organisation in a number of ways. In the present context, it has led to the application of various statistical measures of inequality, initially evolved to study income distribution, to the analysis of concentration. Nevertheless, for reasons that will become apparent, sheer inequality cannot be equated to concentration and we confine our discussion to a few illustrative measures.[12]

The most obvious measure of dispersion or inequality in size is, of course, its variance. But because the variance is sensitive to the units of measurement and the absolute magnitudes involved, a rather purer inequality measure is the *coefficient of variation* (cv). This is the ratio of the standard deviation to the mean and is independent of the units employed. We shall see below that the H index exhibits a simple relation to this measure, as do a number of more sophisticated inequality measures, but it is rarely used on its own in the concentration context. The *Lorenz curve* occupies a respected position in the inequalities literature as, in many respects, the perfect measure. Because most other inequality indices can be interpreted as summary statistics of it, a brief description is justified here. The Lorenz curve shown in Fig. 3.2 plots the cumulative percentage of market size (say sales or employment) against the cumulative percentage of firms (starting with the smallest up to the largest firm). Thus curve I corresponds to an industry in which the smallest 30 per cent of firms account for only 2 per cent of total industry sales, the next smallest 30 per cent account for a further 10 per cent of sales, and the next smallest 30 per cent a further 18 per cent of sales: this leaves the largest 10 per cent of firms accounting for 70 per cent of industry size. Given information on the sizes of all firms in the industry, it would be possible to identify all points intermediate between those just mentioned. Broadly speaking, less inequality in the sizes of firms in a given industry is reflected in higher Lorenz curves; this can be seen if we increase the shares of the smaller groups in the above example to 10, 20 and 30 per cent and reduce the share of the largest firms to 40 per cent. The revised curve II now lies above curve I at all points, reflecting the now more equal size distribution. The two limiting cases are 'perfect equality' (all firms are equal sized and the curve becomes a 45° line) and monopoly (where one firm accounts for virtually all industry size and the curve follows the horizontal until just less than 100 per cent, at which point it rises up the vertical axis.) So just as a particularly unequal income distribution shows as a very low Lorenz curve, so too does an unequal firm size distribution. Where Lorenz curves do not cross, as in Fig. 3.2, there is no ambiguity as to the ranking of the size distributions concerned. Indeed, a property that statisticians usually require of any inequality measure is that it should rank distributions in the same order as the Lorenz curve (in non-intersecting cases). Where the curves do intersect, things are less clear cut and depend on which tail of the distribution is most interesting.[13]

This, and all other pure inequality measures, cannot be taken too seriously as concentration measures for two related reasons. Firstly, they fail to

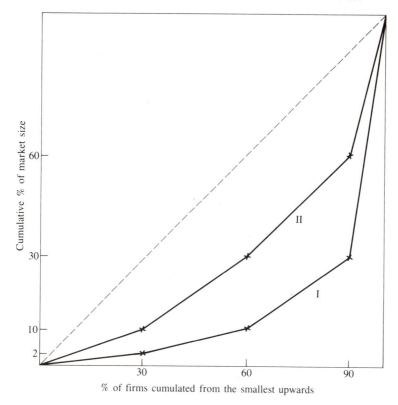

FIG. 3.2 The Lorenz curve

explicitly acknowledge firm numbers. Again a hypothetical example illustrates this: suppose industry A comprises 5 equally sized firms and B 1000 equally sized firms. Unequivocally, A is more concentrated than B yet both record perfect equality and therefore diagonal Lorenz curves. Secondly, and at first blush paradoxically, they are oversensitive to changes in the small-scale end of an industry. Consider the earlier example of an industry with two large firms supplying 90 per cent of the market, and 98 smaller firms supplying the rest; suppose also that the big two are equal in size. Almost certainly it would make little difference to the behaviour of this virtually duopolistic industry whether or not the small firms exist. Yet their inclusion leads to a Lorenz curve indicating extreme inequalities, while their exit would lead to a diagonal curve, indicating a very substantial reduction in inequalities.

One other inequality measure deserves special mention: the variance of the logarithm of firm size, σ^2. While in general this is no better as a measure of inequality than many others, there is extensive evidence that most real-world firm size distributions can be reasonably approximated by the lognormal distribution.[14] Where this is so, this parameter is of considerable interest. Lognormal distributions are described completely by firm numbers, and the mean and variance of log size. Not only is σ^2 then the natural inequality measure, but also it is easily shown (e.g.

Hart 1975) that most other concentration measures can be derived merely from information on N and σ^2. On a theoretical level, there are various models which attempt to explain this wide applicability of the lognormal, and to some extent they provide predictions as to the determinants of the magnitude of σ^2. In turn this implies predictions of the determinants of concentration itself. Thus σ^2 as a measure of inequality will often prove convenient as an aid to understanding concentration, especially if complemented by an explanation of N. Hart and Prais (1956) provide a classic exposition of the value of this measure in these circumstances, including its analytically useful decomposition properties.

(b) POPULAR CONCENTRATION INDICES

The obvious implication of the discussion so far is that any self-respecting index of concentration should reflect both inequalities and firm numbers. Fortunately most of those in common use exhibit this property, and it is to these that we now turn. The *Herfindahl index* (H), which we encountered in the previous section, bears an obvious inverse relation to firm numbers and is positively related to size inequalities. This is most readily apparent when rewriting the sum of squared shares expression as follows:

$$H = \Sigma s_i^2 = \frac{1 + (\text{cv})^2}{N} \qquad [8]$$

where cv is the coefficient of variation of firm size.[15]

As already stated, H must always take on some value between 0 and 1, with larger values indicating higher concentration. With equal sized firms, $H = 1/N$ since $s_i = 1/N$ for all i and $(\text{cv})^2 = 0$. More generally, as inequalities appear, $H > 1/N$ and it is sensitive to the shares of the leading firms; for example, if the leading firm controls half of the market, H must exceed 0.25 no matter how many other firms there are. Another way of looking at H is as the reciprocal of the *equivalent number of equal sized firms*. Thus suppose in an industry of 100 firms, H is 0.2 (which indicates a fair amount of inequality); this may be interpreted as an industry as equally concentrated as one of five equal-sized firms. This is an appealing feature of the index when comparing and interpreting H values for different industries.

For many economists, the main attraction of H is that, as we have already seen, it is often generated by theoretical models as the appropriate measure of the degree of oligopoly. An infrequent criticism (Hart 1975; Hart and Clarke 1980) is that it is too sensitive to firm numbers, in the sense that entry of relatively small firms will lead to non-trivial reductions in H, indicating a significant reduction in concentration which is not really justified. But this contention clearly depends on a subjective view (with no particular theoretical base) as to how much the index 'should' decline. In any event, Davies (1979b), for instance, shows how other popular indexes may be even more sensitive to small-scale entry. A practical problem with the H index is that one requires information on the sizes of all firms in the industry.

Conceptually similar to H is a group of measures known as entropy statistics. The most simple example is the *first-order entropy* defined by:

$$E = - \Sigma \ s_i \log s_i \qquad\qquad [9]$$

When all firms are of equal size, $s_i = 1/N$ for all i and $E = -N(1/N).\log(1/N) = \log N$, but when firms are very unequal in size E will tend to zero. Thus E is related to both dimensions of concentration, although it should be noted that its definition renders it an inverse measure — low values indicating high concentration. This slight inconvenience is avoided in two modified forms of the index, the redundancy and relative entropy indexes, which are defined respectively as (log N) – E and 1 – $(E/\log N)$. But these are best thought of as sheer inequality measures (Hart 1975).

E tends to be more sensitive than most indices to firm numbers (and has been criticised on this count by Hart 1975). Perhaps the most damning criticism, however, is that it appears to have no theoretical justification in this particular branch of economics. Waterson offers a brave attempt at an intuitive justification for the index in this context, employing an example based on information theory, but we are bound to agree with his perplexed conclusion: [This] author finds it difficult to relate this [index] more closely to industrial concentration.' (1984: 172). On the other hand, E scores over H in one respect: that of decomposition. This statistical property means that the index can be decomposed into within- and between-group components. This may be helpful where an industry comprises a number of sub-industries, and one wishes to know how concentration compares between the constituent parts, and how much each contributes to the whole.[16] For this reason E is often preferred in descriptive studies of a statistical nature, but is less popular when testing behavioural relationships generated by economic theory.

Hannah and Kay (1977) suggest an interesting generalisation of the H and E indexes:

$$N(\alpha) = (\Sigma \ s_i^{\alpha})^{1/(1-\alpha)} \quad \alpha > 0, \ \alpha \neq 1 \qquad\qquad [10]$$

Thus instead of squared market shares, this index takes shares to the power of α and then takes the $(1 - \alpha)$th root of the sum. In the case where $\alpha = 2$, $N(\alpha) = (\Sigma \ s_i^2)^{-1}$ which is simply the reciprocal of H, i.e. the Herfindahl numbers equivalent. Indeed this index is termed the 'numbers equivalent' index. The basic idea is that one selects an α value depending on how much weight one wishes to attach to the upper portion of the size distribution relative to the lower ... In general, high α gives greater weight to the role of the largest firms in the distribution: lower α emphasises the presence or otherwise of small firms' (ibid: 56). To simplify only a little, one might say that the value of α selected reflects one's view of the significance of inequalities relative to numbers. Thus at $\alpha = 0$, $N(\alpha) = N$, so only numbers matter, while as $\alpha \to \infty$, $N(\alpha)$ tends to the reciprocal of the leading firm's share — only the top firms matter. More generally, for a given value of α, $N(\alpha)$ shows the number of equal-sized firms which would record the same level of concentration. Thus $N(\alpha)$ is an inverse measure of concentration.

This index has much to commend it — most obviously its generality (another special case is E as $\alpha \to 1$) and flexibility. In addition it satisfies various statistical criteria for acceptability (see below.) Yet, to date it has not been widely used: perhaps this is due to the considerable data and time input required of the potential user, but probably also to the absence of any obvious criterion for selecting the α value. In their own work with the index, Hannah and Kay suggest that a range of $0.6 < \alpha < 2.5$ might be appropriate. One interesting application arises in the aggregation of production functions across plants in which α is determined by the degree of scale economies (Davies and Caves 1987: Ch.2).

In spite of the relative sophistication of these alternatives, the most commonly employed concentration measure remains the traditional concentration ratio. This shows the share of industry sales, or more generally size, accounted for by the K largest firms:

$$CR_k = \sum_{}^{K} s_i$$ [11]

where firms are ranked in descending order of size, with firm 1 therefore the largest. The overwhelming reason for its popularity is pragmatic. It happens to be the only measure of concentration which the authorities are prepared to publish in the Census of Production in most countries. The value of K varies between countries and, within countries, between Census years, it typically takes values such as 3,4,5, or 8; at the moment the UK Census reports the 5-firm ratio, and the US Census, the 4- and 8-firm ratios. It should be stressed, however, that the choice of particular values for K by the Census agencies is arbitrary and has little direct economic significance.

In general terms, CR is a reasonable measure in that large values indicate more dominance for the leading firms; loosely speaking, it does reflect our two dimensions of concentration, albeit rather ambiguously. Hart and Clarke (1980: 104–5) provide a pragmatic defence, and we must admit that it is a more immediately understandable index of concentration than some of the others we have discussed. This may be important for the dialogue between academics and policy makers. Nevertheless there is widespread unease with the concentration ratio precisely because it has little to commend it theoretically. It is true that the price leadership model described in the previous section establishes s_K as an appropriate measure and that this corresponds to CR_K if the number of firms in the colluding group happens to be the same as the K value chosen by those who calculate CR. There is, of course, no reason why this should be so, or why the size of the colluding group should be the same in all industries. Indeed it is somewhat unlikely that this sort of pricing behaviour is common across industries in the first place.

On a more statistical note, the main problem with this measure is that it emphasises inequalities between the top K and the rest of the industry at the expense of all else. In many instances we will be just as interested in inequalities within the top K group. A simple hypothetical example illustrates this problem. Suppose there are two industries, A in which there are 12 equally sized firms, and B with one large firm, accounting for 40 per cent of the market; and 120 small firms each with 0.5 per cent of the market. In both cases $CR_5 = 42\%$, but B is clearly more monopolistic than A. This is an, admittedly extreme, example of a general failing of the measure: it takes no account of differences in size within the top K firms but only compares the top K as a group with all others. More formally, this is because CR reports only one point on the cumulative concentration curve (Clarke 1985: 10–13), and as such the ranking of industries may vary depending on the value of K which is arbitrarily chosen.[17]

(c) COMPARING INDICES

Since most of the above indices are representative of various families of measures,[18] our list could be easily extended. Faced with this choice some economists argue that, although measures may differ in detail, most of the more respectable ones, e.g. CR, H and E, provide roughly the same information and it is unimportant which particular index is chosen. This view is usually based on the general finding that most concentration indexes are highly correlated and tend to yield similar rankings of industries.[19] But this is a dangerous argument: of course different indexes will be correlated, what is at issue is the marginal differences between them. Boyes and Smith (1979) show empirically how different measures can yield significantly different implications when used as alternative explanatory variables in regression analysis.

Given that there is a non-trivial choice to be made, various criteria have been suggested on which to base that choice. Some of these criteria have already emerged above. For example, we have suggested that the H index often appears most appropriate in terms of oligopoly theory. On the other hand, the concentration ratio may be the practical choice — often it is the only alternative available in published sources. However, most of the discussion has centred on statistical criteria. As a very basic requirement, one might insist, as we have here, that a concentration index should reflect both inequalities and numbers. Taking this argument further, we might wish to base a choice on the relative weights different indices attribute to the two constituents. This idea underlies the suggestion by Davies (1979b) that different indices can be compared by investigating the shapes of the 'iso-concentration curves' implied.[20] Another statistical angle involves the decomposition properties of different indices — as already mentioned, the entropy index scores well on this criterion (Cowell 1977).

A more systematic treatment (Hall and Tideman 1967; Hannah and Kay 1977) involves deriving a list of axioms that a concentration measure should satisfy. For example, Hannah and Kay suggest seven axioms, the most interesting of which are as follows. Measured concentration should increase following a merger of two or more firms within the same industry, and following a gain in market share of a large firm at the expense of a small firm, but concentration should decrease following entry of a small firm. They also require that industries' ranking by concentration should map directly on to a ranking by concentration curves (a requirement analogous to non-intersecting Lorenz curves but allowing for firm numbers as well as inequalities). While these axioms have not met with universal approval (see, for example, Hart 1975), they can be useful as a reference point. Unsurprisingly perhaps, the most appropriate index appears to be Hannah and Kay's own! The problem is that none of the popular simple indices satisfy all axioms unambiguously, and unless the data are sufficiently copious to permit estimation of more sophisticated variants such as the Hannah and Kay index, some compromise is necessary. A purely personal view is that the Herfindahl index is perhaps the best all-round alternative. (This preference for H seems to be shared by the US Justice Department: their recent modifications to merger guidelines include a shift from the previous practice of using CR to now employing H in assessing potential monopoly power.)

3. Evidence on concentration and the census of production

The descriptive evidence on how concentration levels vary between industries and how they have changed over time is fairly well documented, especially for the UK, and this is one area of the subject in which there is little argument. For this reason our survey of the evidence will be brief and we refer the interested reader to one of the many excellent and painstaking studies mentioned below for the details. In fact, somewhat unusually for a survey such as this, we shall place the emphasis on the *nature of the data* employed in concentration studies. Although this may appear a mundane and unfashionable issue, it does raise a number of important conceptual and definitional questions which are of wider relevance to virtually all empirical work in industrial organisation.

(a) DEFINITIONAL MATTERS

We have seen that most concentration indices require complete or partial information on the number of sellers and their shares in a given market. This raises two questions: how to define the market, and how to measure shares or firm sizes? The latter is generally less troublesome. There are of course many alternative indicators of firm size, e.g. value of assets, stock market valuation, sales, value added, employment, etc. None is totally satisfactory: the value of sales will tend to exaggerate the size of firms in retailing who add relatively little to the value of products; the value of assets will overrate capital-intensive firms relative to labour-intensive ones; while employment has the opposite effect. However, most of these problems are only serious when comparing firms with radically different technologies/products, i.e. in studies of aggregate concentration, and require less emphasis when, as here, one is concerned with concentration in individual markets.[21]

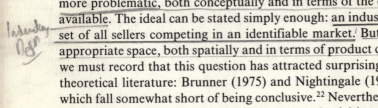 The question of how best to define the market or industry is altogether more problematic, both conceptually and in terms of the data which are typically available. The ideal can be stated simply enough: an industry should represent the set of all sellers competing in an identifiable market. But in practice what is the appropriate space, both spatially and in terms of product characteristics? Frankly, we must record that this question has attracted surprisingly little attention in the theoretical literature: Brunner (1975) and Nightingale (1978) are rare exceptions which fall somewhat short of being conclusive.[22] Nevertheless, in terms of product space, there is a common intuition that cross-elasticities of demand hold the key; see, for example, Clarke (1985: 21). While this intuition makes obvious sense in terms of standard models of oligopoly, there is plainly the problem of where to draw

the line: what value of a cross-price elasticity is sufficiently high to merit including two firms within the same industry, and what value is sufficiently low to assign them to separate industries? Less obviously, turning to potential competition, it may be also desirable to include within the same industry those firms with high cross-elasticities of supply. For example, consider the actual and potential for competition between firms producing packeted dehydrated potatoes, canned potatoes and canned peas.

Spatially, some industries might be sensibly defined at the national level, but others, especially those involving high transport costs, might have a regional flavour; yet others might involve an international market. The possibility that national concentration figures may conceal considerable inter-regional variations is probably unimportant for the UK (but not the US), but the existence of international markets, sometimes dominated by multinational oligopolies, can hardly be denied in certain prominent industries, e.g. aircraft, oil refining, some consumer durables. In these cases the concentration of sellers within a single, relatively insignificant, part of the world economy, such as the UK, is of limited interest. More generally, separate national markets may still be identifiable, but the sellers in those markets will not be confined to domestic producers. This is, of course, the norm for an open economy such as the UK. In these cases concentration of producers within the UK need not be closely related to the concentration of sellers within the UK market, and exporting and importing behaviour becomes important.

Some of these problems are surmountable in principle quite easily given a sufficiently rich data set. In practice, however, estimation of concentration indices across a population of, say, more than 100 industries, perhaps also over time, is extremely data intensive. Very few researchers have been prepared or able to collect such data from the primary sources, i.e. the firms concerned. Instead, the common practice is to rely on the Census of Production. The Census, which is now taken annually in Britain, is based on questionnaire answers from firms concerning output, employment, wage bills, investment, etc. The industry definitions employed by any Census authority are defined in its Standard Industrial Classification (SIC). The SIC employed by the British authorities underwent a fundamental revision at the turn of the 1980s in order to achieve closer comparability with continental Europe.

Although the criteria embodied in the British SIC are by no means always obvious, it appears that supply considerations tend to dominate. The current SIC is based upon four tiers of aggregation. The economy is first split into 10 Divisions (one-digit industries); each Division comprises a number of Classes (two-digit industries); each Class is split into its constituent Groups (three-digit industries); and each Group comprises a number of four-digit Activities. As far as the manufacturing sector is concerned,[23] this accounts for 3 of the Divisions and 104 of the Groups. As an example, Division 2 is 'Extraction, other than fuel, metal manufacture, mineral products and chemicals'. This includes 6 Classes, one of which is 25, 'Chemicals'. In turn, one of the 6 Groups in this Class is 251, 'Basic industrial chemicals', which itself comprises four Activities, one being 2515, 'Synthetic rubber'.

Invariably, the one- and two-digit classifications are too aggregate for our purposes, and since the Census typically reports most data at the three-digit level, it is at this level of aggregation that most empirical work is conducted. Generally however, this is still too aggregate to correspond with theoretical notions of what constitutes a well-defined industry. For example, 'Basic industrial chemicals' is clearly a collection of industries sharing, at best, certain common supply-side properties. Unfortunately, the more appropriate four-digit level of aggregation is rarely reported on an ongoing or systematic basis. So whatever the pros and cons of the supply, as opposed to demand, based criterion for grouping firms, it is the inappropriately high level of aggregation which mars the true information value of the UK Census.[24] Another limitation imposed by Census data follows from the legal requirement that confidentiality must be respected. Thus individual firm sizes are not reported and we must make do with the second best of size distribution tables which group firms into a small number of size class bands. This precludes the possibility of estimating any of the various concentration indices described above with any degree of accuracy.[25] As a compensation, it is the convention in most censuses around the world for the concentration ratio to be reported.

The fact that the Census is production based also presents obvious problems in observing the degree of *seller* concentration in any industry with significant exports or imports. The official concentration ratio merely reports the degree of concentration in domestic production, when for market power purposes we are clearly more interested in concentration of sellers within the domestic market. A moment's contemplation of the UK car industry will confirm the potential difference between the two concepts (the leading domestic producer is also a major importer). In the absence of widespread information on individual firms' export figures or market shares of leading importers on an industry by industry basis, one can only speculate about the practical importance of this problem. Some attempts have been made (HMSO 1978; Utton 1982; Kumar 1985) to 'correct' the concentration ratio for trade. The most simple method is to define the corrected *K*-firm ratio as:

$$CR_K (1 - EXP) / (1 + IMP - EXP) \qquad [12]$$

where EXP and IMP are exports and imports as proportion of industry sales. This adjustment is only 'correct', however, if the *K* largest firms export in proportion to their share of total domestic production, and if importers are not sufficiently large to be properly counted within the top *K*. Cowling (1978) offers a convincing critique of this correction, pointing to the operations of multinational firms (both British and foreign) as a reason why these assumptions may be often wide of the mark. Moreover, Utton, who himself uses this correction, acknowledges that the evidence we do have on intra-industry export performance points to larger firms doing rather more than their share of the exporting and importing.

(b) CENSUS EVIDENCE ON CONCENTRATION ACROSS INDUSTRIES

Inspection of the five-firm sales concentration ratios, CR_5, reported in the latest Census (1982) at the time of writing, reveals considerable variations between three-digit industries. In cases such as tobacco, sugar, man-made fibres, motor vehicles, and wines and cider, $CR_5 > 90\%$, while in others, particularly in the furniture and leather and clothing industries, $CR_5 < 15\%$. To give a rough idea of the distribution across sectors, Table 3.1 reports the average three-digit CR_5 for each of 13 two-digit classes or combinations of comparable classes. Although this consolidation conceals sometimes considerable intra-class variations, it serves to establish a broadly accurate league table of concentration. Without anticipating our later discussion of the determinants of concentration too much, one can detect a tendency for the more concentrated sectors to be more capital intensive and high technology.

Moving down to the more meaningful four-digit level of aggregation, the most recently published data refer to 1977,[26] under the old SIC (although it is doubtful whether things will have changed dramatically in the decade since). At this level concentration is typically higher than at the three-digit level. (This reflects the fact that most three-digit industries comprise two or more 'real' industries each consisting of quite separate sets of firms.) In at least 28 of these four-digit industries,

TABLE 3.1   Market concentration by sectors within manufacturing in 1982

Above average concentration			Below average concentration			
Two-digit sectors Classes	No. of three-digit indust-ries (groups)	Average CR_5 (%)	Sectors Classes		No. of indust-ries	Average CR_5 (%)
35/36 Vehicles & transport engineering	8	66	43	Textiles	9	40
			32	Mechanical engineering	10	33
21–23 Extraction and metal manufacture	7	63	44/45	Clothing, footwear & leather	6	25
41/42 Food, drink & tobacco	16	60	47–49	Other manu-facturing[1]	9	24
24 Non-metal mineral products	8	55	31	Metal goods	5	23
			46	Timber, wooden furniture	7	23
34 Electrical & electronic engineering	7	53				
14/25/ 26 Chemicals & oil refining	8	52				
33/37 Instrument engineering & office & data process-ing machinery	5	50	TOTAL		105	45

Source: Census of Production Summary Tables 1982
Note 1:   'Other manufacturing' includes Paper, printing and publishing, Processing of rubber and plastics, and four other sundry groups.

the concentration ratio exceeds 90 per cent, with more than half of these being in the food, drink and tobacco, and vehicles and related sectors. (See Clarke 1985: table 2.3.)

(c) TIME SERIES EVIDENCE ON CONCENTRATION

Attempts to plot how market concentration has varied over time have been plagued by changing Census industry definitions. The recent radical overhaul of the SIC is the most serious, but not the only, example of this. Nevertheless, a reliable picture has been constructed by Hart and Clarke (1980), Clarke (1985) and Hart (1985) from painstaking study of Censuses dating back to 1935. Over the period 1935–68 a sample of 42 industries for which industry definition had not changed was examined. The mean value of CR_3 was observed to increase fairly steadily from 26.3 per cent in 1935 to 32.4 per cent in 1958. This was followed by a marked acceleration to 37.4 per cent in 1963 and 41.0 per cent in 1968. During the 1970s, however, things appeared to have stabilised: for a different sample of 93 three-digit industries, the average CR_5 increased by only 1 per cent between 1970 and 1979. Since 1979 the picture is less clear-cut, partly because of the revised SIC and partly because of the 2–3 year lag before Census results are reported. Hart's examination of the data for 1979–81 does suggest, however, little or no change in average levels of market concentration.

In other words, the evidence on concentration of producers in the UK points to a dramatic increase in the twenty years following the Second World War, especially during the 1960s, but very little change thereafter on average. But taking into account the substantial increase in imports of manufactures in the 1970s and 1980s, it might be supposed that concentration of sellers has actually fallen in recent years. This is certainly the conclusion of Utton (1982): having adjusted the reported five-firm concentration ratios for the effects of trade in the way described earlier, he finds that the average of a sample of 121 four-digit industries declined from 58.8 per cent in 1968 to 54.8 per cent in 1977. (The unadjusted average showed no change over the period.) It is our view that Utton's adjustments probably overstate the deconcentrating effects of imports for the reasons given earlier. They are, nevertheless, an illustrative first stab at the problem, and it is likely that this is a subject which will attract more attention in the future. Definitive answers will require firm-level data on exporting and importing, especially by multinational corporations.

(d) COMPARISONS WITH OTHER COUNTRIES

Mueller and Hamm (1974) report a more stable pattern over time for the US: for a sample of 166 industries, 1947–70, average CR_4 rose only slightly from 40.9 per cent to 42.7 per cent. Caves and Porter (1980) tell a similar story for their sample of four-digit US industries, average CR_4 rising by only 2.3 points between 1954 and 1972. Both studies show, however, that concentration rose in the consumer good industries, by about 6 points, and it is this which accounts totally for the increase in the overall average. Since these studies and samples are quite independent of those used by Hart and Clarke and other British writers, direct comparison with the UK trends just described is somewhat hazardous. But on the face of it, it seems that the marked increase in UK market concentration, especially in the 1960s, far outstrips anything that may have happened in the US.

A more immediately direct comparison of the two countries is reported in Davies and Caves (1987). In the context of a study of comparative productivity, they had cause to calculate CR$_5$ for a matched sample of 86 industries. On average, concentration was 14 points higher in British industries than in comparable US industries. This is not altogether surprising because of typically smaller UK markets and the more tolerant attitude of successive governments to mergers. What is a little surprising is the relatively low correlation ($r = 0.59$) between the two countries, indicating similar distributions of CR, but not overwhelmingly so.[27]

Comparisons between the UK and continental Europe are more difficult because the Census authorities in the latter tend to treat subsidiaries as separate firms, unlike the UK Census. The most comprehensive study, which is subject to this qualification, is by George and Ward (1975). They find that, on average, concentration levels are higher in the UK than in any of West Germany, France or Italy; and, typically, the correlation between concentration levels in these countries was between 0.5 and 0.8, not especially high. More generally, the two findings which emerge from most international comparisons are that concentration at the market level does tend to decrease with the size of the country's market, although UK levels are usually higher than would be expected given its size. Also levels are correlated across countries, but not very closely. (See Pryor 1972; Horowitz 1970; Phlips 1971; as well as George and Ward.)

As we suggested at the start of this section, there is little controversy over this particular set of facts. In brief, market concentration in the typical UK market is 'high', both by historical and international standards; and it increased significantly between 1950 and 1970, but has probably stabilised since then. The effects of international trade and the operations of multinational firms constitute the outstanding priorities for future research.

4. Determinants of concentration: (a) theory

Theory on the determinants of concentration reminds one somewhat of the Tower of Babel, with different groups of contributors seemingly speaking in different and unconnected tongues. There is nothing which could be labelled an integrated, universally accepted, theory of what determines the level of concentration in a given market. Instead, we have a 'hotch-potch' of ideas and models of quite diverse origins: casual observation of the real world suggests a key role for technology; competition and merger policy clearly affects structure in some industries; the initial insights of the early S–C–P advocates tend to reinforce the technology argument, while also stressing the importance of entry barriers; contributions from the 'new'

I.O. theorists move us towards a world of simultaneous relations, in which concentration is jointly determined along with performance; and then the contributions from the very different stochastic tradition seem to point to an important chance element. At present, these strands to the literature have developed largely independently of each other. Here we shall order and present the material in a way that suggests that there is the potential for a synthesis and we hope this anticipates future developments in this area.

(a) TECHNOLOGY AND BARRIERS: THE TRADITIONAL S–C–P APPROACH

Following Bain, the early proponents of S–C–P viewed concentration as the starting point in the causal chain leading eventually to performance variables such as profitability and productivity. In econometric terms, this was not a simultaneous system and concentration was seen as the consequence of the cost, and to a lesser extent demand, parameters of the market concerned — and these in turn were viewed, by default, as exogenous to the behaviour of firms. In the light of more recent theoretical developments, this can now be seen to be too simplistic, as will become apparent presently. (See also Chapter 5.) In addition, it is clear that technology and entry barriers provide an incomplete explanation of concentration, being relatively strong on firm numbers, but rather weak on inequalities.

The belief that concentration reflects technology, and thus cost structures, is one which is easily understood by the layman. According to this view, concentration is often the result of economic necessity: to be efficient, plants, and thus firms, must be large and some markets may only be big enough to sustain a few efficient firms. By the same token, increasing concentration occurs because technical progress dictates ever-increasing scales for efficient production, and thus fewer firms. The argument is rarely formalised in textbook treatments, but this can be done easily as follows. Suppose all sellers in a given market produce the same good and have access to the same U-shaped long-run average costs curve (shown in Fig. 3.3a) where costs are minimised at c^* for a scale ES, efficient size. Assuming free entry, in the long run the industry settles down to a competitive equilibrium where price $= c^*$ and all firms must produce at ES. If demand at the competitive price is X_C, then the market supports X_C/ES equally sized firms and this ratio alone determines the level of concentration (for instance, the Herfindahl index will be simply ES/X_C). Thus the industry is more concentrated, the larger is efficient size relative to market size.

The determinancy of the model is broken however if, we introduce more realistically, an L-shaped cost curve (Fig. 3.3b), with ES now defined as the minimum efficient size and denoted hereafter as MES.[28] Under these cost conditions we cannot exclude the possibility that some firms will operate at scales in excess of MES even in the long-run competitive equilibrium. Should this happen, X_C/MES only places an upper limit on firm numbers, and similarly MES/X_C is now only a lower limit on the H concentration index. In these circumstances, X_C/MES remains an interesting 'ball-park' figure, but the task of the theorist moves on to explaining how firms will be arrayed along the flat portion of the curve, that is size inequalities.

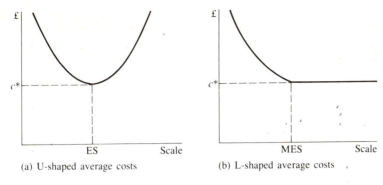

FIG. 3.3 Long-run average costs at the firm level

Traditional S–C–P does not offer much on this question except, somewhat vaguely, the supposition that entry barriers will have a role to play.

   Since entry barriers were discussed extensively in the previous survey, we shall be brief in our treatment here. Very simply, the S–C–P supposition was that, with entry barriers high, entry rates will tend to be low, and because of the consequent lower number of firms, concentration will be high, *ceteris paribus*. In broad terms, this seems reasonable, if rather loose. To explore the effects of barriers a little further, let us return to Fig. 3.3b, and define an entry barrier as something which allows incumbents to price in excess of c^*: three modifications to the simple technological model appear. The first is obvious: with price greater than the competitive level, output $< X_c$ and so the size of market is reduced, tending to increase concentration. But secondly, with $p > c^*$, it now becomes possible to survive in the market profitably at scales less than MES; in that this allows a sub-optimal sector of small-scale firms to survive, concentration may be reduced.[29] Thirdly, without the competitive discipline of new entry, existing large firms may be able to increase their market shares, thus moving out along the cost curve and so increasing size inequalities and concentration. This third argument is particularly difficult to develop formally without some specified model of incumbent behaviour.[30] But this is unsurprising: the very weakness of the technology/barriers model is that it strives for a fully determinate explanation of concentration without recourse to modelling the oligopoly game. It is to this question that later theory turned.

   One other worry with the traditional S–C–P model is the implicit assumption that where entry occurs, concentration will necessarily fall. Consider, for example, the case of diversifying entry by firms from other industries. Given that such firms may have ready access to the capital market and may be able to extend some of their existing consumer loyalty to this new market, it is debatable whether conventionally defined entry barriers will have a deterrent effect (see Chapter 2). Equally, it is not necessarily the case that such entry will be on a small scale.[31] Where entry is at a relatively large scale, concentration may well increase. To see this, suppose an industry with sales initially of S and a Herfindahl index H. Define the typical size of firm in the industry as $Z = SH$. (This definition uses the numbers-equivalent dimension of the H index: just as H^{-1} is the number of equivalent equal-sized firms, so too Z is the equivalent size of firm. That is, an industry of size S and concentration H with identical firms would comprise H^{-1} such firms each of size Z.) Now suppose a new firm enters the industry at size λZ where $\lambda \geq 1$, with all existing firms' sizes unchanged.

The pre- and post-entry values of H are:

$$H = \Sigma \, S_i^2 / S^2 \tag{13}$$

$$H^* = \frac{\Sigma \, S_i^2 + \lambda^2 S^2 H^2}{(S + \lambda \, S \, H)^2} = \frac{S^2 \, H \, (1 + \lambda^2 H)}{S^2 \, (1 + \lambda H)^2} = \frac{H \, (1 + \lambda^2 H)}{(1 + \lambda H)^2} \tag{14}$$

It follows that $H^* > H$ if $1 + \lambda^2 H > (1 + H\lambda)^2$

i.e. if $\lambda^2 H > 2 \, H\lambda + H^2 \lambda^2$

i.e. if $\lambda > 2 + \lambda H$ or $\lambda > 2 / (1 - H)$ $\tag{15}$

It is therefore possible that entry can increase concentration if the entrant is relatively 'large', where 'large' is made precise by [15]. For instance, this is true for an entrant little more than twice typical size in an unconcentrated industry, but larger-scale entry would be required as H increases.

(b) CONDUCT IS IMPORTANT

It is now widely acknowledged that the single direction of causality in the early descriptions of S–C–P was too simple. In particular, it is likely that the structure of an industry will be partly determined by a reverse causality depending on incumbent firms' conduct. In short, structure is endogenous to the system. To be fair, this was always implicit in the limit pricing models of S–C–P (with the decision of whether or not to deter entry having effects on future structure), but what was not recognised was that the nature of competition *between* incumbents will also influence their own market shares and so size inequalities and concentration.

Worcester (1967) provides an early example of a model with this implication. Since it takes up the story with an L-shaped cost curve, coupled with a very simple statement of behaviour, it is a convenient starting point for our purposes. Worcester assumes initially only one firm in the industry, behaving myopically by setting marginal revenue $MR = c^*$ at output X_1 in Fig. 3.4 (to retain clarity MR curves are omitted from the figure). A second firm now enters and assumes, correctly, that the first firm will maintain its output. Thus firm 2 faces the residual demand curve $D_2 D'_2$. Given that firm 2 also optimises myopically, it will produce X_2 where the marginal revenue curve associated with $D_2 D'_2$ equals c^*. This leaves a third firm, which in turn assumes the first two will maintain their output levels, with a residual demand curve $D_3 D'_3$ and a prospective optimal output X_3. To keep things simple, the figure has been drawn such that $X_3 = MES$. This means that no further firms will enter because the residual demand curve left by firm 3 lies everywhere below the cost curve to the left of MES. In this simple case the market can support only three firms of efficient scale or more. More generally, a larger number of firms would be possible given a demand curve further to the right, or given smaller MES. Since this model has 'explained' how firms will be arrayed along

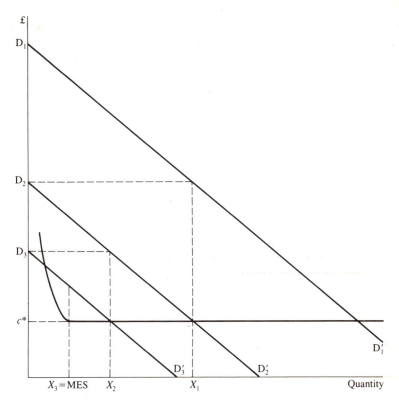

FIG. 3.4 An explanation of size inequalities with L-shaped costs

the cost curve, we now have a fully determinate explanation of concentration: $N = 3$, market shares are 4/7, 2/7, 1/7 and $H = 21/49$. More generally, it is easily shown that $N = \log_2(X_c/\text{MES})$ and $H = (1 + \text{MES}/X_c)/3 (1 - \text{MES}/X_c)$.[32]

Interestingly, this model confirms the significance of the MES/X_c ratio: it alone determines concentration, albeit now in a non-linear way. However, Worcester's description of the oligopoly game is a little crude. Even accepting orderly sequential entry of this type, it is only the first step towards an equilibrium, because none of the firms would choose to maintain these output levels *ex post*. Nevertheless it serves to show how an assumption concerning conduct is required to render the technological explanation determinate in a world of constant returns.

We can develop this theme by reverting to the Cournot equilibrium of the oligopoly game used in section 1. It differs from Worcester's model in that: (1) different firms may face different cost functions, and (2) firms set output simultaneously. We shall assume that each firm has constant marginal costs and a fixed cost (F). This means that average costs will be L-shaped, although there is no longer a unique value for MES. Clarke and Davies (1982) show how this model provides not only a prediction about the aggregate price cost margin (given by eqn [4] above) but also a prediction about the level of concentration in equilibrium. In the case of the H index, this is derived algebraically by squaring eqn [3], substituting for equilibrium price and summing over all firms in the industry to give:

$$H = 1/N + (1 - eN)^2 ((cv_c)^2/N) \qquad [16]$$

where, as before, e and N are the demand elasticity and firm numbers, and cv_c is the coefficient of variation of marginal costs across firms. Thus concentration will be higher (a) the fewer firms there are, (b) the more elastic is demand, and (c) the greater variability there is between firms in the level of marginal costs. In this model the technological influence of scale economies appears indirectly, via the magnitude of fixed costs relative to market size, as a determinant of N. Assuming the industry to be in long-run equilibrium, and a continuous distribution across firms in the magnitude of marginal costs, the marginal firm will be earning zero profits. It follows, for any cost distribution and demand curve, that N will be inversely related to F. Fixed Cost .

So in this model production costs continue to play a key role in determining concentration, but the additional insight is that they explain size inequalities as well as numbers. Equally important, it is clear that the mapping from costs to market shares reflects the nature of conduct of the oligopoly game. Thus structure may vary between industries if conduct varies. This point can be illustrated very conveniently within the Clarke–Davies model by switching from the special Cournot form to their more general case with the α parameter, which represents the degree of collusion in the sense explained earlier. Where $\alpha \neq 0$, Clarke and Davies derive the equilibrium expression for concentration as:

$$H = (1/N) + ((cv_c)^2/N) (1 - N(e - \alpha)/(1 - \alpha)^2 \qquad [17]$$

Consequently the level of concentration also depends positively on the degree of collusion within the industry, *ceteris paribus*, with the effect increasing in cv_c. In other words, for a given set of cost curves and demand curves, concentration will be higher, the more prone are firms to act in a cooperative way. The intuition behind this result is that collusive restriction of output works out unequally across firms, with the largest firms benefiting most and size inequalities thereby increased (just as a monopolist would concentrate output in his most efficient plant). Note however that this prediction is based on the assumption of fixed firm numbers; if the price-raising consequence of collusion attracts new entry, the concentrating effect may be offset.

The endogeneity of concentration within models of oligopoly has been established in a number of other contexts in recent years. Rather than embark on a comprehensive listing, we shall cite two further examples in situations where competition is not confined merely to price/quantity. In the first, Dasgupta and Stiglitz (1980) consider the effect of R & D expenditures within the Cournot model. They posit an industry of identical (implying $c_i = c$ for all i) quantity-setting firms producing a homogeneous product, and in addition, firms compete by undertaking R & D in order to reduce costs of production. Assuming the complete absence of entry barriers, such an industry in long-run equilibrium will be zero-profit, i.e. entry will drive each firm's margin over production costs down to a level just sufficient to cover R & D costs.

Using the same notation as earlier (but ignoring fixed production costs) and defining R_i as expenditure on R & D by firm i, the free entry assumption ensures:

$$R_i = (p - c)X_i \qquad [18]$$

As before (eqn [3]), the first-order condition with respect to output will determine each firm's mark up, assuming Cournot conjectures, as:

$$(p - c)/p = s_i/e \qquad [19]$$

Combining the two and noting that, from symmetry, $s_i = 1/N$,

$$R_i = pX/N^2e \qquad [20]$$

Summing across all firms and denoting aggregate industry R & D by R,

$$R/pX = 1/Ne \qquad [21]$$

Thus the industry's research intensity is inversely related to firm numbers, with the prediction therefore that more concentrated industries undertake relatively more R & D. But as Dasgupta and Stiglitz emphasise, this does not mean that concentration determines R & D; both are jointly determined by the equilibrium conditions of the market. In order to identify the underlying causes of both, we need to consider the first-order condition with respect to R & D. Since R & D expenditures are assumed to reduce marginal production costs, the condition is:

$$\delta\pi_i/\delta R_i = - (dc_i/dR_i) X_i - 1 = 0 \qquad [22]$$

Assuming the elasticity of marginal production cost with respect to R & D is the same for all firms, i.e.

$$\epsilon = - \{dc_i/dR_i. \ R_i/c_i\} \text{ for all } i \qquad [23]$$

then, from simple manipulation of [19] and [22],

$$R/pX = \epsilon (1 - (1/Ne)) \qquad [24]$$

and combining with [21],

$$N = \{(\epsilon + 1)/\epsilon\} 1/e \qquad [25]$$

Therefore, the number of firms sustained by the market in equilibrium will be smaller, and concentration greater, the higher is the demand elasticity and the higher the cost elasticity with respect to R & D. The former corresponds to the Clarke and Davies result, the latter implies higher concentration in industries where technological opportunity (for successful and significant process innovation) is greatest.

Shaked and Sutton (1987) offer an additional insight on the endogeneity of market structure based on their recent developments of the theory of product differentiation. For our purposes the important point to their argument is that the level of fixed costs in an industry characterised by differentiated products may be endogenous.[33] This means that, although we may observe a correlation across industries between concentration and fixed costs (i.e. the extent of scale economies), this need not be causal; both may reflect the outcome of the oligopoly game. In order to explain the argument, we must distinguish two types of product differentiation: horizontal and vertical. Horizontal differentiation is as described in locational models following Hotelling. Namely, there is a distribution of tastes across consumers with respect to a certain attribute of the industry's product (say the news/pictorial/gossip content of newspapers). Different firms offer different brands with different mixes and thus, within limits on price, all producers are able to carve out a niche in the market, supplying those consumers whose needs they most closely satisfy. Brands may also differ vertically, however: vertical differentiation refers to quality differences between brands which will be ranked identically by all consumers. On this count, one brand may be said to be unambiguously better than another; in our example such an attribute might be the quality of the print (i.e. readability and tendency for the ink not to rub off on the reader's hands.) Clearly, if brands differed only with respect to a vertical attribute, lower-quality brands would only sell if priced lower than their better-quality rivals. (Shaked and Sutton offer their own examples of horizontal attributes as the colour of the brand or 'aesthetic' features (e.g. design), and the operating speed of a computer as an example of a vertical attribute.) A second key feature of their model concerns the ways in which firms are able to generate brand improvements. These may require either higher variable costs or higher fixed costs. For instance, faster computer speed may only be possible given an increased R & D effort, i.e. by increasing fixed costs, while the production of higher-quality furniture may necessitate using better quality raw materials, i.e. increasing the variable costs of production.

Shaked and Sutton show how the nature of differentiation and the technology of quality improvements are crucial in determining the degree of concentration which will emerge in a given market. For instance, in the special case where differentiation is horizontal only, and given free entry and fixed costs of entry, it can be shown that the effect of increasing market size is to attract new entrants, offering new brands with attributes located between those of existing firms. That is, there is an increased tendency for each consumer to be able to buy a product more closely fitting his exact tastes. On the other hand, with vertical differentiation too, and where quality improvements are bought predominantly by higher fixed costs, competition forces firms to ever-increasing fixed outlays. In this case with an increase in market size, fixed costs increase too and there is no scope for new entry — concentration remains high. In both cases, the ratio of fixed costs to market size is related to concentration (playing the same role as the MES/X_c ratio in earlier models) but in the latter case, there is no question of scale economies causing concentration because both are endogenous. Interestingly, Shaked and Sutton show that this result holds for both Bertrand and Cournot behaviour, but as they acknowledge, the implications of collusive behaviour remain unexplored at present.

It would be premature to suggest that the 'new I.O.' has provided a new integrated theory of concentration, but the recognition that structure depends as much on the behaviour of firms as on exogenous technological factors constitutes an important development of the original S–C–P model. However, work in this area is still at a relatively preliminary stage and a number of issues remain unanswered. A major limitation of these models is that, for analytical convenience, they treat conduct as exogenous — yet this denies one of the main lessons learnt from traditional S–C–P, namely that conduct will be determined by structure. Perhaps further work will tackle the problem of the truly simultaneous relationship between conduct and structure.

There is another very different criticism which can be levelled against these models, and more generally the whole S–C–P and neo-classical tradition. This is that the underlying notion of competition is largely static and abstracts from most of the interesting features of competition in the real world. Such a view emanates from the Austrian school and modern Schumpeterians (see Chapter 1). Unfortunately, writers from these schools have contributed very little constructively to our understanding of what does determine concentration. One important exception is the work of Nelson and Winter, who develop the theme of endogenous market structure within a Schumpeterian framework. They also provide a rare example of a fully developed economic model of concentration within a stochastic framework and thus a link with the literature discussed in the following section. Since the early 1970s, Nelson and Winter have been developing what they call evolutionary models of change (this work being collected in their 1982 volume.) Conceptually their approach derives more from biological evolution theory than the usual equilibrium analysis of economics (with roots in physics.) In particular, some of their work (part 4 of their book) involves modelling the evolution of industrial structure in a world characterised by (a) firms making decisions in a behavioural, rather than optimising, way, and (b) an environment of Schumpeterian competition: namely the main vehicle of competition is research activity, the results of which are inherently uncertain. Analytically this leads them to computer simulations of hypothetical industries, rather than comparative statics via differential calculus. Although their work is radically different from most of that surveyed so far, they share one important insight with the models of this section; that is the realisation that concentration is endogenous to the process of competition, or in their words: 'industrial concentration is to be understood as a dynamic, historical phenomenon, endogenous to the market system in which it appears' (1978: 543).

The bare bones of the model are as follows. Firms produce at full capacity (regardless of price which is related to aggregate output by an industry demand curve) with fixed-coefficient technologies. Investment is undertaken if they are successful in earning more than a target mark-up over production costs (but the magnitude of investment is limited by access to credit). Crucially, firms also undertake R & D in order to search for better techniques of production to be used in future time periods; the amount of R & D undertaken is proportional to the firm's capital stock (which implies that, as the industry evolves, larger firms do more R & D). However, the results of R & D are uncertain: each period a firm may discover a new technology or imitate a best practice already used by one of its competitors, but also it may achieve neither. Which of these outcomes obtained depends on chance, although bigger firms have a greater chance of being successful precisely because of their higher R & D spending. The underlying latent technology which may be discovered also improves steadily over time.

Against this backcloth the analysis is conducted by running a number of simulations which differ in the values of certain key parameters of the model: (i) the initial concentration level; (ii) the pace at which latent technology improves; (iii) the ease of imitation of other firms' existing technologies; (iv) the variance of research 'draws' around latent technology (i.e. the uncertainty attached to research); and (v) the aggressiveness of investment policies. Two alternatives under (v) are compared (which work through different targets on the mark up): the first corresponds to a sort of Cournot behaviour, and the second to a more aggressive behaviour where firms invest right up to their finance constraints (in effect this amounts to disregarding short-run optimising and behaving in a price-taking manner). Each simulation starts with an industry of equal-sized firms and lasts for 25 'years', at the end of which concentration is recorded. Although the results from comparing the outcomes of a limited number of simulations do not have the generality of comparative statics, Nelson and Winter do derive some fairly general findings. Firstly, whatever parameter values are assumed, concentration has an inexorable tendency to grow over time (this is quite consistent with the stochastic models described below). Secondly, concentration grows more rapidly in conditions of rapid underlying change in latent technology, especially if innovation is not easily imitated. Thirdly, concentration increases more rapidly if starting from lower initial levels. Fourthly, and most interesting here, aggressive investment behaviour also tends to accelerate the increase in concentration. On the face of it, this last result is surprising; it implies that more competitive (aggressive) price-taking behaviour leads to higher levels of concentration, while more restrained Cournot-type behaviour leads to more modest levels.[34] However, the intuition of this result is simple given the restrictive assumptions of the model; aggressive investment means that successful firms become bigger and thereby increase their chances of subsequent innovation and imitation, in turn this increases the chances of future productivity increases and therefore size increases. By assumption then, large firms are larger because they are more progressive and this makes them more progressive in the future.

The policy implications are controversial. Apparently, concentration is the natural consequence of greater technological efficiency of larger firms, but this does rest on the assumption that large firms *are* more likely to make technical advances (since larger firms are assumed to do more R & D and more R & D leads to more technical change). The empirical support for this assumption is, however, inconclusive (see Chapter 6). Our opinion is that this particular model is limited by, among other things, the failure to model new entry which must be an important deconcentrating factor over a 25-year period. But this is not to deny that, more generally, simulation and alternative formulations of the competitive process may prove fruitful in the future.

(c) STOCHASTIC MODELS OF CONCENTRATION

We mentioned earlier the conceptual similarity between explaining distributions of firm size and personal income. It is therefore unsurprising that the stochastic models developed to analyse the latter have been frequently applied to the former. The stochastic tradition in the explanation of concentration dates back to at least the middle 1950s, but until recently it has attracted little attention from the mainstream of industrial organisation. The general opinion seems to be one of mistrust and doubt that this tradition has much to offer to an economic explanation (as opposed to description) of concentration.[35] We believe this view to be short-sighted and insular.

At the heart of the stochastic approach is a Gibrat process (Gibrat 1931) known as the *law of proportionate effect*. In its simplest form this states that the growth of firms is an independent random variable, i.e.

$$\log S_{i,\,t+1} - \log S_{i,\,t} = \epsilon_t \qquad\qquad [26]$$

where ϵ_t is $N(\,m,\,s^2)$ \hfill [27]

$S_{i,t}$ *and* $S_{i,t+1}$ denote the size of firm i at times t and $t + 1$. Thus the rate of proportionate growth (expressed here using the approximation of the difference between logs) for firm i is a random variable, independent of initial size, and exhibiting a normal probability distribution. The expected value of ϵ is m and the variance is s^2. Justification for the normality of ϵ is to be found in the central limit theorem, which states that any variate which itself reflects the sum total effect of many other broadly independent influences will possess a normal probability distribution. The growth rate of a firm may be such a variable since it reflects many diverse factors such as outcomes of advertising and R & D programmes, changes in managerial personnel, labour relations, etc., and, to some extent, sheer luck.

Assuming this law to apply to all firms *in a given population (industry)* (importantly then we assume fixed N) at all points in time, elementary statistical theory establishes three results:

1. The asymptotic distribution of firm size will be lognormal, with log firm size having mean μ and variance σ^2. Where σ^2 is large, the distribution exhibits a pronounced positive skew and the leading firms have an especially large share of the market. If universally applicable, this result would be singularly helpful to the analysis of concentration. As was stated earlier, it can be shown (Hart 1975) that most concentration indices depend only on σ^2 and N when firm size is lognormal. As such, information on the values of these parameters alone would be sufficient to summarise and compare concentration across industries. Another major advantage of the lognormal is its convenient aggregation properties (Aitchison and Brown 1957). Given that theory in industrial organisation often describes behaviour at the individual firm level, but is then tested with data for industry aggregates, the capacity to aggregate is an important one. Without this, we are often reduced to the assumption that industries can be modelled as if they comprised N 'representative' (i.e. identical) firms, which is hardly satisfactory.[36] Unfortunately, the evidence on real-world size distributions is inconclusive. Without doubt, virtually all industries possess positively skewed distributions, and at least half typically follow the lognormal shape closely; but for the remainder the lognormal is a less accurate approximation, depending crucially on the severity of the statistical test procedures used whether the hypothesis of lognormality is rejected or accepted.[37]

2. The variance of log size will be larger in industries where growth prospects are especially variable. Given the random walk described by [26] (strictly speaking, assumption [27] is unnecessary for both this and the following prediction), operating over all firms and over a large time period, the variance of log

size will be the product of s^2 and the number of periods having elapsed (T):

$$\sigma^2 = Ts^2 \qquad\qquad [28]$$

This can open a fruitful line of investigation into the sources of high concentration if we are able to distinguish between industries' innate variability of growth prospects (Weiss 1963). For instance, one might expect that, where competition is practised using less certain weapons such as research design and advertising, growth variability (s^2) will be greater than where price is the main weapon (mistakes are more easily rectified, and effective reaction will tend to be quicker in the latter case).

    3. The variance of log firm size will increase over time. This is what Prais (1976) refers to as 'spontaneous drift', and follows directly from [28]. The implication is that an industry of firms experiencing simple random growth of the above sort will exhibit a pervasive tendency to increasing size inequalities and higher concentration over time. The best intuitive explanation of this is provided by Prais in a simple numerical example (Prais 1976, Ch.2). The basic idea is that, so long as growth is independent of initial size, some 'lucky' firms will tend to string together a series of positive growth rates and emerge from the pack as significantly larger. In fact, it is precisely this mechanism which is at work in the Nelson and Winter model described earlier.

    Evidently this simple model is rich in its range of predictions. On the other hand, it is short on economic theory, and by extension, explanation of the underlying mechanisms. For example, it has nothing of interest for the policy maker intent on controlling concentration. Indeed, one can discern only three assumptions: the supposed random nature of growth rates, fixed N, and the normality of the growth distribution. The third assumption is least important, and is really only required for prediction 1; in any event, it is of little economic interest and is probably reasonable on statistical grounds given enough observations/firms.[38] The second assumption of a constant population is patently unrealistic and limits this explanation of the determinants of concentration to only the inequality dimension. But it is the first assumption which has attracted most debate. Stated at its simplest, it means that all firms have an equal chance of growing at any given rate (although of course that chance differs between rates). Whether or not this is reasonable is partly an empirical matter and partly one of a priori reasoning. The implication sometimes drawn is of constant returns to scale: if all firms face constant costs, it is not unlikely they have the same growth prospects. It is tempting to ask whether it also implies some homogeneity on the demand side (for example, identical income elasticities for different brands in a differentiated market). Even abstracting from this, the cost interpretation does limit the model to those firms in excess of MES scale given the L-shaped cost curve. As for the empirical evidence, this is not really conclusive either way. On balance, the evidence from many studies does not refute the hypothesis that the growth rates of firms are independent of their size. On the other hand, the law also implies that the variance of growth rates should be independent of size, and here the evidence is not convincing. In most studies, growth rates are found to vary less within groups of large firms than within groups of small firms.[39]

For the sceptic this is often sufficient to reject the stochastic approach; not only is it theoretically sterile, but also it is not even empirically 'correct'. Yet this approach has more to offer, with a real potential for future developments of considerably more economic interest. For example, the pioneers in the field, Hart and Prais (1956) and Prais (1976) suggest a modification allowing for 'regression to (or away from) the mean'. This admits the possibility that larger firms may tend to grow faster or slower than small firms, and involves reformulating the basic law as:

$$\log Z_{i,\,t+1} = \beta \log Z_{i,\,t} + \epsilon_t \qquad [29]$$

where $\log Z$ denotes the deviation from mean log size. Where $\beta < 1$, there is a tendency for larger firms to grow slower, and smaller firms faster, than average (regression to the mean); presumably the implication is an optimum size of firm located at the mean. Plainly, $\beta > 1$ implies faster than average growth for larger firms; but either way the lognormal prediction remains. However, if regression to the mean is sufficiently pronounced, this may reverse or cancel the prediction that concentration will drift upwards over time.

Saving (1965) suggests a more fundamental modification based explicitly on economic theory. He posits a technology which places both upper and lower bounds on firm size, with constant returns between the extremes. In this case firm size will have an asymptotic four-parameter lognormal distribution. In spite of some supportive empirical results (from which he draws rather speculative conclusions about the existence and extent of diminishing returns), this has attracted little attention since.[40]

Undoubtedly the weightiest competitor to the standard lognormal model is provided by Simon and Bonini's (1958) variation. Their model uses two basic assumptions. Firstly, it employs a milder form of the law of proportionate effect which requires only that the expected growth of the aggregate size of all firms in a size class be independent of size. (This avoids some of the empirically suspect implications of the basic form of the law concerning variance of growth and size which were mentioned above.) But more important, the law is assumed to apply only for firms in excess of some minimum (MES in our terminology) — this squares neatly with the L-shaped cost curve. Secondly, they allow for new entry, with a constant probability that any increment in industry size will be satisfied by a new entrant. The model has two important conclusions: (i) the steady-state size distribution of the growth process is a Yule distribution which can be approximated in its upper tail by the Pareto curve; (ii) the inequality parameter of the curve, α, (the counterpart to σ^2 in the lognormal) is determined uniquely by the probability of entry: α is equal to the reciprocal of the complement of the entry probability. In later papers with Ijiri (collected in Ijiri and Simon 1977), Simon has developed the model in different directions, allowing for mergers and serially correlated growth, i.e. non-random growth prospects. But confining our attention to the original model, various points of interest emerge. Certainly the underlying economic content is still simple, but it is more explicit and realistic than is typical of the stochastic genre. The alternative prediction of a Pareto size distribution for the larger firms in a given industry has a similar weight of empirical support as the lognormal (in truth, the many test statistics used to assess fits are often unable to differentiate these two very similar curves). For our purposes the most exciting feature of this model is that it can be used to provide a surprisingly far-reaching explanation of concentration. Davies and Lyons (1982) show that the Pareto curve implies the following equation for the five-firm concentration ratio:

$$CR_5 = [MES/X]^{(\alpha-1)/\alpha}[5\alpha/(\alpha - 1)]^{(\alpha-1)/\alpha}(1 - y)^{1/\alpha} \hspace{2cm} [30]$$

where, as earlier, MES/X is the relative magnitude of minimum efficient scale; y is the share of industry output accounted for by sub-optimal firms; α is Pareto's inequality parameter (larger values of α imply smaller size inequalities). Although not obvious from mere inspection, it is easily shown that CR_5 is (a) positively related to MES/X; (b) inversely related to y; and (c) inversely related to α.

For those seeking a reconciliation of the various themes of the determinants of concentration literature, this is a neat and satisfying result — we have a stochastic explanation which includes important roles for both technology and entry barriers. Just as important, it sharpens our understanding of how these factors interact. Firstly, notice that the impact of MES/X depends on the probability of entry: a special case of interest is where $\alpha \rightarrow \infty$, $CR_5 \rightarrow 5MES/X$, in this model very large α values indicate high entry probabilities, and so this result corresponds to the earlier technological prediction for an industry in long-run equilibrium. Secondly, consider the role of α. This describes (inversely) the extent of size inequalities among efficient firms (i.e. in excess of MES), and because α is itself positively related to the probability of entry, we have the prediction that concentration is inversely related to the probability of entry. Assuming, in turn, that the latter is inversely related to the height of entry barriers, a direct relationship is predicted between barriers and concentration.[41] This fills a gap in the traditional S–C–P model of concentration, offering a tight formalisation, rather than mere assertion, of how barriers affect concentration; interestingly, barriers matter here because they determine the extent of size inequalities. Thirdly, while the inverse relation between CR_5 and y, sub-optimal capacity, is something of a tautology, it is consistent with our earlier suggestion that entry barriers may also have a secondary deconcentrating effect if they permit sub-optimal firms to exist, shielded by a high price.

Since we have covered a wide range of literature in this section, a brief overview is in order. We have suggested that the original S–C–P model attributed a central role to technological cost factors and, while more recent theory calls into question the exogeneity of costs, there is little doubt that high concentration will tend to be *associated with* extensive scale economies, especially where market size is small. On the other hand, we should look beyond just technological factors; one of the morals of the 'new I.O.' is that the conduct of incumbent firms will have a crucial effect on the industries in which they operate. Equally, the other cornerstone of traditional S–C–P, barriers to entry, will affect concentration, but not necessarily in the simple way first envisaged. As a generalisation, we can probably accept the proposition that high barriers tend to make for high concentration because of reduced entry rates and thus lower firm numbers. But that is not the end to the story. Firstly, and as always accepted by traditional S–C–P, barriers will be less of a deterrent in growing industries (just as it is the magnitude of MES relative to market size, rather than its absolute value, which derives the technological explanation). Secondly, entry may not always assume a deconcentrating role — it matters how large the entrants are. Thirdly, and rather less obviously, barriers may also influence size inequalities, and the propensity to survive of small inefficient incumbent firms, as signalled in the Simon and Ijiri model. Our final conclusion is that the contribution of stochastic approaches should not be overlooked: our admiration of the work of Simon and Ijiri is obvious from the previous paragraph, but we should also recall the potential for further developments of Nelson and Winter's approach — in spite of any limitations it may have, this remains a rare example of economists working outside of the mainstream, but still retaining a degree of analytical formalism.

(d) MERGERS AND PUBLIC POLICY

We conclude this section with a 'cause' of concentration which would be obvious to the layman but which has remained largely outside the theoretical literature on this subject. It is widely believed that horizontal mergers are a major cause of high and increasing market concentration. Certainly, Bain (1959: 170–2) cites 'the desire to restrict competition' as one of his determinants of concentration, and suggests the horizontal merger as a means of achieving that restriction. At a superficial level we can agree with this suggestion: a natural consequence of profit-maximising objectives is that firms should wish to restrict competition, and it is also true that a merger is one way of reducing the number of competitors in the short run. On the other hand, we must question whether mergers add anything over and above the causes of concentration discussed above. If indeed the desire to restrict competition is an innate tendency in the capitalist economy, should this not apply equally across all industries? If so, there would be little hope of identifying the impact of mergers on concentration by observing inter-industry differences. As a matter of fact, however, the extent of merger activity *does* vary across industries and over time, and this must be (abstracting for the moment from other motives for merger) because the potential for the merger to restrict competition also varies. More specifically, any short-run restriction on competition and raising of prices can only be sustained into the long run if higher profits do not attract new entry. In short, barriers to entry are a necessary condition for competition-restricting horizontal mergers. Or, to change the emphasis, the merger is the *vehicle* by which barriers are exploited.

More generally, there will be other reasons for mergers and takeovers. For instance, the most commonly cited (public) claim of the particpants in horizontal mergers is the commendable desire to attain scale or scope economies. If we accept this then it seems sensible to suggest that scale economies are the cause of any resulting increase in concentration and, again, mergers are merely the vehicle. The case of the merger undertaken to exploit a managerial asset is less clear cut, but even here we might argue that this is another form of scale economy. There is an extensive literature on the motives for merger (and on their effects on the profitability, etc., of the participants),[42] but this is of limited relevance to the present discussion unless one can identify some additional motive for the horizontal merger which does not reflect one or the other of our existing list of the causes of concentration. In this respect, we should concede at least one unresolved issue. A persistent theme in much of the motives for mergers literature is that many mergers have been undertaken primarily in the interests of the managers, rather than the owners.[43] If this is so, we might concede that 'managerial motives' are an additional cause of concentration, and speculate that the scope for managerial discretion depends on the internal organisation of firms, as well as their size and perhaps history. Whether such variables would have much explanatory power as determinants of concentrations is unclear.

Finally, there remains the impact of government competition policy on concentration: there is little doubt that some of the international and inter-temporal differences in concentration can be attributed to the impact of policy, specifically on mergers. We saw earlier that market concentration in the UK is typically much higher than in the US, and it is difficult to avoid the conclusion that this reflects the traditionally more tolerant attitude of British governments to horizontal mergers. (On occasions, such as the Industrial Reorganisation Corporation, mergers have even been encouraged.) It is also sometimes suggested that the 1960s UK merger wave was a response to the Restrictive Practices Legislation. With the outlawing of collusive practices, it appears that some firms substituted amalgamation for collusion as a means of avoiding competition.[44] Neither of these observations necessarily undermines our thesis that the merger is the means by which concentration may be increased, rather than the underlying cause; but they do suggest the likelihood of an important statistical association between mergers and concentration.

5. Determinants of concentration: (b) empirics

A variety of empirical methodologies has been used in this area, probably the most common being the large-scale regression analysis of inter-industry differences. But some studies have used the case study approach to individual industries. Sometimes researchers have worked with time series data on individual firms, usually with the aim of identifying what part of concentration changes can be attributed to mergers as opposed to internal growth (or the stochastic effect).

(a) CROSS-SECTION REGRESSION STUDIES

There exists a long tradition of studies employing cross-section, usually Census, data on large numbers of industries (mainly at the three- or four-digit levels).[45] Simplifying only a little, most involve linear regressions roughly equivalent to:

$$C_j = a_0 + a_1 (MES/X)_j + \Sigma\, a_i B_{ij} + \Sigma\, a_i Z_{ij} \qquad [31]$$

where C_j is some summary concentration index, usually the five-firm concentration ratio, in industry j; MES/X is the relative size of minimum efficient scale; the B_{ij} refer to a vector of entry barriers into j; and the Z_{ij} are sundry other determinants. Sometimes the dependent variable is *changes* in concentration in j over a given time period, and sometimes it is the rate of net entry over a given period. But the unifying theme is inter-industry differences. In our opinion, the vast majority of these studies are seriously flawed because of measurement errors in the key MES variable. We shall substantiate this claim presently, having first provided a brief survey of the main findings.

First and foremost, MES/X is nearly always found to be a strongly significant determinant of concentration,[46] with $a_1 > 0$. Since this variable usually dominates estimated regression results, it suggests a very strong role for the technological explanation of concentration. In some cases MES and X are entered as separate explanatory variables, and, especially in equations with net entry and concentration changes as dependent variables, they are included in first difference form. But whatever the form, the results point to a strong positive relation between concentration and MES and a strong negative relation to market size, or its rate of change.

Second, there is also fairly widespread evidence that concentration, or the rate of entry, is positively (inversely) related to the height of the capital requirement and product differentiation barriers.[47] The capital barrier is usually measured by the capital requirement for a plant of MES scale and, because this is often based on measures of MES itself, it is subject to the measurement error criticisms to be elaborated presently. The differentiation barrier is normally measured by the industry's advertising expenditure-to-sales ratio, presumably on the grounds that where the product is highly differentiated, the industry will spend more on advertising. Quite clearly this is a crude proxy, and we should acknowledge that a number of other studies have found no relation between this variable and concentration (Telser 1964; Guth 1971; Hart and Clarke 1980; Levy 1985).

Relatively few studies have attempted to test the stochastic explanation within a regression context. Weiss (1963), working with US data for 1947–54, finds that the largest increases in CR occurred in the consumer durable and durable equipment industries. He argues that this is consistent with stochastic models of concentration since it is precisely these types of industry in which one might expect substantial inter-firm variability in growth rates, and thus in size inequalities. This is because competition in these industries tends to operate via new product design and/or large advertising campaigns. The outcome of such competition is likely to be highly uncertain (for the individual firm) with the possibility of fairly large changes in market share over a short period of time. Not only is there the prospect of large changes in market share for the firm introducing the new product, but also its competitors will find it difficult to react in the short run. In industries where price competition prevails, mistakes or lags in policy presumably can be rectified more rapidly.[48] Davies and Lyons (1982) test their extension of the Simon and Bonini model, in the form of equation [30] above, for a sample of 100 UK manufacturing industries and report a very close fit $R^2 = 0.9$). This extraordinarily high fit confirms the usefulness of this model as the starting point for empirical analysis; it is not, however, a behavioural explanation of CR — a fully specified model would require explanations of the α and y parameters.[49]

Merges

Turning to the impact of mergers, Hart and Clarke (1980) include an extra explanatory variable measuring merger activity in different UK industries, 1958–68, as a determinant of concentration changes. They report a positively significant result but this should be qualified by pointing to the rather poor quality data employed and the *ad hoc* specification of the impact of mergers.

Conc'

There is therefore apparent support for parts of the theoretical literature discussed earlier, although few studies have recognised the two-way relation between structure and conduct by estimating within a simultaneous system.[50] In addition, as mentioned already, nearly all studies have been undermined by problems in measuring MES. It has been argued by Davies (1980a), Lyons (1980) and Ornstein *et al.* (1973) that most proxy measures for MES are tautologically related to concentration. If this is true this casts doubt not only on the regression coefficients of MES, but also on the identification of entire equations.

General Problems (1)

To see the nature of the problem, we must acknowledge at the outset that it is virtually impossible to observe MES directly in any industry. It is sometimes suggested that 'engineering estimates' on the costs of installing and operating different scales of plant should enable one to construct hypothetical long-run average costs curves and thereby identify MES. This methodology has serious limitations: production economies are not the only determinant of MES — scale economies in finance, R & D, and advertising might all be such as to render the minimum efficient scale of firm considerably larger than that dictated by technology alone. Equally important, engineering data is necessarily hypothetical: it cannot easily allow for managerial diseconomies, potentially greater strike activity in larger plants, inelastic factor supplies, etc. In any event, the sheer magnitude of data required to calculate such estimates for large numbers of industries has deterred researchers from employing engineering estimates in many cross-section regression analyses.

In these circumstances, most research has employed either the 'survivor' technique or simple statistical measures of typical plant/firm size as proxies for MES. The former has fallen out of favour in recent years, partly because it, too, is data intensive, partly because it often fails to provide determinate estimates, and partly because it requires faith that the size distribution in a given industry is always tending to equilibrium.[51] Faced with these problems, the majority of studies proxy MES using some measure of 'typical' plant size derived from Census size tables, and it is these measures which are most dangerous to use in the context of regression analysis to explain concentration.

The argument can be seen most clearly given the simplest measure of typical size: the arithmetic average (which has been used by Pashigian 1968, 1969; and Sawyer 1971). When expressed as a proportion of aggregate industry size, X, this amounts to the reciprocal of plant numbers. It is hardly surprising that this is strongly correlated with concentration, since concentrated industries tend to have fewer plants. It is difficult to see, however, that this tells us much about the impact of technological forces, or any other determinants of concentration for that matter. Most studies use slightly more refined proxies, although the tautology problem remains. Two examples are worthy of note since they continue to figure strongly in the empirical literature. Weiss (1963) suggests as a proxy for MES the 'midpoint

Median.

plant size'. He means by this the median of the first moment distribution, i.e. the size of plant at the midpoint of the size (say employment) distribution in the sense that 50 per cent of industry size is accounted for by plants in excess of the midpoint. Note the implicit, and unlikely, assumption that in every industry sub-optimal plants account for exactly 50 per cent of employment. Unfortunately, the arbitrary nature of the proxy is supplemented by a systematic measurement error. Davies (1980a) shows that where sub-optimally sized plants account for less than 50 per cent of industry size, (empirically, this seems to be the norm[52]), this proxy overstates true MES by more, the larger are size inequalities. In fact, where the size distribution is lognormal, Davies shows that the Weiss proxy, relative to industry size is (a) inversely related to plant numbers, and (b) positively related to the Gini coefficient of inequality. In other words, this proxy is a fairly respectable measure of concentration itself.

The other widely used statistical proxy is due to Comanor and Wilson (1967). This is the average size of plant or firm in excess of the midpoint. When expressed as a ratio to industry size, this is equivalent to the reciprocal of the number of plants needed to produce the top 50 per cent of industry size. This, too, is inversely related to plant numbers and positively related to size inequalities. Indeed, as Davies shows in the lognormal case, the logarithm of this proxy is identical to the entropy measure of concentration!

Since so many regression studies employ these measures unthinkingly, and because they tend to dominate estimated equations it is difficult to read very much of interest into the results reported in this area.

(b) TIME SERIES STUDIES

Time series work has tended to favour the case study methodology rather more than econometrics. A striking example is Hart and Clarke (1980), following Hart, Utton and Walshe (1973), who employ this methodology for a random sample of 30 UK industries at the product level of aggregation for 1958–68. Many of their results are qualitative rather than quantitative. They report instances where increasing concentration derives from: economies of scale and contraction of the market; forward integration; and government intervention (encouragement to mergers). Other industries in their sample provide examples of factors leading to reductions in concentration: market growth; low entry barriers; and high initial levels of concentration. The last of these results suggests that concentration is more likely to decline, *ceteris paribus*, if concentration is already high; Hart and Clarke suggest that this might be due to entry attracted by high initial profit levels (but perhaps, more simply, concentration can really only change, if at all, in a downwards direction when starting at a high level given that it is subject to an upper bound). However, the most important result to emerge from these two studies concerns mergers. Between 1958 and 1968, 20 of 27 industries experienced increasing concentration. On Hart and Clarke's assessment, for 14 of the 20, mergers were the prime cause; they also estimate that for the group as a whole almost half the average increase in concentration could be attributed to mergers.[53]

More generally, the effect of mergers on concentration has attracted considerable attention in case study work. Weiss (1965) finds a significant role for mergers in determining concentration changes in six US sectors between 1930 and 1960, although he also reports an important role for internal growth by the leading firms. More recently, Hannah and Kay's (1977) study of the UK for 1919–76 has generated some startling, but contested, figures. Their analysis is conducted at the aggregate two-digit level and is based on time series data on mainly larger quoted firms. To estimate the consequences of mergers on concentration in a given industry, they calculate the change in the concentration index, their numbers-equivalent measure described earlier, which would have occurred merely from adding together the market shares of the merging firms. The difference between this hypothetical value and the actual change in concentration is then assumed to be the result of internal growth. For the periods 1919–30 and 1930–48 they do not find a particularly dominant influence for mergers, but for 1957–69 in virtually all industries, mergers were the sole cause of concentration increases. These results have been contested by Prais (1976), who argues on various methodological grounds. For example, he shows that the sample overstates the incidence of mergers because the sample of small firms included in the study are included precisely because they were taken over. In addition, he suggests that Hannah and Kay's treatment of takeovers, as opposed to mergers, tends to overstate the impact of takeovers. In a later paper, Hannah and Kay (1981) appear to acknowledge that their estimates may have been too high. Having said this, Prais is in agreement that in the 1950s and 1960s mergers became progressively more important as a cause of increasing concentration.

6. Market concentration: summary and future research prospects

Speculation on how the subject may develop in the future is probably less hazardous than is usual for economics. The literature on indices of concentration is now well established, with little prospect of significant additions. Similarly, after a period of intense activity in the 1960s and 1970s, we now have a reliable picture on the facts of concentration for UK manufacturing. The fundamental change in the British SIC will probably deter much comparative work in the short-run linking trends before and after 1980. The one aspect of measurement which probably deserves immediate attention concerns adjustment of observed concentration levels for the effects of international competition, especially the activities of multinational firms. The empirical literature on the determinants of concentration has, to our mind, failed to rise above the mediocre; we have stressed the sensitivity of results to the unacceptable proxies of MES which most practitioners have been happy to employ. But in truth this is merely symptomatic of a tradition based on imprecise proxies for all variables and *ad hoc* specifications only loosely based on theory. The lively empirical debate on the impact of mergers is unlikely to be repeated for market concentration, although the upsurge in conglomerate mergers in Britain at the time of writing probably means that this issue is not closed as far as aggregate concentration is concerned.

We believe that the most important advances will occur on the theoretical side of the subject. Industrial organisation theory is passing through a fascinating phase and is something of a battleground between conflicting schools of thought. On the one hand, the traditional neo-classical structure–conduct–performance paradigm is being 'beefed-up' by the influx of the new industrial organisation theorists; an example of this is the greater attention to the impact of conduct on structure mentioned above. This work will undoubtedly continue. On the other hand, and far more radically, the very underpinnings of the subject are being questioned from a number of angles. We close this part of the survey with a brief discussion of two of the more prominent critiques.

(a) COMPETITION AS A PROCESS AND DYNAMIC MEASURES OF CONCENTRATION

The neo-Austrian school of thought has consistently criticised neo-classical notions of competition for being static (see our introductory survey). It argues that the so-called perfect competition of neo-classical theory is not only unattainable but is also rather irrelevant as a description of what would normally (i.e. by the layman) be conceived of as competition. The latter, and the true meaning, is a process by which actors strive by their own efforts to get one jump ahead of their rivals. When successful, they enjoy the fruits of having 'won', but are unable to rest on their laurels lest someone else displaces them. In this vision, super-normal profits and monopoly power (unless protected by state-imposed entry barriers) are the just reward for greater efficiency, widely defined. For our purposes, this can be likened to the Schumpeterian view in which monopoly profits are the reward for successful innovation and are essentially transitory (creative destruction). Indeed, this is the gist of the Nelson and Winter argument already described. One implication of this is that static measures of concentration are meaningless if we wish to record the degree of real competition within a given market.

Given this critique, it is fair to ask the question: 'what measures could be derived which might better indicate the state of competition as a process?' Unfortunately there is no answer to be found in the writings of contemporary Austrian economists. On the other hand, the seeds of a potential answer may be found in a strain of the conventional empirical literature which has never quite established itself, and which has fallen into neglect in recent years. This is the investigation of measures of *market share stability*, or what might be called 'dynamic concentration'. In their simplest form, these amount to measuring the correlation of firms' market shares between time periods.[54] The basic idea is that in industries where the thrust and counterthrust of competition are prevalent, market shares will fluctuate accordingly and this will mean a lower correlation over time. On the other hand, collusive agreements will tend to fossilise shares and correlations will be accordingly high. Similarly, new entry will tend to destabilise the shares of incumbents. While there are obvious dangers in equating competition to market share instability (leading firms may sustain their leading position even in a competitive industry if they consistently beat rivals on efficiency), there is surely scope here for further development. In particular, as Nelson and Winter have shown, simulation models are ideally suited to descriptions of Schumpeterian competition, and, by extension, to the identification of suitable summary indices thereof.[55] What is equally clear is that dynamic competition need not be revealed by low levels of static concentration. This can be illustrated by reference to the law of proportionate effect. As already explained, this predicts that concentration will tend to be higher in industries exhibiting larger variances in the probability distributions of growth rates. But it is precisely these industries which will also display the highest mobility of market shares from period to period. Perhaps the lesson is that high concentration only reveals the absence of competition if the identity and ranking of the leading firms always remains the same.

(b) CONTESTABLE MARKET THEORY

To the proponents of contestable market theory (see Chapter 2 for more detail), much of this survey will have been irrelevant. Baumol's recipe (1982: 6) for determining the structure of a given industry involves two steps. 'First, we determine what structure happens to be most efficient for the production of a given output vector by a given industry. Next we investigate when market pressures will lead the industry toward such an efficient structure in equilibrium.' In effect, his solution to the first step adds little to what we have already labelled the technological explanation of concentration. In the case of single-product industries, and relying on either a continually declining cost curve, or a U-shaped curve, the answer must be either natural monopoly or the firm numbers shown in Fig. 3.3a. For multi-product industries the story is a little more interesting. Here there is no unique cost curve and the answer depends also on 'the location of the industry's output vector' (i.e. product mix). But this, in turn, will depend on the prices charged by firms in the industry, and 'since pricing depends on structure, we are brought full circle to the conclusion that pricing behaviour and industry structure must, ultimately, be determined simultaneously and endogenously'. In this respect at least, there is common ground with other contemporary work on the theory of concentration. However, the more important part of the message concerns the second stage to the analysis. *Assuming the market to be perfectly contestable*, market forces will inevitably produce an equilibrium under which only the efficient structure(s) can be sustained. The internal logic of this argument is irrefutable. What is still very much a matter of debate, however, is the outcome once we move away from the fiction/textbook polar case of the contestable market. Baumol himself seems to have little doubt that real-world structures will constitute 'reasonable approximations to the efficient structures' (ibid.: 8). This belief seems to rest on the similarity of concentration in a given industry in different countries. This is hardly conclusive, however: as we have seen, the evidence certainly points to (usually) moderately high correlations across countries. But this merely establishes a role for technological factors — the correlations are by no means perfect and other forces are undoubtedly at work.

It is too early to attempt a definitive assessment of the impact of contestable market theory for the theory of concentration. Quite clearly it reinforces the intuition that technology is important, although the indeterminacy of the explanation in the constant-cost case remains. To some extent the generalisation to multi-product industries, and the ensuing realisation that structure is endogenous, is an important development in the theory of concentration. But the key issue of what happens in markets that are even slightly less than perfectly contestable remains unresolved.

II AGGREGATE CONCENTRATION

Just as market concentration is concerned with the extent to which an individual market is dominated by its leading firms, so aggregate concentration measures the extent to which the macro-economy (or broad sectors thereof) is dominated by the leading, usually conglomerate, firms in the economy as a whole. A standard measure of aggregate concentration is, for example, the share of total industrial output accounted for by the top 100 firms.

Rather strangely, the two subjects have generated traditions of research which are, in the main, quite independent of each other. To be charitable we might account for this by pointing to different theoretical perspectives — the micro/macro distinction, with market concentration relating to oligopoly theory, while aggregate concentration has interested those with somewhat wider social and political concerns, such as the long-run evolution of capitalist economies, and worries about the centralisation of power. But whatever the reason, the absence of cross-pollination between the two subjects means that our survey will display a marked imbalance and this second part to the survey is brief, with only passing reference to the literature outside of industrial organisation. We first set the scene by establishing formally the nature of the relationship between aggregate and market concentration; a brief summary of the evidence is then followed by discussion of the theoretical and empirical explanations offered for the rise in concentration in the UK during the twentieth century.

1. Aggregate and market concentration and diversification

Although it is intuitively likely that the level of concentration in a given economy will depend on concentration within individual markets and the degree of diversification, a formalisation of the exact nature of this relationship has only appeared in recent years (Clarke and Davies 1983). Consider an economy (or broad sector) comprising N firms and K industries. Typically some firms will be diversified and/or integrated, and will therefore operate in more than one industry. For these purposes, define aggregate concentration by the aggregate Herfindahl index[56]:

$$H = \Sigma \, S_i^2 / \, S^2 \qquad\qquad [32]$$

where S_i is the aggregate size of firm i and S is the aggregate size of the economy.

Likewise, concentration in the jth industry is to be measured by the Herfindahl index of market shares in that industry:

$$H_j = \Sigma \, S_{ij}^2 / \, S_j^2 \qquad\qquad [33]$$

where S_{ij} is the size of firm i's operations in j and S_i is the aggregate size of industry j.

Aggregation of [33] across industries and firms yields the following decomposition of aggregate concentration:

$$H = (1 - D)^{-1} \, \Sigma \, w_j \, H_j \qquad\qquad [34]$$

where w_j is the squared share of industry j in the aggregate economy, and D is an aggregate index of diversification:

$$D = \Sigma \, w_i \, D_i \qquad\qquad [35]$$

Thus D is the weighted index of diversification across firms with diversification at the individual firm level being measured by the standard Berry index.[57]:

$$D_i = 1 - \Sigma \, S_{ij}^2 / \, S_i^2 \qquad\qquad [36]$$

In other words, aggregate concentration is proportional to a weighted sum of concentration in individual markets. The factor of proportionality depends positively on the level of diversification within the economy.

2. The evidence on aggregate concentration

The major empirical study in this area, in terms of both its findings and the rigour of data collection, is by Prais (1976). He establishes a time series for the share of the top 100 corporations in manufacturing net output; the key figures are a low initial level of 16 per cent in 1909, rising to 24 per cent in 1935 but then falling back to 22 per cent by 1949 (apparently due to the effects of the Second World War), and then a dramatic increase to 41 per cent by 1970. His study closes at 1970 and comparable figures are difficult to obtain thereafter. Nevertheless, various later studies confined to the 1970s suggest that this was a period of little change in aggregate concentration.[58]

Turning to the US, aggregate concentration is clearly lower; for instance, the top 100 firms in manufacturing accounted for only 34 per cent of value added in 1976 (White 1981). Moreover, the upward trend over the century is far less pronounced than in the UK: following a gradual increase from 22 per cent in 1919 to 30 per cent in 1958, aggregate concentration in the US seems to have remained fairly stable thereafter at around 30 per cent.[59] Evidence for other countries is rather patchy, but the UK Government 1978 Green Paper (HMSO 1978: 60–1) reports aggregate concentration to be lower than the UK in both West Germany and Canada, and in the latter it fell significantly between 1968 and 1977.

3. Explanations of aggregate concentration

Explanations of the causes and consequences of high and rising aggregate concentration are somewhat heterogeneous and tend to depend on the perspective of the researcher. We shall force things a little by grouping perspectives into three main types: the market-based, firm-based, and historical macro.

The market perspective tends to view aggregate concentration merely in terms of a logical extension of the first part of our survey. As revealed by eqn [34], aggregate concentration is, after all, a summary measure of what is happening on average within individual markets in the economy. Thus high aggregate concentration probably reflects typically high market concentration and is a cause for concern for precisely this reason. The level of diversification also matters of course, but this too will have implications at the individual market level if conglomerate power bestows competitive advantages.

As a matter of empirical fact, it does seem that the time paths of aggregate and typical market concentration have been very similar in the UK economy. For the period 1935–68, they moved very closely together (Clarke 1985: 25), and Clarke and Davies (1985), using the decomposition shown here in [34], confirm that this was true for the shorter period 1963–68. On the other hand, their figures suggest a slight reduction in aggregate concentration during 1971–77, while market concentration was largely unchanged on average. (Unfortunately, more recent comparisons are not available at the time of writing.) To some extent then, we can argue that an understanding of the determinants of market concentration goes a long way to explaining changes in aggregate concentration. But it would be wrong to impute unchanged levels of diversification from parallel paths for market and aggregate concentration. As eqn [34] confirms, aggregate concentration is the *product* of market concentration and diversification, and therefore an x per cent increase in market concentration will not, in general, mean an x per cent increase in the aggregate level. Indeed, the rather sketchy information we have on diversification levels suggests that diversification also increased strongly between 1935 and 1968.[60] Abstracting for the moment from the causes of this, the implications for within-market competition have been the subject of some concern. It is certainly clear (Utton 1974) that in most three-digit industries in the UK the leading firm(s) also happen to be among the top 100 corporations in the economy as a whole. The question is, does conglomerate power have implications for the nature of competition within individual markets? This is a question on which theory is speculative and evidence virtually non-existent. The issues include on the one hand the socially beneficial aspects of economies of scope and ease of diversified entry, and on the other hand, the anti-competitive consequences of predatory pricing and mutual forbearance. Clarke (1985: 215–21) provides a brief introduction to this somewhat unsatisfactory literature.

The second identifiable strand in the literature places the individual firm in the centre of the stage. It asks: why have the leading firms become so large? Not surprisingly, answers owe less to the theory of industrial organisation than to its cousin, the theory of the firm. In particular, Williamson's work dominates much of the thinking. His markets and hierarchies approach (e.g. Williamson 1975) offers a powerful framework, in which the growth of large integrated and diversified firms can be explained by an increasing tendency to internalise market transactions. Frustratingly, this approach has still to attract sufficient empirical attention for us to evaluate whether increasing aggregate concentration is explicable in terms of changes in the relative efficiency of firms as opposed to markets. Similarly, his work on internal organisation (1970), and the growth of the M-form at the expense of the U-form, is suggestive but not conclusive. There is no doubt that the multi-divisional form has diffused rapidly within the UK in the post-war period, but whether this is the cause of increased concentration, rather than a consequence or facilitating tendency, is debatable.

On an empirical level, the most impressive studies are Hannah and Kay (1977) and Prais (1976). Hannah and Kay, extending the analysis already described in Part I to the explanation of aggregate concentration, find that all of the post-war increase can be attributed to merger activity. As before, we raise the nagging doubt that this tells us about the vehicle of increasing concentration, but not the underlying cause. Clearly, this leads us in the direction of managerial motives, i.e. sales and growth maximisation, and thus away from our immediate concern here. Perhaps the growth in M-forms has enabled the assimilation of rapid growth by merger in a way which was not feasible with the U-form organisation. Similarly, we have already discussed Prais's stochastic description of the world under market concentration. We might also add here two other points he raises. Firstly, it appears that the increase in aggregate concentration has not involved an equivalent increase in plant level concentration. Prais estimates that the share of the largest 100 plants remained largely unchanged at 11 per cent between 1930 and 1968. Quite obviously, the main feature of rising aggregate concentration has been an increase in the number of plants operated by the leading firms. This is consistent with increasing multi-plant operations both within and across industries. Perhaps more significantly, it offers no support for the contention that increasing scale economies at the factory level have been a prime cause of the growth of the large firm. Economies to firm scale, however, are more likely. Prais himself tends to emphasise financial economies based on easier access to the financial markets and tax advantages over smaller firms. The latter are also stressed by Kay and King (1978).

Finally, we come to the rather more historical and ambitiously 'global' explanations of increasing aggregate concentration. In fact we might interpret the stochastic models as belonging to this group, when applied to the aggregate economy. There is nothing in the law of proportionate effect which is peculiar to specific industries or time periods. As such, this might be claimed as one of the underlying physical laws of a capitalist economy. In this respect alone, a parallel to Marx's prediction of increasing concentration might be drawn. The latter, however, has a rather fuller economic explanation of underlying causes. For Marxists, the 'centralisation of capital' is an inevitable consequence of competition between capitalists in the drive for accumulation. The emergence of technologies (which are capital rather than labour intensive) necessitates large-scale production and drives out smaller-scale, high-cost competitors. Whether the ensuing stage of 'monopoly capitalism' is characterised by more or less competition appears to be a matter of debate within the Marxist camp. But what seems to be beyond debate is that this phase, characterised by mergers and collusion, only serves to reinforce tendencies to higher concentration.

Clearly, a more extended discussion of aggregate concentration would take us away from the main micro themes of this volume. It is unsatisfactory that research within the industrial organisation tradition has failed to seriously address the consequences for behaviour within individual markets of high and increasing aggregate concentration. We add this subject to the inventory of items for future research mentioned at the end of Part I.

Notes

1. Lerner (1934) and Kalecki (1939) were the first to suggest the price–cost margin as a measure of the degree of monopoly or oligopoly power. Scherer (1970: p.50) lists some of its limitations. More recently, Dansby and Willig (1979) have developed what they call the 'industry performance gradient index' as a measure of the rate of potential improvements in welfare performance from government policy intervention. This index is a simple transformation of the Lerner index.
2. Throughout this survey all summations are over $i = 1, \ldots, N$ unless otherwise indicated.
3. The *weighted* average margin is appropriate here since it reflects the mark-up earned on the average unit (which is what is observed at the industry level). That is, it attaches more weight to the margins of those firms selling more units.
4. The intuition of this result is as follows. For a given market demand curve, price is more responsive proportionately to changes in an individual firm's output the larger is its market share. So in an industry of few firms, each will perceive less elastic demand and exploit this by restricting output and so raising price. To put it the other way round, in unconcentrated industries each firm perceives a near horizontal marginal revenue curve (for the usual reasons given in perfect competition analysis) and so has little incentive to restrict output.
5. Note that the perfectly collusive (monopoly) solution requires that all producing firms should have identical marginal costs in this model.
6. Cyert and de Groot (1973) suggest a rather different way of modelling implicit collusion.
7. For example where buyers and sellers enter into contracts on an individual basis, and secret discounts and reciprocal buying may occur.
8. The intuition of this result is fairly clear. Where there are only a few sellers, the random flows of customers switching allegiance are more predictable, that is the variance of the flows will be smaller. As such, any systematic flow due to secret price cutting will be more conspicuous.
9. Hay and Morris (1980: 167–77) offer a more extensive discussion of the conditions facilitating collusion. Spence (1979) provides a rare attempt to make econometrically operational this and other hypotheses in the collusion literature.
10. Other models which point to the Herfindahl as the appropriate index of concentration include, for instance, Hannah and Kay (1977: 13), using a locational analogy, and Nickell and Metcalf (1978), who confirm a positive relation between margins and the Herfindahl index in markets incorporating product differentiation.

11. Examples of symmetric models appear in a number of the surveys of this book. Within this survey, the Dasgupta–Stiglitz model of R & D described in section 4 is one.

12. Cowell (1977) provides a complete and accessible discussion of inequality measures. The reader is also referred to Hannah and Kay (1977: 50–2) for a strong attack on their use as measures of concentration, and to a lively debate between Hart (1981) and Hannah and Kay (1981).

13. The Gini coefficient is sometimes used in these cases: it measures the area between the curve and the diagonal — larger values of the coefficient indicating greater inequalities.

14. See Quandt (1966), Silberman (1967) and Clarke (1979).

15. Equation [8] can be derived by rewriting H as $\Sigma (X_i/N\bar{X})^2$ where X_i is the size of firm i and $\bar{X}$ is average firm size. From the definition of the variance of size, $V = (\Sigma X_i^2/N) - \bar{X}^2$, it follows that $H = (V + \bar{X}^2)/N\bar{X}^2 = (1 + (cv)^2)/N$ where $(cv)^2 = V/\bar{X}^2$. Interestingly, as suggested earlier, in the special case of a lognormal size distribution, $(cv)^2 + 1 = \exp(\sigma^2)$ and H is thus positively related to σ^2 and inversely to N.

16. Jacquemin and Kumps (1971), for example, consider concentration within and between two sub-groups of firms in Europe. See also Jacquemin and de Jong (1977) for a more general discussion.

17. The cumulative concentration curve differs from the Lorenz curve in only one respect: the horizontal axis records the number, rather than proportion, of firms. In the above example CR_3 in A (25%) is significantly lower than in B (41%) but CR_8 in A (67%) is significantly higher than in B (43%), which means that these cumulative concentration curves cross.

18. For instance, we have seen that the $N(\alpha)$ index is a generalisation of H; Hart (1975) discusses the family of entropy measures; and a widely used measure in continental Europe, the Linda index, can be interpreted as a generalisation of the concentration ratio (Waterson 1984: 171).

19. See for instance Kilpatrick (1967) and Bailey and Boyle (1971). However, comparisons of H and CR by Hause (1977), Schmalensee (1977) and Sleuwangen and Dehandschutter (1986) also suggest important empirical differences. Kwoka (1981) also confirms important differences.

20. Davies (1980b) also suggests a more general index which is based explicitly on inequalities and numbers with flexibility built into the weights attributed to the two constituents.

21. But see Hannah and Kay (1977: 42–3).

22. Brunner and Nightingale point to the distinction between markets and industries. Chamberlin (1983: 61) clearly doubts whether there is such a thing as a well defined market. Ederington and Skogstad (1977) develop a methodology based on observing which firms interact with each other in practice, but this is far too data-intensive for widespread applicability.

23. We shall consider only the manufacturing sector here. Unfortunately, evidence on concentration in the service and other sectors of the economy is sparse and unreliable. Aaronovitch and Sawyer (1975: Ch.5) include a useful summary of what is known.

24. The 'old' SIC, in use until 1980 and thus the basis of most empirical research until very recently, involved splitting Manufacturing into 'Orders', 'Minimum list headings' (MLH), and 'Products'. The most critical difference between the new and the old occurs at the three-digit level: the level at which most detailed data is and was published in the Census. The new SIC not only reduces the number of three-digit

industries by about a third, but also changes most of the industry definitions at this level. This makes detailed comparison of pre- and post-1980 data virtually impossible.

25. For example, firms might be grouped into those employing between 1 and 25 employees, 25–100, 100–200, 200–500, and so on. The table will show the total number of firms in each class and its aggregate employment and output. In these circumstances, the H index and other indices might be calculated on the assumption that all firms in each size class are of the same size. But this will yield only an imprecise estimate which will be biased downwards as it will not allow for intra-class variance in size.

26. Business Statistics Office (1980) provides a useful, very detailed, source at this level for 1977, 1976 and 1975.

27. According to the purely technological explanation of concentration, to be described presently, one would expect high correlations, with levels differing only to the extent that market size varies between two countries. Note also that this result is rather awkward for the contestable market theorists' explanation of industry structure; see the discussion of section 6.

28. Note that production diseconomies need not invalidate the L-shaped costs assumption, since firms may avoid them by operating a number of efficiently scaled plants. If, on the other hand, larger firms tend to have worse labour relations and/or experience 'control loss' (Williamson 1967), this will imply an upturn in average costs at some point, at the firm level. Hay and Morris (1980: Ch.2) provide a very thorough discussion of scale economies, and Lyons (1980) lists some of the empirical studies which tend to confirm the L-shaped costs assumption.

29. See the discussion in Chapter 2 on the profits/entry barriers literature.

30. But, as we shall see, the stochastic model of Simon and Bonini (1958) provides a neat explanation of how entry rates will affect inequalities.

31. Of course when entry is effected by takeover, there is no immediate change in concentration, only ownership.

32. To derive these results, note that the output of firm 1 corresponds to monopoly output; for linear demand, this is exactly half of competitive output, $X_1 = X_c/2$. The output of the smallest firm is MES, thus $X_N = $ MES. Since each firm produces twice as much as the next smallest, $X_1 = 2X_2 = 2^2X_3 = 2^{i-1}X_i = \ldots = 2^{N-1}X_N$. Thus $X_c/2 = 2^{N-1}$MES and, therefore, $(X_c/\text{MES}) = 2^N$. When logged, this is the general result shown in the text. To derive H, note that $X_i = 2^{N-1}X_N2^{1-i} = 2^{N-i}$MES. Thus $\Sigma X_i = $ MES $\Sigma 2^{N-i}$ and $H = \Sigma X_i^2/X^2 = $ MES^2 Σ $2^{2(N-i)}/$MES^2 $(\Sigma 2^{(N-i)})^2$. Now $\Sigma 2^{2(N-i)}$ is a geometric progression with a sum of $[1 - 2^{2N}]/1 - 2^2$ and $\Sigma 2^{N-i}$ has a sum of $[1 - 2^N]/1 - 2$. Therefore, substituting for N, $H = \{[1 - (X_c/(\text{MES})^2]/(-3)\}/\{1 - X_c/\text{MES}\}^2$. Simple rearrangement gives the expression in the text. Note that this model implies $H \geq 1/3$ since as MES $\to 0$, $H = 1/3$.

33. Loosely speaking, this repeats the Dasgupta–Stiglitz finding, but the context is rather different. Shaked and Sutton model the case where product quality, rather than the cost of production, is improved by additional outlays.

34. This certainly contrasts with the findings of, say, the Clarke and Davies model in which more cooperative solutions lead to higher concentration.

35. For instance, the survey article by Curry and George (1983: 238) contains a dismissal of the stochastic approach as 'mechanical' and concludes: 'Stochastic models contain little of direct interest to the economist.'

36. Davies (1979a) provides an example of how the aggregation properties of the lognormal allow an explanation of industry-level diffusion performance to be based firmly

on a firm-level model of decision making under uncertainty.

37. See the references in note 14.

38. Interestingly, the lognormal prediction is usually found to be least appropriate to small-number industries. This is consistent with the usual qualification to the Central Limit Theorem, namely that the population be sufficiently large (certainly no less than 30).

39. Studies by Hart (1962), Mansfield (1962) and Ijiri and Simon (1977) all tend to confirm that there is no tendency for large firms to grow faster on average than small firms. But Singh and Whittington (1968) and (1975) report some evidence of a very weak tendency for large firms to grow more rapidly. The last mentioned also find that growth variability tends to decline with firm size; this is also the conclusion of Samuels and Chesher (1975) and others.

40. Probably the main reason for this is that the four-parameter lognormal shares few of the desirable properties of the more popular two-parameter form, e.g. concerning aggregation, decomposition (see Aitchinson and Brown 1957).

41. Davies and Lyons extend the model by examining the probability of entry in a world of demand uncertainty and attempted entry deterrence. They find α depends on the height of entry barriers, the demand elasticity and the degree of uncertainty.

42. A comprehensive summary is provided in Hay and Morris (1980: Ch.14) which can be supplemented with the more recent, but briefer, Clarke (1985: 272–4.)

43. Hay and Morris (Ch.8, especially pp. 243–55) summarise the theoretical and empirical literature on the divorce of ownership and managerial control.

44. Swann et al. (1974) is the classic reference to the Restrictive Practices Legislation in the UK.

45. The list of studies in this tradition is almost endless; our summary is based on: Comanor and Wilson (1967), Guth (1971), Jenny and Weber (1978), Ornstein et al. (1973) (itself a good survey of the literature at that time), Pashigian (1968, 1969), Porter (1974), Sawyer (1971), Strickland and Weiss (1976), Hart and Clarke (1980). Studies of the determinants of changes in concentration include Caves and Porter (1980), Mueller and Hamm (1974), Weiss (1963). Chapter 2 in this book discusses some of the empirical studies of entry determinants in a cross-industry setting. Levy (1985) suggests a methodology somewhere between explaining levels and changes in concentration, using a lagged endogenous variable. This is a precarious procedure in *cross-section*, and as might be expected, lagged concentration dominates the other explanatory variables. Curry and George (1983: 217–27) report the results of many of these studies in more detail.

46. This result applies to virtually all the studies mentioned in the previous note.

47. See, for example, Comanor and Wilson (1967), Guth (1971), Ornstein et al. (1973), Orr (1974), Mann et al. (1967), Greer (1971), Strickland and Weiss (1976).

48. Hay and Morris (1980: 508–10) have a brief discussion of other work in a similar vein. Ornstein et al. (1973), however, report no significant relationship between concentration and a variable measuring the variability of aggregate industry growth rates, implying no stochastic influence. Unfortunately this is not an appropriate test: the stochastic growth model predicts a positive relation between CR and the variance of growth rates across firms. High inter-firm variability need not imply a highly variable growth rate for the industry as a whole over time.

49. The R^2 they report describes the relationship between CR and estimates of MES/X, y and α. As they admit, this relationship is partly tautological (given the Pareto curve). A more complete empirical test would entail the explanation of y and α.

50. Exceptions include Strickland and Weiss (1976), Caves *et al.* (1980), Neumann *et al.* (1979).
51. See Chapter 2 for a summary of the survivor and engineering techniques.
52. Most studies of sub-optimal plants suggest a much lower typical value. Bain (1956: 185) reports a suboptimal share of between 10 and 30 per cent; Weiss himself (1964: 258–9), in a paper not employing his proxy, finds a figure of less than 50 per cent in 52 of 65 industries, with a mean of 35 per cent.
53. This estimate is necessarily hypothetical and a little arbitrary. It is based on the assumption that in the 14 industries where mergers were important, without mergers concentration would have still increased on average by the same amount as it did in the 6 other non merger-intensive industries. This is sheer conjecture of course, although not without interest.
54. See Collins and Preston (1961), Boyle and Sorenson (1971), and Shepherd (1975).
55. A rare theoretical contribution in this area, but with a neo-classical perspective, is provided by Grossack (1972), with his concept of 'permanent levels of concentration'. This tends to miss the point in our opinion because fluctuations tend to be equated to transitory factors and reveal nothing about the underlying dynamic. The analogy to Friedman's permanent income hypothesis is also rather crude.
56. Clarke and Davies (1983, 1985) show that similar decompositions are possible for most concentration indices.
57. Clarke (1985: 197–201) provides a brief survey of diversification indices.
58. Hughes and Kumar (1984a,b) present estimates for the 100 firm employment concentration ratio for the whole economy (and not just manufacturing) which suggest a very marginal increase between 1968 and 1980. Clarke and Davies (1983), using Census data, report a very slight reduction in the Herfindahl index for aggregate manufacturing 1971–77.
59. White's claim of stable aggregate concentration was contested by Feinberg (1981), who estimates that the share of the top 0.05 per cent of firms rose from 25 per cent in 1947 to 42 per cent in 1977. These figures can be easily reconciled with White's since this period was one in which total firm numbers increased noticeably. In other words, the top 0.05 per cent was a much larger number of firms in 1977 than 30 years earlier. But why Feinberg should prefer this measure (which amounts to an inequality index) is obscure.
60. Again Clarke provides a useful summary. Clarke and Davies's own results suggest a slight reduction in diversification in 1971–77.

References

Aaronovitch, S. and **Sawyer, M. C.** (1975) *Big Business: Theoretical and Empirical Aspects of Concentration and Mergers in the U.K.*, Macmillan: London.

Aitchinson, J. and **Brown, J. A. C.** (1957) *The Lognormal Distribution*, Cambridge University Press: Cambridge.

Bailey, D. and **Boyle, S. E.** (1971) The optimal measure of concentration, *Journal of the American Statistical Association,* **66**, 702–6.

Bain, J. S. (1956) *Barriers to new Competition*, Harvard University Press: Cambridge, Mass.

Bain, J. S. (1959) *Industrial Organisation*, John Wiley: New York.

Baumol, W. J. (1982) Contestable markets: an uprising in the theory of industry structure, *American Economic Review,* **72**, 1–15.

Boyes, W. J. and **Smyth, D. J.** (1979) The optimum concentration measure: theory and evidence for Canadian manufacturing industries, *Applied Economics*, **11**, 289–302.

Boyle, S. E. and **Sorenson, R. L.** (1971) Concentration and mobility, *Journal of Industrial economics*, **19**, 118–32.

Brunner, E. (1975) Industrial analysis revisited, in Andrews, P. W. S. and Brunner, E., *Studies in Pricing*, Macmillan: London.

Business Statistics Office (1980) *Statistics of Product Concentration of U.K. Manufactures for 1975, 76 and 77*, P01006, HMSO: London.

Caves, R. E. *et al.* (1980) *Competition in the Open Economy*, Harvard University Press, Harvard: Mass.

Caves, R. E. and **Porter, M. E.** (1980) The dynamics of changing seller concentration, *Journal of Industrial Economics*, **29**, 1–15.

Chamberlin, E. H. (1933) *The Theory of Monopolistic Competition*, Harvard University Press: Cambridge, Mass.

Clarke, R. (1979) On the lognormality of firm and plant size distributions: some U.K. evidence, *Applied Economics*, **11**, 415–33.

Clarke, R. (1985) *Industrial Economics*, Basil Blackwell: Oxford.

Clarke, R. and **Davies, S. W.** (1982) Market structure and price-cost margins, *Economica*, **49**, 277–87.

Clarke, R. and **Davies, S. W.** (1983) Aggregate Concentration, Market Concentration and Diversification, *Economic Journal*, **93**, 182–92.

Clarke, R. and **Davies, S. W.** (1985) On measuring diversification and concentration, *Economics Letters*, **15**, 145–52.

Collins, N. R. and **Preston, L. E.** (1969) Price-cost margins and industry structure, *Review of Economics and Statistics*, **51**, 271–86.

Comanor, W. S. and **Wilson, T. A.** (1967) Advertising, market structure and performance, *Review of Economics and Statistics*, **49**, 423–40.

Cowell, F. (1977) *Measuring Inequality*, Philip Allan: Oxford.

Cowling, K. (1978) Monopolies and Mergers Policy: a view on the Green Paper, *Economic Research Paper no. 139*, Warwick University.

Cowling, K. (1982) *Monopoly Capitalism*, Macmillan: London.

Cowling, K. and **Waterson, M.** (1976) Price-cost margins and market structure, *Economica*, **43**, 267–74.

Curry, B. and **George, K. D.** (1983) Industrial concentration: a survey, *Journal of Industrial Economics*, **31**, 203–55.

Cyert, R. M. and **de Groot, M. H.** (1973) An analysis of cooperation and learning in a duopoly context, *American Economic Review*, **63**, 24–37.

Dansby, R. E. and **Willig, R. D.** (1979) Industry performance gradients, *American Economic Review*, **69**, 249–60.

Dasgupta, P. and **Stiglitz, J.** (1980) Industrial structure and the nature of innovative activity, *Economic Journal*, **90**, 266–93.

Davies, S. W. (1979a) *Diffusion of Process Innovations*, Cambridge University Press: Cambridge.

Davies, S. W. (1979b) Choosing between concentration indices, *Economica*, **46**, 67–75.

Davies, S. W. (1980a) Measuring industrial concentration: an alternative approach, *Review of Economics and Statistics*, **62**, 306–9.

Davies, S. W. (1980b) Minimum efficient size and seller concentration: an empirical problem, *Journal of Industrial Economics*, **28**, 287–301.

Davies, S. W. and **Caves, R. E.** (1987) *Britain's Productivity Lag*, Cambridge University Press: Cambridge.

Davies, S. W. and Lyons, B. R. (1982) Seller concentration: the technological explanation and demand uncertainty, *Economic Journal*, **92**, 903–19.

Dixit, A. and Stern, N. (1982) Oligopoly and welfare: a unified presentation with applications to trade and development, *European Economic Review*, **19**, 123–44.

Ederington, L. and Skogstad, A. (1977) Measurement of banking competition and geographic markets, *Journal of Money, Credit and Banking*, **9**, 469–82.

Feinberg, R. M. (1981) On the measurement of aggregate concentration, *Journal of Industrial Economics*, **30**, 223–30.

George, K. D. and Ward, T. (1975) *The Structure of Industry in the E.E.C.*, Cambridge University Press: Cambridge.

Geroski, P. A. (1983) Some reflections on the theory and applications of concentration indices, *International Journal of Industrial Organisation*, **1**, 79–94.

Gibrat, R. (1931) *Les Inegalities Economiques*, Sirey: Paris.

Gort, M. (1983) Analysis of stability and change in market shares, *Journal of Political Economy*, **71**, 51–63.

Greer, D. D. (1971) Product differentiation and concentration in the brewing industry, *Journal of Industrial Economics*, **19**, 201–19.

Grossack, I. M. (1972) The concept and measurement of permanent industrial concentration, *Journal of Political Economy*, **80**, 745–60.

Guth, L. S. (1971) Advertising and market structure revisited, *Journal of Industrial Economics*, **19**, 179–98.

Hall, M. and Tideman, N. (1967) Measures of concentration, *Journal of the American Statistical Association*, **62**, 162–8.

Hannah, L. and Kay, J. A. (1977) *Concentration in Modern Industry*, Macmillan: London.

Hannah, L. and Kay, J. A. (1981) The contribution of mergers to concentration growth: a reply to Professor Hart, *Journal of Industrial Economics*, **29**, 305–13.

Hart, P. E. (1962) The size and growth of firms, *Economica*, **29**, 29–39.

Hart, P. E. (1971) Entropy and other measures of concentration, *Journal of the Royal Statistical Society*, series A, **134**, 423–34.

Hart, P. E. (1975) Moment distributions in economics: an exposition, *Journal of the Royal Statistical Society*, series A, **138**, 423–34.

Hart, P. E. (1981) The effects of mergers on industrial concentration, *Journal of Industrial Economics*, **29**, 315–20.

Hart, P. E. (1985) Recent trends in concentration in British industry, *National Institute of Economic and Social Research Discussion Paper 82*.

Hart, P. E. and Clarke, R. (1980) *Concentration in British Industry, 1935–75*, Cambridge University Press: Cambridge.

Hart, P. E. and Prais, S. J. (1956) The analysis of business concentration: a statistical approach, *Journal of the Royal Statistical Society*, series A, **119**, 150–91.

Hart, P. E., Utton, M. A. and Walshe, G. (1973) *Mergers and Concentration in British Industry*, Cambridge University Press: Cambridge.

Hause, J. C. (1977) The measurement of concentrated industrial structure and the size distribution of firms, *Annals of Economic and Social Measurement*, **6**, 73–107.

Hay, D. A. and Morris, D. J. (1980) *Industrial Economics: Theory and Evidence*, Oxford University Press: Oxford.

HMSO (1978) *A Review of Monopolies and Mergers Policy*, (Green Paper), Cmnd 7198, HMSO: London.

Horowitz, I. (1970) Employment concentration in the Common Market: an entropy approach, *Journal of the Royal Statistical Society*, **133**, 463–79.

Hughes, A. and **Kumar, M. S.** (1984a) Recent trends in aggregate concentration, *Cambridge Journal of Economics,* **8,** 235–50.

Hughes, A. and **Kumar, M. S.** (1984b) Recent trends in aggregate concentration: revised estimates, *Cambridge Journal of Economics,* **8,** 401–2.

Ijiri, Y. and **Simon, H. A.** (1977) *Skew Distributions and the Size of Business Firms,* North Holland: Amsterdam.

Jacquemin, A. P. and **de Jong, H. W.** (1977) *European Industrial Organisation,* Macmillan: London.

Jacquemin, A. P. and **Kumps, A-M.** (1971) Changes in the size structure of the largest European firms: an entropy measure, *Journal of Industrial Economics,* **20,** 59–70.

Jenny, F. and **Weber, A.** (1978) The determinants of concentration trends in the French manufacturing sector, *Journal of Industrial Economics,* **26,** 193–207.

Kalecki, M. (1939) *Essays in the Theory of Economic Fluctuations,* Allen and Unwin: London.

Kay, J. A. and **King, M.** (1978) *The British Tax System,* Oxford University Press: Oxford.

Kilpatrick, R. W. (1967) The choice among alternative measures of industrial concentration, *Review of Economics and Statistics,* **49,** 258–60.

Kumar, M. S. (1985) International trade and industrial concentration, *Oxford Economic Papers,* **37,** 125–33.

Kwoka, J. E. (1981) Does the choice of concentration measure really matter?, *Journal of Industrial Economics,* **29,** 445–53.

Lerner, A. P. (1934) The concept of monopoly and the measurement of monopoly power, *Review of Economic Studies,* **1,** 157–75.

Levy, D. (1985) Specifying the dynamics of industry concentration, *Journal of Industrial Economics,* **34,** 55–68.

Lyons, B.R. (1980) A new measure of minimum efficient plant scale in U.K. manufacturing industry, *Economica,* **47,** 19–34.

McKinnon, R. I. (1966) Stigler's theory of oligopoly: a comment, *Journal of Political Economy,* **74,** 281–5.

Mansfield, E. (1962) Entry, Gibrat's law, innovation and the growth of firms, *American Economic Review,* **52,** 1023–51.

Mueller, W. F. and **Hamm, L. G.** (1974) Trends in industrial market concentration, *Review of Economics and Statistics,* **56,** 511–20.

Nelson, R. R. and **Winter, S. G.** (1978) Forces generating and limiting competition under Schumpeterian competition, *Bell Journal of Economics,* **9,** 524–48.

Nelson, R. R. and **Winter, S. G.** (1982) *An Evolutionary Theory of Economic Change,* Harvard University Press: Cambridge, Mass.

Neumann, M., **Bobel, I.** and **Haid, A.** (1979) Profitability, risk and market structure in West Germany, *Journal of Industrial Economics,* **27,** 227–42.

Nickell, S. and **Metcalf, D.** (1978) Monopolistic industries and monopoly profits; or are Kellogg's cornflakes overpriced? *Economic Journal,* **88,** 254–68.

Nightingale, J. (1978) On the definition of 'Industry' and 'Market', *Journal of Industrial Economics,* **27,** 1–12.

Ornstein, S. I., **Weston, J. F., Intriligator, M. D.** and **Shrieves, R. E.** (1973) Determinants of market structure, *Southern Economic Journal,* **39,** 612–25.

Orr, D. (1974) An index of entry barriers and its application to the structure performance relationship, *Journal of Industrial Economics,* **23,** 39–49.

Pashigian, B. P. (1968) Market concentration in the U.S. and Great Britain, *Journal of Law and Economics,* **11,** 299–319.

Pashigian, B. P. (1969) The effects of market size on concentration, *International Economic Review,* **10,** 291–314.

Phlips, L. (1971) *Effects of Industrial Concentration: A Cross-sectional Analysis for the Common Market*, North Holland: Amsterdam.

Porter, M. E. (1974) Consumer behaviour, retailer power and market performance in consumer goods industries, *Review of Economics and Statistics,* **56,** 419–36.

Prais, S. J. (1976) *The Evolution of Giant Firms in Britain*, Cambridge University Press: Cambridge.

Pryor, F. L. (1972) The size of production establishments in manufacturing, *Review of Economics and Statistics,* **82,** 547–66.

Quandt, R. E. (1966) On the size distribution of firms, *American Economic Review,* **56,** 416–32.

Rees, R. (1985) Cheating in a duopoly supergame, *Journal of Industrial Economics,* **33,** 387–401.

Samuels, J. M. and **Chesher, A. D.** (1975) Growth, survival and the size of companies 1960–9, in Cowling, K. (ed.), *Market Structure and Corporate Behaviour*, Gray-Mills: London.

Saving, T. R. (1965) The four parameter lognormal, diseconomies of scale and the size distribution of manufacturing establishments, *International Economic Review,* **6,** 87–104.

Saving, T. R. (1970) Concentration ratios and the degree of monopoly, *International Economic Review,* **11,** 139–46.

Sawyer, M. C. (1971) Concentration in British manufacturing, *Oxford Economic Papers,* **23,** 352–83.

Scherer, F. M. (1970) *Industrial Market Structure and Economic Performance*, Rand McNally: Chicago.

Schmalensee, R. (1977) Using the H index of concentration with published data, *Review of Economics and Statistics,* **59,** 186–93.

Shaked, A. and **Sutton, J.** (1987) Product differentiation and industrial structure, *Journal of Industrial Economics* (forthcoming).

Shepherd, W. G. (1975) *The Treatment of Market Power: Antitrust, Regulation Public Enterprise*, Columbia University Press: New York.

Silberman, I. H. (1967) On lognormality as a summary measure of concentration, *American Economic Review,* **57,** 807–31.

Simon, H. A. and **Bonini, C. P.** (1958) The size distribution of business firms, *American Economic Review,* **48,** 607–17.

Singh, A. and **Whittington, G.** (1975) The size and growth of firms, *Review of Economic Studies,* **42,** 15–26.

Sleuwangen, L. and **Dehandschutter, W.** (1986) The critical choice between the concentration ratio and the H index in assessing industry performance, *Journal of Industrial Economics,* **35,** 193–208.

Spence, M. (1979) Tacit coordination and imperfect information, *Canadian Journal of Economics,* **11,** 490–505.

Stigler, G. J. (1964) A theory of oligopoly, *Journal of Political Economy,* **72,** 44–61.

Strickland, A. D. and **Weiss, L. W.** (1976) Advertising, concentration and price-cost margins, *Journal of Political Economy,* **84,** 1109–21.

Swann, D. *et al.* (1974) *Competition in British Industry: Restrictive Practices Legislation in Theory and Practice*, Allen and Unwin: London.

Telser, L. G. (1964) Advertising and competition, *Journal of Political Economy*, 537–62.

Utton, M. A. (1974) Aggregate versus market concentration: a note, *Economic Journal,* **84,** 150–55.

Utton, M. A. (1982) Domestic concentration and international trade, *Oxford Economic Papers,* **34,** 479–97.

Waterson, M. (1984) *Economic Theory of the Industry*, Cambridge University Press: Cambridge.

Weiss, L. W. (1963) Factors in changing concentration, *Review of Economics and Statistics, 45*, 70–7.

Weiss, L. W. (1964) The survival technique and the extent of sub-optimal capacity, *Journal of Political Economy, 72*, 246–61.

Weiss, L. W. (1965) An evaluation of mergers in six industries, *Review of Economics and Statistics, 47*, 172–81.

White, L. W. (1981) What has been happening to aggregate concentration in the U.S.?, *Journal of Industrial Economics, 29*, 223–30.

Williamson, O. E. (1967) Hierarchical control and optimum firm size, *Journal of Political Economy, 75*, 123–38.

Williamson, O. E. (1970) *Corporate Control and Business Behaviour*, Prentice-Hall: Englewood Cliffs, N.J.

Williamson, O. E. (1975) *Markets and Hierarchies*, Free Press: New York.

Worcester, D. A. (1967) *Monopoly, Big Business and Welfare in the Postwar U.S.*, University of Washington Press: Seattle.

CHAPTER FOUR

Oligopoly theory made simple

Huw Dixon[1a]

Oligopoly theory lies at the heart of industrial organisation (I.O.) since its object of study is the interdependence of firms. Much of traditional micro-economics presumes that firms act as passive price-takers, and thus avoids the complex issues involved in understanding firms' behaviour in an interdependent environment. As such, recent developments in oligopoly theory cover most or all areas of theoretical I.O., and particularly the 'new' I.O. This survey is therefore very selective in the material it surveys: the goal is to present some of the basic or 'core' results of oligopoly theory that have a general relevance to I.O.

The recent development of oligopoly theory is inextricably bound up with developments in abstract game theory. New results in game theory have often been applied first in the area of oligopoly (for example, the application of mixed strategies in the 1950s — see Shubik 1959, and more recently the use of subgame perfection to model credibility). The flow is often in the opposite direction: most recently, the development of sequential equilibria by Kreps, Milgrom, Roberts, and Wilson arose out of modelling reputational effects in oligopoly markets. Over recent years, with the new I.O., the relationship with game theory has become closer. This chapter therefore opens with a review of the basic equilibrium concepts employed in the new I.O. — Nash equilibrium, perfect equilibrium, and sequential equilibrium.

The basic methodology of the new I.O. is neo-classical: oligopolistic rivalry is studied from an equilibrium perspective, with maximising firms, and uncertainty is dealt with by expected profit or payoff maximisation. However, the subject matter of the new I.O. differs significantly from the neo-classical micro-economics of the standard textbook. Most importantly, much of the new I.O. focuses on the process of competition over time, and on the effects of imperfect information and uncertainty. As such, it has expanded its vision from static models to consider aspects of phenomena which Austrian economists have long been emphasising, albeit with a rather different methodology.

The outline of the chapter is as follows. After describing the basic equilibrium concepts in an abstract manner in section 1, the subsequent two sections explore and contrast the two basic static equilibria employed by oligopoly theory to model product market competition — Bertrand (price) competition, and Cournot (quantity) competition. These two approaches yield very different results in terms of the degree of competition, the nature of the first-mover advantage, and the relationship between market structure (concentration) and the price–cost margin.

Section 4 moves on to consider the incentive of firms to precommit themselves in sequential models; how firms can use irreversible decisions such as investment or choice of managers to influence the market outcome in their favour. This approach employs the notion of subgame perfect equilibria, and can shed light on such issues as whether or not oligopolists will overinvest, and why non-profit maximising managers might be more profitable for their firm than profit maximisers. Section 5 explores competition over time, and focuses on the results that have been obtained in game-theoretic literature on repeated games with perfect and imperfect information. This analysis centres on the extent to which collusive outcomes can be supported over time by credible threats, and the influence of imperfect information on firm's behaviour in such a situation. Alas, many areas of equal interest have had to be omitted — notably the literature on product differentiation, advertising, information transmission, and price wars. References are given for these in the final section. Other omissions are dealt with elsewhere in the book — entry deterrence in Chapter 2, R & D in Chapter 6.

Lastly, a word on style. I have made the exposition of this chapter as simple as possible. Throughout the chapter I employ a simple linearised model as an example to illustrate the mechanics of the ideas introduced. I hope that readers will find this useful, and I believe that it is a vital complement to general conceptual understanding. For those readers who appreciate a more rigorous and general mathematical exposition, I apologise in advance for what may seem sloppy in places. I believe, however, that many of the basic concepts of oligopoly theory are sufficiently clear to be understood without a general analysis, and that they deserve a wider audience than a more formal exposition would receive.

1. Non-cooperative equilibrium

The basic equilibrium concept employed most commonly in oligopoly theory is that of the *Nash equilibrium*, which originated in Cournot's analysis of duopoly (1838). The Nash equilibrium applies best in situations of a one-off game with perfect information. However, if firms compete repeatedly over time, or have imperfect information, then the basic equilibrium concept needs to be refined. Two commonly used equilibrium concepts in repeated games are those of *subgame perfection* (Selten 1965), and if information is imperfect, *sequential equilibria* (Kreps *et al.* 1982).

We shall first introduce the idea of a Nash equilibrium formally, using some of the terminology of game theory. There are n firms, $i = 1, \ldots, n$, who each choose some strategy a_i from a set of feasible actions A_i. The firm's strategy might be one variable (price/quantity/R & D) or a *vector* of variables. For simplicity, we will take the case where each firm chooses one variable only. We can summarise what each and every firm does by the n-vector $(a_1, a_2, \ldots, a_n)$. The 'payoff' function shows the firm's profits π_i as a function of the strategies of each firm:

$$\pi_i = \pi_i(a_1, a_2, \ldots, a_n) \tag{1}$$

The payoff function essentially describes the market environment in which the firms operate, and will embody all the relevant information about demand, costs, and so on. What will happen in this market? A Nash equilibrium is one possibility, and is based on the idea that firms choose their strategies non-cooperatively. A Nash equilibrium occurs when each firm is choosing its strategy optimally, given the strategies of the other firms. Formally, the Nash equilibrium is an n-vector of strategies $(a_1^*, a_2^*, \ldots, a_n^*)$ such that for each firm i, a_i^* yields maximum profits given the strategies of the $n - 1$ other firms a^*_{-i}.[1] That is, for each firm:

$$\pi_i(a_i^*, a^*_{-i}) \geq \pi_i(a_i, a^*_{-i}) \tag{2}$$

for all feasible strategies $a_i \epsilon A_i$. The Nash equilibrium is often defined using the concept of a *reaction function*. A reaction function for firm i gives its best response given what the other firms are doing. In a Nash equilibrium, each firm will be on its reaction function.

Why is the Nash equilibrium so commonly employed in oligopoly theory? Firstly, because no firm acting on its own has any incentive to deviate from the equilibrium. Secondly, if all firms expect a Nash equilibrium to occur, then they will choose their Nash equilibrium strategy, since this is their best response to what they expect the other firms to do. Only a Nash equilibrium can be consistent with this rational anticipation on the part of firms. Of course, a Nash equilibrium may not exist, and there may be multiple equilibria. There are many results in game theory relating to the existence of Nash equilibrium. For the purpose of industrial economics, however, perhaps the most relevant is that if the payoff functions are continous and strictly concave in each firm's own strategy then at least one equilibrium exists.[2] Uniqueness is rather harder to ensure, although industrial economists usually make strong enough assumptions to ensure uniqueness.[3]

If market competition is seen as occuring over time, it may be inappropriate to employ a one-shot model as above. In a *repeated game* the one-shot *constituent* game is repeated over T periods (where T may be finite or infinite). Rather than simply choosing a one-off action, firms will choose an action a_{it} in each period $t = 1, \ldots, T$. For repeated games, the most commonly used equilibrium concept in recent oligopoly theory literature is that of subgame perfection which was first formalised by Selten (1965), although the idea had been used informally (e.g. Cyert and De Groot 1970). At each time t, the firm will decide on its action a_{it} given the past history of the market h_t, which will include the previous moves by all firms in the market.

A firm's 'strategy' in the repeated game[4] is simply a rule σ_i which the firm adopts to choose its action a_{it} at each period given the history of the market up to then, h_t:

$$a_{it} = \sigma_i(h_t)$$

If we employ the standard Nash equilibrium approach, an equilibrium in the repeated game is simply n strategies $(\sigma_1^*, \sigma_2^*, \ldots, \sigma_n^*)$ such that each firm's strategy

σ_i^* is optimal given the other firms' strategies σ^*_{-i}. Thus no firm can improve its payoff by choosing a different strategy, given the strategies of the other firms.

However, a major criticism of using the standard Nash equilibrium in repeated games is that it allows firms to make 'threats' which are not *credible*, in the sense that it would not be in their interest to carry out the threat. For example, consider the example of entry deterrence from Chapter 2, with two periods. In the first period, the entrant decides whether or not to enter. In the second period, the entrant and incumbent choose outputs. The incumbent could adopt the following strategy: if entry does not occur, produce the monopoly output. If entry does occur, produce a very large output which drives down the price below costs at whatever output is chosen by the entrant. In effect, the entrant is posed with a powerful threat by the incumbent: 'if you enter, I'll flood the market and we'll both lose money'. Clearly, with this powerful threat, the incumbent will be able to deter entry. However, it is not a *credible* threat: if entry *were* to occur, then the incumbent would not wish to carry out this potent threat. Thus the incumbent's strategy is not credible, since he would be making unnecessary losses.

Subgame perfection was formulated to restrict firms to *credible* strategies. The basic idea of subgame perfection is quite simple. In a Nash equilibrium the firm chooses its strategy σ_i 'once and for all' at the beginning of the game, and is committed to it throughout the play (as in the above example). To rule out non-credible threats, however, in a subgame-perfect equilibrium at each point in time firms choose their strategy for the rest of the game. The 'subgame' at any time t is simply the remainder of the game from t through to the last period T. Subgame perfection requires that the strategies chosen are Nash equilibria in each subgame. This rules out non-credible threats, since in effect it requires a firm to choose its strategy optimally at each stage in the game. In our example, the incumbent's threat to expand output is not 'credible': in the subgame consisting of the second period, it is not a Nash equilibrium. Indeed, if the market is Cournot, and there is a unique Cournot equilibrium, then the unique subgame-perfect strategy for the incumbent involves producing the Cournot output if entry has occurred. One of the major attractions of subgame perfection is that it narrows down the number of equilibria: there are often multiple Nash equilibria in repeated games and imposing 'credibility' on strategies can reduce the number considerably, at least in finitely repeated games.

With imperfect information, a commonly used equilibrium concept is that of a 'sequential' equilibrium (Kreps *et al.* 1982). This is formally a rather complex concept, but we shall provide a simple example in section 5. The basic idea of subgame perfection is employed, with the added ingredient of Bayesian updating of information.[5] Firms may be uncertain about each others' payoff functions (e.g. they do not know each others' costs or each others' objectives). At the start of the game, firms have certain prior beliefs, which they then update through the game. Firms may be able to learn something about each other from each others' actions. In such a situation, firms of a certain type may be able to build a 'reputation' by taking actions which distinguish themselves from firms of another type. For example, in Milgrom and Roberts' (1982b) paper on entry deterrence, low-cost incumbents are able to distinguish themselves from high-cost incumbents by following a 'limit pricing' strategy which it is unprofitable for high-cost firms to pursue. These reputational equilibria are very important, since they can explain how firms might behave against their short-run interest in order to preserve their reputation intact, for example as a low-cost firm or as an aggressive competitor.

2. Cournot and Bertrand equilibria with homogeneous products

The previous section considered the concept of a Nash equilibrium in purely abstract terms. To make the concept concrete, we need to specify the exact nature of the strategies chosen, and define the payoff function. Corporate strategy is of course very broad, embracing all the activities of the firm — price, output, investment, advertising, R & D, and so on. In practice, oligopoly theory abstracts from the complexity of real-life corporate strategy, and concentrates on just one or two strategic variables. There are two basic ways of modelling how firms compete in the market. The first takes the view that the firm's strategic variable is its output, and originates in Cournot (1838). The second takes the view that the firm's basic strategic variable is price, and originates in the work of Bertrand (1883), Edgeworth (1925) and more recently in models of imperfect competition with product differentiation (e.g. Chamberlin 1933; Dixit and Stiglitz 1977).

As we shall see, whether price or output is the strategy makes a difference to the equilibrium outcome. For example, one of the basic issues of interest to industrial economists is the relationship between concentration and the price–cost margin. The standard notion that higher concentration leads to a higher price–cost margin is based on the Cournot view, and does not hold in the Bertrand framework, where there can be a perfectly competitive outcome with two or more firms. The distinction between price and quantity setting in the context of oligopoly is not present in monopoly, where it makes no difference whether the monopolist chooses a price or quantity (the monopolist simply chooses a point on its demand curve). In order to capture the distinction between the Cournot and Bertrand framework in its starkest form, we will first consider the simplest case of homogeneous goods. We will then discuss what arguments there are for choosing between the two competing approaches to modelling product market competition. In the next section, we will pursue this fundamental dichotomy further in the context of the more realistic case of differentiated commodities.

(a) COURNOT–NASH EQUILIBRIUM WITH HOMOGENEOUS GOODS

The basic view of the market taken by Cournot was that firms choose their outputs, and that the market then 'clears' given the total output of firms. There are n firms $i = 1, \ldots, n$, which produce outputs x_i, industry output being $x = \sum_{i=1}^{n} x_i$. We will make the simplest possible assumption about demand and costs:

A 2.1 Industry demand

$$P = 1 - \sum_{i=1}^{n} x_i \qquad\qquad [3]$$

A 2.2 Firm's costs

$$c(x_1) = c\,x_i \qquad (0 \leq c < 1)$$

Equation [3] is called the *inverse industry demand function*. Normally, the industry demand curve is seen as arising from the utility-maximising behaviour of consumers — the market demand curve tells us how much households wish to buy at a given price. The mathematical operation of taking the inverse, as in [3], has important economic implications: it assumes that there can only be one 'market' price. Thus firms have no direct control over the price of their output, only an indirect control via the effect that changes in their own output have on the total industry output.

Given A2.1–A2.2, we can define the firm's payoff function which gives firm *i*'s profits as a function of the outputs chosen:

$$\pi_i\,(x_1, x_2, \ldots, x_n) = x_i\left(1 - \sum_{j=1}^{n} x_j\right) - c\,x_i$$

$$= x_i - x_i^2 - x_i \sum_{j \neq i} x_j - cx_i \qquad [4]$$

Each firm has a reaction function, which gives its profit-maximising output as a function of the outputs chosen by the other firms. Since firm *i* treats the output of the other firms $j \neq i$ as fixed, the first-order condition for maximising [4] with respect to x_i is[6]:

$$\frac{\partial \pi_i}{\partial x_i} = 1 - \sum_{j \neq i} x_j - 2x_i - c = 0$$

Solving this defines the reaction function for firm *i*:

$$x_i = \frac{1 - \sum\limits_{j \neq i}^{n} x_j - c}{2} \qquad i = 1, \ldots, n \qquad [5]$$

Each firm has a similar reaction function, and the Nash equilibrium occurs when each firm is on its reaction function (i.e. choosing its optimal output given the output of the other firms). There will be a symmetric and unique Cournot–Nash equilibrium which is obtained by solving the *n* equations [5] for outputs (which are all equal by symmetry),

$$x_i^* = x^c = \frac{1-c}{n+1} \qquad \textit{Cournot–Nash equilibrium output} \qquad [6]$$

which results in equilibrium price:

$$p^c = \frac{1}{n+1} + \frac{n}{n+1}\,c \qquad [7]$$

For example, if $n = 1$ (monopoly) we get the standard monopoly solution. For $n = 2$, $x^c = (1-c)/3$, $p^c = 1/3 + (2/3)c$. The price cost margin for each firm is:

$$\mu^c = \frac{p^c - c}{p^c} = \frac{1-c}{1+nc} \qquad [8]$$

There is a clear inverse relationship between the equilibrium price–cost margin and the number of firms. As the number of firms become infinite ($n \to \infty$), the price–cost margin tends to its competitive level of 0: as the number falls to one, it tends to its monopoly level $(1-c)/(1+c)$, as depicted in Fig. 4.1.

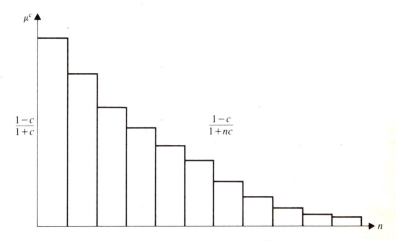

FIG. 4.1 The price–cost margin and the number of firms in the Cournot–Nash equilibrium

What is the intuition behind this relationship between number of firms and the price–cost margin? Very simply, with more firms, each firm's own demand becomes more elastic. With an infinite number of firms, the firm's elasticity becomes infinite, and hence the firms behave as competitive price-takers. The representative firm's elasticity η_i can be related to the industry elasticity η:

$$\eta = \frac{p}{x}\frac{dx}{dp} \tag{9a}$$

$$\eta_i = \frac{p}{x_i}\frac{dx_i}{dp} = \frac{x}{x_i}\left(\frac{p}{x}\frac{dx_i}{dp}\right) \tag{9b}$$

Under the Nash assumption firms treat the other firms' outputs as given, and the change in industry output x equals the change in firm i's output. Hence $dx_i/dp = dx/dp$. Of course, x_i/x is the ith firm's market share, which for our example is in equilibrium $1/n$. Hence [9b] becomes:

$$\eta_i = n.\eta \tag{10}$$

In equilibrium, each firm's elasticity is equal to n times the industry elasticity of demand. As n gets large, so does η_i, leading to approximately 'price-taking' behaviour.

(b) BERTRAND COMPETITION WITH HOMOGENEOUS PRODUCTS

In his famous review, Bertrand criticised Cournot's model on several counts. One of these was the reasonable one that firms set prices, not quantities: the output sold by the firm is determined by the demand it faces at the price it sets. What is the equilibrium in the market when firms set prices, the Bertrand–Nash equilibrium?

If firms set prices, the model is rather more complicated than in the Cournot framework, since there can be as many prices in the market as there are firms. In the Cournot framework, the inverse industry demand curve implies a single 'market' price. In the Bertrand framework each firm directly controls the price at which it sells its output, and in general, the demand for its output will depend on the price set by each firm and the amount that they wish to sell at that price (see Dixon 1987b). However, in the case of a homogeneous product where firms have constant returns to scale, the demand facing each firm is very simple to calculate. Taking the case of duopoly, if both firms set *different* prices, then all households will wish to buy from the lower-priced firm, which will want to meet all demand (so long as its price covers cost), and the higher-priced firm will sell nothing. If the two firms set the *same* price, then the households are indifferent between buying from either seller, and demand will be divided between them (equally, for example). If firms have constant marginal cost, there exists a unique Bertrand–Nash equilibrium with two or more firms, where each firm sets its price p_i equal to marginal cost — the competitive equilibrium. This can be shown in three steps:

Step 1: If both firms set different prices, then that cannot be an equilibrium. The higher-priced firm will face no demand, and hence can increase profits by undercutting the lower-priced firm, so long as the lower-priced firm charges in excess of c. If the *lower*-price firm charged c, it could increase profits from 0 by raising its price slightly while undercutting the higher-priced firm. Hence any Bertrand–Nash equilibrium must be a single-price equilibrium (SPE).

Step 2: The only SPE is where all firms set the competitive price. If both firms set a price *above* c, then either firm can gain by undercutting the other by a small amount. By undercutting, it can capture the whole market, and hence by choosing a small enough price reduction it can increase its profits.

Step 3: The competitive price is a Nash equilibrium. If both firms set the competitive price, then neither can gain by raising its price. If one firm raises its price while the other continues to set $p_i = c$, the lower-priced firm will face the industry demand, leaving the firm which has raised its price with no demand.

The Bertrand–Nash framework yields a very different relationship between structure and conduct from the Cournot–Nash equilibrium: with one firm, the monopoly outcome occurs; with two or more firms the competitive outcome occurs. Large numbers are not necessary to obtain the competitive outcome, and in general price-setting firms will set the competitive 'price-taking' price.

Clearly, it makes a difference whether firms choose prices or quantities. What grounds do we have for choosing between them? First, and perhaps most importantly, there is the question of the *type* of market. In some markets (for primary products, stocks and shares) the people who set prices (brokers) are different to the producers. There exists what is essentially an *auction* market: producers/suppliers release a certain quantity into the market, and then brokers will sell this for the highest price possible (the market clearing price). The Cournot framework would thus seem natural where there are *auction* markets. While there are auction markets, there are also many industrial markets without 'brokers', where the producers directly set the price at which they sell their produce. Clearly, the 'typical' sort of market which concerns industrial economists is not an auction market, but a market with price-setting firms. How can the use of the Cournot framework be justified in markets with price-setting firms?

It is often argued that the choice of Bertrand or Cournot competition rests on the *relative* flexibility of prices and output. In the Bertrand framework, firms set prices and then produce to order. Thus, once set, prices are fixed, while output is perfectly flexible. In the Cournot framework, however, once chosen, outputs are fixed, while the price is flexible in the sense that it clears the market. Thus the choice between the two frameworks rests on the relative flexibility of price and output. This is of course an empirical question, but many would argue that prices are more flexible than quantities (e.g. Hart 1985), and hence the Cournot equilibrium is more appropriate.

A very influential paper which explores this view is Kreps and Scheinkman (1983). They consider the subgame perfect equilibrium in a two-stage model. In the first stage, firms choose capacities; in the second stage firms compete with price as in the Bertrand model, and can produce up to the capacity installed. The resultant subgame-perfect equilibrium of the two-stage model turns out to be equivalent to the standard Cournot outcome. This result, however, is not general, and rests crucially on an assumption about contingent demand (the demand for a higher-priced firm given that the lower-priced firm does not completely satisfy its demand) — see Dixon (1987a). An alternative approach is to allow for the flexibility of production to be endogenous (Dixon 1985; Vives 1986). The Bertrand and Cournot equilibria then come out as limiting cases corresponding to when production is perfectly flexible (a horizontal marginal cost curve) or totally inflexible (a vertical marginal cost curve at capacity).

Another reason that the Cournot framework is preferred to the Bertrand is purely technical: there is a fundamental problem of the non-existence of equilibrium in the Bertrand model (see Edgeworth 1925; Dixon 1987a). In our simple example, firms have constant average/marginal costs. If this assumption is generalised — for example, to allow for rising marginal cost — non-existence of equilibrium is a problem.[7]

A common argument for the Cournot framework is its 'plausibility' relative to the Bertrand framework. Many economists believe that 'numbers matter': it makes a difference whether there are two firms or two thousand. Thus the prediction of the Bertrand model — a zero price–cost margin with two or more firms — is implausible (see, for example, Hart 1979; Allen and Hellwigg 1986). The Cournot equilibrium captures the 'intuition' that competition decreases with fewer firms. There are two points to be raised here: one empirical, one theoretical. Firstly, on the empirical level, there exists little or no evidence that there is a smooth monotonic relationship between the level of concentration and the price–cost margin (see Chapter 5). Secondly, on the theoretical level, the stark contrast in the Bertrand and Cournot formulations has been exhibited here only in the case of a simple one-shot game. In a repeated game, numbers may well matter. For example, Brock and Scheinkman (1985) consider a price-setting super-game, and show that there is a relationship between numbers and the prices that can be sustained in the industry (although the relationship is not a simple monotonic one). A related point is that the Nash equilibrium is a non-cooperative equilibrium. Numbers may well matter when it comes to maintaining and enforcing collusion, and one of Bertrand's criticisms of Cournot was that collusion was a likely outcome with only two firms.

3. Cournot and Bertrand equilibria with differentiated commodities

In this section, we will explore and contrast the Bertrand and Cournot approaches within a common framework of differentiated products with symmetric linear demands. As we shall see, there are again significant contrasts between markets where firms compete with prices and quantities. Firstly, we will compare the equilibrium prices and show that the Cournot equilibrium yields a higher price than the Bertrand equilibrium. Thus, as in the case of homogeneous products, Cournot competition is less competitive than Bertrand competition, although the contrast is less.

Secondly, we contrast the 'Stackelberg' equilibrium (where one firm moves before the other) and the corresponding 'first-mover' advantage. In the Cournot framework, the leader increases his own output and profits at the expense of the follower, and total output increases, reflecting a more competitive outcome than the standard Nash equilibrium. In the Bertrand framework the Stackelberg leader will raise his price and increase his profits. The follower will also raise his prices, and indeed his profits will increase by more than the leaders. Unlike the Cournot case, there is then a 'second-mover advantage' in the Bertrand case. Overall, with price competition the Stackelberg equilibrium leads to higher prices and profits, and a contraction in total output. These differences between the behaviour of markets with price and quantity competition have important policy implications, which will be discussed at the end of this section in the context of the recent literature on strategic trade policy.

We continue to assume that firms have constant average/marginal cost, A2.2. However, we will drop A2.1 and assume that there is a symmetric linear demand system; in the case of two firms with differentiated products we have:

A3.1

For $0 < \alpha < 1$

$$x_1 = 1 - p_1 + \alpha p_2 \qquad \text{[11a]}$$

$$x_2 = 1 - p_2 + \alpha p_1 \qquad\qquad [11b]$$

where $\alpha > 0$ implies the two outputs are *substitutes* (e.g. margarine and butter): if α were negative then they would be complements (e.g. personal computers and software). In the exposition, we will assume throughout that the firms produce *substitutes*, and for technical reasons that $\alpha < 1$ (i.e. quite plausibly the firm's own price has a greater absolute effect on its demand than the other firm's price).

The above equations express outputs (or, more precisely, demands) as a function of prices.[8] If we want to explore the Cournot framework with differentiated products, we need to invert [11] to give the prices that will 'clear' the markets for chosen outputs.

Inverting [11] we have:

$$p_1 = a_0 - a_1 x_1 - a_2 x_2 \qquad\qquad [12a]$$

$$p_2 = a_0 - a_1 x_2 - a_2 x_1 \qquad\qquad [12b]$$

where $a_0 = \dfrac{1-\alpha}{1-\alpha^2}$; $a_1 = \dfrac{1}{1-\alpha^2}$; $a_2 = \dfrac{\alpha}{1-\alpha^2}$

Since $\alpha > 0$, both prices are decreasing in both outputs. Thus an increase in x_1 by one unit will decrease p_1 by a_1, and p_2 by a_2 (of course $a_1 > a_2$ for $\alpha < 1$).

(a) COURNOT–NASH EQUILIBRIUM

There are two firms which choose outputs, the resultant prices given by the inverse demand system [12]. Firm 1's 'payoff' function is:

$$\pi_1 = x_1[(a_0 - a_1 x_1 - a_2 x_2) - c]$$

To obtain firm 1's reaction function, x_1 is chosen optimally given x_2:

$$\frac{\partial \pi_1}{\partial x_1} = a_0 - 2a_1 x_1 - a_2 x_2 - c = 0$$

Solving for x_1 this yields:

$$x_1 = r_1(x_2) = \frac{a_0 - c - a_2 x_2}{2a_1} \qquad\qquad [13]$$

The slope of the reaction function is given by:

$$\left.\frac{dx_1}{dx_2}\right|_{r_1} = \frac{-a_2}{2a_1} = -\frac{\alpha}{2} < 0$$

With substitutes, each firm's reaction function is downward sloping in output space, as in Fig. 4.2.

The firms are identical, and there is a unique symmetric equilibrium at N with $x_1 = x_2 = x^c$:

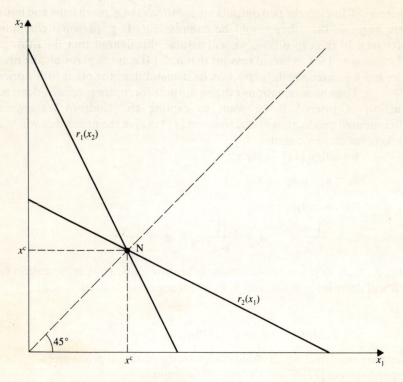

FIG. 4.2 Cournot reaction functions

$$x^c = \frac{a_0 - c}{2a_1 + a_2} = \frac{1 + \alpha - c(1-\alpha^2)}{2 + \alpha} \tag{14}$$

with resultant price:

$$p^c = \frac{1 + c(1-\alpha)}{(2+\alpha)(1-\alpha)} \tag{15}$$

(b) BERTRAND–NASH EQUILIBRIUM

Turning now to the Bertrand case, firms choose *prices*, so that we use the direct demand system [11]. Firm 1's profits are:

$$\pi_1 = p_1(1 - p_1 + \alpha p_2) - c(1 - p_1 + \alpha p_2) \tag{16}$$

$$\frac{\partial \pi_1}{\partial p_1} = 1 - 2p_1 + \alpha p_2 + c = 0$$

Hence firm 1's reaction function in price space is:

$$p_1 = s_1(p_2) = \frac{1 + c + \alpha p_2}{2} \tag{17}$$

The slope is:

$$\left.\frac{dp_1}{dp_2}\right|_{s_1} = \frac{\alpha}{2} > 0$$

Thus, the two firms' reaction functions are upward sloping in price space as depicted in Fig. 4.3.

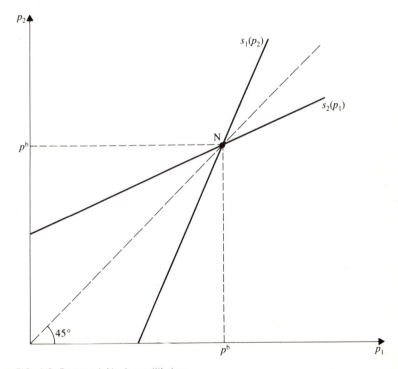

FIG. 4.3 Bertrand–Nash equilibrium

There is a unique symmetric equilibrium price $p_1 = p_2 = p^b$, with corresponding output, price, and price–cost margins:

$$p^b = \frac{1 + c}{2 - \alpha} \tag{18}$$

$$x^b = \frac{1 - c(1-\alpha)}{2 - \alpha} \tag{19}$$

$$\mu^b = \frac{1 - c(2-\alpha)}{1 + c} \qquad [20]$$

How do the Cournot and Bertrand equilibria compare? Direct comparison of [18] with [15] shows that $p^b < p^c$: i.e. the Bertrand equilibrium prices are *lower* than Cournot prices. We formulate this in observation 1:

Observation 1: If firms demands are interdependent, $\alpha \neq 0$, then:

$$p^c > p^b; \quad x^c < x^b; \quad \mu^c > \mu^b$$

If $\alpha = 0$, then each firm is in effect a monopolist, since there are no cross-price effects, and the two outcomes are of course the same. It should be noted that observation 1 remains true when the goods are complements ($-1 < \alpha < 0$).

With differentiated products, then, Bertrand competition will be more competitive than Cournot competition, although the difference is less stark than in the case of homogeneous products. With product differentiation, firms have some monopoly power even with price competition, and do not have the same incentives for undercutting their competition as in the homogeneous goods case.

What is the intuition behind observation 1, that price competition is more competitive than quantity competition? Clearly, for a monopoly, it makes no difference whether price or quantity is chosen; it simply chooses the profit-maximising price–output point on its demand curve. There is a sense in which this is also true for the oligopolist: *given* what the other firm is doing, it faces a demand curve, and chooses a point on that demand curve. However, the demand curve facing firm 1 will be different if firm 2 keeps x_2 constant (and hence allows p_2 to vary) from when firm 2 keeps p_2 constant (and hence allows x_2 to vary). From [11], if firm 2 has price as its strategy, and holds p_2 constant, firm 1's demand is:

$$x_1 = (1 + \alpha p_2) - p_1 \qquad [21]$$

with slope

$$\left. \frac{dx_1}{dp_1} \right|_{p_2} = -1 \qquad [22a]$$

and elasticity

$$\left. \eta_1 \right|_{p_2} = \frac{p_1}{x_1} \qquad [22b]$$

If, on the contrary, firm 2 has output as its strategy, it allows its price p_2 to vary as p_1 varies (to keep x_1 constant):

$$p_2 = 1 - x_2 + \alpha p_1 \qquad [23]$$

Substituting [23] into [11a] we obtain firm 1's demand when x_2 is held constant:

$$x_1 = (1 + \alpha) - (1 - \alpha^2)p_1 - \alpha x_2 \qquad [24]$$

with slope and elasticity:

$$\left.\frac{dx_1}{dp_1}\right|_{x_2} = -(1-\alpha^2); \qquad \left.\eta_1\right|_{x_2} = -\frac{p_1}{x_1}(1-\alpha^2) \qquad [25]$$

Clearly, comparing elasticities [22] and [25]:

$$\left.\eta_1\right|_{p_2} < \left.\eta_1\right|_{x_2} < 0$$

Thus the demand facing firm 1 is *more* elastic when firm 2 holds p_2 constant (and allows x_2 to vary) than when x_2 is held constant (and p_2 allowed to vary). For example, suppose that firm 1 considers moving up its demand curve to sell one less unit of x_1, with substitutes ($\alpha > 0$). If firm 2 holds x_2 constant, then as firm 1 reduces its output and raises its price, the price for x_2 will rise (via [11b]). Clearly, the demand for firm 1 will be more elastic in the case where firm 2 does not raise its price and expands output.

We have derived observation 1 under very special assumptions A2.1, A3.1: how far can we generalise this comparison of Cournot and Bertrand prices? This has been the subject of much recent research — see for example Cheng (1984), Hathaway and Rickard (1979), Okuguchi (undated), Singh and Vives (1984), Vives (1985a,b). Vives (1985a) considers a more general differentiated demand system, which need not be linear or symmetric (ibid. 168) and derives fairly general conditions for which the Bertrand price is less than the Cournot price. Of course, there need not be unique Cournot or Bertrand equilibria: with multiple equilibria, the comparison becomes conceptually more complex. Vives (1985b) has established a result that for very general conditions, there exists a Bertrand equilibrium which involves a lower price than any Cournot equilibrium.

Of course, there are other contrasts to be drawn between Cournot and Bertrand–Nash equilibria. For example, there is the question of welfare analysis employing standard consumer surplus. A simple example employing the linear demand system ([11],[12]) is provided by Singh and Vives (1984: 76) which shows that the sum of consumer and producer surplus is larger in Bertrand than in Cournot–Nash equilibrium, both when goods are substitutes and complements.

(c) STACKELBERG LEADERSHIP AND THE ADVANTAGES OF MOVING FIRST

The differences between Cournot and Bertrand competition go deeper than the simple comparisons of the previous section. To illustrate this, we will examine the advantages of moving first in the two frameworks. The standard Nash equilibrium assumes that firms move simultaneously. However, Heinrich von Stackelberg (1934) suggested an alternative in which one firm (the leader) moves first, the other (the follower) moves second. Thus, when the follower chooses its strategy it treats the leader's choice as given. However, the leader will be able to infer the follower's choice and take this into account in its decision. The explicit algebraic analysis of the Stackelberg equilibrium is rather complicated, and we will rather employ the familiar iso-profit loci.[9] In the following analysis, it is important to note that under A2.1, A3.1 the model is perfectly symmetric; thus whether in price or quantity space, the firms' reaction functions are 'symmetric' in the sense that firm 1's reaction function is a reflection of firm 2's in the 45° line (see Figs 4.2, 4.3). Similarly, firm 1's iso-profit loci are simply reflections of firm 2's in the 45° line, and vice versa.

Firstly we analyse the Stackelberg equilibrium in the Cournot case. The follower (firm 2) will simply choose its output to maximise its profits given x_1, so that $x_2 = r_2(x_1)$. The leader, however, will choose x_1 to maximise its profits given that x_2 depends on x_1 via r_2. Thus, by moving first, the leader can pick the point on firm 2's reaction function that yields it the highest profits: this is represented in Fig. 4.4 by the tangency of iso-profit loci π^L to r_2 at point A.

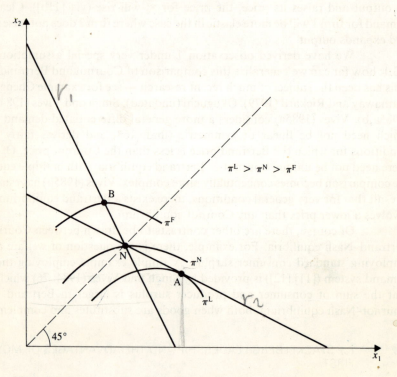

FIG. 4.4 First-mover advantage in Cournot model

If firm 2 were the leader, and firm 1 the follower, then by symmetry firm 2's Stackelberg point would be at point B — the reflection of A in the 45° line (at this point firm 2's iso-profit locus is tangential to firm 1's reaction function). Comparing points A, B and the Nash equilibrium at point N, we can see that if firm 1 is the leader it earns, π^L, which is greater than in the Nash equilibrium π^N. If firm 1 is a follower, it will end up at point B, and earn only π^F which is *less* than π^N. Hence, in the Cournot framework, we have:

$$\pi^L \; > \; \pi^N \; > \; \pi^F \qquad (Cournot)$$

profits	Nash	profits
of	profits	of
leader		follower

There is thus a first-move advantage in two senses: the leader earns more than in the simultaneous move case ($\pi^L > \pi^N$); the leader earns more than the follower ($\pi^L > \pi^F$). The leader increases his output and profits at the expense of the follower (in fact, the decline in the follower's profits from π^N to π^F is *larger* than the increase in the leaders from π^N to π^L: industry profits fall).

In the Bertrand case, the story is rather different: there is a 'second-mover' advantage. The reaction functions and iso-profit loci of firm 1 depicted in price space are shown in Fig. 4.5, and again are symmetric. The iso-profit loci for firm 1 are higher, the further away they are positioned from the x-axis (firm 1 will earn higher profits, the higher p_2 is). N is the Nash equilibrium, A occurs if 1 is the leader, B if 2 is the leader.

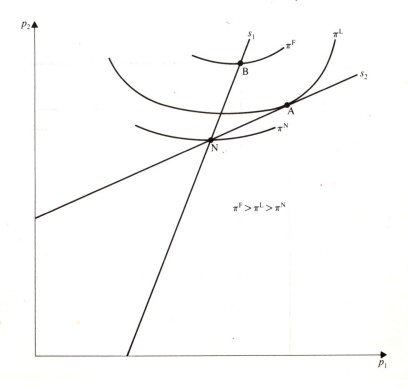

FIG. 4.5 First-mover advantage in Bertrand model

If firm 1 is the leader, it will choose to raise its price, moving along firm 2's reaction function S_2 from N to A and profits will increase from π^N to π^L. However, if firm 1 is the follower, it will end up at B with profits π^F. Note that the follower raises his price by less than the leader, and that $\pi^F > \pi^L$. Thus the leader will set a higher price than the follower, produce a lower output and earn *less* profits:

$$\pi^F > \pi^L > \pi^N \quad (Bertrand)$$

There is an advantage to moving 'second'. This second-mover advantage goes beyond Bertrand equilibria, and extends to any game with upward-sloping reaction functions (Gal-Or 1986). There is still a first-mover advantage in the sense that the leader earns more than in the simultaneous move case ($\pi^L > \pi^N$). In contrast to the Cournot case, in the Bertrand case Stackelberg leadership leads to higher prices, profits and lower outputs.

(d) PRICES v QUANTITIES

Price and quantity competition have very different implications for the nature of product market competition between firms. Most importantly, from the firms' point of view, price competition leads to lower profits than does quantity competition in Nash equilibrium. As was discussed in section 2, whether firms should be viewed as competing with price or quantity can be seen as depending on structural or institutional characteristics of the market — the flexibility of production, whether the market is an auction market, etc.

An alternative approach is to treat the firm's decision to choose price or quantity as itself a strategic decision (Klemperer and Meyer 1986; Singh and Vives 1984). While it is perhaps not quite clear how firms might achieve this, it is at least a useful 'experiment' and will reveal the incentives which firms have to achieve one or the other type of competition.

Without uncertainty, this 'experiment' is not fruitful: firms are *indifferent* between choosing price or quantity. The reason is that from the individual firm's perspective, it simply faces a demand curve, and — like a monopolist — chooses a point on that demand curve. It can achieve any point on the demand curve by choosing either price or quantity. The firm's own price/quantity decision does not affect this demand curve, which is rather determined by the *other* firm's choice. Firm 1's choice has a pure externality effect on the demand faced by firm 2: if 1 chooses price, 2's demand is more elastic than if firm 1 had chosen quantity. However, in the Nash framework, each firm will ignore this externality: given the other firm's choice, each firm will face a particular demand curve, and will be indifferent between setting price or quantity itself. In the case of duopoly, there will be four Nash equilibria in this strategic game: one where both set quantities (Cournot); one where both set prices (Bertrand); and two asymmetric equilibria where one sets price, the other quantity. With certainty, then, allowing firms to choose price or quantity tells us nothing about which may be more appropriate.

The presence of uncertainty (adding a stochastic term to A3.1, for example) can mean that firms have a *strict* preference between price and quantity setting. The results depend very much on the exact assumptions made (is demand uncertainty additive or multiplicative; is demand linear in prices?). For the simple linear demand system A3.1 with an additive stochastic term, firms will prefer quantity setting if marginal costs are increasing; they will be indifferent if marginal costs are constant (as in A2.1); they prefer price setting if marginal costs are decreasing (Klemperer and Meyer 1986: próposition 1). While this and related results are at present rather specific, they do suggest that the presence and nature of uncertainty provide some insights into how firms view the alternatives of price and quantity setting.

4. Precommitment: strategic investment and delegation

In the previous section, we explored the nature of the first-mover advantage in the Cournot and Bertrand framework. Clearly, if we start from the Nash equilibrium, there is an incentive for the firm to precommit its output/price to obtain this first-mover advantage. By 'precommitment' it is meant that the firm takes some action prior to competing in the product market which commits it to a certain course of action. In the standard Cournot model, it is not credible for one firm to produce the Stackelberg output in the simultaneous move game. For example, in terms of Fig. 4.6, firm 1's Stackelberg point A is not on its reaction function — so that given firm 2's output x_{2A}, firm 1 would like to produce x_1'. The only credible equilibrium is the Nash equilibrium at N. In order to move towards its Stackelberg point, the firm must be able to precommit its output in some way. In section 3 we

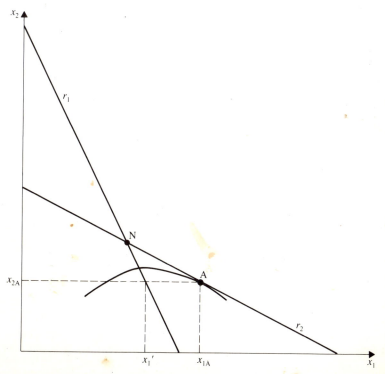

FIG. 4.6 Non-credibility of Stackelberg point

simply assumed that the leader was able to move first. In some situations it is natural to assume a particular sequence of moves (e.g. entrant/incumbent, dominant firm). However, in the case of active incumbents which are competing on even terms, simultaneous moves seem more natural.

Given that there is an incentive for the firm to precommit, how can this be achieved? This section will look at two methods of precommitment which have received much recent attention — precommitment through investment, and precommitment through delegation. The basic idea is simple: the firm can take actions prior to competing in the market, which will alter the Nash equilibrium in the market. Firms can take actions, such as investment decisions,[10] choice of managers, that are irreversible (in the sense of being 'fixed' over the market period), and which alter the firm's reaction function, thus shifting the Nash equilibrium in the market. We will first consider how investment by firms can be used strategically to alter the market outcome.

For a wide range of industrial processes, economists since Marshall have taken the view that it is appropriate to treat the capital stock decision as being taken on a different time scale (the 'long run') to price/output decisions (the 'short-run'). When firms compete in the product market, it follows that they treat their capital stock as fixed. The capital stock chosen by the firm will influence its *costs* when it competes in the market. The fact that capital is committed 'before' output/price decisions means that it can use investment strategically, to influence the market outcome. In essence, through its choice of capital stock, the firm will determine the short-run costs which it will have when it chooses output/price; the firm's marginal costs will determine its reaction function, and hence the Nash equilibrium in the product market. Schematically:

$$\text{investment} \rightarrow \begin{array}{c}\text{short-run}\\\text{marginal cost}\end{array} \rightarrow \begin{array}{c}\text{reaction}\\\text{function}\end{array} \rightarrow \begin{array}{c}\text{market}\\\text{equilibrium}\end{array}$$

For example, in the Cournot case, the firm can increase its investment, reduce its marginal cost, and hence shift its reaction function out, so that the product market equilibrium moves towards the Stackelberg point. Of course, this precommitment is not costless: capital costs money, and as we shall see, such use of capital leads to productive inefficiency. Again, there is an important dichotomy between the Cournot and Bertrand approaches: if the product market is Cournot, then the firm will want to overinvest; if the product market is Bertrand, then the firms will want to underinvest. We will briefly illustrate both situations.

The structure of strategic investment models is very simple: there are two stages to capture the distinction between the short and the long run. In the first 'strategic' stage, the firms choose their capital stock; in the second 'market' stage, firms choose output/price. The choice of capital stock in the first stage will determine the cost function which the firm has. In sections 2 and 3 we assumed constant average/marginal cost at c (A2.2). This can be conceived of as the long-run cost function. In order to keep the exposition consistent, we will assume that firms have a production function of the form:

A4.1

$$x_i = k_i^{1/2} L_i^{1/2}$$

where L_i is labour input. If capital costs r, and labour's wage is normalised to unity, the resultant short-run cost function given investment is:

$$c(x_i, k_i) = rk_i + \frac{x_i^2}{k_i} \tag{26}$$

with linear increasing marginal cost:

$$\frac{\partial c}{\partial x_i} = \frac{2}{k_i} x_i \tag{27}$$

Thus an increase in investment lowers the marginal cost of producing output. The production function A4.1 displays constant returns to scale, and hence the long-run cost function has constant average/marginal cost in terms of A2.2,[11] minimum average cost $c = 2\sqrt{r}$.

We will first outline the strategic investment model with Cournot competition in the product market, a simple version of Brander and Spencer's (1983) article. If investment is used non-strategically, then the firm simply operates on its long run cost function given by A2.2: capital and labour are chosen to minimise production costs. In the strategic investment framework, however, the firm's costs will be given by its short-run cost function [26]. Turning to the market stage, the firm's profits are:

$$\pi_i = x_i(a_0 - a_1 x_i - a_2 x_j) - rk_i - \frac{x_i^2}{k_i} \tag{28}$$

The reaction function which the firm has in the market stage, conditional on k_i, is derived by setting $\partial \pi_i / \partial x_i = 0$:

$$x_i = r_i(x_j, k_i) = \frac{a_0 - a_2 x_j}{2a_1 + (2/k_i)} \tag{29}$$

By increasing its investment, firm i will reduce its marginal costs, and from [29] it will shift its reaction function out, as in Fig. 4.7. Given the level of investment by the two firms (k_1, k_2) the Cournot–Nash equilibrium in the market stage is given by solving for the intersection of the two firms' reaction functions, as in Fig. 4.8. Thus the equilibrium outputs conditional on (k_1, k_2) are obtained by solving [29] for x_1 and x_2 (we leave this as an exercise for the reader). In general form:

$$x_i = x_i(k_i, k_j) \tag{30}$$
$$(+) \ (-)$$

This notation signifies that firm i's equilibrium output in the market stage depends positively on its own investment, and negatively on investment by the other firm. Suppose we start off at point A in Fig. 4.9: an increase in k_1 to k_1' shift out r_1, so that the market equilibrium goes from A to B, x_i rising and x_2 falling. Conversely, an

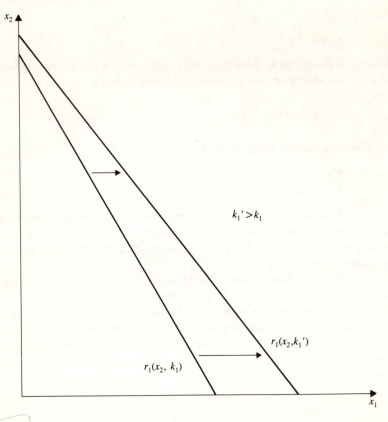

FIG. 4.7 Investment shifts from 1's reaction function out

increase in k_2 shifts the equilibrium from A to C. Thus by altering their investment, the firms can alter their reaction functions, and hence the market stage equilibrium.

How is the optimal level of investment in the first strategic stage determined? Firms choose investment levels k_i, *given* that the second-stage outputs will be as in [30]. We can see their profits as a function of capital stocks. For firm 1 we have profits:

$$u_i(k_1,k_2) = x_1(k_1,k_2)[a_0-a_1x_1(k_1,k_2)-a_2x_2(k_1,k_2)] -c(x_1(k_1,k_2),k_1) \qquad [31]$$

The RHS term in square brackets is the price, which is multiplied by output to obtain revenue, from which are substracted costs.

The firm will choose k_1 to maximise its profits [31], hence:

$$\frac{\partial u_1}{\partial k_1} = \frac{\partial x_1}{\partial k_1}\left[a_0-2a_1x_1-a_2x_2- \frac{\partial c}{\partial x_1} \right] - a_2x_1 \frac{\partial x_2}{\partial k_1} - \frac{\partial c}{\partial k_1} = 0 \qquad [32]$$

Since firm 1 chooses x_1 to maximise profits given x_2 and k_1 in the second stage, the bracket on the right-hand side of [32] is zero (it is simply its reaction function [29]). Hence [32] becomes:

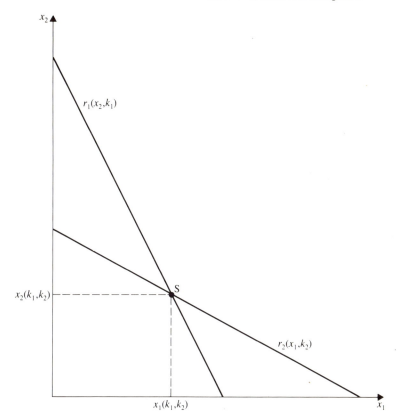

FIG. 4.8 Market stage equilibrium given investment k_1, k_2

$$\frac{\partial c}{\partial k_1} = -a_2 \frac{\partial x_2}{\partial k_1} x_1 > 0 \qquad\qquad [33]$$

What does [33] tell us? $\partial c/\partial k_1$ gives the effect of investment on the total costs of producing x_1. If $\partial c/\partial k_1 = 0$, as in the standard non-strategic case, then k_1 *minimises* the cost of producing x_1. If $\partial c/\partial k_1 > 0$, as in [33], then there is 'overcapitalisation', more investment than would minimise costs (a reduction in k_1 would reduce average costs). If $\partial c/\partial k_i < 0$, then there is 'undercapitalisation': less investment than would minimise costs.

With a Cournot market stage, then, there is overcapitalisation of production in the market stage. The intuitive reason is quite simple. Given the other firm's reaction function, each firm can shift its own reaction function out towards its Stackelberg point. Of course, there is a cost to this: more investment leads to higher capital costs and inefficient production. The firms will shift out their reaction functions beyond their 'innocent' level, and the final product market equilibrium will be at a point such as S in Fig. 4.10. At the equilibrium level of investment, the additional cost of investment equals the additional gains from moving out the

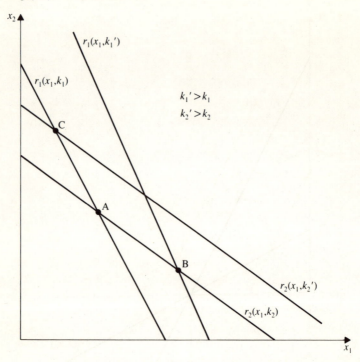

FIG. 4.9 Market stage equilibrium and changes in investment

reaction function further. In the strategic investment equilibrium S then, both firms produce a larger output than in the non-strategic equilibrium N.

In the Bertrand case, an exactly analogous argument applies for strategic investment: however, there is the opposite result of _undercapitalisation_. The Stackelberg equilibrium results in higher prices and lower outputs in the Bertrand case. Thus firms will _restrict_ investment relative to the innocent Bertrand equilibrium, in order to shift their reaction function _out_ in price space, as in Fig. 4.11. Starting from the 'innocent' Bertrand equilibrium at N, if firm 1 restricts its investment, its marginal costs _rise_, and its reaction function shifts outwards to s_1 (an outward shift because with higher marginal costs, it will wish to set a higher price and produce a smaller quantity given the price chosen by the other firm). If both firms underinvest strategically, the resultant equilibrium will be at S, with higher prices and lower output.

We will briefly sketch the algebra underlying this result. Under A2.1, A4.1, the firm's profits are:

$$\pi_i = p_i - p_i^2 - \alpha p_i p_j - \frac{1}{k_i}(1 - p_i - \alpha p_i p_j)^2 - rk_i \qquad [34]$$

Setting $\partial \pi_i / \partial p_i = 0$, firm i's reaction function $p_i = s_i(p_j)$ is:

$$P_i = \frac{1 + 2/k_i}{2 + 2/k_i} + \frac{\alpha(1 + 2/k_i)}{(2 + 2/k_i)} p_j \qquad [35]$$

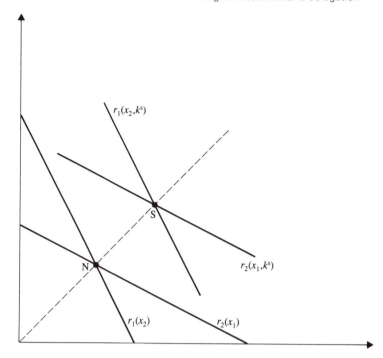

FIG. 4.10 Strategic investment equilibrium – the Cournot case

Solving for p_i to p_j given k_i and k_j, in general terms we have:

$$P_i = p_i\,(k_i,\,k_j) \qquad i,j = 1,2,\ i \neq j \tag{36}$$
$$(+)\ (-)$$

The firms chooses k_i to maximise [34] given that in the market subgame firms prices are given by [36] (i.e. a Betrand–Nash equilibrium occurs).

$$\frac{d\pi_i}{dk_i} = \frac{\partial\pi_i}{\partial p_i}\cdot\frac{dp_i}{dk_i} + \frac{\partial\pi_j}{\partial p_j}\cdot\frac{dp_j}{dk_i} + \frac{\partial\pi_i}{\partial k_i} = 0 \tag{37}$$
$$\phantom{\frac{d\pi_i}{dk_i} =\ }(0)\quad\ (-)\quad\ (+)\quad\ (-)\quad\ (+)$$

Note that $\partial\pi_i/\partial p_i = 0$, since firms are in their market stage reaction function [35], and further that $\partial\pi_i/\partial k_i = -\partial c_i/\partial k_i$. Hence [37] can be expressed as:

$$\frac{\partial c}{\partial k_i} = \frac{\partial\pi_i}{\partial p_j}\frac{dp_j}{dk_i} < 0 \tag{38}$$
$$\phantom{\frac{\partial c}{\partial k_i} =\ }(+)\quad (-)$$

That is, *undercapitalisation* of production results from the strategic use of investment with Bertrand product market competition.

　　Clearly, the result of strategic investment models depends on the nature of product market competition. Other papers have made different assumptions than the simple Cournot–Nash and Bertrand–Nash equilibria. Dixon (1985) considers the case of a *competitive* product market; Eaton and Grossman (1984) and Yarrow

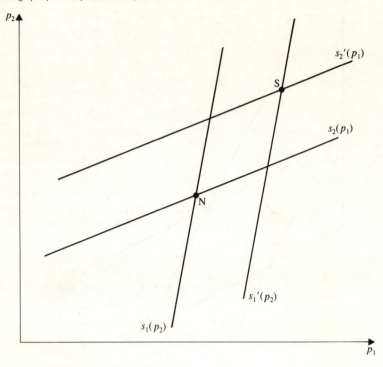

FIG. 4.11 Underinvestment raises prices

(1985) a *conjectural* Cournot equilibrium; Dixon (1986b) a *consistent conjectural variation* equilibrium in the product market.

Since production will generally be inefficient in a strategic investment equilibrium, firms have an incentive to try and precommit their labour input at the same time as their capital. By so doing, firms will be able to produce any output efficiently, while being free to precommit themselves to a wide range of outputs. In Dixon (1986a), precommitment is treated as a strategic choice by the firm: the firm can precommit either, neither, or both capital and labour in the strategic stage. Because of the strategic inefficiency in production that occurs when only capital is precommited, under almost any assumption about the nature of product market competition, firms would prefer to precommit both factors of production (Dixon 1986a: Theorem and p.67). If firms precommit both factors of production in the strategic stage, then in effect they have chosen their output for the market stage, and the resultant equilibrium is equivalent to the standard Cournot equilibrium. How might firms be able to precommit their output in this manner? One important method that may be available is choice of technology. More specifically, the firm may have a choice between a putty–putty technology that allows for smooth substitution of capital for labour in the market stage, or an otherwise equivalent putty–clay technology that is Leontief in the market stage. If the firm chooses a putty–clay technology, then its choice of investment and technique in the strategic stage effectively ties down its output and employment in the market stage. If possible, then, firms would prefer to have totally inflexible production in the market stage. This strong result ignores uncertainty, of course. If demand or factor prices are uncertain, there will be a countervailing incentive to retain flexibility.

In strategic investment models it is firms themselves which precommit. Governments, however, can undertake precommitments which firms themselves cannot make. In the context of trade policy, there has been much recent research on how governments can improve the position of their own firms competing in international markets (see Grossman and Richardson 1984; Venables 1985, for excellent surveys). If domestic firms are competing in foreign markets, the net benefit to the home country in terms of consumer surplus is the repatriated profits — total revenue less the production costs (with competitive factors markets, production costs represent a real social cost to the exporting country). Government trade policy may therefore be motivated by what is called 'rent extraction', that is, helping their own firms to make larger profits which are then repatriated. Trade policy, usually in the form of an export subsidy or tax, is a form of precommitment by the government which enables domestic firms to improve their position in foreign markets. Brander and Spencer (1984) presented the first model based on the rent-extraction principle, and argued for the use of export subsidies in the context of a Cournot–Nash product market. Subsidies have the effect of *reducing* the marginal costs faced by exporters, and can thus be used to shift out their reaction functions to the Stackelberg point (the cost subsidies 'cost' nothing from the point of view of the exporting country, since they merely redistribute money from the taxpayers to shareholders). As Eaton and Grossman (1983) argued, the exact form of the trade policy will be sensitive to the nature of product market competition. With a Bertrand product market, of course, rent extraction arguments lead to the imposition of an export *tax*, since this will shift the Bertrand competitor's reaction function outwards in price space towards its Stackelberg point.

The incentive to precommit in oligopolistic markets also sheds light on one of the perennial issues of industrial economics — what are the objectives of firms? The divorce of ownership from control can be viewed as an act of delegation by shareholders. This act of delegation can be employed as a form of precommitment by shareholders. What sort of managers do shareholders want to manage their firms? There is an obvious answer to this question, which underlies the managerialist view of Marris (1964): shareholders want managers who maximise profits (share valuation) and work hard. This may be true in the context of monopoly: in an imperfectly competitive framework, matters are rather different. Several recent papers (Fershtman 1985; Lyons 1986; Vickers 1985a) have shown how higher profits for shareholders can be obtained when they have non-profit maximising shareholders. The reaction functions of firms in the standard Cournot and Bertrand models are based on the assumption of profit maximisation. By choosing managers with different objectives (e.g. a preference for sales, or an aversion to work) the firms' reaction functions will be shifted. We will illustrate this with a very simple example adapted from Lyons (1986). Managers maximise utility, which depends on profits (remuneration) and sales R (power, prestige, and so on). The utility is a convex combination of the two:

$$u = \gamma\pi + (1-\gamma)R \qquad 0 \leq \gamma \leq 1$$
$$= R - \gamma c$$

since $\pi = R-c$. The coefficient γ represents the weight put on *profits*: $\gamma=1$ is profit maximisation, $\gamma=0$ yields sales maximisation.

Using the common framework A2.1, A2.2, assuming that managers choose outputs to maximise utility, we can derive the firm's reaction functions:

$$u_1 = x_1(a_0 - a_1x_1 - a_2x_2) - \gamma cx_1$$

$$\frac{\partial u_1}{\partial x_1} = a_0 - 2a_1x_1 - a_2x_2 - \gamma c = 0$$

which yields the reaction function:

$$x_1 = r_1(x_2, \gamma_1) = \frac{a_0 - \gamma c - a_2x_2}{2a_1}$$
$$ (-) \ (-)$$

By choosing managers with a preference for sales (i.e. γ smaller than unity), shareholders can push out their firm's reaction function. In Fig. 4.12 we depict the two extreme reaction functions: the one nearest the origin corresponding to profit maximisation $\gamma=1$, the other to sales maximisation $\gamma=0$. Given firm 2's reaction function, firm 1 can move to any point between N and T by choosing the appropriate value of γ. If, as depicted, the Stackelberg point A lies between N and T, then firms will be able to attain their Stackelberg point — note that since A will lie to the left of N, the choice of γ will surely be less than unity, reflecting non-maximisation of profits due to some sales preference. In such a market, if one firm is a profit maximiser with $\gamma=1$ and the other has management with $\gamma<1$, the non-profit maximising firm will earn *more* than the the profit-maximising firm! Of course, in a Bertrand market, the shareholders would wish to choose managers who would restrict output and raise prices — perhaps lazy managers with an aversion to work (see Dixon and Manning 1986, for an example). While we have talked about different 'types' of managers, the precommitment made by shareholders can be seen as taking the form of different types of remuneration packages which elicit the desired behaviour from managers.

In an imperfectly competitive market then, it can pay shareholders to have non-profit maximising managers. There need not be the conflict of interest between owners and managers that is central to managerialist theories of the firm. Also, 'natural selection' processes need not favour profit maximisers in oligopolistic markets, since (for example) sales-orientated managers can earn larger profits than their more profit-orientated competitors. This is a comforting result given the apparent prevalence of motives other than profits in managerial decisions.

The presence of a first-mover advantage means that firms competing in an oligopolistic environment have an incentive to precommit themselves in some way. We have explored *two* methods of precommitment: through investment, and through delegation. Strategic investment leads to productive inefficiency, and from

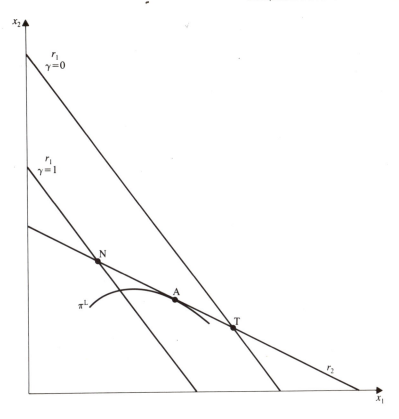

FIG. 4.12 Equilibrium outcome and managerial preferences

the point of view of the firm, it may be cheaper to make its precommitment through its choice of managers rather than its choice of capital stock.

5. Competition over time

In general, Nash equilibria are 'inefficient' in the sense that in equilibrium, profits of all the firms can be increased. The fundamental reason is that firms' profits are interdependent (via the payoff function): each firm's profits depend partly on what the other firms are doing. There is thus an 'externality' involved when each firm chooses its strategy. For example, in the Cournot framework, if one firm raises its output, it reduces the prices obtained by the other firms, thus reducing their profits (a negative externality). In the Bertrand case, a rise in price by one firm is a positive externality, since it raises the demand for other firms. Under the Nash assumption, each firm chooses its own strategy taking into account only the impact on its *own* profits, ignoring the externality.

   The inefficiency of Nash equilibria can easily be demonstrated using the abstract notation of section 1. For simplicity we will take the case of duopoly. To obtain an *efficient* (Pareto optimal) outcome between the two firms, simply maximise a weighted sum of firms' profits:

$$\max_{a_1, a_2} \quad \lambda \pi_1 (a_1, a_2) + (1 - \lambda) \, \pi_2(a_1, a_2) \qquad [39]$$

where $0 \leq \lambda \leq 1$. The first-order conditions for [39] are:

$$\gamma \, \frac{\partial \pi_1}{\partial a_1} + (1 - \gamma) \, \frac{\partial \pi_2}{\partial a_1} = 0 \qquad [40a]$$

$$\gamma \, \frac{\partial \pi_1}{\partial a_2} + (1 - \gamma) \, \frac{\partial \pi_2}{\partial a_2} = 0 \qquad [40b]$$

The leading diagonal terms represent the effect of a_i on π_i, the firm's strategy on its own profits. The off-diagonal terms reflect the 'externality', the effect of a firm's strategy on the other firm's profits. Depending on the weight λ, a whole range of Pareto-optimal outcomes is possible (corresponding to the contract curve of the Edgeworth box). These outcomes can be represented as the profit frontier in payoff space, as in Fig. 4.13. On the frontier, each firm's profits are maximised given the other firm's profits. As λ moves from 0 to 1, more weight is put on firm 1's profits and we move down the profit frontier.[12]

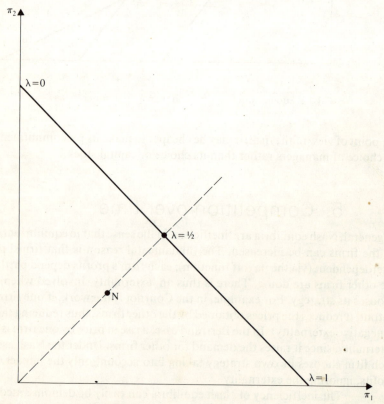

FIG. 4.13 The profit frontier

The Nash equilibrium profits are not Pareto optimal, and lay *inside* the profit frontier at point N, for example. To see why, note that for a Nash equilibrium to occur, both firms choose a_i to maximise their own profits (they are both on their reaction functions). Thus the first-order equations defining the Nash equilibrium are:

$$\frac{\partial \pi_1}{\partial a_1} = \frac{\partial \pi_2}{\partial a_2} = 0 \qquad\qquad [41]$$

If we compare [41] with [40], we can immediately see that if there is some interdependence captured by a non-zero cross-effect ($\partial \pi_i / \partial a_j \neq 0$), then [41] will not be efficient. If there is a *negative* cross-effect, then at the Nash equilibrium *N*:

$$\left.\frac{\lambda \partial \pi_1}{\partial a_1}\right|_N + (1 - \lambda)\left.\frac{\partial \pi_2}{\partial a_1}\right|_N < 0 \qquad\qquad [42]$$
$$\quad (0) \qquad\qquad\qquad (-)$$

The marginal effect of a_1 on the weighted sum of industry profits is *negative*: there is too much output chosen. Conversely, in the Bertrand case, at the Nash equilibrium, the marginal effect of a price rise on the weighted sum of industry profits is *positive*.

  This inefficiency of Nash equilibria means that there is an incentive for firms to collude — to choose their strategies (a_1, a_2) *jointly*, and move from N towards the profit frontier. Of course, if the two firms could merge, or write legally binding contracts, it would be possible for them to do this directly. However, anti-trust law prevents them from doing so: firms have to behave non-cooperatively. However, since the efficient outcomes are not Nash equilibria, each firm will have an incentive to *deviate* from the efficient outcome: it will be able to increase its profits, e.g. from [40] at an efficient outcome where partial $\partial \pi_i / \partial a_j$ is positive (negative), then $\partial \pi_i / \partial a_i$ will be negative (positive), so that a slight reduction (increase) in a_i will increase *i*'s profits.

  Given that firms have an incentive to cooperate, how can they enforce cooperative behaviour if there is also an incentive for firms to deviate from it? One response is to argue that firms compete over time: firms can enforce cooperative behaviour by punishing deviation from a collusive outcome. Since firms are involved in a repeated game, if one firm deviates at time *t*, then it can be 'punished' at subsequent periods. In a repeated game, might not such 'threats' enable firms to enforce a collusive outcome over time? This question has provided the impetus for much research in recent years.

  In a finitely repeated game with perfect information, it turns out that the unique subgame-perfect equilibrium will be to have the Nash equilibrium in each period (assuming that there is a unique Nash equilibrium in the constituent game). That is, if we restrict firms to *credible* punishment threats, then those credible threats will not enable the firms to do better than their Nash equilibrium profits in each period. The argument is a standard backwards induction argument. Consider the subgame consisting of the last period. There is a unique Nash-equilibrium for this subgame, which is that the firms play their Nash-strategies. Any other strategy in the last period would not be 'credible', would not involve all firms adopting their best response to each other. Consider the subgame consisting of the last two periods. Firms know that whatever they do in the penultimate period, the standard Nash-equilibrium will occur next period. Therefore, they will want to choose their action to maximise their profits in the penultimate period, given what the other firms do. If all firms do this, the standard Nash-equilibrium will occur in the penultimate period. By similar arguments, as we go backwards, for any period t, given that in subsequent periods the Nash-equilibrium will occur, the Nash-equilibrium will occur in period t as well. Hence finite repetition of the game yields the standard Nash outcome in each stage of the history of the market. This backwards induction argument goes back to Luce and Raiffa's analysis of the repeated prisoner's dilemma (1957).

In finitely repeated games, then, there is no scope for threats/punishments to move firms' profits above their Nash-level. The argument relied upon a known terminal period, 'the end of the world'. An alternative approach is to analyse *infinitely* repeated games, reflecting the view that market competition is interminable. This raises a different problem: there are generally many subgame perfect equilibria in infinitely repeated games. Clearly, the above backwards induction argument cannot be employed in infinitely repeated games, because there is no last period to start from! It has proven mathematically quite complex to characterise the set of subgame perfect equilibria in infinitely repeated games. There are two types of results (commonly called 'Folk theorems') corresponding to two different views of how to evaluate the firm's payoffs over an infinitely repeated game. One approach is to view the firm maximising its discounted profits for the rest of the game at each period (Lockwood (1984), Abreu (1985), Radner (1986)). The other is to view that the firm does not discount but maximises its average per-period payoff.

Let us first look at the 'Folk theorem' for infinitely repeated games without discounting, which is based on work by Rubenstein (1979). The key reference point is the '*security level*' of firms: this represents the worst punishment that can be inflicted on them in the one-shot constituent game. This is the 'minimax' payoff of the firm, the worst payoff that can be imposed on the firm given that it responds optimally to the other firm(s). For example, take the simple Cournot model in Section 3: the lowest level to which firm 1 can drive firm 2 is zero — this corresponds to where firm 2's reaction function cuts the x-axis, and firm 2's output and profits are driven to zero. In the framework we have employed each firms' security level corresponding to the worst possible punishment it can receive is equal to zero. An individually rational payoff in the constituent game is defined as a payoff which yields both firms their security level. The basic result is that *any* individually rational payoff in the constituent game can be 'sustained' as a perfect equilibrium in an infinitely repeated game without discounting. By 'sustained' it is meant that there corresponds equilibrium strategies that yield those payoffs for each firm. In our example, this means that *any* combination of non-negative profits is possible! This will include the outcomes on the profit frontier, of course, but also outcomes that are far worse than the standard Cournot–Nash equilibrium! In terms of Fig. 4.13, the whole of the area between the axes and the profit frontier (inclusive) represents possible payoffs of some subgame perfect equilibrium!

With discounting, the range of possible equilibria depends on the discount rate δ. At period t, the future discounted profits for the rest of the game are:

$$\sum_{s=0}^{\infty} \delta^s \pi_{it+s}$$

where $0 \leq \delta < 1$ (if the interest rate is r, then $\delta = 1/(1+r)$). The larger is δ, the more weight is put on the future: as δ tends to one, we reach the no-discounting case (since equal weight is put on profits in each period); with δ equal to zero, the future is very heavily discounted, and the firm concentrates only on the current period. The analysis of infinitely repeated games with discounting is rather more complex than the no-discounting case, not least because it is more difficult to define the firm's security level which itself varies with δ (see Fudenberg and Maskin 1986). The basic Folk theorem is that: (a) as $\delta \to 0$, then the set of perfect equilibrium payoffs shrink to the one-shot Nash payoffs; (b) as $\delta \to 1$, then any individually rational payoff is an equilibrium payoff. Again, the analysis is rather complicated here, and the reader is referred to Lockwood (1987) for an excellent analysis of the issues. The basic message for games with discounting is that the set of perfect equilibria depends on the discount rate, and may be very large.

From the point of view of industrial economics, the game-theoretic results for repeated games are far from satisfactory. With finite repetition, the equilibrium is the same as in the one-shot case: with infinite repetition there are far too many equilibria — almost anything goes! There seems to be little middle ground.

However, recent advances involving games of imperfect information may provide some answer to this dilemma (Kreps *et al.* 1982). The basic idea is very simple. Suppose that the firms are uncertain about each other's objectives. In a repeated game, firms can learn about each other's 'character' from observing their actions through time. In this circumstance, firms are able to build up reputations. Let us take a very simple example: there are two firms A and B with two strategies, cooperate (*c*) or defect (*d*). The resultant profits of the two firms are of the familiar prisoner's dilemma structure:

		B		
		c		*d*
A	*c*	1 1		–1, 2
	d	2, –1		0 0

Defection is the 'dominant' strategy: whatever the other firm does, defection yields the highest profits, hence the unique Nash equilibrium is for both firms to defect. This outcome is Pareto-dominated by the outcome where both firms cooperate. If there is perfect information, and the game is repeated over time, then the unique subgame-perfect equilibrium is for both firms to defect throughout (by the standard backwards induction argument).

Now, following Kreps *et al.* (1982), introduce some uncertainty. We will take the case where firms are uncertain about each other's motivation. In general, firms are of two types: a proportion α are 'Rats' and play rationally; proportion $(1-\alpha)$ are 'Triggers' and play 'trigger' strategies. A trigger strategy means that the firm will play cooperatively until the other firm defects, after which it will punish the defector by playing non-cooperatively for the rest of the game.

In a multi-period game like this where there is imperfect information, each firm may be able to infer the other firm's type from its past actions. For example, if one firm defects when they have previously both been cooperative, then the other firm can infer that the other firm is a Rat (since a Trigger only defects in response to an earlier defection). By playing cooperatively, then, a Rat can leave the other firm guessing as to his true type; if a Rat defects, he knows he will lose his reputation and 'reveal' his true nature.

To illustrate this as simply as possible, we will consider what happens when the above game is repeated for three periods, and firms have discount rates δ. For certain values of α and δ, it will be an equilibrium for both firms to cooperate for the first two periods, and defect in the last period. Consider the following strategy from a Rat's point of view (a Trigger will of course follow a trigger strategy).

Period 1:　　Cooperate
Period 2:　　Cooperate if the other firm cooperated in period 1, defect otherwise.
Period 3:　　Defect.

We will now show that this can be a perfect-equilibrium strategy for a Rat. Recall that the Rat does not know whether his opponent is a Trigger, or a Rat following the same strategy.

In period 3, it is clearly subgame perfect to defect — whatever the type of the opponent, be he Rat or Trigger, defection is the dominant strategy and yields the highest payoff. In period 2, the decision is a little more complex. If the other firm (B, say) defected in period 1, then of course he has revealed himself to be a Rat, and so defection is the best response for A for period 2. If firm B did not defect in period 1, then he may be a Trigger or a Rat (with probability $(1-\alpha)$ and α respectively). If firm A defects in period 2, then whatever the type of firm B, it will earn two units in period 2, and nothing in period 3 (since firm B will retaliate whether a Rat or a Trigger). Its expected discounted profits are 2. If, however, firm A cooperates in period 2, it will earn 1 unit of profit in that period: in period 3 its profit will depend on firm A's type — with probability α the other firm is a Rat and will defect anyway: with probability $(1-\alpha)$ the other firm is a Trigger, and will cooperate in the last period. Thus, if A cooperates in period 2, its expected period 3 profits are $\alpha 0 + (1-\alpha)2$. In period 2, firm A's expected discounted profits if it cooperates will be $1 + \delta(1-\alpha)2$. Clearly, firm A will cooperate in period 2 if the expected discounted profits doing so exceed those from defection, i.e.

$$\begin{array}{ccc} \text{defect in} & 2 < 1 + \delta(1-\alpha)2 & \text{cooperate in} \\ \text{period 2} & & \text{period 2} \end{array}$$

This is satisfied for $\delta(1-\alpha) > 1/2$. In period 1 the decision is similar. If it defects in period 1, it earns 2, then nothing thereafter. If it cooperates, then it expects to earn 1 in period 1, 1 in period 2 (from the foregoing argument), and $(1-\alpha)2$ in period 3. The expected discounted profits from cooperation in period 1 are thus $1 + \delta + \delta(1-\alpha)2$. If $\delta(1-\alpha) > 1/2$, then again cooperation in period 1 yields higher expected profits than defection. Thus the above strategy is subgame perfect if the proportion of Triggers is high enough $(1-\alpha) > 1/2\delta$.

With uncertainty then, it can be an equilibrium to have both firms cooperating initially during the game, and only to defect towards the end of the game (the last period in the above example). The intuition is simple enough: by playing cooperatively in the first two periods, the Rat hides his true nature from his competitors. There is a 'pooling' equilibrium early on: both Rats and Triggers cooperate, so that cooperation yields no additional information about the firm's type to alter the 'priors' based on population proportions α, $(1-\alpha)$. One problem with this account — for neo-classical economists at least — is the need to assume the existence of non-rational players to sustain the collusive outcome. This is a problem in two senses. Firstly, there are an indefinite number of ways to be non-rational: alongside the Trigger, the bestiary of the non-rational includes the 'Tit-for-Tats' (Kreps *et al.* 1982), and many other fantastical possibilities. Secondly, the methodology of most economics is based on an axiom that all agents are rational maximisers: yet here we have an explanation which presumes that only some are rational maximisers. It might be said that all that is required for such equilibria is the *belief* that there are some non-rational players. While this may be so, it would seem less than satisfactory if the belief were not justified by the existence of the required proportion α of Triggers.

This sort of equilibrium with imperfect information is called a *sequential equilibrium*, and has the added ingredient that firms use the history of the game to learn about each others' type, by Bayesian updating. The equilibrium strategies in the example need not be unique: for some values of δ and α, it is also an equilibrium for Rats to defect throughout the game, as in the full-information case. However, there exists the possibility of sustaining cooperative behaviour for some part of the game even with a limited period of play. The use of sequential equilibria has been applied to several areas of interest and industrial economists — most notably entry deterrence (Milgrom and Roberts 1982a,b).

6. Conclusions

This chapter has tried to present some of the basic results in the recent literature on oligopoly theory in relation to product market competition. Given the vastness of the oligopoly literature past and present, the coverage has been limited. For those interested in a more formal game-theoretic approach, Lockwood (1987) is excellent (particularly on repeated games and optimal punishment strategies). On the growing literature on product differentiation, Ireland (1986) is comprehensive. Vickers (1985b) provides an excellent survey of the new industrial economics, with particular emphasis on its policy implications.

Notes

1a.   The material of this chapter is based on MSc lectures given at Birkbeck over the period 1985–86. I would like to thank students for their comments and reactions, from which I learned a lot. I would also like to thank Ben Lockwood for invaluable comments, as well as Bruce Lyons, Steve Davies and the editors. Errors, alas, remain my own.

1. a^*_{-i} is the $n-1$ vector of all firms' strategies excepting i's.
2. See Debreu (1952), Glicksburg (1952), and Fan (1952). Strict concavity is a stronger condition than we need — it can be relaxed to quasiconcavity.
3. A sufficient condition for uniqueness is that each firm's reaction function is a 'contraction mapping' — see Friedman (1978) for a formal definition.
4. Note the change in the use of the word 'strategy'. In a one-shot game, the firm's strategy is simply the action it pursues. In a repeated game 'action' and 'strategy' cease to be equivalent, 'strategy' being its 'game plan', the rule by which the firm chooses its action in each period.
5. Bayesian updating means that firms have subjective probabilities which they update according to Bayes rule. Firms start the game with 'prior' beliefs, and revise these to take into account what happens. This is a common way to model learning in neoclassical models.
6. This simply states that x_i is chosen to equate marginal revenue with marginal cost.
7. The reason for this non-existence is quite simple — step 3 of our intuitive proof breaks down, and the competitive price need not be an equilibrium. The competitive price is an equilibrium with constant returns because when one firm raises its price, the other is willing and able to expand its output to meet all demand. However, if firms have rising marginal cost curves, they are supplying as much as they want to at the competitive price (they are on their supply functions). If one firm raises its price, there will be excess demand for the firm(s) still setting the competitive price. The firm raising its price will thus face this unsatisfied residual demand, and in general will be able to raise its profits by so doing (see Dixon 1987a: Theorem 1). One response to this non-existence problem is to allow for *mixed* strategies (rather than firms setting a particular price with probability one, they can set a range of prices each with a particular probability). Mixed-strategy equilibria exist under very general assumptions indeed (Dasgupta and Maskin 1986a,b) and certainly exist under a wide range of assumptions in the Bertrand framework (Dasgupta and Maskin 1986a; Dixon 1984; Dixon and Maskin 1985; Maskin 1986). However, the analysis of mixed-strategy equilibria is relatively complex, and it has yet to be seen how useful it really is. It can be argued that it is difficult to see that mixed strategies reflect a genuine aspect of corporate policy.
8. The standard models of Bertrand competition assume that outputs are demand-determined (see 11): each firm's output is equal to the demand for it. This was the assumption made by Chamberlin (1933) in his analysis of monopolistic competition. This is appropriate with constant costs, since firms will be willing to supply any quantity at the price they have set (for $p_i \geq c$, profits are increasing in output). More generally, however, it is very strong. Surely firms will only meet demand insofar as it raises the firm's profits. With rising marginal cost, the output that the firm wishes to produce given the price it has set is given by its supply function, (the output that the firm wishes to produce given the price it has set is given by its supply function). If demand exceeds this quantity, and there is *voluntary trading*, then the firm will turn customers away (otherwise marginal cost would exceed price). This approach is similar to Edgeworth's (1925) analysis of the homogeneous case — see Dixon (1987b), Benassy (1986). Benassy (1986) has analysed the implications of including an Edgeworthian voluntary trading constraint on price-setting equilibria. While the Nash equilibrium prices will be

the same there is, however, an existence problem: if demand is highly cross-elastic between firms, then no equilibrium may exist.

9. The formula can be obtained by total differentiation of the implicit function $\pi_i(a_i, a_j) = \theta$.

10. 'Investment' can be taken as any fixed factor — capital, R & D, firm-specific human capital, and so on).

11. Long-run average cost is derived as follows. Minimise total costs $rK + L$ with respect to the production function constraint A4.1. Since the production function displays constant returns, long-run average and marginal cost are equal.

12. The profit frontier in Fig. 4.13 is derived under the common framework A2.1–2. Linearity comes from constant returns with a homogeneous product. The actual solution is that *total* output on the frontier equals the monopoly output M, with total profits at their monopoly level μ. L determines the firms' share of output and profit:

$$x_1 = \lambda M \; ; \; \pi_1 = \lambda \, \mu \; ; \; x_2 = (1-\lambda) \, M \; ; \; \pi_2 = (1-\lambda)\mu$$

With diminishing returns, i.e. a strictly convex cost function, the profit frontier will have a concave shape.

References

Allen, B. and **Hellwig, M.** (1986) Bertrand–Edgeworth oligopoly in large markets, *Review of Economic Studies*, **53**, 175–204.

Benassy, J. P. (1986) On the role of market size in imperfect competition: A Bertrand–Edgeworth–Chamberlin synthesis, *CEPREMAP No. 8610*.

Bertrand, J. (1983) Review of Cournot's 'recherches sur la theorie mathematique de la Richess', *Journal des Savants*, pp. 449–50.

Brander, J. and **Spencer, B.** (1983) Strategic commitment with R & D: the symmetric case, *Bell Journal*, **14**, 225–35.

Brander, J. and **Spencer, B.** (1984) Export subsidies and international market share rivalry, *NBER Working Paper 1404*.

Brock, W. and **Scheinkman, J.** (1985) Price-setting supergames with capacity constraints, *Review of Economic Studies*, **52**, 371–82.

Chamberlin, E. (1933) *The Theory of Monopolistic Competition*, Harvard University Press: Cambridge, Mass.

Cheng, L. (1984) Bertrand equilibrium is more efficient than the Cournot equilibrium: the case of differentiated products, Mimeo, Florida.

Cournot, A. (1838) *Recherches sur la theorie mathematique de la Richesse*.

Cyert, R. and **De Groot, M.** (1970) Multiperiod decision models with alternating choices as a solution to the duopoly problem, *Quarterly Journal of Economics*, **84**, 410–29.

Dasgupta, P. and **Maskin, E.** (1986a) The existence of equilibrium in discontinuous economic games, I: Theory, *Review of Economic Studies*, **53**, 1–26.

Dasgupta, P. and **Maskin, E.** (1986b) The existence of equilibrium in discontinuous economic games, II: Applications, *Review of Economic Studies*, **53**, 27–42.

Debreu, G. (1952) A social equilibrium existence theorem, *Proceedings of the National Academy of Sciences*, **38**, 886–93.

Dixit, A. and **Stiglitz, J.** (1977) Monopolistic competition and optimum product diversity, *American Economic Review*, **67**, 297–308.

Dixon, H. (1984) The existence of mixed-strategy equilibria in a price-setting oligopoly with convex costs, *Economics Letters,* **16,** 205–12.

Dixon, H. (1985) Strategic investment in a competitive industry, *Journal of Industrial Economics,* **33,** 205–12.

Dixon, H. (1986a) Cournot and Bertrand outcomes as equilibria in a strategic metagame, *Economic Journal,* Conference Supplement, pp.59–70.

Dixon, H. (1986b) Strategic investment and consistent conjectures, *Oxford Economic Papers,* **38,** 111–28.

Dixon, H. (1987a) Approximate Bertrand equilibria in a replicated industry, *Review of Economic Studies,* **54,** 47–62.

Dixon, H. (1987b) The general theory of household and market contingent demand, *The Manchester School,* **55,** 287–304.

Dixon, H. and **Manning, A.** (1986) Competition and efficiency, Mimeo, Birkbeck College.

Dixon, H. and **Maskin, E.** (1985) The existence of equilibrium with price-setting firms, Mimeo, Harvard University.

Eaton, J. and **Grossman, G.** (1983) Optimal trade and industrial policy under oligopoly, *NEBR Working Paper 1236.*

Eaton, J. and **Grossman, G.** (1984) Strategic capacity investment and product market competition, *Woodrow Wilson School Discussion Paper 80,* Princeton.

Edgeworth, F. (1925) The pure theory of monopoly, collected in *Papers Relating to Political Economy,* Vol. I, Macmillan.

Fan, K. (1952) Fixed point and minimax theories in locally convex topological spaces, *Proceedings of the National Academy of Sciences,* **38,** 121–6.

Fershtman, C. (1985) Managerial incentives as a strategic variable in a duopolistic environment, *International Journal of Industrial Organisation,* **3,** 245–53.

Friedman, J. W. (1978) *Oligopoly and the Theory of Games,* N.H.P.C.

Fudenberg, D. and **Maskin, E.** (1986) The Folk theorem for repeated games with discounting and incomplete information, *Econometrica,* **54,** 533–44.

Gal-Or, E. (1986) First and second mover advantages, *International Economic Review* (forthcoming).

Glicksberg, I. (1952) A further generalisation of the Kakutani fixed point theorem with application to Nash-equilibrium points, *Proceedings of the National Academy of Sciences,* **38,** 170–4.

Hart, O. (1979) Monopolistic competition in a large economy with differentiated commodities, *Review of Economic Studies,* **46,** 1–30.

Hart, O. (1982) Perfect competition and optimal product differentiation, in Mas-Collel (ed) *The Non-Cooperative Foundations of Perfect Competition,* Academic Press.

Hathaway, N. and **Rickard, J.** (1979) Equilibria of price-setting and quantity setting duopolies, *Economic Letters,* **3,** 133–7.

Ireland, N. (1986) *Product Differentiation and the Non-Price Decisions of Firms,* Blackwell: Oxford.

Klemperer, P. and **Meyer, M.** (1986) Price competition vs quantity competition: the role of uncertainty, *Rand Journal of Economics,* **17** No.4.

Kreps, D. and **Scheinkman, J.** (1983) Quantity pre-commitment and Bertrand competition yield Cournot outcomes, *Bell Journal of Economics,* **14,** 326–37.

Kreps, D. and **Wilson, R.** (1982a) Sequential equilibria, *Econometrica,* **50,** 863–94.

Kreps, D. and **Wilson, R.** (1982b) Reputation and imperfect information, *Journal of Economic Theory,* **27,** 253–9.

Kreps, D., **Milgrom, P.** and **Wilson, R.** (1982) Rational cooperation in the finitely repeated prisoner's dilemma, *Journal of Economic Theory,* **27,** 245–52.

Lockwood, B. (1984) Perfect equilibria in repeated games with discounting, *Cambridge University Economic Theory Discussion Paper 65.*

Lockwood, B. (1987) Some recent developments in the theory of non-cooperative games and its economic applications, in Pearce and Rau (eds) *Economic Perspectives.*

Luce, R. and **Raiffa, H.** (1957) *Games and Decisions,* Wiley.

Lyons, B. (1986) Mixed-motive duopoly, Mimeo, UEA.

Marris, R. (1964) *Managerial Capitalism,* Macmillan.

Milgrom, P. and **Roberts, J.** (1982a) Predation, reputation and entry deterrence, *Journal of Economic Theory,* **27,** 280–312.

Milgrom, P. and **Roberts, J.** (1982b) Limit pricing and entry under incomplete information: an equilibrium analysis, *Econometrica,* **50,** 443–55.

Radner, R. (1986) Repeated principle agent games with discounting, *Econometrica,* **53,** 1173–97.

Rubenstein, A. (1979) Equilibrium in supergames with the overtaking criterion, *Journal of Economic Theory,* **21,** 1–9.

Selten, R. (1965) Spieltheoretic Behandlung eines Oligopolmodells mit Nachtragetrgheit, *Zeitschrift fur die Gesamte Staatswissenschaft,* **121,** 301–24, 667–89.

Shubik, M. (1959) *Strategy and Market Structure,* John Wiley and Sons: New York.

Singh, N. and **Vives, X.** (1984) Price and quantity competition in a differentiated duopoly, *Rand Journal of Economics,* **15,** 540–54.

Venables, A. (1985) International trade, industrial policy, and imperfect competition, *CEPR Discussion Paper 74.*

Vickers, J. (1985a) Delegation and the theory of the firm, *Economic Journal,* **95,** 138–47.

Vickers, J. (1985b) Strategic competition among the few — some recent developments, *Oxford Journal of Economic Policy.*

Vives, X. (1985a) On the efficiency of Cournot and Bertrand equilibria with product differentiation, *Journal of Economic Theory,* **36,** 166–75.

Vives, X. (1985b) Nash equilibrium with monotone best responses, Mimeo, University of Pennsylvania.

Vives, X. (1986) Commitment, flexibility, and market outcome, *International Journal of Industrial Organisation,* **2,** 217–30.

von Stackelberg, H. (1934) *Marketform und Gleichgewicht,* Vienna and Berlin.

Yarrow, G. (1985) Measures of monopoly welfare loss in markets with differentiated products, manuscript, *Journal of Industrial Economics,* **33,** 515–30.

CHAPTER FIVE

Competition policy and the structure–performance paradigm

Paul Geroski[1a]

1. Introduction

While it is by no means the only influence, the 'structure–performance' paradigm has long been an important element of the case for competition policy. This influential body of thought stresses the importance of various structural characteristics of markets as determinants of price and non-price behaviour, and thus ultimately of industry performance. In calling attention to the environment within which market conduct occurs, it has directed attention away from factors internal to firms and towards the stable and exogenous features of markets which are thought to constrain and condition the behaviour of all industry members to an overwhelming degree. Both as a research programme and as a guide to action, the 'structure–performance' paradigm has been very successful. It has provided an organising set of ideas, an impressive body of empirical results suggesting that market structure is systematically linked with market performance, and has led policy makers to be concerned with the level of and increase in industry concentration in the formulation of their policy objectives. It has, however, not been without its critics, and even those who work within this intellectual tradition have recently modified the line of argument in various important ways. This survey identifies a number of the problems, new approaches to solving them, and new interpretations which have emerged in recent studies, and indicates how they may affect the anti-trust policy conclusions and recommendations that emerge from this intellectual tradition.

The organization of the survey is as follows. Section 2 states the basic structuralist hypothesis, outlines the empirical methodology typically used to examine it, and sketches the policy conclusions which appear to follow from it. Section 3 examines three developments and modifications of the basic methodology, and highlights what seem to be the important modifications in policy conclusions that follow from them. The discussion of sections 2 and 3 roughly characterises the position a persuaded structuralist might adopt towards his/her empirical work and its policy implications. Section 4 looks at three of the more important problems which need to be answered by proponents of this position. In each case, some possible resolutions are examined, and the major implications for anti-trust policy that result from these objections are summarised. Partly as a result of the perceived need to answer problems of this form and partly because interesting research generates its own dynamic motion, there have been a number of interesting innovations in methodology in this area recently. Section 5 highlights the more important ones and discusses the policy questions which seem to follow from each development. Section 6 contains some brief conclusions.

2. The basic structuralist hypothesis

The basic 'structure–performance' paradigm isolates market structure as the major exogenous variable of interest because it is thought to be the ultimate determinant of market performance. That is, it looks to structural factors like market concentration and barriers to entry to provide most of the explanation of differences in profitability across industries. There are, of course, other views that one can take. A hint of an alternative paradigm can be found in the experimental work surveyed by Plott (1982), which suggests that it may be the methods by which prices are set rather than the structural conditions in which this occurs which are of major importance. Another alternative has emerged from recent theoretical developments in industrial organisation which have stressed the importance of conduct and strategic activity, arguing that any given set of structural conditions can give rise to a rich variety of alternative behavioural patterns.[1] Nevertheless, it is interesting to focus on the role played by market structure, defined as that vector of stable industry attributes which are thought to condition the price and non-price behaviour, that is the conduct, of industry members. Of the fairly wide range of possibilities that present themselves as candidates for this role, interest has in practice centred upon variables such as the number of firms operating in the market, or on indices of market concentration which reflect the size distribution of firms. Either way, the basic notion is that the fewer the firms or the more dominating are the leading few, the easier will be tacit or overt collusion over price and, perhaps, other choice variables. The next step in the argument links such conduct to market performance. If we define market performance relatively narrowly in terms of the elevation of prices above marginal costs,[2] then it is clear that by affecting market conduct in a manner which facilitates collusion, market structure ultimately affects market performance. The basic structuralist hypothesis is a strong version of this argument which tends to see market structure as *the* main determinant of conduct, and hence as the important ultimate cause of acceptable or unacceptable market performance.

The policy interest in the structure–conduct–performance paradigm springs from a recognition of the allocative inefficiencies and possible distributional distortions that arise when price exceeds marginal costs. Such an outcome involves a redistribution of consumer surplus from consumers to producers of size equal to the gap between price and marginal cost on all units of output sold, and a dead-weight loss of consumer surplus occasioned by the exit from the market of marginal consumers. Essentially, those consumers who still elect to purchase the good must pay higher price and so forgo consumption in other areas, while those who leave prefer not to make this sacrifice. Since neither of these sacrifices would need to be made were prices set equal to marginal costs, it is clear that elevating prices above marginal costs creates unnecessary losses to consumers. However, it is not entirely clear that the whole of the redistribution of surplus from consumers to producers reduces welfare. There are two important caveats. Firstly, if these profits are used to finance research and development, then losses of consumer surplus in the current period may be compensated for by gains in the near future from new products, or the economising on resources used in production. Here what matters is not only whether profits are spent on research and development efficiently and in sufficient quantities, but also on whether the ultimate gains to consumers arrive sufficiently quickly and whether other investment possibilities would have yielded more gains. However, not all such expenditure raises consumer welfare. To the extent that resources are spent simply to acquire monopoly positions, then consumers definitely lose. This is discussed in Tullock (1967), Posner (1975), Hillman (1984), Hillman and Katz (1984), Lyons (1986), and others, with much interest centring on the proposition that competition among rent seekers will lead to the full quantity of monopoly profits being squandered in pursuit of monopoly positions. This loss arises because such expenditures simply secure profits for those who control the property rights to monopoly positions, and do not lead to new products or more efficient production processes. Secondly, it is generally agreed that there are situations (frequently characterised by production with economies of scale) where one might be willing to 'trade-off' some dead-weight loss for the superior cost efficiency a monopolistic market structure may bring. That is, to achieve the productivity gains associated with large-scale operations in a narrow market, one may be forced to tolerate the existence of a monopolist in that market. To obtain maximum social gains by avoiding the elevation of price that this can be expected to occasion, it is necessary to regulate that monopolist. If such regulation is not feasible or is too costly, the gains in social resources saved from large-scale production must exceed the consumer welfare losses caused by high prices if monopolisation is to be defended on efficiency grounds; this trade-off is outlined in Williamson (1968); Cowling *et al.* (1980) is a good illustration of its application in evaluating a number of horizontal mergers in the UK.[3] Despite these two qualifications, it remains the case that large deviations of price from marginal cost do give serious cause for concern, and the appeal of the structuralist hypothesis is that it suggests that the source of this problem is fairly easily identified, being most likely to appear in industries with highly concentrated market structures.

Following the classic study of Bain (1951), empirical examination of the basic structuralist hypothesis has involved looking for a systematic association between average industry profits and levels of industry concentration. Denoting the average level of profits in industry j by π_j, and the level of industry concentration by C_j, the structuralist hypothesis has been most commonly tested using a cross-section regression model of the form

$$\pi_j = \beta_0 + \beta_1 C_j + \mu_j \qquad [1]$$

where μ_j is a residual summarising 'all other factors'. Estimating [1] across a range of industries j in a given year is a natural way to ascertain the extent to which variations in industry performance are attributable to differences in structure. If the estimated value of $\beta_1 > 0$, then it is natural to conclude that firms in more highly concentrated industries are relatively more successful in raising prices above competitive levels; i.e. that they have market power. Thus, considered as a hypothesis to be tested, the structure–conduct–performance paradigm seems to resolve itself into a causal association between the level of industry profits on average and industry concentration levels.[4] While not as precise an examination of pricing conduct as can be found in case studies, this cross-section regression formulation does at least enable one to make rough-and-ready generalisations about pricing behaviour which are applicable to a wide range of industries. As such, it carries two rather strong implications for anti-trust policy.

In the first place, verification of (or, more accurately, failure to reject) the profits–concentration hypothesis suggests an important role for structure as a *guide* to policy intervention. The basic causal nature of the hypothesis naturally transforms itself into the notion of using market structure and, in particular, the level of industry concentration, as a rough-and-ready predictor of performance. This focuses scarce anti-trust resources on the relatively inexpensive task of examining only industries with high levels of concentration (and their likely change following, say, a horizontal merger). Having identified potential problem industries, the bulk of anti-trust resources can be devoted to the necessary and far more time-consuming task of examining industry pricing practices in greater detail. However, the structure–conduct–performance hypothesis carries a second, rather more profound and controversial implication for policy. Since structure is the ultimate determinant of industry performance, then it clearly serves as a *goal* for policy intervention. There is obviously no sense in formulating a policy action directed towards altering 'endogenous' variables, and it is clearly very difficult to construct a wide-ranging and easily applicable policy based on the (in general) not easily observable features of industry conduct. The great simplification introduced by the structuralist version of the structure–conduct–performance hypothesis is to suggest the sufficiency of attacking highly concentrated market structures. Again, in a rough-and-ready sense, a policy of deconcentration, or, at least, a policy preventing mergers which lead to unduly high levels of concentration, can be expected to remove important structural conditions which facilitate overt or tacit collusion, and so open up the possibility that the natural rivalrous behaviour of firms will compete away excess profits and lower prices towards marginal costs. Needless to say, such a policy should be completed by detailed and more industry-specific injunctions of particular types of competitive practices which may persist even after industry market structure has reached 'workably competitive' levels. Nevertheless, it is clear that the primary focus of policy ought to be structural.

3. Some subsequent developments

The basic exercise of searching for a significant relationship in the data between average industry profitability and industry concentration has now been repeated sufficiently often for all but the most obdurate to be persuaded that more highly concentrated industries are generally associated with rather higher levels of profits than less concentrated ones. Most of this work has been done for the US on post-war data for large samples of manufacturing industries at highly disaggregated levels, and good surveys of most of the literature can be found in Cubbin (1986), Schmalensee (1986b), Weiss (1974), and Scherer (1980: Ch.9); Jacquemin and de Jong (1977) look at this material from a European perspective, and highlight specifically European work. Critical examinations of the methodology of this work include Phillips (1976), Cowling (1976), Sawyer (1982) and Cooley *et al.* (1984). This weight of evidence has been taken by most to provide a solid empirical support for the types of anti-trust policies indicated above. There are three subsequent developments in the literature which have served to refine these policy recommendations in important ways: the 'critical concentration ratio' hypothesis, the 'full structural' hypothesis and the 'appropriate' concentration measure.

(a) THE CRITICAL CONCENTRATION LEVEL HYPOTHESIS

The basic form in which Bain tested the structure–conduct–performance hypotheses in his pioneering 1951 study was fundamentally non-linear. Indeed, he found little compelling evidence to suggest the kind of linear association between industry profitability and concentration suggested in eqn [1]. In his view, '... the major distinction ... is not between industries of oligopolistic and atomistic structure, but between the more highly concentrated oligopolies and all other industries' (1951: 194, footnote 5). This argument entails a straightforward generalization of [1] in which the main parameter of interest, β_1, is allowed to vary across industries. The simplest version of this hypothesis posits two regimes: 'highly concentrated oligopolies' where market power is translated into high price–cost margins and so $\beta_1 = \bar{\beta} > 0$, and 'all other industries' where conditions are fairly competitive and so $\beta_1 \simeq 0$. If the critical concentration level which separates these two regimes is C^*, then the critical concentration level hypothesis can be written as

$$\pi_j = \beta_0 + \beta_{1j}C_j + \mu_j \qquad [2]$$

where $\beta_{1j} = \bar{\beta}$ if $C_j \geq C^*$ and $\beta_{1j} =$ if $C_j < C^*$.

Empirically, Bain discovered that if an industry's eight-firm concentration ratio exceeded 70 per cent, it would enjoy average profits of about 12 per cent, a little over five percentage points higher than would have been the case had the eight-firm concentration ratio fallen below this critical threshold. Somewhat neglected in the great rush of subsequent literature, this 'critical concentration level' hypothesis has nevertheless attracted a certain amount of interest (e.g. see Geithman *et al.* 1981; White 1976; Meechan and Duchesneau 1973; Dalton and Penn 1976). A particularly interesting application is that of Bradburd and Over (1982), who posit two critical thresholds depending on whether industry concentration levels are rising or falling. Of course, there need not be only two types of competitive 'regime', and Geroski (1981) builds up an association between profits and concentration as a series of linear segments which, in effect, allows the data to reveal a number of 'critical concentration levels'. While linear regressions have generally found positive and significant associations between profits and concentration, the overall strength of the relation has not generally been impressive. Modifications like the critical concentration level hypothesis have frequently been rather more successful in this respect. As a rough generalisation, there seems to be very little evidence to suggest that linear associations are anything like the best descriptions of the data possible. Indeed, some of the results suggest that high excess profits are characteristic of only a relatively few, very highly concentrated industries.

This work carries an important implication for anti-trust policy. In particular, it lays to rest the false optimism that intervention rules can be tied in a simple way to industry concentration levels. A simple rule globally applied to all industries (such as 'the higher the level of concentration, the more likely the need for intervention') seems to be dangerously simple. At the very least, one can often classify industries into two sorts, 'cooperative' and 'competitive', by using a critical concentration level. Those industries above the critical threshold are likely to be worth a closer look and, should structural manipulation be deemed necessary, it must be sufficiently extensive to take them down again below the dividing line. It also follows that what is as important to test as the association between concentration and profitability is the shape that the association takes. That is, one must *derive* a policy rule from the data by testing for the right functional description of it, and must avoid *imposing* a rule (e.g. a linear rule) on the data.

(b) THE FULL STRUCTURALIST HYPOTHESIS

So far, we have presumed that the relatively rich and complex notion of market structure could be adequately represented by a single variable like a concentration index. In fact, Bain (1951: 295) argued that this would be the case only if one holds '... demand and cost conditions and entry conditions constant' across industries. The problem that arises here is that the residual in [1], μ, which describes 'all other things', may contain components correlated with C. If this were the case, then estimates of β would be biased. That is, one would erroneously attribute to industry concentration the effects that emanated from these other factors. Following the influential paper of Comanor and Wilson (1967), the structure–conduct–performance paradigm has most often been implemented in regressions in which concentration and a host of other factors are used jointly to explain industry profitability. Thus, it is generally supposed that

$$\mu_j = \sum_k \alpha_k x_{kj} + \epsilon_j \qquad [3]$$

where the k variables x_j are the important causes of non-constancy in demand, cost, and entry conditions which may be correlated with C_j, and ϵ_j is a residual. Numerous variables have been used to proxy cost, demand and entry conditions. Trade variables are likely to be particularly important, particularly in a European context (see Jacquemin 1982, and Caves 1985, for surveys, and, for some measurement of industry specific, trade-induced profit differentials over time, see de Ghellinck *et al.* 1983). Advertising has always proved to be an important variable since its introduction be Comanor and Wilson, and is, perhaps, the most robust element of [3]. Other popular conditioning variables include average industry growth, industry diversification, and measures of minimum efficient scale. Equation [3] embodies the notion that market structure is a complex, multi-dimensional phenomenon inadequately described by just a concentration index. What is more, and what is worse from the point of view of the implementation of policy, is the almost immediate corollary that those various elements of market structure are all interdependent. On the one hand, this leads to purely statistical problems arising from multi-collinearity (especially prevalent between measures of minimum efficient scale and industry concentration) which makes it difficult to attribute effects to specific variables. On the other hand, interdependence can also arise from mutual causation, and this had led some scholars to look at simultaneous equation models (Strickland and Weiss 1976; Martin 1979, 1980; Geroski 1982c). In these studies, entry conditions, cost conditions, demand conditions and industry concentration are seen to be mutually interacting, and jointly determine industry profitability.

In principle, this extension significantly modifies the policy recommendations which emerge from the basic structuralist hypothesis. Evidently, one can no longer suppose that concentration indices taken alone are a good guide for policy intervention. Further, it is no longer obvious that structural manipulations of concentration levels alone are the best policy response to the existence of persistently high levels of excess profits. It is difficult, however, to know just how hard to push these conclusions. While in some long-run sense the various dimensions of market structure clearly determine each other, there may still be scope for substantial short-run gains through manipulating only concentration levels. Further, there are some fairly well-known patterns of association between levels of concentration and other elements of market structure which enable one to use concentration indices to guide intervention with some awareness about the total effects such manipulations have on performance via other elements of market structure. Subject to fairly obvious qualifications, this second extension of the structuralist hypothesis suggests a somewhat wider vector of guiding instruments to use and a wider range of structural manipulations open up themselves to policy manipulation. However, the basic presumption of working from the exogenous elements of market structure towards performance remains intact, if used with care.

The much more substantive policy implication that follows from this work concerns entry. Many of the additional elements of market structure introduced in the full structuralist hypothesis purport to describe the structural barriers to entry which enable a profitable position to be maintained more or less persistently. This generally accounts for the inclusion of advertising and minimum efficient scale proxies; import intensity is, of course, a direct measure of foreign sourced competition. Entry is often thought of as the natural market response to the problem of excess profits, and it is desirable to base an anti-trust policy on it, strengthening its force and impact if possible. Following from the commonplace observation that a monopoly unprotected from entry will either not remain a monopoly for long, or will at least fail to achieve anything like full monopoly profits, this observation suggests a shift in emphasis from a 'concentration level policy' towards one which uses the level of entry barriers to guide intervention designed largely to lower these barriers.[5]

(c) THE APPROPRIATE CONCENTRATION MEASURE

Let us return to the basic structuralist hypothesis embodied in eqn [1] for a final set of remarks. In that approach, market structure has come to be thought of primarily in terms of the level of market concentration. However, there are a number of ways one might choose to measure market concentration and this raises the natural question of whether it matters if one uses a five-firm concentration ratio or, say, a Herfindahl index of concentration. There has been much debate on this question, and it has largely been treated as an empirical issue.[6] Although it is well known that various concentration measures are fairly highly correlated with each other, there nevertheless appear to be good grounds for thinking that the choice of an appropriate index may still be important (see Schmalansee 1977; Kwoka 1979, 1981; Geroski 1983a). In particular, any policy which is geared towards reducing concentration levels below a certain level and which has a differential impact on large and small firms is going to be fairly sensitive in detail towards the choice of which concentration index to use as a policy guide. The implication is that one must, as it were, go *within* an industry and consider in detail where and to what extent policy ought to be applied. This, in turn, raises the idea that an appropriate policy ought to use *inter-industry* work as a stepping-off point which is understood to require subsequent *intra-industry* analysis. This is a theme we shall return to below.

4. Some problems

The structuralist hypothesis, even with its modifications, has not, of course, been without its critics. Given the oft replicated positive and significant correlation found between concentration (and other dimensions of market structure) and average industry profitability,[7] much of the substantive criticism of the structure–conduct–performance hypothesis has turned on the interpretation of these correlations. The first two topics of discussion in this section cover the two most important of these, the market power–efficiency ambiguity, and the question of endogeneity. A third problem which is of great importance is the question of whether inter-industry analysis is, in fact, the appropriate level of aggregation at which to analyse the problems of monopoly power.

   Before we pursue these issues, however, it is necessary to develop a somewhat more precise interpretation of the parameter β_1 in eqn [1]. Suppose that firms $i = 1, \ldots, N$ in industry j produce a homogeneous good with demand $P = P(Q)$, where $Q \equiv \Sigma \, Q_i$ is industry output and Q_i the level of output selected by firm i. Further, suppose that all firms have fixed assets of F and produce at constant unit costs, c_i. The important calculations that firm i must make when it chooses its output level are the output choices of its $(N-1)$ rivals, and how their choices might change were firm i to change its production programme. This latter response, the change in Q occasioned by a change in Q_i, is often called i's *conjectural variation*. If $dQ/dQ_1 \equiv \lambda_i$ is zero, then firm i expects no change in industry output (and thus price) to result from a change in its production programme. It is natural to describe such beliefs as 'price-taking' behaviour, and to expect a competitive outcome to emerge if all firms had such beliefs. Clearly, this situation could be expected to prevail if N were 'large'. By contrast, if λ_i is close to unity, then industry output rises and falls as if i were the only member of the industry, and this apparent control over price would enable it to elevate prices somewhat above marginal costs.

Let us assume that $\lambda_i = \lambda$ for simplicity, that is, that all firms have the same beliefs. Then, using conjectural variations, all the variable components of firm i's profit function,

$$\pi_i(Q_i) = P(Q)Q_i - cQ_i - F \qquad [4]$$

can be linked to its choice variable Q_i, and it becomes possible to describe rational choice in a simple fashion. The first-order conditions for profit maximisation are

$$\lambda P'(Q)Q_i + P(Q) - c_i = 0 \qquad [5]$$

which can be rearranged as

$$\frac{P - c_i}{P} = \frac{P'(Q)}{P} \lambda Q S_i \qquad [6]$$

where $S_i \equiv Q_i/Q$ is firm i's market share. Weighting by market share and summing [6] over all firms yields

$$\pi_j = \frac{\lambda}{\eta} H_j \qquad [7]$$

where π_j is the average industry price–cost margin, $\eta \equiv (-P'(Q)Q/P)^{-1}$ is the elasticity of industry demand, and $H_j \equiv \sum_i S_i^2$ is the index of concentration.[8] Comparing eqn [7] with eqn [1] suggests that estimated values of β_1 can be interpreted as average measures of λ/η across all industries, and so one expects to observe $\beta_1 = 0$ if competitive conditions prevail on average across industries j. This, of course, implies that $\beta_1 > 0$ signals resource misallocation.

This more rigorous interpretation of the parameter of interest, β_1, in [1] is useful for several reasons. For example, it provides an obvious interpretation of the critical concentration ratio hypothesis in eqn [2]. If $C_j < C^*$, then we expect firms to be competitive, so that $\lambda = 0$. This implies $\beta_1 = 0$. If, by contrast $C_j > C^*$, then we expect some degree of monopoly to emerge from collusion facilitated by these market conditions. This implies $\lambda > 0$, so that $\beta_1 > 0$. However, the principal reason for elaborating this interpretation of β_1 is that much recent controversy has centred on whether it is the correct one, or whether β_1 might reflect something other than the exercise of monopoly power.

(a) THE MARKET POWER–EFFICIENCY AMBIGUITY

The simplest, most straightforward response to the empirical findings and policy implications discussed above is to assert that positive and significant correlations between profits and concentration merely reflect a superior efficiency of large firms which are, in consequence, rewarded with high profits and large market shares. Equation [5] indicates that the optimal choice of output by firm i depends on rivals' choices, λ, on marginal costs c_i and on the parameters of the demand function. Holding all other factors constant, a lower level of c_i leads to a higher Q_i and hence S_i, and so to a higher level of $(P-c_i)/P$. Hence, the superior relative efficiency of a few firms can increase both industry concentration and average profitability simultaneously. The precise details of the argument can take one of two forms. The first path is to commence from the observation that extensive economies of scale imply high concentration levels, and also generate an equilibrium in which firms lucky enough to be participating in the industry can earn excess profits due to the natural barrier to entry that such economies represent. There is clearly something to this argument, although the importance of such economies is frequently exaggerated; for a survey of the empirical work, see the excellent discussion in Scherer (1980: 81–118). In general, and particularly for the US, there is some agreement that concentration levels are in excess of those strictly implied by the need to achieve full realisation of economies. Also, what are frequently referred to as scale economies are often pecuniary in nature, and thus do not represent a substantive saving of society's scarce resources (Scherer 1974 – McGee 1974, is a useful contrast in views on these points). Nevertheless, this argument represents a substantive caveat to the earlier policy analysis, and suggests that anti-trust policy may take the form of a 'trade-off' between the efficiency gains and the welfare losses due to excess monopoly power (as discussed above in section 2).

The second path is a little different. To the extent that average industry profits are dominated by the profits of large firms and to the extent that such firms are large and profitable due to their superior efficiency (reflected in a lower c_i), then the observed correlation between concentration and industry average profitability may well be due solely to this superior efficiency; this point was originally made by Demsetz (1974). This argument is obviously important and directly challenges the interpretation of β_1 developed above. However, Caves and Pugel (1980), Schmalensee (1986a), Mueller (1981), Clarke *et al.* (1984), and others have questioned its empirical validity using various alternative tests. These tests all hinge on the notion that if superior efficiency does explain the observed correlation between industry concentration and average profits, then the profitability of small firms in highly concentrated industries should be no different from the profitability of small firms in less highly concentrated industries. The power to raise prices is, by contrast, a public good that ought to bring benefits to all firms in the highly concentrated industries where it is exercised. This implies that the profits of small firms in highly concentrated industries ought to exceed the levels achieved by small firms in less concentrated industries. In a somewhat different type of test, Salinger (1984) has recently suggested that the market power argument applies only where barriers to entry exist. This leads to an extension analogous to [2]: $\beta_{1j} = \bar{\beta}$ if industry entry barriers are substantial, and $\beta_{1j} = 0$ otherwise. Since the differential efficiency argument does not involve barriers, this gives a basis for comparing the two interpretations.

In fact, despite first appearances, this differential efficiency argument represents only a qualification of the conventional conclusions. Even if one were to concede that the correlation is entirely due to superior efficiency and that no market power is being exercised, there still remains a policy problem because the limited diffusion of such superior techniques is clearly sub-optimal: industry price remains too high. In fact, 'superior efficiency' could arise from all sorts of merely pecuniary economies which do not obviously lower social costs. Perhaps the most obvious of these are the capital-raising advantages that large firms seem to enjoy (e.g. see Prais 1976: Ch.5; Reinganum and Smith 1983; and others). In any case, it is hard to imagine a firm enjoying superior efficiency not translating that advantage into some elevation of prices above marginal costs, and this rules any of the strong versions of this argument well out of the bounds of plausibility.

The resolution of the ambiguities raised here concerning profits–concentration regressions is, in principle, straightforward. The problem arises largely because one is examining propositions about pricing behaviour by looking at profits. Theory suggests that prices will be raised relative to costs. Since it is generally difficult to observe prices and costs, profits are used as a proxy. There has, in fact, been substantial controversy about how best to measure the dependent variable, profitability, in these types of studies. See the discussions and references in Weiss (1974) and Scherer (1980: Ch.9). Recently, Fisher and McGowan (1983) have regenerated controversy on this subject with a number of somewhat extravagant claims about the difficulties of drawing conclusions about economic profits from accounting data (see Kay and Mayer 1986 for a careful reassessment of these points). Partly in response to these problems, there has also been some recent work using Tobin's q rather than profits as a dependent variable (see Salinger 1984, and the references cited therein), the idea here being that Tobin's q, being based on stock market valuations, is more likely than accounting data to pick up expected future monopoly profits. The dispute about the relative merits of price–cost margins, rates of return on shareholders' equity, Tobin's q, and so on, obscures the point that it is the relative deviation of prices from marginal costs that is thought to be affected by monopoly. That is, one should examine the effect of monopoly on prices, holding marginal costs constant. Profits are not really the appropriate variable to use in examining this conditional prediction, as they do not satisfactorily hold constant the various influences that market structure may have on costs. Clearly, bias is bound to result if variations in marginal costs across industries are correlated with market structure variables of interest, and this means that β_1 will reflect more than the effects of monopolistic pricing. The solution to this classic measurement errors problem involves trying to develop independent estimates of industry marginal costs, and then examining the departure of prices from these marginal costs at observed industry outputs. However, it is virtually impossible to develop satisfactory measures of price, let alone marginal costs, across a wide range of industries. Thus, in resolving this 'market power or efficiency' ambiguity, one is likely to have to trade-off the ability to make broad statements applicable to a wide range of industries with the ability to make fairly precise, bias-free statements applicable to only a handful of industries. In short, the major import of this type of criticism to traditional profits–concentration regressions suggests a reorientation away from the broad brush of inter-industry work towards the finer analysis made possible by intra-industry analysis.

(b) THE QUESTION OF ENDOGENEITY

The question of endogeneity presents a much more substantive problem for structuralist thinking on anti-trust policy. The model set out in eqns [4]–[6] describes a firm's output or price choices given their cost functions, demand functions, and the expectations they hold regarding rivals' behaviour. In equilibrium, market price and the outputs of all firms are jointly determined by the solution of [5] for all $i = 1, \ldots, N$ industry members. But this implies that both profits and industry concentration are endogenous variables whose values in different industries depend on the ultimate exogenous variables of costs, demand, and the expectations held by firms in those industries (which, in turn, may be affected by post-market structure and conduct). That is, industry concentration as a summary statistic reflecting current output flow choices cannot be considered as a causal determinant of current period profits, since both are jointly determined by the exogenous variables of the problem (see Geroski 1982a; Clarke and Davies 1982; Donsimoni et al. 1984).

The neglect of this rather simple point may have originated from a too rapid translation of the basic structural hypothesis into operational form. There is no doubt that the ultimate determinants of behaviour are structural, although one may legitimately quibble with how tightly structure really determines conduct. The problem lies in the use of concentration measures, which are defined in terms of current output flows to reflect these ultimate exogenous structural attributes of an industry. The implications for anti-trust policy are fairly sweeping. Since one cannot reasonably give a causal interpretation to the correlation between profits and concentration, one certainly cannot use a positive and significant correlation in the usual regressions (i.e. $\beta_1 > 0$) to make simple policy recommendations in the form of manipulating market structure. While one might, nevertheless, be tempted into hazarding some policy recommendations in the form of structural intervention, the justification for this is a good deal more tortuous than in the basic structuralist hypothesis. Policy must be directed at the exogenous determinants of performance and this means that it must look at the basic conditions of costs, demand, market conduct, and potential entry. The old and attractive notion that acting on market structure in a broad way, and avoiding the problem of trying to operate on conduct (which is both difficult to observe directly and hard to alter by anything other than very detailed policy intervention) would seem to rest on a very insecure basis.[9] It may well be the case that systematic associations between conduct and structure, however defined, exist, but it is probably the case that a correlation between concentration and profits casts very little light on it.

It will not do, however, to push this point too far. Since concentration and profits are jointly determined, it is not sensible to use concentration indices as a predictor of performance. But, being jointly determined, they both clearly contain similar information on the exogenous variables of costs, demand, and market conduct. Thus, one can say that when profits are difficult to observe, an appropriately chosen concentration index may be a good proxy for unobserved market performance. This is, in a sense, consistent with the notion that concentration might be a good guide for policy. Subject to the proviso that it is appropriately chosen to reflect the conduct characteristic of the industry and that it is chosen to maximise its worth as a proxy, then use of a concentration index is probably a good way to screen large numbers of industries, prior to a more detailed analysis when performance cannot easily be observed.

(c) INTER-INDUSTRY OR INTRA-INDUSTRY ANALYSIS?

Suppose, for a moment, that one accepts that it is reasonable to use levels of industry concentration, among other variables, to try to identify industries which are likely to be engaged in monopolistic pricing abuses. This could be consistent with a number of alternative views about what is really happening *within* the industries concerned, and, in particular, with how the gains from monopolistic pricing are distributed among industry members. One might argue that all industry members share the benefits from output restriction, so that high levels of concentration identify *broad pools* of excess profits across industries. Alternatively, one might take the view that only the largest firms within industries benefit from monopolistic practices, so that high levels of concentration point to the possible existence of rather *narrow pockets* of market power within different sectors. Given that many of these large firms are likely to be diversified, is there any point at all in proceeding with analysis at the industry level? To put the same question another way, is it the case that the intra-industry variation in profits statistically dwarfs inter-industry variations in average industry profits?

There are a number of recent studies that seem to suggest that intra-industry analysis may be an attractive alternative to conventional inter-industry work. Equations [6] and [7] provide a helpful way of interpreting much of this work. Rather than summing eqn [6] across all firms i in industry j to obtain an industry-level relation like [7], one can recognize that [6] is a structure–performance relation expressed at the firm level, relating firm i's market share to its price–cost margin. Hence the firm-level regression analogue of [1] is

$$\pi_i = \gamma_0 + \gamma_1 S_i + \mu_i \qquad [8]$$

where γ_1 can be interpreted as the ratio of firm i's conjecture to the elasticity of demand it faces. If $\gamma_1 > 0$, then clearly firms in industry j with larger market shares gain a larger share of the gains from monopoly pricing: if $\gamma_1 = 0$ (as when $\lambda=0$), then all share such gains more or less equally. Equation [8] applies only to firms i in industry j, and much work in this area has broadened this model into a combination of inter- and intra-industry analysis by using a combination of [1] and [8] to look at the profit, π_{ij}, of various (usually large) firms i in industries j.

$$\pi_{ij} = \beta_0 + \beta_1 C_j + \gamma_1 S_i + \mu_{ij} \qquad [9]$$

This type of model emerges, for example, if one allows the average profits per firm, γ_0, in industry j to vary across industries in response to variations in the level of industry concentration. Using models like [9], a number of scholars have examined inter-industry variations in firm-level profitability, and have discovered that market share is an apparently far more important determinant than industry concentration. That is, generally they have found that $\gamma_1 > 0$ and $\beta_1 = 0$ or, occasionally, $\beta_1 < 0$, and that while γ_1 is almost invariably significant, β_1 is generally not. (See, among others, Shepherd 1972; Gale 1972; Hall and Weiss 1967; Mueller 1986; Porter 1979; Martin 1983; Ravenscroft 1983).[10] Since market shares and industry concentration are not independent variables, it is very hard to read anything substantive about the size of monopoly profits across industries from these studies; one certainly cannot say that industry level concentration is irrelevent. It would seem more natural to read the coefficient on market shares (i.e. γ_1) as describing the distribution of monopoly rewards within industries, subject to the 'market power or efficiency' caveat raised earlier, leading one to the conclusion that it is large-sized firms which gain the preponderant share of such gains. The fact that it is market share and not concentration which seems to account for much of the variation in profitability would seem to suggest that the 'shared asset' of monopoly power is so unevenly distributed within industries that it might as well be considered as largely a private good exploited and appropriated by the dominant firms in markets.

This type of conclusion carries fairly strong implications for anti-trust policy. Systematically unequal distributions of power across industries direct attention away from basing policy at an industry level. Instead, the natural policy course is to focus attention in the first instance at the level of the firm. Keeping within the broad spirit of the structuralist philosophy, but accepting the caveats discussed above, one inclines naturally towards a policy of monitoring firms which are large relative to the markets in which they operate.[11] This step can be thought of in terms of sheer economy of effort. If it really is the case that market power is distributed in a very skewed manner within industries, then analysis at the industry level introduces a lot of more or less extraneous noise. It seems more reasonable to concentrate in the first instance on large, dominating firms and then to spread out within industries, following such interactions with rival firms as is necessary. Rather than monitoring events in several hundred industries using rather rough-and-ready indices of market power, regular monitoring of the several hundred largest firms in the economy using the altogether more precise firm-level data which exists may not only enable one to focus on market power more exactly, but may also be rather more economical.

5. Some recent developments

There is a persistent drift in the remarks that we have been making whose threads should be gathered together before proceeding to highlight some recent work of interest. Clearly there are several reasons for treating structuralist anti-trust policy recommendations with some caution. The basic goal of developing simple predictors of industry performance from exogeneous structural traits of an industry seems not to have lived up to its promise, for at least two reasons. First, the association between structure as conventionally defined and performance is subject to several ambiguities in interpretation, and certainly cannot be given a single causal interpretation. Second, it is not even clear that prior analysis at the industry level is the best route to follow because it is important to go underneath the correlation to be sure that it really reflects market power and because the distribution of power within industries may be such as to limit interest to the behaviour of a relatively small set of the industry members. For those who do not wish to follow the argument so far, the most tenable position to take seems to be a kind of two-step screening procedure. That is, first one scans industries using rather simple screening rules, perhaps built around notions of critical levels of an appropriate concentration ratio and high entry barriers indicating particularly high levels of excess profits. Then one goes beneath these indicators to investigate the precise causes of such excess profits and their distribution within the industry. Given the existence of abuses among several industry members, one is then in a position to devise a policy to affect industry conduct, and so ameliorate performance.[12]

In my view, the likely gains from such an exercise are perhaps not overwhelming. A reasonable case can be made to concentrate policy resources at the level of the firm by focusing on large, dominant firms, and then, in cases where a firm's interaction with other firms is particularly extensive, perhaps to expand outwards towards the industry level. What follows highlights three further strands of empirical work which are germane in this context. The appeal of this newer work depends on the level at which one feels that policy ought to be directed, and the various developments will be taken up in an order which starts with those more appropriate to an industry-level policy.

(a) ESTIMATING AND INFERRING CONDUCT

Dissatisfaction with simple correlations between concentration indices and average industry profitability, as well as recent developments in the theory of oligopoly, have prompted industrial economists to attempt the more ambitious task of inferring the existence of monopoly power from observations of prices, quantities produced, costs, and demand. It is clear from our discussion of eqns [4]–[7] that λ is the interesting parameter reflecting monopoly power. $\lambda = 0$ identifies price-taking behaviour, and increases in λ signify an increasing degree of output restriction. Since it seems clear that what happens within industries is as interesting as what happens between them, it is natural to try to measure a value of λ for each firm, or at least, a broad systematic pattern across firms in each industry. In precisely the same way that one uses information on outputs and inputs to infer the parameters of a production function, or data on prices and quantities to infer the parameters of consumer utility functions, so one can use basic data on prices, outputs, costs, and demand, together with the marginal cost equals marginal revenue condition of eqn [5], to infer what the conduct of industry members must have been in order to have generated the observed price and output data (see Appelbaum 1979, 1982; Sumner 1981; Gollop and Roberts 1979; Iwata 1974; Roberts 1985; Geroski 1982b; Baker and Bresnahan 1985; Bresnahan 1981; Cubbin 1975. Geroski *et al.* 1985 contains a brief critical survey of this literature). Indeed, one can go somewhat further. Having isolated conduct in this manner, it is then a natural step to examine its variations over time (see Porter 1983; Lee and Porter 1984; Geroski *et al.* 1986).

This kind of work is a natural development of the traditional structuralist line. Let us suppose that one has employed a two-step intervention rule to select industries for further examination by inspection of their concentration levels, among other things. It then becomes crucial to proceed to analyse the markets so chosen in more detail. From our earlier discussion, it is clear that, in this context, the interesting exogenous variables pertain to conduct (i.e. the λ_i). Not only can more or less direct observation of conduct reveal whether monopolistic pricing is occurring and where within the industry it is occurring, but a dynamic explanation of conduct patterns opens up possibilities of more fundamental causal testing, and prediction. That is, examination of movements in λ over time may enable causal links from market structure in time t to conduct in $t+1$ to be identified, so enabling one to predict the effects of mergers, etc., on future industry behaviour and performance.

(b) STRATEGIC GROUPS AND MOBILITY

Dissatisfaction with the definition of industries has led a number of economists to define and begin to use the concept of strategic groups. The major theoretical paper is Caves and Porter (1977); empirical analysis has been reported by Newman (1978), Porter (1979), Donsimoni and Leoz-Arguelles (1982), and Oster (1982). The crucial notion is based on a generalisation of the concept of entry barriers to describe those obstacles to movement within industries. Such barriers to mobility within industries create pockets of market power among relatively homogeneous groups of firms, separating them and protecting them from the competitive challenges of other industry members and entrants. The traits which define strategic groups emerge as a by-product of the different types of competitive strategies selected by firms, and the structure of strategic groups within industries can facilitate the development of within-group patterns of tacit or overt collusion.

   The major research problems with the strategic-group approach is how to identify the different strategic groups in practice, and how to allocate firms within an industry to the different groups which make up the industry's internal structure. Once this has been done in an appropriate fashion, testing is fairly straightforward. Strategic groups are a way of formalising the notion that there are important heterogeneities within industries. If these heterogeneities truly exist, then firms in different groups will experience different effects of industry concentration (among other things) on their profits. Hence, if firms $i = 1, \ldots, N_0$ and $i = N_0 + 1, \ldots, N_1$ in industry define two strategic groups, then one can estimate models like [1], [2], [3], [8] or [9] separately for each group, say

$$\begin{cases} \pi_{ij} = \beta_0^1 + \beta_1^1 C_j + \gamma_1^1 S_j + \mu_{ij}^1 \quad \text{for } i = 1,\ldots,N_0 \\ \\ \pi_{ij} = \beta_0^2 + \beta_1^2 C_j + \gamma_1^2 S_j + \mu_{ij}^2 \quad \text{for } i = N_0 + 1,\ldots,N_1 \end{cases} \qquad [10]$$

and test the null hypothesis of no heterogeneities within the industry by examining whether $\beta_0^1 \neq \beta_0^2$, $\beta_1^1 \neq \beta_1^2$, $\gamma_1^1 \neq \gamma_1^2$, and so on. If these inequalities hold, then the firms in the two different strategic groups are affected in significantly different ways by market structure. Since this could only arise in the presence of heterogeneities between firms, it is sufficient evidence to reject the null hypothesis of no strategic groups. Most of the work reported thus far suggests that strategic groups exist, although it seems that many of the differences between firms that one observes are, in the main, size related.

The strategic groups research programme is a half-way house between the traditional emphasis on an industry-based anti-trust policy, and a more micro-economic stress on dominant firms as the centre of attention. It enables policy makers to economise on scarce resources by concentrating attention on identifiable pockets of market power within industries without losing the important emphasis on inter-firm interaction that a more micro-economic policy runs the danger of overlooking. The main problem with this approach is to develop measurable indicators of monopoly power which both screen across industries and explore the market structure within them. It is an open question whether or not more workable measures reflecting the varieties of corporate strategic policy will emerge with more research.

(c) THE PERSISTENCE OF PROFITABILITY

There is one element of the structuralist hypothesis that we have until now hardly touched upon. It is clear that relatively transitory positions of monopoly power are unlikely to be of much interest, and in this connection, entry seems to have been somewhat neglected in the overwhelming attention paid to concentration indices. Entry is the natural market response to excess profits, and the assurance that entry forces are strong and operate in a very pro-competitive fashion would reduce the need for a strong and vigorous anti-trust policy, regardless of concentration levels. Conversely, if entry barriers were high, then even relatively small elevations of price above marginal cost would be costly as they are likely to persist for long periods of time. The implication of this point for anti-trust policy is straightforward. Since, in principle, markets operate to remove monopolistic abuses through entry, anti-trust policy can only be justified by showing both that such abuses exist *and* that the anti-trust authorities can eliminate them more quickly and cleanly than the market would anyway. This naturally turns attention towards the analysis of market dynamics. In general, cross-section analyses of concentration and average industry profitability do not yield a great deal of information on the persistence of profits, but there seems to be ample ground for development of this kind of analysis at the industry level, and, even more interestingly, at the firm level.[13] The basic idea is to develop time series descriptions of the profitability experience of firms taken in isolation, or grouped together to capture what shared industry or strategic group effects as do exist. The simple theory of competitive markets predicts that positions of monopoly power gradually erode, with profitability returning towards competitive levels. This, in turn, yields a relatively simple predicted pattern of profitability over time which can be compared with the data.

More precisely, suppose that we have a structure–performance model analogous to [8],

$$\pi_i(t) = \gamma S_i(t) + \mu_i(t) \qquad [11]$$

where $\mu_i(t)$ captures all other factors including the constant. The natural consequence of excess profits ($\pi_i(t) > 0$) is entry in subsequent periods. Denoting entry into the market niche occupied by firm i by $E_i(t)$, then it is natural to suppose that

$$E_i(t) = \tau \pi_i(t-1) + \epsilon_i(t) \qquad [12]$$

Equation [12] is the basic form of the equation estimated in the entry literature cited in note 5. The quantity $\epsilon_i(t)/\tau$ is that level of profits which is sustainable for ever against entry (so-called 'limit profits'), for if $\pi_i(t-1) = \epsilon_i(t)/\tau$, then $E_i(t) = 0$. Since the height of these limit profits depends on various entry barriers, then, in the manner of eqn [3], most research with cross-section data extends the model [12] to allow $\epsilon_i(t) = \sum_l \phi_l B_{li} + e_i(t)$, where the l variables B_l are different entry barriers. Measurement of the parameters ϕ_l is then a way to assess which barriers are most important. Our concern here is less with the height of particular entry barriers and more with how fast markets converge to long-run competitive positions. Thus, to [11] and [12] we must add an equation describing the consequences of entry. The effect of entry into i's market niche is to reduce i's market share, so

$$\Delta S_i(t) = -\theta E_i(t) \qquad [13]$$

where $\Delta S_i(t) \equiv S_i(t) - S_i(t-1)$. Thus, eqn [13] describes the effects of successful entry on the market shares of leading firms, and so on industry market structure. Equations [11]–[13] describe a complete feedback loop from profits at time t to entry in $t+1$, and thence to market structure and performance in $t+1$. That is, high profits are caused by a highly concentrated market structure, and attract entrants who bid away sales from incumbents and so cause the initially high level of profits to fall. This process occurs until no excess profits are left, and the resulting long-run level of profits attracts no further entry. Whether or not these entry-forestalling profits exceed competitive levels depends on the height of entry barriers. To estimate the speed with which these effects work their way through the system, we can combine [11]–[13] to yield

$$\pi_i(t) = \delta_0 + \delta_1 \pi_i(t-1) \qquad [14]$$

where $\delta_1 \equiv (1-\tau\gamma\theta)$ and $\delta_0 = \mu_i(t) - \gamma\theta\epsilon_i(t)$. Clearly, the stronger is the effect of entry (i.e. the higher is θ), and the more it responds to profits (i.e. the higher is τ), the quicker profits will erode. If all of this happens instantaneously, profits are always at their long-run equilibrium positions and so $\pi = \delta_0$ (i.e. $\delta_1 = 0$). If, by contrast, entry barriers are large and prevent entrants from responding to profits or effectively challenging incumbents, then δ_1 will be close to unity. In this case, profits will persist above competitive levels for long periods of time.

Empirical work on this subject has been built around equations like [14] (for a critical analysis of work done on the three equations [11]–[13] separately, and an examination of its implications for the reduced form [14], see Geroski and Masson 1986). While such work has only just begun, most of the signs are that market power persists. Dominant firms with large market shares show only very weak tendencies towards decline (see Geroski 1986; Utton 1986; Pascoe and Weiss 1983; Caves *et al.* 1983, for empirical work along these lines; the survey by Davies in Chapter 3 of this volume also considers the related question of measures of 'dynamic concentration' based on the stability of market shares). Excess profits appear to erode somewhat more rapidly, but such erosion is noticeably slower for firms with large market shares (Mueller 1977, 1986 is the pioneering work in this area; further work can be found in Cubbin and Geroski 1986; Geroski and Jacquemin 1986; Connolly and Schwartz 1985; Odagiri and Yamawaki 1986; and, for work at industry level, Levy 1986). Since this work does tend to suggest that competitive processes work rather slowly, it appears that there is an important role for a prompt and well directed anti-trust policy to be applied not so much to make markets work well, as to make them work faster.

From the point of view of policy, this seems to lead towards a sensible empirical basis upon which to erect a micro-economic anti-trust policy. It is more than clear that the fortunes of large firms are becoming increasingly divorced from the immediate vagaries of the industry they principally operate in. Given this, and given a generally unequal distribution of market power within industries, it is natural to direct attention at firm level. Anti-trust policy can only really be conceived as a supplement to natural market forces, as a policy based on the presumption that markets in general work fairly well. Since corrective market forces like entry work only very gradually over time, it is necessary to look at the monopoly problem in a dynamic context, and to examine the performance of firms or industries over time. Their response to shocks, and the effect of the market's response to excessive profit positions are all reflected in profit performance over time. Such an analysis of the persistence of profits at high or low levels, and the identification of the factors which seem to be responsible for this performance is a natural way to approach the question of where and how market forces ought to be supplemented.

6. Conclusions

The 'structure–performance' paradigm has played a major role in guiding competitive policy in the post-war period, and it still exerts a major influence. Scholars now are less inclined to see market structure as the dominant influence on market conduct, and regressions of average industry profits on industry concentration command less attention than formerly. The paradigm has evolved from its strict structuralist roots into one concerned increasingly with examining what happens within industries, and with the properties of competitive processes. Yet concern with its distribution and its persistence does not hide the fact that monopoly profits remain a problem, and, despite all the caveats, market structure remains part of the key to identifying and solving that problem.

Notes

1a.   I am obliged to C.E.P.S. in Brussels and the I.I.M. in Berlin for assistance, and to R. Clarke, S. Davies, A. Jacquemin, B. Lyons, R. Masson, D. Hay, W. Hall, D. Mueller, R. Feinberg, and M. Waterson for helpful comments on earlier drafts. The usual disclaimer applies. J. Fairburn drew my attention to the survey by Paulter (1983) after most of the revision of this paper was completed.

1. A flavour of this work can be found in the volume edited by Mathewson and Stiglitz (1986); surveys include the paper by Encaoua *et al.* in that volume, and Geroski and Jacquemin (1984).

2. Bain (1951: 294, footnote 4) notes that: 'the profit rate for a firm or industry should not be regarded as a sole or an infallible index of the workability of competition. Clearly it is one of several dimensions of market performance . . . .' In contrast to Bain's broad notion of what constitutes satisfactory industry performance, I shall use the relatively narrow definition in the text since that seems to me the only real aspect of performance that conventional structure–performance studies shed light upon.

3. The discussion of monopoly welfare loss in the text is slightly casual in being couched in terms of consumer surplus, and a more precise statement can be found in Varian (1978); see also Kay (1983), who provides a rigorous justification for some common empirical approximations. Easily the most important empirical work done on estimating monopoly welfare loss is Cowling and Mueller (1978), who produced controversial estimates suggesting that these losses are rather large in the US and UK; Cowling *et al.* (1980) survey much of the empirical work on this subject.

4. A rather different hypothesis, positing an association between market structure and the rate of price adjustment to cost and demand shocks (that is, between industry structure and price dynamics rather than price levels), has also commanded attention since the days of Means (1935). For recent work see Domberger (1983), and, for opposite results, Encaoua and Geroski (1984). Unlike the conventional structure–conduct–performance hypothesis, this work on price dynamics carries no straightforward policy implications. In particular, it is not obvious that a rapid pricing response to short-term cost and demand shocks is a 'good thing'.

5. For some theoretical work which places almost the whole burden of performance regulation on entry, see the 'contestability' theory of Baumol *et al.* (1982). Unfortunately, structure–conduct–performance regressions like eqn [1] are not ideally suited to shed light on the effects of entry on market performance because they neither address the causes and consequences of entry directly, nor the persistence of profits at super-competitive levels to which high entry barriers give rise. For some inter-industry work which models entry flows directly see Orr (1974), Harris (1976), Gorecki (1975, 1976), Khemani and Shapiro (1983), Baldwin and Gorecki (1983) and Masson and Shaanan (1982) (for surveys, see Geroski 1983b); Geroski and Masson 1986; and the survey by Lyons in Chapter 2 of this volume); work on the persistence of profits is discussed below in section 5.

6. Some of the trade-offs involved in choosing different measures are discussed in Hart (1975) and Davies (1979). Some scholars have attempted to deduce the appropriate concentration index from precise prior specifications of what one means by acceptable performance; see Hannah and Kay (1977: Ch.4), Encaoua and Jacquemin (1980), Blackorby *et al.* (1982), Geroski (1983a), and Donsimoni *et al.* (1984). A good survey of this material is that by Davies in Chapter 3 of this volume.

7. Weiss (1974) gives a fairly thorough going over and a satisfactory explanation of early 'perverse' results. Work in the UK (e.g. Clarke 1984; Hart and Morgan 1977) has, at times, produced non-significant correlation, but one answer to this is non-linearity in the relationship — see Geroski (1981).

8. This derivation follows Cowling and Waterson (1976) (see also the survey by Dixon in Chapter 4 of this volume). Alternative assumptions about intra-industry

variations in λ will generate alternative concentration indices. For instance, Saving (1970) and Geroski (1983a) show how the concentration ratio is the appropriate index in price leader models. See Chapter 3 of this volume for more detail.

9. One could read this observation as suggesting that restrictive practices policy and policy generally directed towards anti-competitive practices ought to bear the main brunt of anti-trust efforts. Feinberg (1980, 1984a,b,c) has detected important effects on the prices and price–cost margins of firms indicted by anti-trust activities for various forms of horizontal conspiracy.

10. In a rather different type of exercise, Schmalensee (1985) tried to separate out the relative importance of 'industry' and 'firm' effects on profitability, and concluded that the former is of major importance (at least in the US). Quite different results from a related methodology are obtained for the UK by Cubbin and Geroski (1986).

11. Cowling (1978: 8) reaches very similar conclusions, arguing in favour of creating an 'additional institutional framework for the regulation of major centres of economic power'; see also Cowling (1982). One further source of support for this notion emerges from Cowling and Mueller's (1978) estimates of the apparently large monopoly dead-weight losses created by large US and UK *firms*.

12. This raises the interesting question of whether there ought to be *per se* rules governing mergers which raise industry concentration (or, the market share of individual firms) above some threshold level. However attractive this course is for those who fear the creation of large and more or less unregulated centres of economic power, it is hard to see a really substantive basis for such a rule. A more attractive approach to this question is to shift the burden of proof. There is a widely agreed upon presumption among those who proclaim the virtues of democratic decision making that the decentralisation of economic decision making ought to be pushed as far as possible, perhaps subject to some constraints on efficiency. Hence, any merger which increases size and market power ought to be frowned upon, *unless those who initiate the amalgamation* can clearly demonstrate efficiency gains and are willing to accept restrictions on their ability to exploit the enhanced market power that the merger gives them.

13. There is a large and growing theoretical literature which examines how positions of dominance, once achieved, are maintained (see Geroski and Jacquemin 1984 for a survey), but what follows is not a test of these kinds of arguments. Rather than asking how dominant positions are maintained, we are interested in how long they are maintained, whatever the means.

References

Appelbaum, E. (1979) Testing price taking behaviour, *Journal of Econometrics,* **9,** 283–94.

Appelbaum, E. (1982) The estimation of the degree of oligopoly power, *Journal of Econometrics,* **19,** 187–299.

Bain, J. (1951) Relation of profit rate to industry concentration: American manufacturing, 1936–1940. *Quarterly Journal of Economics,* **65,** 293–324.

Baker, J. and Bresnahan, T. (1985) The gains from merger or collusion in product-differential industries, *Journal of Industrial Economics,* **33,** 427–44.

Baldwin, J. and Gorecki, P. (1983) Entry and exit to the Canadian manufacturing sector, Mimeo, Economic Council of Canada.

Baumol, W., Panzar, J. and **Willig, R.** (1982) *Contestable markets and the theory of industry structure*, Harcourt-Brace-Jovanovich: San Diego.

Blackorby, C., Donaldson, D. and **Weymark, J.** (1982) A normative approach to industrial performance evaluation and concentration indices, *European Economic Review*, **19**, 89–122.

Bradburd, R. and **Over, A.** (1982) Organisational costs, 'sticky equilibria' and critical levels of concentration, *Review of Economics and Statistics*, **64**, 50–8.

Bresnahan, T. (1981) Departures from marginal-cost pricing in the American automobile industry: estimates for 1977–1978, *Journal of Econometrics*, **9**, 1010–19.

Caves, R. (1985) International trade and industrial organization: problems, solved and unsolved, *European Economic Review*, **22**, 377–95.

Caves, R., Fortunato, M. and **Glemawat, P.** (1984) The decline of dormant firms, *Quarterly Journal of Economics*, **99**, 527–46.

Caves, R. and **Porter, M.** (1977) From entry barriers to mobility barriers: conjectural decisions and contrived deterrence to new competition, *Quarterly Journal of Economics*, **91**, 421–34.

Caves, R. and **Pugel, T.** (1980) Intra-industry differences in conduct and performance: viable strategies in U.S. manufacturing industries, *Monograph Series in Finance and Economics*, N.Y.U. Graduate School of Business Administration.

Clarke, R. (1984) Profit margins and market concentration in the manufacturing industry 1970–76, *Applied Economics*, **16**, 57–71.

Clarke, R. and **Davies, S.** (1982) Market structure and price cost margins, *Economica*, **49**, 277–88.

Clarke, R., Davies, S. and **Waterson, M.** (1984) The profitability–concentration relation: market power or efficiency? *Journal of Industrial Economics*, **32**, 435–50.

Comanor, W. and **Wilson, T.** (1967) Advertising, market structure and performance, *Review of Economics and Statistics*, **49**, 423–40.

Connolly, R. and **Schwartz, S.** (1985) The intertemporal behaviour of economic profits, *International Journal of Industrial Organization*, **3**, 465–72.

Cooley, T., Bothwell, J. and **Hall, T.** (1984) A new view of the market structure–performance debate, *Journal of Industrial Economics*, **32**, 397–418.

Cowling, K. (1976) On the theoretical specification of industrial structure–performance relationships, *European Economic Review*, **8**, 1–14.

Cowling, K. (1978) Monopolies and mergers policy: a view on the Green Paper, Mimeo, University of Warwick.

Cowling, K. (1982) Monopolies and merger policy, *Socialist Economic Review*, The Merlin Press: Whitstable, Kent.

Cowling, K. and **Mueller, D.** (1978) The social costs of monopoly power, *Economic Journal*, **88**, 727–48.

Cowling, K. and **Waterson, M.** (1976) Price-cost margins and market structure, *Econometrica*, **43**, 275–86.

Cowling, K., Stoneman, P., Cubbin, J., Cable, J., Hall, G., Domberger, S. and **Dutton, P.** (1980) *Mergers and Economic Performance*, Cambridge University Press: Cambridge.

Cubbin, J. (1975) Quality change and pricing behaviour in the U.K. car industry, 1956–1968, *Economica*, **42**, 43–58.

Cubbin, J. (1986) Industry structure and performance: the empirical work, Mimeo, Queen Mary College.

Cubbin, J. and **Geroski, P.** (1986) The convergence of profits in the long run: inter-firm and inter-industry comparisons, *Journal of Industrial Economics* (forthcoming).

Dalton, J. and **Penn, D.** (1976) The concentration–profitability relationship: is there a critical concentration ratio?, *Journal of Industrial Economics,* **25,** 133–42.

Davies, S. (1979) Choosing between concentration indices: the iso-concentration curve, *Economica,* **46,** 67–75.

de Ghellinck, E., Geroski, P. and **Jacquemin, A.** (1983) Inter-industry and inter-temporal variations in the effect of trade on industry performance, Mimeo, Louvain la Neuve.

Demsetz, H. (1974) Two systems of belief about monopoly, in Goldschmid *et al.* (eds), *Industrial Concentration: The New Learning,* Little and Brown: Boston.

Domberger, S. (1983) *Industrial Structure, Pricing and Inflation,* Martin Robertson: Oxford.

Donsimoni, M-P. and **Leoz-Arguelles, V.** (1982) Strategic groups: an application to foreign and domestic firms in Spain, *Recherches Economiques de Louvain,* **47,** 291–306.

Donsimoni, M-P, Geroski, P. and **Jacquemin, A.** (1984) Concentration indices and market power: two views, *Journal of Industrial Economics,* **32,** 419–34.

Encaoua, D. and **Geroski, P.** (1984) Competition and price flexibility in five countries, Mimeo, University of Southampton.

Encaoua, D. and **Jacquemin, A.** (1980) Degree of monopoly, indices of concentration and threat of entry, *International Economic Review,* **21,** 87–105.

Feinberg, R. M. (1980) Antitrust enforcement and subsequent price behaviour, *Review of Economics and Statistics,* **62,** 609–12.

Feinberg, R. M. (1984a) The timing of anti-trust effects on pricing, *Applied Economics,* **16,** 397–410.

Feinberg, R. M. (1984b) Strategic and deterrent pricing responses to anti-trust investigations, *International Journal of Industrial Organization,* **2,** 75–84.

Feinberg, R. M. (1984c) The effects of EEC competition policy on pricing and profit margins, Mimeo, Pennsylvania State University.

Fisher, F. and **McGowan, J.** (1983) On the misuse of accounting rates of return to infer monopoly profits, *American Economic Review,* **73,** 82–97.

Gale, B. (1972) Market share and rate of return, *Review of Economics and Statistics,* **54,** 412–23.

Geithman, F., Marvel, H. and **Weiss, L.** (1981) Concentration, price and critical concentration ratios, *Reviews of Economics and Statistics,* **63,** 346–53.

Geroski, P. (1981) Specification and testing the profits–concentration relationship: some experiments for the U.K., *Economica,* **48,** 279–88.

Geroski, P. (1982a) Interpreting a correlation between profits and concentration, *Journal of Industrial Economics,* **30,** 305–18.

Geroski, P. (1982b) The empirical analysis of conjectural variations in oligopoly, Mimeo, Universite Catholique de Louvain.

Geroski, P. (1982c) Simultaneous equations models of the structure–performance paradigm, *European Economic Review,* **219,** 145–58.

Geroski, P. (1983a) Some reflections on the theory and application of concentration indices, *International Journal of Industrial Organization,* **1,** 79–94.

Geroski, P. (1983b) The empirical analysis of entry: a survey, Mimeo, University of Southampton.

Geroski, P. (1986) Do dominant firms decline?, In Hay, D. and Vickers, J. (eds), *The Economics of Market Dominance,* Basil Blackwell: Oxford.

Geroski, P. and **Jacquemin, A.** (1984) Dominant firms and their alleged decline, *International Journal of Industrial Organization,* **2,** 1–28.

Geroski, P. and **Jacquemin, A.** (1986) The persistence of profits: a European comparison, Mimeo, Louvain la Neuve.

Geroski, P. and **Masson, R.** (1986) Dynamic market models in industrial organization, *International Journal of Industrial Organization* (forthcoming).

Geroski, P., Philips, L. and **Ulph, A.** (1985) Oligopoly, welfare and competition: some recent developments, *Journal of Industrial Economics*, **33**, 369–86.

Geroski, P., Ulph, A. and **Ulph, D.** (1986) A model of the crude oil market in which conduct varies over time, *Economic Journal* (forthcoming)

Gollop, F. and **Roberts, M.** (1979) Firm interdependence in oligopolistic markets, *Journal of Econometrics*, **10**, 313–31.

Gorecki, P. (1975) The determinants of entry by new and diversifying enterprises in the U.K. manufacturing sector, *Applied Economics*, **7**, 139–47.

Gorecki, P. (1976) The determinants of entry by domestic and foreign enterprises in Canadian manufacturing industries, *Review of Economics and Statistics*, **58**, 485–8.

Hall, M. and **Weiss, L.** (1967) Firm size and profitability, *Review of Economics and Statistics*, **49**, 319–31.

Hannah, L. and **Kay, J.** (1977) *Concentration in Modern Industry*, Macmillan: Basingstoke.

Harris, M. (1976) Entry and barriers to entry, *Industrial Organization Review*, **4**, 165–74.

Hart, P. (1975) Moment distributions in economics, *Journal of the Royal Statistical Society*, series B, **138**, 423–34.

Hart, P. and **Morgan, E.** (1977) Market structure and economic performance, *Review of Economics and Statistics*, **25**, 177–93.

Hillman, A. (1984) Preemptive rent seeking and the social cost of monopoly power, *International Journal of Industrial Organization*, **2**, 227–81.

Hillman, A. and **Katz, E.** (1984) Risk averse rent seekers and the social cost of monopoly power, *Economic Journal*, **94**, 104–10.

Iwata, G. (1974) Measurement of conjectural variations in oligopoly, *Econometrica*, **42**, 947–66.

Jacquemin, A. (1982) Imperfect market structure and international trade, *Kyklos*, **35**, 75–93.

Jacquemin, A. and **de Jong, H.** (1977) *European Industrial Organization*, Macmillan: London and Basingstoke.

Kay, J. (1983) A general equilibrium approach to the measurement of monopoly welfare loss, *International Journal of Industrial Organization*, **1**, 317–32.

Kay, J. and **Mayer, C.** (1986) On the application of accounting rates of return, *Economic Journal*, **96**, 199–207.

Khemani, R. and **Shapiro, D.** (1983) Alternative specifications of entry models, Mimeo, Bureau of Competition Policy, Ottawa.

Kwoka, J. (1979) The effect of market share distribution on industry performance, *Review of Economics and Statistics*, **61**, 101–9.

Kwoka, J. (1981) Does the choice of concentration measure really matter?, *Journal of Industrial Economics*, **20**, 445–53.

Lee, L-F. and **Porter, R.** (1984) Switching regression models with imperfect sample separation information — with an application on cartel stability, *Econometrica*, **52**, 391–418.

Levy, D. (1986) The speed of the invisible hand, *International Journal of Industrial Organization* (forthcoming).

Lyons, B. (1986) The welfare loss due to strategic investment in excess capacity, *International Journal of Industrial Organization*, **4**, 109–19.

McGee, J. (1987) Efficiency and economies of scale, in Mann, M. *et al.* (eds), *Industrial Concentration: The New Learning*, Little, Brown and Co.: Boston.

Martin, S. (1979) Advertising, concentration and profitability: the simultaneity problem, *Bell Journal of Economics*, **10**, 639–47.

Martin, S. (1980) Entry barriers, concentration and profits, *Southern Economic Journal*, **46**, 471–88.

Martin, S. (1983) *Market, Firms, and Economic Performance*, NTU Graduate School of Business Administration.

Masson, R. and Shannan, J. (1982) Stochastic dynamic limit pricing: an empirical test, *Review of Economics and Statistics*, **64**, 413–23.

Mathewson, I. and Stiglitz, J. (eds) (1986) *New Developments in the Analysis of Market Structure*, MIT Press, Cambridge, Mass.

Means, G. (1935) Industrial prices and their relative inflexibility, *Senate Document 13*, 74th Congress, 1st Session, Washington, D.C., U.S. Government Printing Office.

Meehan, J. and Duchesneau, T. (1973) Theoretical level of concentration: an empirical analysis, *Journal of Industrial Economics*, **22**, 21–30.

Mueller, D. (1977) The persistence of profits above the norm, *Economica*, **44**, 369–80.

Mueller, D. (1981) Economics of scale, concentration and collusion, Mimeo, Federal Trade Concessions.

Mueller, D. (1986) *Profits in the Long Run*, Cambridge University Press: Cambridge.

Newman, M. (1978) Strategic groups and the structure–performance relationship, *Review of Economics and Statistics*, **60**, 417–27.

Odagiri, J. and Yamawaki, H. (1986) A study of company profit rate time series: Japan and the U.S., *International Journal of Industrial Organization*, **4**, 1–24.

Orr, D. (1974) The determinants of entry: a study of Canadian manufacturing industries, *Review of Economics and Statistics*, **61**, 58–66.

Oster, S. (1982) Intra-industry structure and the ease of strategic change, *Review of Economics and Statistics*, **64**, 376–83.

Pascoe, G. and Weiss, L. (1983) The extent and performance of market dominance, Mimeo, Federal Trade Concessions.

Paulter, P. (1983) A review of the economic basis for broad-based horizontal merger policy, *The Antitrust Bulletin*, **Fall**, 571–651.

Phillips, A. (1976) A critique of empirical studies of relations between market structure and profitability, *Journal of Industrial Economics*, **24**, 241–9.

Plott, C. (1982) Industrial organization theory and experimental economics, *Journal of Economic Literature*, **20**, 1485–27.

Porter, M. (1979) The structure within industries and companies performance, *Review of Economics and Statistics*, **61**, 214–28.

Porter, R. (1983) A study of cartel stability: the Joint Executive Committee, 1880–1886, *Bell Journal of Economics*, **14**, 301–14.

Posner, R. (1975) The social costs of monopoly and regulation, *Journal of Political Economy*, **83**, 807–27.

Prais, S. (1976) *The Evolution of Giant Firms in Britain*, Cambridge University Press: Cambridge.

Ravenscroft, D. (1983) Structure–profit relationships at the line of business and industry level, *Review of Economics and Statistics*, **61**, 214–28.

Reinganum M. and Smith, J. (1983) Investor preferences for large firms: new evidence on economies of size, *Journal of Industrial Economics*, **32**, 213–28.

Roberts, M. (1984) Testing oligopolistic behaviour: an application of the variable profit function, *International Journal of Industrial Organization*, **4**, 367–84.

Salinger, M. (1984) Tobin's q, unionization and the concentration–profit relationship, *Rand Journal of Economics*, **15**, 159–70.

Saving, T. (1970) Concentration ratios and the degree of monopoly, *International Economic Review*, **11**, 139–46.

Sawyer, M. (1982) On the specification of structure–performance relationships, *European Economic Review,* **17,** 295–306.

Scherer, F. (1974) Economies of scale and industrial concentration, in Mann, M. *et al.* (eds), *Industrial Concentration: the New Learning*, Little, Brown and Co.: Boston.

Scherer, F. (1980) *Industrial Market Structure and Economic Performance*, Rand McNally: Chicago.

Schmalensee, R. (1977) Using the H-index of concentration with published data, *Review of Economics and Statistics,* **59,** 186–93.

Schmalensee, R. (1985) Do markets differ much? *American Economic Review,* **75,** 341–51.

Schmalensee, R. (1986a) Testing the differential efficiency hypothesis, *Journal of Industrial Economics* (forthcoming).

Schmalensee, R. (1986b) Inter-industry studies of structure and performance, in Schmalensee, R. and Willig, R. (eds), *Handbook of Industrial Economics*, North Holland, Amsterdam (forthcoming).

Shepherd, W. (1972) The elements of market structure, *Review of Economics and Statistics,* **54,** 25–37.

Strickland, A. and Weiss, L. (1976) Advertising, concentration and price-cost margins, *Journal of Political Economy,* **84,** 1109–21.

Sumner, D. (1981) Measurement of monopoly behaviour: an application to the cigarette industry, *Journal of Political Economy,* **89,** 1010–19.

Tullock, G. (1967) The welfare costs of tariffs, monopolies and theft, *Western Economic Journal,* **5,** 224–32.

Utton, M. (1986) *Profits and Stability of Monopoly*, Cambridge University Press: Cambridge.

Varian, H. (1978) *Microeconomic Theory*, W. W. Norton Inc.: New York.

Weiss, L. (1974) The concentration–profits relation and anti-trust, in Mann, M. *et al.* (eds), *Industrial Concentration: The New Learning*, Little, Brown and Co.: Brown.

White, L. (1976) Searching for the critical concentration ratio: an application of the switching of regimes technique, in Goldfeld, S. and Quandt, R. (eds), *Studies in Non-Linear Estimation*, Ballinger: Boston.

Williamson, O. (1968) Economies as an anti-trust defense: the welfare trade offs, *American Economics Reviews,* **68,** 18–34.

CHAPTER SIX

Technical change, productivity and market structure

Stephen Davies

1. Introduction

(a) INTRODUCTORY DEFINITIONS

Technical change in the industrial context can be usefully characterised as having three more or less distinct stages. It is set in motion by *invention*, which may be based on new scientific knowledge or which, more commonly, uses well known scientific prinicples. The *innovation* stage occurs when and if the invention is first commercially introduced by a firm, often called the innovator. Then as the new product or process is recognised as superior to competing existing technologies, this results in its further application within the innovating firm and its introduction by other firms in the industry: that is, imitation or *diffusion* occurs. We shall adopt this three-way distinction, partly for presentational convenience, but, more importantly, because it establishes at the outset that technical change is a process stretching through time. During this process, which will often involve a decade or much more than a decade for a particular new technology, various intertemporal choices will be made by the firms concerned, and these are the subjects of much of the following discussion. We should acknowledge however that these terms will be sometimes misleading, especially in cases when it is difficult to ascertain where one stage ends and the next begins. Also, they can be the source of confusion: for example, 'innovation' is sometimes used, as above, to indicate a stage in the process, and sometimes to indicate the new technology itself.

Additionally, new technologies are usually defined as being either *process* or *product* innovations. To use Blaug's (1963) amusing definitions, the process innovation is 'a novel way of making old goods', while the product innovation involves 'old ways of making novelties'. But again this distinction is not always clear cut. For instance, new products often require modifications, if not more, to the processes previously used in the industry. Moreover, for capital goods industries, all product innovations are some other industry's process innovations.

Two activities in inventive and innovative activity are *patenting* and *research and development expenditures (R & D)*. Generally, patents are viewed as an output of inventive activity, and R & D as an input into both the inventive and innovative stages.[1] In turn, the research component of R & D might be identified primarily with invention and development with innovation.[2] However, neither of these measures provides much assistance to those interested in measuring the output of innovation or, more generally, technical change itself. But this is hardly surprising since as Stoneman (1983: 15) puts it, 'the output of the process of advancing technology is, by tautology, technological advance'. However, it is possible to be a little more positive than this. Considering for the moment only new processes, a successful innovation will generally be associated with significant cost reductions and, therefore, productivity increases. Leaving until later a precise definition of productivity, we believe this to be a compelling reason for including in this survey a section on the relevant literature on market structure and productivity. Quite obviously, productivity growth will reflect more than just technical change, and it is unlikely to capture the effects of product innovation adequately.[3] But in the absence of better measures of the output of innovative activity, its inclusion in this survey is justified and desirable.

Putting these definitions together, we have stylised the process of technical change as follows. Inventions are often made as the consequence of research expenditures and result in patents. Following further development expenditures the innovations appear on the commercial scene. At this point, for process innovations at least, best practice productivity has been increased, but it is only with diffusion that actual productivity levels approach the new best practice.

Finally, this stylised picture can be re-interpreted within the structure–conduct–performance framework. Loosely speaking, invention and innovation can be identified as elements of industry conduct, measured perhaps by R & D expenditure and output of patented inventions. The effects of conduct are translated through to performance (productivity) via diffusion. Whether diffusion is classified as conduct or performance is immaterial, so long as this sequence of things is acknowledged. Our primary concern in this survey is to investigate the influence of industry structure, concentration and firm size, on these dimensions of conduct and performance. An important qualification to bear in mind, however, is that these relationships are rarely uni-dimensional; part of the concentration survey elsewhere in this volume (Ch. 3) discusses the impact of technology on market structure, and in the present survey this theme is repeated on a number of occasions.

(b) SOME IMPORTANT CONCEPTS

To understand the direction taken by the literature on the industrial economics of technical change, it will be helpful to enumerate some of the key dimensions of the generation of technical change which set it apart, to a greater or lesser extent, from other activities of the firm.

First and foremost, the intrinsic *uncertainty* of the exercise has figured centrally in the theoretical literature. There is the technical uncertainty as to whether R & D will successfully generate a new technology and, if so, when. There is the market uncertainty concerning the impact of the technology when it hits the market – by how much will a process innovation reduce costs, what sort of demand curve will the new product attract? And, relatedly, there is uncertainty as to how rivals will react – rivalry uncertainty – will they match our R & D programmes, will they attempt to beat us to innovation, or will they imitate? Increasingly, in all areas of economics, standard theorems have been reworked within a framework of uncertainty but often this is by way of an 'optional extra'. In the economics of invention, innovation and diffusion, however, uncertainty has been acknowledged as critical, from the early writings of Schumpeter through to the neo-classical theorists discussed below. Indeed it is difficult to take seriously any model in this area which does not place uncertainty at the front of the stage, though some such models do exist as we shall see.

Secondly, any firm engaged in inventive activity will contemplate the *appropriability* of the results of its activity. How far will these results be internalised and how far will they constitute a public good? Consider the case of a firm with a process innovation in a perfectly competitive market subject to free entry. The moment the new process is introduced, others will imitate, driving price down to a new lower level and wiping out profits from innovation. The patent is, of course, a governmental device designed to grant the inventor a limited period during which the monopoly profits of innovation may be earned.

Thirdly, *timing* is often crucial. This is most conspicuous in the so-called time–cost trade-off or 'patents race' in developing new technologies. While there are obvious advantages in being first, development programmes have a significant learning dimension, and speeding up development may incur exorbitantly escalating costs. Likewise, in deciding when to adopt a new process, sold say by a capital goods producer, should we opt for early adoption to gain a competitive edge over rivals, or for late adoption when teething troubles have been eradicated? At a more general level, the theoretical modelling of technical change without explicitly introducing the time dimension would seem to be even more ostrich-like than usual in economics. Nevertheless, comparative static models survive and even flourish in this area, as with all areas of the subject.

(c) JOSEPH SCHUMPETER

Writing in the first part of this century, Schumpeter (1934, 1939, 1942) propounded the twin ideas that monopoly power and large scale of firm were the ideal vehicles for generating technical advance. Since these hypotheses have occupied the attention of numerous subsequent writers in this field, a few introductory remarks on Schumpeter are necessary. His basic argument in favour of large firms is that they have the wherewithal (large scale of production and capacity plus the infrastructure in marketing, finance and R & D) to exploit new technologies quickly. In Schumpeter's view of the world (see section 2 of Chapter 1) this is important because capitalist competition involves rapid imitation with innovations continually superseding each other, so there is an incentive to innovate only if one feels confident of being able to exploit that innovation rapidly. For the same sort of reason, monopoly or imperfect competition provides a better setting in which to exploit. More formally, large oligopolistic firms are better able to internalise the benefits of innovation and are generally more certain of their environment. These hypotheses have been embellished in subsequent years, and the 'Schumpeterian hypotheses' are couched often also in terms of the efficiency of organised R & D. As an activity R & D displays scale economies, or so it is said, and therefore large firms with large R & D departments will be more efficient in generating innovation, as well as having greater incentives. In addition, Schumpeter argued that market power, the ability to raise price above average costs, was the reward for innovation. On one level this is obvious and very few contemporary economists would deny that there is at least some element of super-normal profits which can be interpreted in this way. But one implication, which is often ignored, is that market structure is to some extent the product of technical change. In econometric terms, the two are simultaneously related or jointly determined.

In fact Schumpeter had a lot more to say than this: the intricate classification and explanation of cycles generated by clusters of innovations, the idea that capitalism will be destroyed by its own success, and the view of democracy as competition for votes. It is a pity that for many modern economists his name is treated only as a synonym for the hypotheses described in the previous paragraph. Nevertheless, even confining ourselves to these narrow issues of bigness and fewness and their effects on technical change, as we do for present purposes, a little more needs to be said about Schumpeter's theory of technical change and the firm. First, innovation is typically discontinuous and lumpy: 'it arises from within the system [and] so displaces its equilibrium point that the new one cannot be reached from the old one by infinitesimal steps. Add successively as many rail coaches as you please, you will never get a railway thereby.' (1934: 64). Second, innovation is a wider concept than that discussed so far. It includes the opening up of markets, the conquest of new sources of supply of materials, new forms of organisation of an industry, including the creation or breaking up of monopoly positions, as well as what we have called process and product innovations. Third, his entrepreneur is not the narrow profit maximiser of neo-classical theory. Rather, he stresses more basic psychological drives such as empire building, the 'will to conquer', that is success for its own sake rather than for what it brings, and the joy of creating (1934: 93–4). There are real doubts therefore whether Schumpeter conceives the motives and expectations of the innovator as being rational in the neo-classical sense of the word. We make these remarks, not as a brief excursion into the history of economic thought, but as a backcloth to the ensuing literature survey of this chapter. A number of writers have claimed to be modelling Schumpeter's ideas on the generation of technical change. Invariably they employ neo-classical notions of equilibrium, profit-maximising firms, marginal products of R & D expenditures, etc. Whatever may be the intrinsic value of these contributions, one may doubt that they provide appropriate formulations or tests of the Schumpeterian hypotheses, *as he saw them*.[4]

(d) LAYOUT OF THE SURVEY

Section 2 is devoted to the theoretical literature on invention and innovation. It starts with Arrow's famous analysis of the relative attraction of inventing for competitive and monopolistic product markets, and then turns to the question of rivalry between firms in being the first to introduce innovations. The third part of the section discusses the literature most obviously at variance with Schumpeter's view of discontinuous innovation, in which R & D is subjected to the most extreme form of neo-classical marginal analysis. Section 3 surveys the empirical literature on these subjects, a literature which has developed over the years almost independently of the theory, and which, incidentally, falls short of corroborating the Schumpeterian hypotheses. Section 4 considers diffusion – an area in which theory and empirics have moved more or less in tandem. Section 5 surveys the largely empirical literature on market structure and productivity.

2. The theory of invention and innovation

(a) THE INCENTIVE TO INVENT

Any survey of modern, formal neo-classical theory of technical change should begin with Arrow's (1962) seminal analysis of the incentives to invent. This compares the potential returns to invention of a new process for a using industry which is alternatively competitive or monopolistic; and it compares both with what is socially optimal. The scenario described is undoubtedly restrictive in abstracting from problems of uncertainty and appropriability, and there is really no distinction between invention and innovation – for the purpose of this section the two terms are virtually synonomous. Nevertheless, in focusing on comparative market structures and the social optimum, Arrow anticipated two issues which were to dominate the literature over the following quarter of a century. He also served notice that Schumpeterian arguments in favour of bigness and fewness would not go unchallenged.

For presentational purposes, we introduce the analysis by distinguishing between an independent inventor who is to supply a new process and the industry which is to use it. The using industry is described by Fig. 6.1, in which DD is its demand curve and pre-invention constant average costs are CC. If monopolised, the using industry will supply Q_m at price P_m and earn profit π_A; on the other hand, if the industry is perfectly competitive, quantity and price are Q_c and P_c and there are zero profits. Now consider the returns to the inventor from supplying a process innovation which will lower production costs to C'C'. In the competitive case suppose the inventor charges using firms a royalty, r, for each unit of output produced using the new technology. So long as this leaves their marginal costs, now $C' + r$, below the initial level, C, competitive pressures ensure that they all adopt immediately with price falling to $p = C' + r$. The inventor's optimising decision therefore involves maximising rQ with respect to r, subject to $r \leq p_c - C'$. In effect the inventor can control product price by varying his royalty charge and his return will be the surplus of the using industry's sales revenue over its production costs, i.e. $(p - C')Q$. Assuming for the moment that the constraint is inoperative, he is able to extract the full monopoly profit from the demand curve, and will therefore set r such that industry marginal revenue equals C'. The solution is shown by r^* which generates a return of π_B.

If, alternatively, the using industry is monopolistic, it is in the inventor's interest to charge a lump sum rather than a per unit royalty since the latter would cause the monopolist to restrict output while a lump sum payment would avoid this.

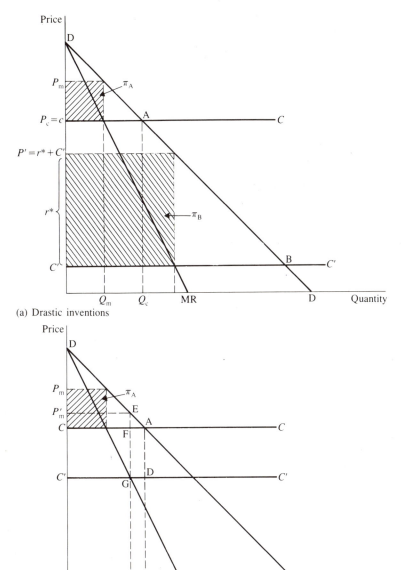

(a) Drastic inventions

(b) Non-drastic inventions

FIG. 6.1 The incentive to invent

But even with a lump sum levy, the most that the inventor can extract is the user's increase in profits between the pre- and post-invention situations. Since the monopolist user will price where marginal revenue equals C' in the post-invention case, his profits will be π_B, and the increase in profits therefore $\pi_B - \pi_A$. Even assuming the inventor were able to claim the entire increase in profits, in what amounts to a bilateral monopoly problem, this must be less than the return he can earn in the competitive case, π_B. The key to this result lies in the fact that the inventor is able to extract the full monopoly profit associated with the lower cost curve in the competitive case, but not in the monopoly case since profits were already being made in the pre-invention world. Loosely speaking, this conclusion may be likened to the somewhat vague assertion sometimes made that monopolists may be less motivated to innovate precisely because they are able to earn super-normal profits in the first place.

Arrow's second important conclusion concerns the divergence between private and social benefits from the new technology. If the market were to be socially managed, that is to maximise the sum of producer and consumer surplus, it would be optimal for price to be equated to new lower marginal costs, $C'C'$. This would generate an increase in surplus equal to the trapezium CABC'. Since this exceeds π_B, it follows that, even under perfect competition, the private benefit is less than the potential for social benefit.[5]

Before turning to subsequent cricitisms of this analysis, the conclusions can be extended in various ways. Firstly, we have confined out representation of the model to what Arrow calls a drastic invention: that is one which yields such a drastic cost reduction that the inventor's optimising problem is unconstrained with $r^* < C-C'$. For non-drastic inventions, the cost saving is more moderate: for example, the cost curve may only be lowered as far as shown in Fig. 6.1b and the most that the inventor can earn in the competitive case is $(C - C') Q_{\hat{c}}$. It may still be shown that this exceeds the maximum which can be earned in the monopoly case.[6] Secondly, we have described the scenario as one in which an independent inventor sells to a separate using industry. The results of the analysis are still the same, however, if the inventor is the monopolist. All that changes is that there is no haggling over the shares of the post-invention increase in profits. If, alternatively, the inventor is one of the firms in the competitive industry, he has nothing to gain by withholding his new technology from competitors since, as we have seen, he is able to extract full monopoly profit from the market anyway by choosing an appropriate royalty rate. Thirdly, we have said nothing about the more likely real-world state of oligopoly in the using industry. But the key point to the analysis would seem to carry over to oligopoly. To the extent that oligopolists are already earning super-normal profits before the invention appears, it follows that the maximum that the inventor can extract from them will be less than under perfect competition.

Finally, we should avoid the obvious error of concluding that, although different structures yield different returns, in all cases these are positive and so innovation will occur whatever the market structure. The fallacy with this is that the invention also involves costs, which have been ignored for simplicity in the above. Arrow's implication is that some inventions will never proceed to innovation because costs exceed returns for the inventor given a monopolistic using industry, while they would not if the using industry were competitive. Similarly, some innovations will never take place under either market structure even although the social benefits exceed the costs. It is in this sense that Arrow can conclude that competitive markets will attract more research and inventive activity than will monopolistic industries, and that both will lead to under-investment in research when compared with what is socially optimal.

The best known criticism of this model is due to Demsetz (1969) who argues that competition and monopoly are compared on unequal terms. Although the Arrow diagrams describe monopoly and competition with identical demand and cost conditions, the output, and thus industry size, under monopoly is far smaller than under competition (in fact 50% smaller given linear demand). As such it is hardly surprising that an inventor will find it more profitable to invent for the larger industry. To make the comparison 'fair', Demsetz suggests that the pre-invention outputs of the two hypothetical industries should be identical. In terms of Fig. 6.1a this can be illustrated by making MR the demand curve in the competitive case and pre-invention output is then Q_m, as for monopoly. To derive the incentive to invent for the competitive industry in these revised conditions, we must draw in the marginal revenue curve associated with MR. This is left as an exercise for the reader, who will confirm that the incentive to invent for the competitive industry is now less than $\pi_B - \pi_A$, at least in the special case of linearity. Thus Demsetz claims to have reversed Arrow's conclusion. The essence of this argument is that Arrow's conclusion is nothing more than the usual criticism of monopoly, namely that it restricts output and thus its use of inputs, including new inventions. Nevertheless, it seems to us that Arrow has established an additional argument against monopoly power: not only will it lead to conventional static welfare losses, but also to more dynamic losses. As Clarke (1985) points out, the standard of comparison used by Arrow is surely the more appropriate for policy issues concerning the monopolisation, or deconcentration, of existing industries.

To our mind, more compelling criticisms concern the restrictive setting employed by Arrow:

1. There is no competition in the inventive process, only in the product market, i.e. the using industry. Thus the inventor faces no uncertainty that he will be first to produce the new process, and similarly, once innovation has occurred, there is no chance that he will be imitated. Where the latter is not so, i.e. imperfect patent protection, it may be preferable to supply a monopoly user who has less to gain from supplying information about the technology to others.

2. Diffusion of the innovation is assumed to be instantaneous in the competitive case.

3. The new process is taken as given. Its technical characteristics are known with certainty, that is, it *will* reduce costs from C to C'. Also the crucial question for an inventor is ignored, namely how quickly to develop his invention.

4. Only a single discrete invention is considered. It may be more reasonable to conceive of R & D generating a continuous stream of innovations, some major, but some minor, building on learning about previous innovations.

Some of the theoretical literature which followed Arrow's work can be viewed as attempts to meet such criticisms.[7]

(b) THE PACE OF DEVELOPMENT AND THE TIMING OF INNOVATION

We now consider an issue ignored by Arrow, the speed of innovation with rivalry among potential innovators, while retaining the notion of a single predetermined invention with known technical characteristics. This aspect of innovation has attracted considerable attention in the recent theoretical literature which is perhaps just starting to tail off at the time of writing. The technological scenario is, in effect, one in which there is a known invention with a number of firms racing to be the first to bring it to the market. For this reason, the phrase 'patent race' is sometimes used. The types of questions posed are: how is the optimal pace of innovation affected by the competitive environment in which the firm is located; and, at the industry level, do monopolistic and oligopolistic industries innovate more rapidly than competitive ones, and how do they compare with what is socially optimal?

An early contribution concerned with product innovation was by Scherer (1967b), later summarised (1970: 366–70) less rigorously but more accessibly using Fig. 6.2 and the concept of the time–cost trade-off. We consider the decision for a given firm of how quickly to develop an invention in order to introduce it on to the market. On the one hand, a very rapid 'crash' development programme will entail

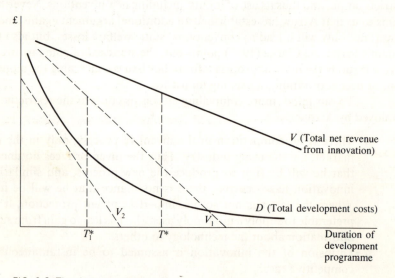

FIG. 6.2 The time–cost trade-off

much higher R & D costs compared to more leisurely development. A crash programme is more costly because: (a) errors are made when stages in development overlap instead of waiting for the information emanating from early experiments; (b) parallel, potentially duplicative, experimental approaches may be required; (c) more traditional diminishing returns, overtime premiums may result in each stage of the programme as more resources are used. (Mansfield *et al.* 1971 provide evidence for these assumptions.) On the other hand, the returns from the innovation will be higher, the more quickly it is introduced to the market. Early introduction allows the market to be tapped for a longer time, and provides the innovator with a competitive edge over rivals and a consequent increased market share which may extend into the longer run if early adoption establishes brand loyalty. These effects are represented by the D- and V-curves in the figure which show how total R & D costs and revenues (net of production costs and marketing expenditures) decline as the development programme is lengthened and innovation is delayed. As drawn, the optimal development period is T^*, at which the curves are parallel and the surplus $V - D$ is maximised.

The competitive environment in this model affects the location of the V-curve in two ways. V becomes steeper and lower as market concentration declines. Sherer argues that in industries with relatively more, and smaller, firms, the conjectured advantages of early innovation/the disadvantages of late innovation are more pronounced because firms anticipate greater scope for increased market share at the expense of rivals. On the other hand, the monopolist can benefit from no market share effect and increased revenues can only result from success in expanding the market and/or extracting a higher price in recognition of improved new product quality. These are the reasons for expecting steeper V-curves in less concentrated industries. Lower curves, on the other hand, reflect the likelihood of faster imitation in a more competitive environment, and possibly also new entry and price wars. Analytically, steeper curves mean faster optimal development, as in V_1, but if the accompanying inwards shift is too severe, as in V_2, profitable innovation is considered unlikely, whatever the length of the development programme.

Scherer's conclusion, then, is that more rapid innovation is likely where the number of sellers is greater, and concentration is lower, but beyond some lower limit on concentration, the stimulus to innovtion may be killed off by fears that a failure to internalise the returns from innovation for very long will prevent development costs from being covered. Turning to the effect of firm size, Scherer uses the potential for increased market share argument to suggest that there are greater incentives for small firms to innovate rapidly. If and when this happens, however, the larger firms will be under pressure to retaliate quickly to protect their market share.

Subsequent work in this vein has been more rigorously specified, but many of Scherer's initial insights have been confirmed. The main contributors, stimulated one suspects by Scherer, but also by Barzel (1968), have been Kamien and Schwartz in a series of articles throughout the 1970s, and since summarised in their 1982 book. Their main theme can be viewed in our terms as further exploration of the V revenue function. Specifically, they model the decision of the individual firm allowing explicitly for uncertainty about the date of rivals' innovation.[8] In this setting, the advantage of rapid development is that it increases the chances of being first; on the other hand, the expected revenues from the innovation will decline the longer is its introduction delayed, since this increases the chances of being beaten to the market. The basic idea can be explained with the following notation.[9] Suppose initially 'our' firm is selling an existing product which yields a net profit flow at any point in time of π_0. In the absence of rivals, this flow would continue until we introduce our new product at time T; the new product then generates a new higher profit flow π_N. However, there is a chance that rivals will beat us to innovation and, if so, the flow from our existing product will fall to π_{01} and from our new product to

π_{N1}. Alternatively, if we win the race to innovation, our new product will yield π_N until the rival's new product arrives, at which time the yield changes to π_{N2} which is probably, but not certainly, less than π_N.

If the rival's innovation date is V and ours T, the profit yields can be summarised as:

we innovate first: π_0 until T, π_N between T and V, π_{N2} after V
we innovate second: π_0 until V, π_{01} between V and T, π_{N1} after T

Which of these outcomes will obtain is unknown at the start of the period because V is unknown. Our firm's problem is then to choose T so as to maximise expected profits. This is the surplus of expected revenue over development costs where expected revenue is the weighted average of the two above alternatives, with more weight attaching to the first more favourable outcome the lower is T, i.e. the more rapid is our development. Now in order to specify expected revenue our firm must be able to attach probabilities to the rival having innovated at each date. In other words this is a standard neo-classical formulation of uncertainty: the date of rival innovation is unknown, but there is supposed to be sufficient information for precise probabilities to be attached to different possibilities.

More formally, if we denote the probability of rival innovation by time t as $F(t)$, then the expected revenue for our firm at any point in time before our date of innovation ($t < T$) is

$$\pi_0 (1 - F(t)) + \pi_{01} F(t) \tag{1}$$

Expected profit at $t > T$, i.e. after we have innovated, is

$$\pi_N (1 - F(t)) + \pi_{N1} F(T) + \pi_{N2} (F(t) - F(T)) \tag{2}$$

where $1 - F(t)$ is the probability that the rival has not innovated by t, $F(T)$ is the probability that the rival has already innovated by T and thereby beaten us, and $F(t) - F(T)$ is the probability that he has innovated by t but had not by T, that is we have beaten him. Summing [1] over all periods between 0 and T, and [2] over all periods after T and discounting back to 0, yields expected revenue at time 0 from innovating at T. Expected profit is derived as the difference between this and a costs function which exhibits the same characteristics as D in the figure, and optimal T is then located where expected marginal revenue equals marginal development costs. Kamien and Schwartz derive the following predictions from comparative static analysis of the solution:

The firm will choose to innovate more rapidly, that is select a lower T:

    (a) the larger are π_N and π_{N2}, the greater are the rewards from being first;
    (b) the smaller are π_0 and π_{01}, the less profitable is the existing product;
    (c) the larger is $\pi_0 - \pi_{01}$, the greater the loss from being beaten to innovation.

While none of these results is especially startling, they are of some interest. Firstly, (a) and (c) capture rather neatly the 'carrot' and 'stick' effects making for rapid innovation. Secondly, for firms already making good profits, perhaps monopolists, the incentive to innovate is reduced according to (b). By the same token, firms initially making no profits, that is potential entrants, or for whom the new product will not supplant an existing product, that is firms contemplating diversification, will innovate more rapidly.

In addition to these results, the intensity of competition affects the speed of innovation in a more direct way through what Kamien and Schwartz call the hazard parameter, h. This is a parameter of the $F(t)$ probability distribution; larger values of h indicate faster expected rival innovation and can therefore be equated with more intense rivalry. Analytically the relationship between optimal T and the value of h is not straightforward, but using an indirect proof and some reasonable assumptions,[10] Kamien and Schwartz are able to establish that one of two alternative possibilities will obtain. The first is where optimal T increases with h, in other words the value of h most conducive to speedy innovation is zero, which can presumably be equated to pure monopoly. But the second possibility is that optimal T will be smallest at some intermediate value of h; in this case the speed of innovation is maximised for firms in industries characterised by some middling level of competition. Unfortunately, Kamien and Schwartz can offer no intuition as to the circumstances under which each alternative holds.

In a series of subsequent studies they introduce various modifications to this model to investigate the effects of patents, the source of funding, the contractual nature of costs, etc. Here we confine ourselves to just one of these modifications which explores the outcome when, if our firm does innovate first, rivals are able to change their own development pace in response. (This is not allowed in the basic form of the model in which the probability distribution of rival entry is assumed to be insensitive to our firm's innovation.) In this modified form the results of the basic model are confirmed and, importantly, it is now possible to say a little more about the role of h. Kamien and Schwartz show that the case where innovation speed is maximised under monopoly occurs for new products offering only moderately good returns. The other case, in which intermediate levels of rivalry maximise innovation speed, appears to be identified with highly profitable new innovations. The intuition offered for this result is that:

> Initially, the fear of losing the race spurs additional expenditure on development but as the intensity of competition continues to grow, the firm begins to fear that it will not get the reward from being the first and will also lose the development costs. It then reduces investment in development and thereby postpones the planned introduction date.
>
> (ibid: 142)

Within the wider debate on the effects of market structure on conduct and performance, these findings are among the most interesting to emerge from the technical change literature. However, they have been bought at some cost. For example, we have been asked to believe that a potential innovator has perfect information on the future characteristics of his invention before embarking on the development phase; he is also supposed to be able to predict with certainty how long the development will require once R & D outlays have been decided.

In addition, in focusing on the individual firm's decision, taken in isolation from that of other firms, we have ignored certain important game-theoretic dimensions. As an illustration of how things change with a game-theoretic perspective, suppose there is an industry of n identical firms each making the development decision simultaneously, and each knowing how much its rivals intend to spend. Since all firms are identical, all would presumably plan to innovate by the same time. But this will significantly reduce the returns from the new product and each firm might be tempted to spend a little more than its rivals to ensure being first (on Cournot conjectures). However, if all firms act in this way they will all be frustrated and probably incur losses. In fact so long as all firms perceive this to be the case *ex ante*, none will consider it worth while to incur R & D expenditures and no innovation will occur, even though for the individual firm taken in isolation it would appear that innovation is profitable. (This argument is analogous to Scherer's case in which the V-curve lies everywhere below the D-curve.)

In recent years there has been an impressive series of game-theoretic papers, taking the story further than Kamien and Schwartz. Notable contributions include Loury (1979), Kami (1979), Reinganum (1979, 1982) and Lee and Wilde (1980). But undoubtedly the most influential work of this type is that of Dasgupta and Stiglitz (1980a, b). One of their speed-of-innovation models describes a context similar to Arrow's in which a process invention with certain technical characteristics will reduce unit production costs from C to C' (1980a). They accept Arrow's comparison of a monopolistic inventor and the socially managed market, but criticise his characterisation of competition for the reason we have already mentioned, namely competition abounds only in the product market. Their own model allows instead for competition in R & D, with the possibility of a large number of firms competing to bring the invention to the market; the reward for being first is a patent on the innovation permitting monopoly profits to be earned. They posit that each firm knows the strategies of all others and entertains Cournot conjectures; it also fears the threat of potential entry by new firms. Under these circumstances Dasgupta and Stiglitz show that the only equilibrium which could exist is with only one firm operating and that this firm will earn zero profits. That a Cournot equilibrium will only involve at most one firm follows from the argument of the previous paragraph – if two or more firms were active, each investing the same amount, this could not be an equilibrium since any one of these firms could increase R & D marginally, so ensuring that it wins the race and corners the entire profit from the innovation. That the one firm which does operate will earn zero profits follows from the free entry assumption – the firm will feel it necessary, if adopting Stackleberg conjectures about potential entrants, to invest in R & D an amount equal to the present value of the future monopoly returns from innovating. The lesson Dasgupta and Stiglitz wish to emphasise is that, even though there may be only one firm active in the innovative stage, this does not necessarily signal a lack of competition. In this case, competition is potentially intense and no super-profits are earned. They proceed by investigating the magnitude of equilibrium R & D expenditure in these circumstances and show that it is (a) larger, *ceteris paribus*, in industries characterised by greater demand, and (b) may well be greater than the social optimum (see also Dasgupta and Stiglitz 1980b: 11). The latter is in contrast of course with Arrow's original finding and derives from the fact that the threat of potential competition pushes the innovator too fast.

Perhaps the most important contribution of this model is of a 'ground clearing' nature rather than as a 'realistic' description of the real world. It is certainly difficult to see what would identify the single firm which does operate actively while all others remain on the sidelines. As Kamien and Schwartz suggest, we might suppose that one entrepreneur is cleverer than the rest in anticipating that all others will refrain from entering the race, but this supposition sits uneasily with an industry of supposedly identical firms. We might also question why any sort of equilibrium *should* exist. On the other hand, the model concentrates the mind by establishing that, for a multi-firm equilibrium to exist, one or another of the assumptions employed so far must be relaxed. In another model Dasgupta and Stiglitz (1980b) turn to *technical uncertainty* as the way forward. It should be clear that the reason why at most one firm can be active in the above model is that all participants could guarantee being equal first in the race by spending as much as their rivals. Suppose now, however, that a given R & D expenditure only fixes the *expected* date of innovation. Where this is so, there can be no certainty that any one firm will be first and, paradoxically, there is an inducement for several firms to participate in the race. Assuming now that increased R & D only increases the probabilities that the innovation will come sooner rather than later,[11] and assuming that the development activities of each of the firms are uncorrelated (which means that there must be several routes to successful innovation), they proceed to show that a competitive equilibrium with more than one active firm can exist. In this equilibrium it is shown that (a) the market always provides inadequate research, relative to the social optimum, for small innovations, and (b) for sufficiently long patent lives, it spends too much on research. Under monopoly, on the other hand, the certainty result is sustained – innovation is delayed relative to what is socially optimal.

In summary, this branch of the literature has added a little more, by way of realism, to the Arrow world. The introduction of rivalry, either actual or potential, in the conversion of invention to innovation was clearly necessary, although the conclusions are obviously highly sensitive to how uncertainty is introduced. An incisive survey of the recent patent race literature can be found in Reinganum (1984), and, more extensively but now rather datedly, in Kamien and Schwartz (1982: Ch. 5). While this literature has become extremely technical, it offers rather modest predictive implications, and we shall now move on to consider the relaxation of another of Arrow's assumptions.

(c) INNOVATION AND R & D AS A CONTINUOUS ACTIVITY

So far we have considered a very limited characterisation of technical change. It is one in which there is a given single invention and R & D is undertaken in order to develop it into an innovation; the technical characteristics of the innovation are known in advance, and the amount of expenditure on R & D merely determines how quickly the transformation takes place (or with technical uncertainty, the expected duration of the development phase.) An alternative approach, more obviously amenable to the traditional structure–conduct–performance framework, has modelled R & D in a more general, if looser, way. It is assumed that innovation and R & D are rather more continuous activities, with the generalised effects of pushing the firm's demand curve outwards (for product innovation) or its cost curve downwards (for process innovation). With this approach, more R & D means more innovations and greater shifts in the demand/cost curves. This is a pure 'black-box' view of technology generation, in which R & D goes in one end and product/process improvements come out the other, with more coming out the more that goes in. No longer do we assume that all firms are chasing the same glamorous innovation. Improvements may be marginal or significant, depending on how much R & D is spent, and different firms may be developing different new technologies. Nevertheless, models within this group usually assume identical innovation production functions for all firms in the sense that equal spending will generate equal improvements. In other words, we have moved to a world with firms undertaking similar research but with different outputs and thus independent patents, and innovation is a continuous, not discrete activity.

An example is Needham's (1975) model of R & D in a product innovation context. He posits an individual firm facing the demand curve:

$$Q = Q(p, D) \text{ where } Q_p < 0, Q_D > 0 \tag{3}$$

and with costs:

$$C = c(Q) + D \tag{4}$$

Q is demand, p is price, $c(Q)$ is production costs, D is R & D expenditure, and subscripts indicate partial derivatives. The demand curve is downward sloping with respect to price, indicating at least some market power for the firm, and increased R & D leads to increased demand at any given price. There is some ambiguity about the meaning of a demand curve in the context where R & D generates an entirely new product and thus a new demand curve. Perhaps the easiest way to resolve this is to think of R & D as generating continuous improvements in the *quality* of the product.[12]

In order to optimise, the firm should spend the following amount of R & D[13]:

$$D/pQ = e_D/e_p \tag{5}$$

where $e_D = (\delta Q/\delta D)(D/Q)$ and $e_p = -(\delta Q/\delta p)(P/Q)$ are, respectively the elasticities of demand with respect to R & D spending and price.[14] Thus the firm should spend relatively more on R & D the more elastic is demand with respect to D and the less elastic it is with respect to price. In turn, e_D can be interpreted as the product of two effects: one reflecting the extent to which R & D improves quality, and the other the extent to which demand is responsive to the improved quality. If we now suppose that the firm's actual R & D behaviour is optimal, we can predict the circumstances in which the R & D sales ratio will be higher. In truth, however, these predictions are fairly obvious. Thus Needham points to e_D, and thus D/pQ, being higher in cases of greater technological opportunity. A firm will spend more in conditions where R & D generates greater, rather than less, improvements in quality!

An extension in which rivalry is introduced is more interesting. Now suppose that demand for 'our' firm's product depends also on its rivals' spending $(\bar{D})$[15]:

$$Q = Q(p, D, \bar{D}) \text{ where } Q_{\bar{D}} < 0 \qquad [6]$$

Optimising now requires a revised R & D to sales ratio:

$$\frac{D}{pQ} = \frac{e_D + ke_{\bar{D}}}{e_p}, e_{\bar{D}} < 0 \text{ and } k \geq 0 \text{ (probably)} \qquad [7]$$

$e_D = (\delta Q/\delta\bar{D})(\bar{D}/Q)$ is the elasticity of our demand with respect to rivals' R & D, and $k = (\delta\bar{D}/\delta D/(\bar{D}/D))$ is the reaction elasticity. This shows the (percentage) reaction we expect from our rivals in increasing their R & D in response to an increase in our R & D spending. In general, rivalry may or may not lead to increased R & D. Two special cases are: (a) when *no* reactions are expected, $k=0$, with Cournot type behaviour [7] degenerates to the original condition [5]; (b) when the firm expects rivals to match any changes in R & D, $k=1$, the numerator reduces to $e_D + e_{\bar{D}}$; and a special case of this is where $e_D = -e_{\bar{D}}$, implying that equal quality improvements by us and our rivals will leave our demand unchanged. In that case quality improvements have only a market share effect, leaving total market size unchanged. In these circumstances R & D will only take place if each firm believes its rivals will *not* exactly match any changes in quality.

Needham proceeds to draw a series of tentative predictions about how research intensity (D/pQ) will vary between firms and industries in the light of suggestions of how the various elasticities will differ between different market structures. While speculative and non-rigorous, these comparisons do generate some suggestive pointers. First, price elasticities, at the firm level will tend to be higher, depressing D/pQ, in more competitive industries. Second e_D will tend to be greater, the better able the firm is to internalise the benefits (e.g. through patent protection). This suggests higher research intensities in less competitive industries (or, at least, where significant product differentiation exists). The extreme case of monopoly means $k=0$, tending to lead to greater optimal outlays, but under monopoly it is also true that there is no market share consideration and $e_D > 0$ only to the extent that the market as a whole can be expanded. So even in this simple case it is by no means clear whether more or less R & D will ensue.

Various theoretical developments of this model have been made, some of which correspond to standard well-known developments of the analogous Dorfman–Steiner condition for advertising (see Hay and Morris 1980: Ch. 12, in which the effects of R & D are allowed to decay over time, for example). More substantively, the model has been applied to process innovation alongside product innovation by Stoneman and Leech (1980) and Hughes (1986). In the simplest form (abstracting from rivals' reactions and assuming constant returns in production) this generates a revised condition for optimality:

$$\frac{D}{pQ} = \frac{e_D - e_{CD}(e_p - 1)}{e_p} \qquad [8]$$

where $e_{CD} < 0$, the elasticity of costs with respect to R & D. This elasticity clearly measures the scope for reducing costs through process innovation, and since it is negative, larger values will lead to increased R & D expenditures. This result is as expected and its various developments (for more details of which, see Stoneman and

Leech) are useful in completing the picture started by Needham, but essentially it takes us no further on the matter of the expected relation between market structure and R & D.

Dasgupta and Stiglitz (1980a) in the article described previously also include a model in this vein in which R & D expenditure is directed at process innovation. The main interest is their aggregation up from the firm-level decision to derive an expression for industry R & D/sales. In order to do this they assume a homogeneous good industry in which output-setting firms have Cournot conjectures. So if a firm i's profit function is:

$$\pi_i = pQ_i - c_iQ_i - D_i \tag{9}$$

where c_i declines as D_i increases, and p = the *industry* price (dependent on the outputs of all firms including i). Optimality for firm i implies setting[16]:

$$\frac{D_i}{pQ_i} = \frac{-e_{cD}\,(e_p - Q_i/Q)}{e_p} \tag{10}$$

and

$$p - c_i = \frac{Q_i}{Q}\frac{p}{e_p} \tag{11}$$

On the assumption of a symmetric equilibrium, i.e. all firms of equal size (requiring identical costs), each firm has a share $1/n$th of the market. So $c_i = c$ and $Q_i/Q = 1/n$ for all i. Now the number of firms in the industry will depend upon entry conditions. Dasgupta and Stiglitz consider two cases:

1. *Free entry.* In this case the number of firms will be just sufficient to ensure zero profits. This means that:

$$(p - c)Q = D \tag{12}$$

and so

$$\frac{D}{pQ} = \frac{p-c}{p} \tag{13}$$

But from [11], $p-c = (1/n)\,p/e_p$ and so

$$\frac{D}{PQ} = \frac{1}{ne_p} \tag{14}$$

Taking n as an inverse measure of the degree of concentration, [14] tells us that the R & D to sales ratio *for the industry* rises with concentration (for given e_p). In this sense, then, the Schumpeterian prediction is confirmed. However, Dasgupta and Stiglitz stress that this does not mean that greater concentration *causes* greater research intensity. Both are endogenous to the system and are determined by the underlying parameters (e_p, c and e_{cD}). In fact, it can be shown, by substitution, that:

$$\frac{D}{pQ} = \frac{e_{cD}}{1-e_{cD}} \tag{15}$$

and

$$n = \frac{1-e_{cD}}{e_pe_{cD}} \tag{16}$$

In other words, R & D intensity and firm numbers will vary between industries as the scope for cost improvements (e_{cD}) varies; they will tend to move together, giving the impression of causality, but this is spurious.[17] The same comment applies if, alternatively, we measure the level of concentration by the mark-up of price over cost (the Lerner index). In this case, concentration and research intensity are identical [13], and this follows directly from the assumption of free entry. Dasgupta and Stiglitz go on to compare the magnitude of D in this market equilibrium with what is socially optimal (D_s). Using specific constant elasticity functional forms, which imply that e_p and e_{cD} are invariant with respect to the levels of P and D, they find that the market will always achieve less cost reduction than is socially optimal. Moreover, if demand is highly price inelastic, the market will also undertake *more* R & D than would a socially managed economy. This apparently paradoxical result derives from the fact that all R & D would be concentrated in one unit in the managed economy while the market economy encourages too much repetition dissipated over many units. Note incidentally that this is not the same reason for excessive R & D as in their model discussed in the previous section; this resulted from competitive pressures to win the innovation race.

2. *Entry barriers*. In this case the number of firms is fixed exogenously and the absence of entry means that in general there is no reason to suppose zero profits (i.e. condition [12] no longer applies). Nevertheless, [10] and [11] still hold and this is enough information for us to compute the relationship between the industry level of D and firm numbers (in the special case of fixed e_p and e_{cD} as above). It turns out that as n increases, so does the industry's equilibrium D, but less than proportionately. In other words, less concentrated industries do more R & D than more concentrated ones, but the amount done *per firm* falls, the lower is concentration. Thus the amount of cost reduction is lower, the less concentrated the industry – greater industry expenditures merely reflect more repetition. Also, whatever the number of firms, it is again shown that the amount of cost reduction is less than what is socially optimal.

The two key points of this paper are well taken: (a) market structure and R & D will be jointly determined in many cases and this has important implications for empirical research; and (b) the market, as opposed to socially managed economy, may well involve excessive duplication. Yet in some ways, the model is stacked against more competitive market structures by construction; the assumption that each firm must undertake its own research to achieve the same process innovations as its competitors (i.e. each firm is perfectly protected by its own patent) makes duplication inevitable. Perhaps a more realistic story would involve diversity and only limited appropriability for each firm of its own innovations, but with this supplemented by partial imitation of its rivals' innovations.

Drawing together these various strands to the literature, it is difficult to establish a series of unambiguous predictions on technical change and market structure which may be readily tested empirically. The 'Schumpeterian hypotheses', that technical change is fostered by monopoly power and large firm size, gain a limited degree of support from more recent theoretical models. There is Kamien and Schwartz's finding that development speed will be greatest under monopoly for new products with moderately high returns, and Dasgupta and Stiglitz's finding that per firm spending on R & D is higher in more concentrated industries. On the other hand, there is Arrow's initial result that competitive industries will tend to attract more innovation, and Scherer's suggestion that speed of development may be fastest for small firms in unconcentrated industries. However, the possibility that competition may deter innovation has been established by Scherer and Dasgupta and Stiglitz. Finally, and what sounds to be a rather comforting compromise, we have Kamien and Schwartz's prediction that, for major innovations, development speed may be maximised by intermediate degrees of rivalry. What is clear from this summary is that the market structure – technical change relationship is highly sensitive to the ways in which innovative activity is modelled. Probably the strongest lead for empirical research is the cautionary point made by Dasgupta and Stiglitz, echoed elsewhere in this volume, that market structure and innovation are jointly determined. Econometric work which fails to recognise this may well be seriously flawed.

3. Empirical studies of innovation and invention

Given the initial stimulus of the Schumpeterian hypotheses, reinforced by the type of subsequent theoretical work just described, it is inevitable that most empirical work in this area by industrial economists has focused on the relationships of inventive and innovative activity to firm size and industrial concentration. In the main, empirical studies have employed multivariate regression analysis using largely cross-section observations on inventive/innovative activity at either the level of individual firms or of industries. It is not unfair to suggest that invariably such studies have employed *ad hoc* theorising, with little attempt to specify regression equations rigorously, or to formulate *precise* tests of the sometimes finely defined hypotheses generated by theory. In short, apart from obligatory remarks about testing Schumpeterian hypotheses that bigness and fewness are conducive to technical progress because of lower uncertainty and a greater ability to finance research and innovation, very many empirical studies are virtually devoid of theory. Other empirical methodologies have been employed of course, notably the case study and descriptive analysis of various R & D and innovation data sets. We preface our discussion with reference to some of the more striking descriptive results to emerge from such studies.

First, it is clear that invention is by no means the prerogative of the organised corporate R & D laboratory. Jewkes *et al.* (1969) find that of 64 major twentieth-century inventions only 24 emanated from formal R & D: the other 40 being attributed to individual inventors. A number of other studies corroborate this result in different contexts, and also point to a tendency for the corporate R & D laboratory to concentrate on relatively minor innovations and/or to rely on others (independent inventors) to supply the original thinking which they may then develop.[18] Second, in all Western economies, formalised R & D is dominated by the large corporations and by relatively few industries. For example, in the US, the largest 100 firms typically account for about four-fifths of all R & D spending, about double their share of overall employment, and the picture is similar for the UK. The industrial distribution of the spending is also heavily concentrated in the same industries: aircraft, pharmaceuticals, electronics, instrument engineering and the chemicals sector, for most countries.[19] Third, innovation, as opposed to invention, is also dominated by larger firms. Freeman (1971), for instance, reports on a major UK study, in which it was found that only 10 per cent of some 1200 post-war innovations were due to small firms (under 200 employees), compared with their share of net output of over double that figure. Descriptive 'facts' such as these help to clear the mind on some issues, while suggesting caution on others.

A stylised picture emerges of the 'little man' being more than able to hold his own at the imaginative inventive stage,[20] but with the resource-endowed R & D laboratory better able to carry invention forward to innovation. Certainly it is clear that R & D is apparently a large-firm activity, but it is also likely that official statistics under-record R & D activity in small firms where, for example, the entrepreneur owner devotes part of his time to product and process improvement without thinking of this as R & D. Moreover, R & D is only at best an input, and greater inputs by larger firms do not automatically imply greater outputs. The fact that greater R & D is consistently observed in certain industries in all countries suggests a point which has also figured prominently in the studies surveyed presently. The technological opportunity for technical advance varies between industries regardless of their structure and typical size of firms[21]; as such, inter-industry comparisons of invention and innovation should normalise for those differences before attempting to identify differences due to structure and size. This argument applies much less for comparisons of firms within given industries, for whom technological opportunity is, in principle, likely to be more equal.

As a final preliminary remark, we should also refer in passing to the relative importance of technological opportunity and economic opportunity as stimuli for inventions. This subject is most widely associated with the work of Schmookler (1966), who argued from a study of the histories of hundreds of important inventions in four fields, that it was always the perception of an economic problem to be solved, rather than a new scientific discovery which stimulated invention. Although this view has attracted much attention (Kamien and Schwartz 1982: 58–64, provide a summary), Schmookler's finding is perhaps on reflection neither surprising nor significant. It is surely self-evident that successful inventions are only successful if they satisfy an economic need. That is, demand, existent or potential, is a necessary condition for success. On the other hand, economic need may not be sufficient – Schmookler's identification of technological opportunity with new scientific discoveries seems unnecessarily restrictive. Employing technological opportunity as a wider (and admittedly looser) concept, there is ample evidence, as we shall see, that it does have an impact. More positively, some of Schmookler's empirical results are of considerable interest. He finds, from a comparison of patent figures, that capital goods invention tends to be distributed across industries in proportion to the relative scale of overall investment in the using industries; that is, invention will be more intense in industries with buoyant demand and investment.

(a) MEASUREMENT ISSUES

Turning now to the econometric analysis of inventive and innovative activity in terms of market structure and firm size, as always in industrial economics, we confront severe measurement difficulties. As far as size and structure are concerned the problems are not unique to this area.[22] But we should emphasise the real difference between measures of concentration, which are widely used as indicators of the degree of competition, and notions such as Kamien and Schwartz's intensity of rivalry. The latter has as much to do with potential competition from without the industry, as the size distribution of firms within it. Indeed, in this respect Kamien and Schwartz's approach has more in common with Schumpeterian notions of competition than the neo-classical view.

In measuring inventive and innovative activity, empirical researchers have employed three main alternatives:

1. head-counts of the number of patents issued;
2. expenditure or employment of personnel on R & D;
3. head-counts of the number of innovations, sometimes confined to 'significant' innovations as defined by either the researcher himself or by 'industry-experts'.

By common agreement, R & D is viewed as an input to the innovative process and patent counts as a measure of the output. Clearly, neither is a perfect measure. Not all patents are of equal significance, many inventions are not patented, and even the granting of a patent by no means assures the eventual appearance of a successful innovation.[23] R & D data does not represent all inputs into the process. As mentioned already, R & D activity is not confined to formal R & D departments and it is doubtful whether the inputs of, say, production managers making on-the-job modification to their processes are recorded in the officially collected R & D statistics. Perhaps more important, while a firm's R & D to sales ratio is usually interpreted as a measure of research intensity, it may also be seen as a crude inverse measure of the productivity of R & D.[24] Nevertheless, these are problems we must live with in the absence of better alternatives.

(b) THE INNOVATIVE PRODUCTION FUNCTION

There is no doubt that R & D intensity is typically correlated with most measures of inventive/innovative activity. McLean and Round (1978) report a strong positive relationship when the latter is measured by the output of new products, thus confirming, for Australia, an earlier finding by Comanor and Scherer (1969) for the pharmaceutical industry in the US. Mansfield (1968), Comanor (1965), Pavitt and Wald (1971) also report, in various contexts, high correlations between R & D and the 'output' of invention and innovation, variously measured. Perhaps the simplest, but in some ways most compelling, evidence is provided by Scherer's early study (1965b) of the 500 largest US firms. He finds a virtually linear relationship between the number of patents issued to a firm and its (lagged) size of R & D workforce. We interpret this to mean that for the very largest firms at least, R & D and patents may be used interchangeably, if with caution, as measures of inventive/innovative activity.[25]

(c) R & D INTENSITY

From a comprehensive survey of studies, Weiss (1971) concluded that there was strong evidence for a positive relationship between firm size and the size of the firm's R & D expenditures or employment. However, in general, R & D was found to rise with firm size at a slightly less than proportionate rate, meaning that R & D intensity tends to fall as size increases. As he points out (1971: 390), some of these results may be biased in two respects: they typically exclude small firms from samples and they fail to exclude R & D conducted in large firms but financed by government, such as military-related research. The latter tends to overstate the positive effect of firm size, while the former means that the drastically lower R & D intensity of smaller firms is not reflected in these estimates. Indeed, we know that below a threshold size, little or no formal R & D is conducted. See, for example, Freeman's (1974) consistent UK case study finding that there is a threshold size required for entering the innovation race. Thus we may *stylise* the relationship between R & D expenditure and firm size, as in Fig. 6.3a, which implies the relationship between R & D *intensity* and firm size as in Fig. 6.3b. In broad terms a

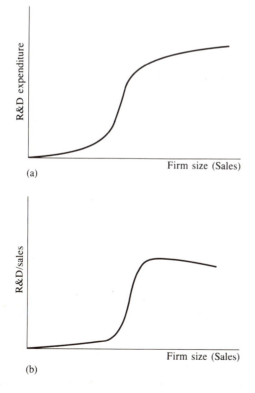

FIG. 6.3 R & D and scale of firm

Schumpeterian view is sustained if we simply compare large with small firms, but contradicted if we investigate the effect of firm size within the set of large firms. In studies since 1970,[26] this picture has been sustained in general, and for countries other than the US. Without doubt, in virtually all industries in all countries studied, there is a threshold size of firms below which formal R & D is hardly conducted at all. Above this, research intensity increases with firm size, only to fall back at very large sizes of firm. It should be noted that in smaller countries, the typically lower sizes of firms observed means that only a few firms may exceed the maximum intensity level (Phillips 1971 provides an example).

Turning to the relationship between R & D and market structure, the value of econometric results depends crucially on whether or not and how well the researcher has standardised for inter-industry differences in technological opportunity. The usual econometric devices for controlling for unmeasurable influences, such as dummy variables and splitting the sample, have been well in evidence.

As often is the case in this area, an early study by Scherer (1967a) sets the scene well. He examined the inter-industry variance in the R & D workforce relative to the total workforce over 56 US industries for 1960, finding that the four-firm concentration ratio was generally positively significant, in broad support of the Schumpeterian hypothesis. However, the impact of concentration varies markedly between experiments depending on how differences in technological opportunities and other qualitative industry differences are incorporated into the model. Quite clearly multi-collinearity serves to render regression coefficients unstable due to correlation between technological opportunity and concentration itself. Problems of interpretation are further aggravated if we recall the above warning that R & D and concentration are jointly determined in equilibrium. If so, this calls for a more detailed model based on simultaneous estimation techniques. Various steps in this direction have been made in subsequent research (e.g. Farber 1981; Howe and McFetridge 1976; Buxton 1975). While they tend to suggest that a positive relation running from concentration to R & D is still sustained, the models and/or data employed are relatively crude and, in our opinion, hardly conclusive.

In further research with the same data set, Scherer pointed to the possibility (not without strong statistical support) of a non-monotonic relation, with R & D intensity peaking at moderate levels of concentration (i.e. with four-firm concentration ratios in the region of 55%). A more refined examination was conducted by Comanor (1967) (and developed by Shrieves 1976), allowing a variable effect for concentration which depended on the importance of product differentiation in the competitive process. His result was that high concentration was associated with high R & D but only where differentiation of products was largely absent. This suggests that where product innovation is important, R & D will be conducted regardless of how concentrated is the industry. Again in more recent years, studies for countries other than the US have appeared. For Belgium, Phlips (1971) found that a positive relationship only existed within the chemicals and electrical equipment sectors of industry. Even this limited support for the Schumpeterian hypothesis was subsequently undermined by Finet (1975), who showed that with a more appropriate acknowledgement of technological opportunity, the relationship becomes even weaker. Globerman (1973) finds no support for the hypothesis in Canada; indeed, among high technological opportunity industries, the reverse is true, with higher concentration associated with lower research intensities. For the UK, we have one recent study which identifies a positively significant effect for concentration (Hughes 1986) in the context of a simultaneous model of exports and R & D. In another study, however, Leech and Stoneman (1976), using admittedly more aggregate data, find no significant effect.

While most of the empirical emphasis has been on concentration, the effects of other elements of market structure have also been investigated. Grabowski (1968), for example, found a significant positive effect on R & D intensity of an index of diversification, but Comanor (1967) had previously found the reverse, with Scherer (1965a) finding no effect either way! This seems to be an area worthy of further research, on both the theoretical and empirical levels. We already have the theoretical prediction of Kamien and Schwartz's model (noted earlier) that R & D expenditures will be greater, the less profitable are firms' existing products. This has direct implications for differences between diversified and specialised firms. Moreover, there is considerable anecdotal evidence that R & D programmes directed at solving problems in one area sometimes throw up solutions in other unrelated areas. Diversified firms are more likely to be able to internalise any such effects.

Barriers to entry have sometimes been included in estimating equations, albeit usually rather crudely with dummy variables. Comanor (1967) finds that, *ceteris paribus*, moderately high entry barriers are most conducive to high R & D intensities. This result is in direct accordance with Kamien and Schwartz's prediction of medium levels of rivalry intensity being most amenable to high research intensity. More generally, there are theoretical reasons for supposing a two-way relation between entry barriers and research intensity. It is argued that some innovative activity may be motivated by the desire to raise entry barriers.[27] For example, Levin (1978) suggests that incumbents may search out scale-augmenting technology when faced with a serious entry potential. The idea that R & D might be directed at increasing product differentiation and brand loyalty, to make the penetration of the market by potential entrants more difficult, is longer established. But as far as is known, this has never been rigorously tested with an appropriate simultaneous dynamic model.

(d) PATENTS AND INVENTION COUNTS

The most thorough early study of patents and firm size was Scherer's (1965b). In a study of the US top 500 companies, he reports, from a cubic regression, that the number of patents issued to firms increases, but at a decreasing rate, thereby confirming a tendency among the very largest firms for diminishing intensity of patents as scale increases. Scherer also finds that smaller firms perform rather better using the patents criterion than, as above, when R & D is examined. He reports that relatively small firms (with less than 5,000 employees) accounted for about 40 per cent of all patents in manufacturing, roughly equal to their share of manufacturing

rly three times their share of R & D). This tends to confirm our earlier
at much R & D in small firms goes unrecorded.

ually, the poorer performance of large firms on patents, compared to R
-, also tends to confirm the suggestion that large-firm patenting may under-record their inventive activity *especially* where research is government funded and needs of secrecy deter patenting. In a relatively rare UK study of 86 firms in chemicals, electrical engineering and electronics, and machine tools, Smyth *et al.* (1972) report a tendency for patent intensity to *increase* with firm size in chemicals and in electrical engineering and electronics, except for the very largest firms in the latter, but to decrease with firm size in the machine tool industry. Similar results emerge for Sweden (Johannison and Lindstrom 1971) especially concerning the performance of larger firms in chemicals.

Turning to the effect of market structure,there are studies of patents and concentration. Scherer (1965b) for example, finds no evidence that the largest firms in industries tend to perform especially well when concentration is highest. But the most interesting study is due to Mansfield (1968), who looks directly at important innovations. Three industries are studied and, for each, the most important innovations are listed and attributed to the firms responsible. Mansfield finds that in the coal and petrol refining industries the four largest firms accounted for more than their share of industry innovations, while in steel very much the reverse was true. Williamson (1965) subsequently re-worked these data in two time periods to show that the largest firms' share of innovations was negatively related to the level of concentration. This is not necessarily inconsistent with Mansfield's own finding but it adds the rider that large firms' innovative performance will depend on the competitive environment in which they are located. For these specific industries, the finding implies that they perform worse when in concentrated markets.

We could go further in this survey of empirical work. Many studies have not been included in the above description and the reader wishing to learn more should consult the outstanding survey in this field (Kamien and Schwartz 1982: Ch. 3). On balance, there does not appear to be a strong consensus in favour of the Schumpeterian hypotheses. Although beneficial effects from increased size do appear up to a point (and certainly above some minimum as far as R & D is concerned), beyond that point larger firms do not increase their innovative or inventive activity: if anything the reverse is true. Likewise, there is no compelling evidence that increased market power (at least measured by concentration) is conducive to greater activity. Here Kamien and Schwartz suggest that the evidence hints at intermediate market structures being most beneficial in this respect. This is certainly consistent with one of the predictions of their own theoretical model and one might be excused for chiding them for a wishful interpretation of the evidence! Our view at this stage is that the evidence is not sufficiently pervasive to support any strong conclusions either way. One is also struck by the feeling that too much of the empirical work has been unashamed 'number crunching' with little regard for theory or even econometric good practice.

In one sense, of course, it is as if we have stopped the film before the final reel. In the last resort none of the measures we have discussed is a true performance measure. R & D is an input, patents are at best an intermediate output, often coming to nothing. Even head-counts of major innovations are subjective and miss the multitude of minor product and process improvements which taken together may be as important in their effects on the performance of industries. In short, we suggest that the logical conclusion to the story should involve an examination of productivity (and of all factors of production, not just those engaged in research) in order to ascertain the effects of inventive and innovative activities of firms and industries. This we shall do in the final section of this survey following our discussion of the important intermediate process of diffusion by which best becomes actual practice.

But finally, we should recall a comment in our introduction. Throughout both the empirical and theoretical literature in this field, there are frequent claims that Schumpeterian views are being modelled and tested. At a trivial level this may be correct. Schumpeter did suggest that big oligopolistic firms would be most progressive, and as we have seen this issue has dominated the post-war literature. On another level, however, these claims are quite misguided. Recall that Schumpeter's world view was one in which equilibrium has no interesting role to play but where the competitive process is one of ebb and flow and essentially dynamic. Moreover, the optimising theories described above and the cross-section econometrics inevitably can only make sense as a description of inter-industry differences in equilibrium, that is, the quantitative counterpart of comparative statics. For Schumpeter, the entrepreneur need not be the cool calculating optimiser and, therefore, it is hard to see how such studies can be amenable to Schumpeterian interpretation. This is not to deny their importance, only to deny their spurious connection with Schumpeter.

On the other hand, more research is now being conducted in the Schumpeterian spirit, with the aid of simulation models rather than from direct observation of the real world. The basic idea is that one sets up a hypothetical industry of firms who behave according to various rules, concerning for example investment, and with their performance determined partly by their own previous behaviour but also partly by a chance element, reflecting for instance the effects of R & D. The way in which firms and the industry then evolve is studied by running a computer program reflecting these assumptions. After a given number of hypothetical time periods, the program is stopped and the resultant structure and performance of the industry are then examined. By varying the basic parameters of the model and re-running the programme one can then determine how far the evolution of the industry is sensitive to the particular values of those parameters.

In the context of technical changes and market structure, the most noteworthy contributions are those of Nelson and Winter (summarized in 1982). In particular, in one paper (1978) they explore the way in which industry structure may evolve as the result of what they call Schumpeterian competition in innovation. The most important features of the model are:

1. firms follow satisficing, not optimising, rules in decision making;
2. innovation and imitation are alternative strategies;
3. firms plan one period ahead and are not overtly racing against their rivals;
4. the chance element is introduced by assuming that the results of R & D are

uncertain, but with the chances of success being higher the more the firm spends;

5. large firms spend more than small firms on R & D because, by assumption, R & D is internally financed.

In other words, the behaviour of these hypothetical firms is modelled in a way which the authors believe is consistent with observations from the real world. There is no assumption that the industry is ever in equilibrium; instead the emphasis is on its evolution over time. The parameters which they vary between runs of the program include: the underlying technological base, aggressiveness in R & D, that is innovation versus imitation, the ease of imitation, etc. The most famous prediction they generate is that, in all simulations, concentration increases, but by less the higher the initial level of concentration. To our mind, this is not surprising since they rule out the possibility of new entry and, in effect, they apply a Gibrat-type effect to existing firms. The outcome for an industry such as this was established much earlier, and more simply, in the work of Hart and Prais (1956) (see our Chapter 3). Indeed, for our purposes, the main conclusion to be drawn is essentially negative. Technical change has important implications for market structure, and any modelling of the effects of structure on innovative performance ignores this reverse causality at its peril.

4. Diffusion

The diffusion of new technologies is the process by which new innovations spread and come into common usage in the industries concerned. To state the obvious, a firm, industry or nation with an impressive inventive and/or innovative record may still lag behind its competitors in performance if it fails to diffuse those innovations sufficiently rapidly.[28]

In this section we shall concentrate on the diffusion of process innovations. The diffusion of product innovations such as video recorders, colour televisions, etc., falls largely outside our present scope, with most of the relevant literature belonging most naturally to the economics of consumer behaviour. We do not wish, however, to force this distinction too far. For one thing, there is more than passing commonality between the literature on process diffusion and diffusion of new consumer durables. (Davies 1979: 32–4). For another, not all product innovation is for consumers; if the new product is a capital good to be sold to other using firms then the diffusion of new products is merely the supply side of the subject of the present section.

To clarify these and other definitional issues, consider a specific example – say the *shuttleless loom*[29] used in weaving. This was a cost-saving process innovation for the weaving industry, but a product innovation for the textile machinery industry. In this case the new technology was generated by firms outside the industry which was to use it. This need not always be the case, especially when the using industry has a substantial 'in-house' R & D tradition. The diffusion process commences with the first adoption by a weaving firm and it proceeds as further weavers adopt and as those who have already adopted use it more widely in their operations. Overall diffusion then reflects the aggregate usage of the technology measured perhaps by the proportion of the industry's stock of looms which are shuttleless or the proportion of output produced using shuttleless looms. In turn this reflects the extent of inter-firm diffusion, that is the proportion of firms having adopted and, for each firm, the extent to which it has adopted, intra-firm diffusion. In some cases, usually lumpy innovations or small firms, if the firm adopts at all it must immediately turn over its entire operations to the new technology, and so intra-firm diffusion is instantaneous and we need consider only inter-firm diffusion. (This is not the case for shuttleless looms where large weaving firms operate scores or hundreds of looms which are usually replaced gradually over time.) One final preliminary remark establishes an important perspective. For virtually all process innovations inter-firm diffusion is far from instantaneous. The shuttleless loom, for example, had been adopted by only about 1 in 8 of all relevant firms in the UK even 13 years after its date of innovation (ibid.: 171).[30]

The literature in this area has addressed three main issues: at the industry level, what determines the speed of diffusion, usually inter-firm; at the firm level, why do some firms adopt earlier than others; and also at the firm level, what determines the pace of intra-firm diffusion?

(a) INTER-FIRM DIFFUSION

Building on earlier work by Griliches (1957),[31] in 1961 Mansfield established a model of diffusion which was to go largely unchallenged for almost twenty years. The key to his model lies in the notion that, once diffusion is under way, the proportion of firms not having adopted the new technology to date ('holdouts') who decide to adopt in a given time period will be critically influenced by the proportion of their competitors who have already adopted. Defining $m(t)$ as the number having adopted by time t, out of an industry population of n firms, this hypothesis can be written algebraically as:

$$\frac{m(t+1)-m(t)}{n-m(t)} = \beta \, \frac{m(t)}{n} \qquad \text{where } \beta > 0 \qquad [17]$$

Thus, the number adopting for the first time in the period t to $t+1$, as a proportion of those not yet having adopted, $n-m(t)$, is assumed to be simply related to the proportion already having adopted, $m(t)/n$. Interestingly, this is identical to the key equation used in simple models of the spread of contagious diseases,[32] and for this reason Mansfield's is often referred to as the epidemic diffusion model. Mansfield rationalises this equation by discussing the reasons why non-adopters would revise their attitude towards the new process. He argues that the proportion of non-adopters adopting should be greater when m/n is higher for three reasons. 'As more information and experience accumulate, it becomes less of a risk to begin using [the new process]. Competitive pressures mount and bandwagon effects occur' (1968: 137). He goes on to develop the informational point by suggesting that 'where the profitability of using the innovation is very difficult to estimate, the mere fact that a large proportion of competitors have introduced it may prompt a firm to consider it more favourably' (1968: 137–8).

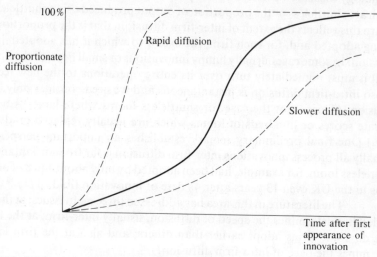

100%

Proportionate diffusion

Rapid diffusion

Slower diffusion

Time after first appearance of innovation

FIG. 6.4 Logistic/cumulative normal diffusion

Replacing discrete time by continuous time and integrating shows that diffusion will follow the logistic curve (Fig. 6.4):

$$\frac{m(t)}{n} = [1 - \exp\{\alpha + \beta t\}]^{-1} \tag{18}$$

where α is the constant of integration. As shown in the diagram, the logistic curve is a symmetrical S-shaped curve with point of inflexion always occuring at $m/n = 0.5$. The steepness of the curve is determined by the value of β, larger values yielding steeper curves and thus more rapid diffusion. For this reason β is usually referred to as the speed of diffusion. Mansfield argues that the value of β will reflect the characteristics of the innovation and of the industry in which it is diffusing. His reasoning is plausible if *ad hoc*. He suggests that β will be larger, that is diffusion faster, the greater is the profitability (π) of the innovation and the smaller is the relative size of the investment outlay required to install it (S), more costly innovations being viewed as inherently more risky. Thus for innovation i in the jth industry:

$$\beta_{ij} = a_0 + a_1\pi_{ij} + a_2S_{ij} \quad \text{where } a_1 > 0, a_2 < 0 \tag{19}$$

Testing the model against data collected on the diffusion of the 12 major new processes in four industries in the US, he finds strong statistical support for the model. First, the logistic curve is transformed[33] to make it amenable to (weighted) least squares regression in the form:

$$\log\left(m(t)/n - m(t)\right) = \alpha + \beta t \tag{20}$$

For all 12 innovations the fit is 'good' in the sense that the correlation coefficient between the dependent variable and time exceeds 0.89 in all cases. Second, using the 12 estimates of β as the dependent variable in a cross-section analysis of the speed of diffusion based on [19],he reports an R^2 of 0.99, with π strongly positively significant and S rather less strongly negatively significant. Most important for present purposes, he also includes dummy intercept variables to represent the four industries concerned, and finds that their relative magnitudes are not inconsistent with the hypothesis that diffusion is more rapid, *ceteris paribus*, in less concentrated industries.

Commenting first on the narrow issue of the last result, it would be wrong to read too much into a comparison of just four observations (industries), but on the face of it, this is a rejection of Schumpeterian type hypotheses. While Mansfield does not develop a strong theoretical case for expecting concentration to affect diffusion speeds, he does suggest that β should be higher, *ceteris paribus*, in 'markets which are more keenly competitive' (1968: 138). This presumably derives from a 'competitive pressures' type argument. For instance, if one assumes that the process is cost saving, the cost disadvantage of a non-adopter may well not result in any loss of market share in industries characterised by price fixing, collusion, price leadership, or the kinked demand curve. In those circumstances the incentive to adopt is not necessarily lower than in more competitive industries, but the pressures on a non-adopter may be substantially smaller. Likewise, in industries characterised by highly differentiated products, price reductions on the part of adopters, passing cost savings on to the consumer, will make smaller inroads into the market shares of non-adopters (see Davies 1979: 142–6).

Mansfield's (1961) paper has had a significant effect on the literature. A number of authors subsequently applied the model to various other innovations, usually with seemingly good results.[34] On the positive side of things, Mansfield, his followers and others, have shown beyond much doubt that diffusion curves *are* invariably S-shaped. This, incidentally, corresponds to the general finding in other social sciences that innovations, epidemics, fashion, rumour, etc., all follow S-shaped diffusion curves.[35] Within economics, the same finding also invariably holds for new consumer durables.[36] On more specific issues, however, Mansfield's work has been criticised by, among others, Davies (1979: Ch. 2) and Stoneman (1983: notably Ch. 7). On an empirical level, neither his curve fitting based on [20] nor his cross-section analysis of diffusion speed based on [19] involved sufficient degrees of freedom to be convincing. Moreover, in collecting data, he considered only the larger firms in each industry, thus installing a spurious homogeneity within his samples and increasing the chances of a good fit for the logistic (Davies 1979: 17). On the theoretical level, the model is disappointing in its lack of any underlying model of decision making under uncertainty and in this respect it is similar to Needham's model discussed earlier. Indeed, because he models only the behaviour of firms in aggregate, Mansfield can, here, offer no reason why some firms adopt early, and others late. Finally, Davies (1979) shows that the conditions required for a logistic epidemic solution are sufficiently restrictive to suggest that it will not be applicable, in general, to new process innovations. (For example, the profitability of adoption must remain constant over time, and the probability of adoption at any point in time should be the same for all firms.)

From the results of Mansfield's followers, one in particular is worthy of comment given our present interest in market structure. Romeo (1977), having fitted Mansfield's model to data on the diffusion of numerically controlled machine tools in various engineering industries, finds that β tends to be higher in industries with a larger number of firms (N) and lower in industries with a larger variance of the logarithm of firms size (σ_s^2). As explained in Chapter 3, virtually all concentration indexes are inversely related to N, and positively related to σ_s^2. Therefore, both these results are consistent with Mansfield's earlier findings that diffusion speed is lower in more concentrated industries.

An alternative approach has employed probit analysis (based on models first used in experimental biology; see Finney 1957). In contrast to epidemic models, this approach explicitly recognises that potential adopters of a new technology will be heterogeneous. Typically this heterogeneity is represented by some key firm characteristic which is supposed to be crucially important in determining responsiveness to the technology. Necessarily, models within this tradition focus directly on the individual firm's decision making and aggregate up to generate industry level predictions. One example is Davies's (1979) model in which firm size is the key characteristic. He places the decision as to whether or not to adopt a new process in a behavioural setting in which the firm compares the *expected pay-back* period, *ER*, with some *target pay-back* period *R**. Both *ER* and *R** depend on a multitude of characteristics of the firm and the new technology; but only firm size is recognised explicitly, the others being represented by stochastic disturbance terms. Typically, both firm size and the stochastic factors vary across potential users, but for all firms, *ER* will decrease over time (representing more favourable expectations about the technology) and *R** will increase over time (representing less stringent targets as the perceived risks attached to adoption are assumed to decline). Some of these assumptions are based on a priori reasoning, and some on a study made of the technical characteristics of a sample of process innovations. For instance, Davies suggests from the latter that process innovations typically involve scale economies. For this and other reasons he suggests that the expected profitability of the technology is typically higher for large firms. But he also finds from his survey that the profitability of adoption varies between firms for a host of technical reasons, for example the nature of their products and the vintage of their existing technology. These are represented by the disturbance term. He suggests that expectations will improve over time partly because information becomes clearer. For example, non-adopters observe the successful application of the new technology by their competitors. Also the technology itself is refined and improved as a result of learning by doing; a feature which Davies shows is well documented for his sample of innovations and which is presumably commonplace among most if not all new technologies. Turning to *R**, the target rate used in investment appraisal, he suggests that larger firms will tend to apply more liberal targets as the consequences of potential failure are relatively less pronounced than for small firms. But, again there are many other factors causing inter-firm differences in *R**, and these are reflected by the disturbance term determining *R**. *R** tends to increase over time because firms reassess favourably the risk of adoption, again on the basis of the experience of others.

Assuming that $R*$ and ER are both multiplicative functions of firm size, time and the disturbance terms, Davies manipulates the adoption decision so that it can be rewritten as:

$$S > S* \qquad [21]$$

Thus i will have adopted if its actual size exceeds some critical level, $S*$.[37] From the specifications of ER and $R*$, this critical size will vary between firms and will tend to decrease over time. This means that the chances of any firm having adopted increase over time, and while there is a *tendency* for large firms to adopt earlier, some small firms will adopt more rapidly than large firms. There will always be some small firms with small critical sizes, and some large firms with large critical sizes.

Assuming that both actual size and critical size are lognormally distributed,[38] he aggregates [21] up to the industry level to show that the aggregate diffusion curve will follow some sort of S-shape. The exact form of the S-shape will depend on the form of the time paths of ER and $R*$, and thus $S*$. Here, Davies suggests two broad alternatives:

$$\text{Group A innovations: } S_t* = S_0*t^{-\psi} \qquad \psi > 0 \qquad [22]$$

$$\text{Group B innovations: } S_t* = S_0*e^{-\psi t} \qquad \psi > 0 \qquad [23]$$

where S_t* and S_0* refer to the levels of critical size at times t and 0 (the date of origin of the innovation). Group A innovations are relatively cheap and simple; they experience major improvements in their early years but thereafter there are fewer improvements. This is reflected in [22], which represents how the profitability and learning about such techniques will improve over time – rapidly at first, but then tailing off. Group B innovations are more expensive and technically complex, and experience more sustained improvements for many years after they are first introduced. He goes on to show that for the Group A type of innovations, diffusion will follow a cumulative lognormal time path (Fig. 6.5), while for the Group B innovations diffusion will be cumulative normal. The essential difference between these curves is that the former is positively skewed with a point of inflexion (maximum growth) relatively early, while the latter is symmetric, and broadly similar to Mansfield's logistic.[39]

The speed of diffusion in this model is determined by the magnitude of ψ, reflecting obvious factors such as the pace of learning, improvements in information and any other time-variant determinants of ER and $R*$. It is also, less obviously, determined by the extent of inter-firm differences in S and $S*$. The intuition behind the latter result is that in industries where firms are largely homogeneous, once diffusion starts all firms are clustered close to the point $S = S*$. Only small changes in ER and $R*$ are required to bring them below the critical point at which adoption is sanctioned.

Davies tests the model against data collected for the diffusion of 22 post-war innovations in the UK. Fitting the appropriate curve to the appropriate innovations yields satisfactory fits in terms of R^2 and Durbin–Watson values. But fitting the 'wrong' curve gives poor results, as would be hoped for if there was any

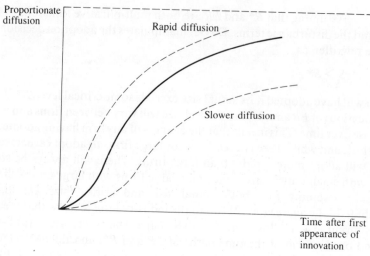

FIG. 6.5 Cumulative lognormal diffusion

validity in the Group A/Group B distinction. In a second stage, similar to Mansfield's, he explains inter-industry and inter-innovation differences in the estimated speed of diffusion. Like Mansfield, he finds the profitability of the innovation to have a positive effect on diffusion speed. Among his other significant explanatory variables, the two most interesting for present purposes are N, firm numbers, and σ_s^2, the variance of log firm size. Diffusion is slower in industries with more firms, perhaps because information dissemination is slower. The inverse effect of size inequalities reflects greater heterogeneity between firms in ER and R^*; this is the logical consequence of the central role of firm size in the model. Thus Davies confirms Romeo's earlier finding on σ_s^2, but not on firm numbers. The overall effect of concentration is therefore unclear. Market structure will influence diffusion speed, but not monotonically.

Other applications of the probit approach include David (1969), Bonus (1973),[40] and Stoneman and Ireland (1983). It is also clear how Salter's vintage model (1960) could be developed to yield a probit model of diffusion in which the heterogeneity of firms' vintages of existing capital stock would take on the role of firm size in Davies's model (see Davies 1979: 29–30; Stoneman 1983). Of these other models we shall concentrate on that of Stoneman and Ireland (1983), partly because it addresses an important omission in Davies, the role of the innovation supplying industry, and partly because it builds on David's earlier work which is unpublished and therefore inaccessible to the interested reader. Like Davies, Stoneman and Ireland construct a model with the implication that a firm will have adopted by t if its actual size exceeds some critical level. But this is derived from a simpler more specific context based on David's earlier work. They assume the new technology requires the purchase of a capital good, with price p. This reduces labour requirements (relative to the old technology) by L^s per unit of output. With interest rate r, wage rate w and ignoring depreciation, it therefore pays to adopt when savings on the wage bill exceed the capital cost of using the technology. Since the output level of the firm is its size S, the critical size satisfies:

$$S^* w L^s = pr \qquad [24]$$

Hence

$$S^* = \frac{pr}{wL_s} \qquad [25]$$

At any point in time, therefore, only firms with actual size in excess of S^* will be users.[41] Over time, wages grow at an exponential rate, lowering S^* and increasing the proportion of firms which will find the new technology profitable. In effect this is the Davies model without the stochastic element and it therefore predicts that firms adopt in exactly descending order of size.

However, Stoneman and Ireland now posit a supplying industry which is aware of the demand curve implied by [25] and the size distribution of firms. They suggest that the supplier(s) has a cost curve embodying a learning mechanism. The unit costs of producing the new technology equipment decline over time and as their cumulative output increases.[42] Assuming long-run optimising behaviour by suppliers, they then explore how the innovation will be priced over time, and thus the form of the diffusion curve and its speed, under different forms of market structure in the supplying industry. Unfortunately, the complexity of the model makes tractable solutions difficult without relaxing various assumptions in different contexts. For more detail, the interested reader is referred to the original paper or Stoneman's own summary (1983: 128–34). For the sake of brevity here, we content ourselves with his own conclusion: 'We have shown that the market structure of the supplying industry, the objectives of the firms in that industry, the degree of learning economics, and the extent of any financial constraints can be important influences on the diffusion path.'

A third, purely theoretical, approach is due to Reinganum (1981). In order to focus attention on the main point of her contribution, she investigates diffusion in a world free of uncertainty and where all potential adopters are identical, precisely the conditions under which diffusion is trivial (instantaneous) under the probit approach. She shows, on the contrary, that even in such a world all firms would not adopt instantaneously, but sequentially. The bare bones of her model involve present value-maximising firms who undertake strategic behaviour, that is bearing in mind the behaviour of their rivals as in the game-theoretic models described above. On the twin assumptions that the profitability of adoption is greatest for early adopters but the costs of adjustment involved in quick adoption are higher, she shows that a Nash equilibrium of adoption dates will exist. This equilibrium involves an orderly sequence of adoption, the pace of which is sensitive to the number of firms (concentration). Unfortunately it is impossible to establish, in general, whether increased firm numbers will increase or retard diffusion. But the main lesson to be learned does not concern any specific prediction to be tested against real-world data. Rather, Reinganum suggests that the effects of strategic behaviour emanating from oligopolistic rivalry may be, in principle, just as important as imperfect information and/or heterogeneity of potential adoptors in understanding the mechanics of diffusion.[43]

The study of the diffusion process seems to be an area of considerable potential future development. Certain empirical 'facts' have been established; the S-shaped curve, the importance of the innovation's profitability and the industry's market structure. Building on these, a theoretically richer understanding is beginning to emerge. There remains the challenge to theoreticians to develop a tractable model incorporating simultaneously strategic behaviour and an explicit supply side, alongside the more traditional elements of imperfect information and heterogeneity among potential adopters.

(b) WHY DO SOME FIRMS ADOPT EARLIER THAN OTHERS?

The answer to this question, in the probit approach, has been provided already. In the theoretical models of David and of Stoneman and Ireland, firm size is a positive (in fact the only) determinant of diffusion speed. In the Davies model the prediction is less stringent: large firms will tend to adopt more quickly; just how strong that tendency will depend, in his theory, on how strongly firm size affects ER and $R*$ relative to the other unspecified determinants. In the epidemic model, because the key equation [17] is defined at the aggregate level, there are no predictions on this matter.

In a quite separate paper, however, Mansfield (1963) did examine inter-firm differences in the speed of adoption,[44] using data on 167 firms adopting 14 different innovations in various US industries. His dependent variable was d_{ij}, the number of years the ith firm waits before adopting innovation j. His strongest finding was that the size of firm was a negatively significant determinant. While there are flaws in his econometric methodology (Davies 1979: 22–5), one suspects that these are insufficiently serious to completely undermine the result, and on the face of it this offers strong support for the central role attributed to firm size in the probit models. In addition to the reasons already discussed in favour of early adoption by large firms, including scale economies in the application of the new process, Mansfield suggests that larger firms tend to adopt earlier: (a) because they are better able to bear the costs and risks, (b) because there is a greater probability of large firms needing to replace old equipment at any point in time, and (c) because they are likely to encompass a wider range of operating conditions than smaller firms; as some innovations have only limited applicability initially (Davies 1979: Ch. 3) there is greater likelihood that large firms will have the appropriate conditions for adoption of the new innovation in its early years. Mansfield also tests a variety of other potential determinants of speed of diffusion, including firms' growth rates, profitability, liquidity and profit trends, and the age of the firms' presidents. None is significant, except for proxy measures of the profitability of adoption and then for only two of the sample innovations. In three other papers using similar methodology to Mansfield (Hakonson 1974; Nabseth and Ray 1974; Smith 1974) results are also disappointing – with some patchy evidence on firm size consistent with Mansfield's being the only generally significant result.

As explained, Davies's model rests on the prediction that larger firms will tend to be quicker at adopting, but beyond this he has nothing specifically to say on the causes of inter-firm differences. On the central issue of firm size, however, data for his sample innovations offers strong support for the hypothesis. Using what he calls the industrial Engel curve,[45] which shows the incidence of adopters among different size classes at a point in time, he finds a positive relationship to firm size for all innovations (and monotonically so for all but 2 of the 22). This part of his work is subject to worries about fewness of observations for individual innovations. But taken together, and with Mansfield and others' earlier work, they offer fairly strong support for the conclusion that, within industries, larger firms tend to adopt earlier than small firms.

This does not, however, imply that large firms are 'more progressive'. As Weiss points out, it is not so much whether larger firms tend to be quicker but whether 'they are quicker than groups of smaller firms with about the same number of investment decisions to make' (1971: 396).[46] In answering Weiss's question, Davies shows (1979: 148–50) that his own results are consistent with larger firms being more progressive, in this relative sense, for only two of his sample innovations. Thus firm size is important but not necessarily conducive to more progressive industry performance in this context.

(c) INTRA-FIRM DIFFUSION

Partly because data is less readily available on the diffusion of new processes within individual firms and partly, as noted already, because in many instances the decision to adopt implies 100 per cent adoption, there have been fewer studies in this area. Again Mansfield (1968) is the innovator, using an epidemic type model. In this case he applies the equivalent of [17] where $m(t)$ refers to the firm's stock of capital embodying the new technology at time t, and n as its saturation level, that is the amount it will have when the changeover to the new technology is completed. Redefined in this way, [17] is meant to apply to any date after the initial introduction, and the rate at which old technology is converted to new is positively dependent on the level of penetration ($m(t)/n$) because the latter reflects inversely the degree of risk involved in changing over. In other words, firms learn from their own experience to successively discount the risk associated with the new technology.

It follows that intra-firm diffusion will also exhibit an S-shaped logistic curve, the speed or shape of which depends by assumption on π, the profitability of the new technology, L, the firm's liquidity, T, the date of its first adoption, and S, its size. The model is tested against data on the spread of dieselisation in 30 US railroads in 1925–60. As before, the logistic curves seems to fit the time series data satisfactorily (with an average $R^2 \approx 0.90$). In the second stage, cross-section examination of differences between firms, the speed of intra-firm diffusion is found to depend positively and significantly on π, L and T, but S is insignificant. The results on profitability and liquidity are as expected and require no further comment. The date of first adoption result implies that firms who adopted relatively later then proceeded to catch up by conducting faster intra-firm diffusion, presumably because of the lower risk attached to dieselisation as time passed, and the favourable experiences of others was observed. The insignificance of firm size confirms Mansfield's own expressed uncertainty as to which way, if at all, it should influence intra-firm diffusion.

Apart from a few empirical studies (Romeo 1975; Nabseth and Ray 1974[47]), the only other major work on this subject is Stoneman's (1981) theoretical contribution using a Bayesian learning model. The basic idea is of a firm choosing between two technologies, the old and the new, on the basis of the mean-variance theory of choice. Over time the firm learns about the characteristics of the new technology from its own experiences. This learning causes revision in the comparison, via changes in the anticipated mean and variance of returns from the new technology. Intra-firm diffusion proceeds or not, depending on what is learnt. The main attraction of this model is that it explicitly incorporates what is implicitly assumed by Mansfield, namely learning by doing. Its drawback, acknowledged by Stoneman, is its empirical intractability.

Drawing together the three strands of the diffusion literature, one is struck by the relative inattention the subject has received. Given the crucial role of diffusion as the link between innovation and productivity, this is surprising especially in the UK, a nation which suffers chronically low productivity by international standards. On the other hand, from the work that has been done, we have something approaching a consensus on the role of concentration and firm size. The regular observations of S-shaped diffusion curves also come close to establishing a 'physical law'. Theoretically, advances have been made on Mansfield's early work, although unfortunately some of the better recent theoretical work proves difficult to translate into empirical tests.

5. Productivity and market structure

As will be apparent, the theoretical and empirical literature on the technical progressiveness of different market structures defies simple generalisations or clear-cut policy implications. Both theory and empirics offer reasons for supposing that some aspects of technical change would appear to benefit from oligopolistic structures and large scale, while others are better encouraged by more competitive structures, as shown for instance by the evidence on R & D as opposed to diffusion. In these circumstances, it is natural to ask whether we have any means of establishing what is the net effect of market structure. Ideally this might be handled empirically using some overall index representing the joint effects of invention, innovation and diffusion taken together. Unfortunately no such index exists, nor is it likely to do so.[48] However, as a second best we can observe the indirect consequences of technical change to the extent that they are revealed in the overall productivity or efficiency of different industries. For example, subject to important qualifications elaborated presently, we might suppose that more technically progressive industries will record higher levels of productivity and efficiency, and faster *growth* thereof, *ceteris paribus*.

In this section, therefore, we briefly survey what is a fairly small empirical literature addressed to the question of inter-industry differences in productivity and efficiency. We concentrate, in particular, on studies employing explanatory variables measuring the structure of the industries concerned.[49] In some ways then, this section serves as an overview for the chapter as a whole. Having said this, we should be clear that there is only a very imprecise connection between progressiveness and the productivity or efficiency of the industry concerned. First, the productivity of inputs used in a given industry may reveal something about its progressiveness and with respect to new processes, but probably little about new products. Second, inasmuch as many industries rely on their suppliers for new technologies, it is not always clear whose progressiveness is reflected in productivity and efficiency measures. Third, technical progressiveness is only one of many influences on efficiency and productivity. Others which are likely to be equally, if not more, important include X inefficiency[50] and the ability of firms to respond optimally to changing factor prices. Since these other influences may also reflect the effects of market structure, there is an obvious under-identification problem. For instance, it is often argued that greater X inefficiency and/or non-optimising managerial behaviour may be tolerated in more concentrated, 'less competitive' industries.[51] If so, such industries may come off poorly in productivity and efficiency comparisons even if they generate more new innovations with superior best-practice capabilities. Similarly, a rapid growth in labour productivity is not necessarily indicative of more rapid technical change. It may merely reflect increasing capital intensity, which may, or may not, be an optimal response to changing factor prices.

(a) EFFICIENCY AND MARKET STRUCTURE

Most empirical studies of efficiency appear to derive in spirit from Farrell's seminal contribution (1957). This is based on the familiar isoquant diagram shown in Fig. 6.6a, in which the isoquant shows the locus of all best-practice factor combinations yielding a given output X_0, AB representing relative factor prices. For simplicity we consider only the two-factor case for capital and labour, K and L. As usual, cost-minimising efficient production implies point C.

But now suppose that a given firm operates at some point F off the isoquant and with an inappropriate factor intensity. Farrell suggests that we measure that firm's technical, or productive efficiency by the ratio OE/OF, and its price efficiency by OD/OE. Total efficiency, the product of the two, is then equal to OD/OF. Note then that this ratio is smaller, that is efficiency is lower, (a) the greater the firm's distance from the best-practice isoquant, and (b) the less appropriate is its chosen factor intensity, that is, the greater the divergence of the ray OF from the optimal ray OC. An obvious problem in making this measure empirically operational is that one can rarely identify the best-practice frontier in the real world. As a substitute, therefore, practitioners usually construct a convex frontier from the innermost set of observations in the sample concerned. For example, suppose that the crosses in Fig. 6.6b each refer to different firms in a given industry. Points (firms) such as G, H and I are designated as technically perfectly efficient.[52] The isoquant is

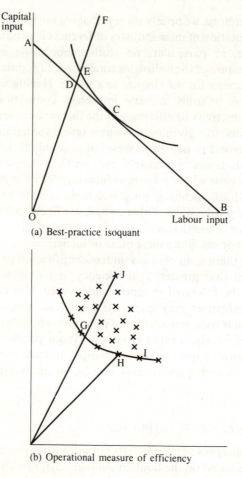

(a) Best-practice isoquant

(b) Operational measure of efficiency

FIG. 6.6 The Farrell measure of technical efficiency

then derived by joining all such points and the efficiency rating of any firm lying beyond the isoquant (e.g. J) can be deduced as already described.

This approach to efficiency has been criticised on a number of counts. For present purposes we consider only what we think is the most damning one. In replacing the hypothetical best practice by an 'isoquant' showing best attained input requirements, we effectively lose any pretensions to measuring efficiency in an absolute sense. Rather the efficiency of J, say, is expressed merely relative to the best elsewhere in the industry. There is not certainty that the best in any way corresponds to the best that could be achieved in absolute terms. It might be, for example, that all firms in a given industry are operating old vintage technology, perhaps failing to take up new technologies available elsewhere, either overseas or in other industries. In these circumstances, one might even observe all firms lying on the best attained isoquant because all are equally sluggish at introducing new techniques. In short, in practice, the Farrell measure tells us more about the distribution of efficiency within an industry than about how that industry compares to what is technologically feasible.

Carlsson (1972) provides an interesting application of this approach for a set of Swedish three-digit industries. Using establishment level data he generates, for each industry, a weighted average measure of efficiency. This is then used as the dependent variable in cross-industry analysis, with explanatory variables reflecting various elements of industry structure. His main findings are that efficiency was greatest (a) in more concentrated industries, and (b) in industries with lower protection from tariffs. However, Carlsson is disinclined to interpret the former result as evidence that market power is conducive to efficiency. In a very open small economy such as Sweden, he argues, competition is more accurately reflected by the absence or existence of tariffs. Thus he concludes that protection reduces competition and breeds inefficiency, while the effects of internal concentration reflect the benefits of scale economies and specialisation.

In a rare UK study of Farrell inefficiency, Hart (1978) failed to detect any discernible influence either way for concentration. In this case, individual observations referred to industries, not individual plants or firms, and thus the 'isoquant' was aggregate in the sense of apparently applying over all industries. It is difficult to see what the technical efficiency measure represents at this level of aggregation. The implicit assumption appears to be that all industries share the same production function, which seems somewhat unlikely. One suspects that inter-industry differences in location in the space described in Fig. 6.6 are due more to differences in technological opportunity than to technical progressiveness, or, for that matter, X inefficiency.

Largely because of problems such as those just mentioned, the Farrell measure has fallen into comparative disuse in recent years, although Todd (1985) has produced estimates again at the industry level for German manufacturing.[53]

A rather more sophisticated variation on the Farrell theme was suggested by Spence in Caves et al. (1980). He argues that there are four dimensions to inefficiency. In addition to Farrell's two concepts of efficiency, a firm or industry may be inefficient because, firstly, in minimising costs, 'it may have faced (or set, depending on its power in the factor markets in relation to the power of the factors themselves) inappropriate factor prices ... For example, *monopoly* power, unions, and imperfect capital markets may produce distortion of this type.' Secondly, 'it may fail to achieve minimum average costs because of small scale' (1980: 258). Spence considers that this fourth dimension may be of particular concern to Canada, the subject of his study. A key feature of Spence's study is to measure technical efficiency in each of his Canadian industries relative to its US counterpart, thus avoiding our worries above concerning inter-industry differences in technological opportunity. After some manipulation, Spence shows that the overall measure implied is equivalent to value added per worker in the Canadian industry relative to that in the counterpart US industry, but corrected for US–Canadian differences in product and input prices and in capital intensity. In cross-industry regression analysis (both Ordinary Least Squares and within a wider simultaneous model) a number of interesting determinants of technical efficiency are identified but there are few signs of a significant influence for direct market structure-type variables. The most important determinants identified relate to returns to scale in both production and marketing. In addition it appears that efficiency is positively influenced by foreign ownership, that is it is higher where a large proportion of the industry is controlled by foreign-owned multinational enterprises. It is only weakly influenced by trade exposure, thus offering only limited support for Carlsson's finding that in an open economy international competition is the most relative discipline. The result concerning multinationals is obviously consistent with the hypothesis that multinationals are conducive to rapid international technology transfer.

(b) PRODUCTIVITY AND MARKET STRUCTURE

There have been rather more inter-industry studies on productivity; unfortunately many have used rather limited, *ad hoc*, models leading to empirical work which is open to severe specificational worries. In general terms, productivity reflects the productiveness of the inputs used in a particular firm or industry. More specifically, most studies have concentrated on labour productivity or total factor productivity. One way of illustrating the relationship of these measures to technical progressiveness is to suppose that the relation between inputs and output can be described by the well-known Cobb–Douglas production function, with constant returns to scale,[54]

$$X = AK^{\alpha}L^{1-\alpha}$$ [26]

where X, K and L are net output, capital and labour services respectively. A is usually referred to as the efficiency parameter and is equivalent to a measure of Farrell technical efficiency. The rate of change of A reflects the rate of Hicks neutral disembodied technical change.[55] It follows that the level of labour productivity may be written as:

$$X/L = A(K/L)^{\alpha}$$ [27]

and, by differentiating the logged form of [27] with respect to time, the rate of growth of labour productivity is:

$$(\dot{X}/L)/(X/L) = \dot{A}/A + \alpha[\dot{K}/L)]/(K/L)$$ [28]

where the dot notation refers to a derivative with respect to time. The rate of growth of total factor productivity (TFP) represents the joint productivity of labour and capital, suitably weighted, and may be written here as:

$$\text{TFP} = (\dot{X}/X) - \alpha(\dot{K}/K) - (1-\alpha)(\dot{L}/L) = \dot{A}/A$$ [29]

In each case, the productivity measure is clearly related to A, or its rate of growth, $\dot{A}/A$. It is reasonable to suppose therefore, that *ceteris paribus*, productivity, or its rate of growth, will vary between industries depending on their technical progressiveness. But, as for Farrell efficiency, one would also expect X inefficiency to have an important part to play in the story. This provides a simple justification for the use of multiple regression models in which productivity is the dependent variable and in which a number of explanatory variables are included, including concentration, as determinants of A or $\dot{A}/A$. However a number of cautionary points need to be made.

First, labour productivity will clearly vary between industries depending on capital intensity, or its rate of growth, and it is essential that inter-industry differences in capital intensity be controlled for. Unfortunately most early studies failed to do this and their findings are correspondingly difficult to interpret.[56] Total factor productivity measures do not suffer from this problem since they reflect the combined effect of capital and labour.[57] The main problem here is in identifying the 'correct' value of α, i.e. the relative weights to attach to capital and labour growth. In practice α is usually estimated from observed factor shares using the restrictive assumption of marginal productivity pricing. See, for example. Peltzmann (1977) and Gisser (1984), who use this index.

Second, and a now familiar point, industries will differ in technological opportunity. Such differences, which will operate via A or $\dot{A}/A$ in this context, will arise in part because industries will be at different stages in their technological life cycle. But in addition, their underlying technological bases can be expected to differ significantly. Consider, for instance, hand-made pottery as opposed to motor vehicles. What this suggests is that comparisons should be made of performance relative to what is feasible. In recent years, a number of studies have employed performance in a second country in attempt to control this problem, but such studies are still very much in a minority. Third, the relationship between productivity and the potential determinants of A, including concentration, is most sensibly seen as only part of a larger simultaneous system.[58] In econometric terms this suggests that the prevailing use of ordinary least squares is misplaced. Again the implication is that estimates of the effects of concentration, and other variables, may be subject to bias.

We shall start our summary with a group of early studies which merely examined the correlation, or simple regression, of labour productivity growth on concentration. Therefore, they suffer from all three failures just mentioned. Perhaps not surprisingly, they also present a somewhat confused picture. Stigler (1956) examined differences in the growth of labour productivity in 29 US industries, 1899–1937, and found what appeared to be strong evidence against high concentration. Apparently, productivity increased more rapidly in low-concentration industries and especially so where concentration was declining. His conclusion was that it is the competition of new entrants which most spurs rapid technological change. Strangely however, Phillips (1956), who used a partially overlapping data set, found almost exactly the reverse: a positive correlation between productivity growth and concentration.[59] To add to the confusion, Allen (1969) found no significant difference in productivity growth between differently concentrated groups of industries when updating Stigler's data for 19 industries over various periods during 1939–64. In a British study for 12 industries 1907–48, Carter and Williams (1959) established a weakly positive correlation between labour productivity and concentration.

Following these early studies, productivity appears to have been largely overlooked by industrial economists until the late 1970s. But in more recent years further work has appeared in a number of areas. The first was largely stimulated by

Demsetz's (1973) assertion that the widely observed correlations between concentration and profitability derive more from efficiency considerations than from collusive price raising. The most recent study in this vein is by Gisser (1984), who establishes a significant positive relationship between productivity growth, both total factor and just labour, and concentration, for a sample of 314 US industries over the period 1963–72. In addition, he finds that productivity growth is higher among industries in which concentration is increasing than in those in which it is decreasing. His theoretical explanation of this involves a price-leader model in which the leading firms are responsible for inventing and innovating major new technologies, with the competitive following fringe subsequently imitating. Thus there is an initial period during which innovation by the leaders causes faster than average productivity growth and increasing concentration. The secondary phase when the smaller firms follow suit implies lower than average productivity growth and declining concentration. While Gisser fails to formalise this model, it does appear to be consistent with the 'facts' as he had identified them. Unfortunately his empirical work, and thus the reliability of those facts, is open to question. First, the explanatory power of his regression is low, typically about 10 per cent. Second, no other explanatory variables are included and no allowance is made for differences in technological opportunity. Putting this paper into an historical perspective, it belongs to a group, including Peltzman (1977), Lustgarten (1979), Kendrick and Grossman (1980) and Gisser (1982), all of which take a similar theoretical stance and establish similar sorts of results. Unfortunately, all are subject to similar criticisms.

Other recent inter-industry studies of productivity have used a much broader perspective in which concentration is only one of many explanatory variables investigated. Indeed these studies are usually more concerned with other issues, e.g. the interrelation between productivity and trade performance, or the operation of Verdoon's law at the micro level, and concentration is often included in regression equations as little more than an afterthought. Paradoxically perhaps, this more catholic approach may yet provide a sharper unbiased test of the influence of concentration than regressions such as those just described in which all other explanatory variables are ignored. For instance, Wragg and Robertson's (1978) work on the growth of labour productivity in 82 UK industries, 1963–73, employs a range of potential explanatory variables relating to labour relations, trade and capital intensity as well as concentration and plant size. Their findings of most interest for our purpose are that the level of concentration has a significantly negative impact, plant size a significantly positive impact, and exposure to foreign trade appears to have beneficial effects. Productivity growth tends to be greatest among the set of producer good industries where exports account for a larger proportion of production, and imports a larger share of the market. While there must be doubts about these authors' specificational approach,[60] and their failure to control for technological opportunity, on the face of it their results offer obvious support to the view that competition, both domestic and international, is conducive to greater technical progressiveness.

A rather more promising approach followed in a small number of recent studies involves inter-industry regression in a bilateral international context. These seem to be the most serious attempts to date to solve the technological opportunity problem. Caves (1980) examines labour productivity levels across 71 UK industries for 1968 in terms of a number of UK explanatory variables, but having first measured UK productivity relative to productivity in the corresponding US industry. One way of looking at this productivity differential is to think of it as the ratio of actual UK productivity, relative to what is attainable, or best practice.[61] Turning to Caves's results, he identifies a number of suggestive findings on the determinants of productivity, including a negative impact of managerial and labour relations, but on the issue which concerns us here, concentration, there appears to be no significant influence.[62] In another study, Saunders (1980) investigates Canadian industries, relative to their US counterparts, and again finds no significant impact for a concentration variable.

Caves's work has since extended with Davies. In their study (Davies and Caves 1987) both productivity levels and growth rates are examined for nearly 100 industries for 1977 as well as 1968. The equations are estimated within a formal production function context as part of a fuller simultaneous system in which the effects of productivity on trade performance, market and plant size, concentration and profitability are examined. Once more, however, concentration appears to have no significant influence on productivity. Their most interesting results for the present survey concern the effects of international competition, plant size and R & D. They find that the UK–US productivity differential is least *ceteris paribus* in industries which are more prone to import competition or which export on a significant scale. The differential is positively related to the R & D differential, i.e. the UK industry performs relatively better when its R & D expenditure comes closer to that of its US counterpart. The effect of plant size is less straightforward, but intriguing. They find no significant effect on comparative productivity of a variable measuring comparative plant size, but a strongly negative effect for a variable measuring absolute plant size. They interpret this to mean that UK industries perform comparatively worse in industries characterised by large plants. This is not because UK plants are bigger or smaller than their US counterparts (on average they are roughly similar) but because, where plants need to be large for technological reasons, UK industries appear to be particularly inept.[63] One suspects that this result reflects factors which are mainly to do with X inefficiency,such as inferior labour relations, loss of managerial control, rather than sluggishness among larger plants in introducing new technologies. Overall, however, the picture emerging from Davies and Caves is that, contrary to Schumpeterian expectations, concentration and large scale are not particularly conducive to rapid technical change, at least as far as it is reflected in productivity. The degree of competition does matter, but more in international than domestic terms.[64]

It seems likely that productivity and efficiency will play an increasing part in the development of the literature on industry structure and performance. At present, however, we believe that little conclusive evidence has emerged. We form this conclusion in part because of the criticisms already made concerning empirical methodology, and in part because most studies suggest that concentration has little effect. The latter is a negative finding, but one worth having. While it is dangerous to equate this directly with the statement that concentration, on balance, neither encourages nor discourages technical progress, it is fair to say that the Schumpeterian arguments are far from confirmed in this part of the literature. Perhaps this is to be expected given the theory and empirics described earlier in the chapter on the component parts of technical change.

Notes

1. Just how satisfactory patents and R & D are as observable measures of the outputs and inputs of inventive and innovative activity is discussed later. It is evident, however, that by no means all successful innovations are patented and, even more strikingly, most patented inventions never see the marketable light of day. Equally, R & D expenditures are neither necessary nor sufficient for successful innovations.

2. In practice R & D expenditures are typically dominated by the development component, research only accounting for about one-quarter of all expenditures on average in the UK since 1945.

3. Defining productivity generally as the ratio of output to inputs employed, the effects of product innovation will depend crucially on how output is measured. Normally it will be measured in value terms, the only practicable way of aggregating heterogeneous products. If the improved quality of new products is reflected by higher prices, there will be a correlation, albeit imperfect, between product innovation and productivity.

4. For a different, more technocratic, discussion of whether the Schumpeterian hypotheses are correctly interpreted, especially in modern empirical studies, see Stoneman (1983: 13–14) and the references therein. This is probably best consulted after the whole of this survey has been read.

5. It is clear that if the post-invention price were C', rather than P', the inventor could be recompensed by consumers (either directly or indirectly) with π_B, still leaving a net surplus of CABC'$-\pi_B$.

6. Graphically, a non-drastic invention generates a cost curve intersecting the MR curve at an output level less than the original competitive output, Q_c. To see that the incentive to invent is still greater for the competitive industry, proceed as follows: (i) Profit in the competitive case is CADC', and in the monopoly case P'_mEGC' – π_A; (ii) CADC' $>$ CFGC' (by inspection); (iii) P'_mEFC $<$ π_A (otherwise the monopolist would have charged P'_m pre-invention); (iv) since CFGC' = P'_mEGC' – P'EFC, from (ii) and (iii) CADC' $>$ P'_mEGC'$-\pi_A$.

7. For further work on the Arrow model, but still within the terms of reference set out by Arrow, that is not involving criticisms 1–4 above, see Kamien and Schwartz (1970), Ng (1971), Waterson (1982).

8. Since this model is concerned with the behaviour of the individual firm, with no analysis of interactions within the set of rivals, they can be viewed for these purposes as a single entity. Moreover, they may be actual rivals, already in the industry, or potential new entrants. As such the analysis may also be applicable to monopolists not protected by cast-iron entry barriers. In this sense, rivalry is a wider concept than is usual. It is, in fact, more in keeping with Schumpeterian notions of competition in that it is not equated narrowly to the level of concentration in the industry concerned.

9. In a few inessential respects we simplify the Kamien and Schwartz model. For example, we assume a static market; they allow for growth or decline. We assume the magnitudes of π_{N1} and π_{N2} do not depend on the length of the lag V-T or T-V, but they allow this possibility. Also for increased clarity our notation in [1] and [2] differs from theirs.

10. See their book for the relevant assumptions.

11. More formally, the probability that the innovation will have been made by t is $1 - \exp\{-h(D)t\}$, where D is development expenditure. For any value of t, this probability will be greater the larger is D, with h increasing with D at an increasing rate initially, but at a decreasing rate thereafter.

12. Hay and Morris (1980: Ch. 13) offer an alternative interpretation in which increased R & D leads to more new products, with P defined as a weighted average price. The specification of Needham's model is sufficiently loose to permit either.

13. The marginal conditions here are that the last £1 spent on R & D should add £1 to its sales revenue net of production costs and marginal revenue and production costs should be equal.

$$\pi = pQ(p,D) - c(Q) - D \tag{i}$$

$$\delta\pi/\delta p = Q + pQ_P - MC.Q_P = 0 \tag{ii}$$

$$\text{and } \delta\pi/\delta D = pQ_D - MC.Q_D - 1 = 0 \tag{iii}$$

To derive [5] from (iii), $(p-MC)/p = 1/pQ_D = D/pQe_D \tag{iv}$

and from [ii], $(p-MC)/p = -[Q/pQ_P] = 1/e_P \tag{v}$

Therefore $D/pQe_D = 1/e_P$ and $D/pQ = e_D/e_P$

14. This is exactly the same as the well known Dorfman–Steiner condition for optimal advertising outlays; see Waterson (1984: Ch. 7).

15. Treating all rivals as a homogeneous bloc, and abstracting for simplicity from cross-price effects. As far as the latter is concerned, think of e_p hereafter as *net* of any cross-price effects generated by rivalry over price.

16. Note that [10] corresponds to [8] with $e_D = 0$, i.e. no product innovation, and $Q_i=Q$ in [10], i.e. firm i is the only seller of this particular product. Expression [11] refers to optimality with respect to output, which also applies equally to the earlier models with $Q_i = Q$.

17. See also our discussion of this model in Chapter 3.

18. See Hamberg (1966), Mueller (1962), Peck (1962), Enos (1962).

19. For an analysis of similar UK data, both official and survey, see Pavitt *et al.* (1987); for an international comparison, see Freeman and Young (1965) and Schott (1981).

20. It is sometimes suggested that freedom from bureaucratic decision making and the need to produce results, even if trivial, puts the independent inventor at an advantage *vis-à-vis* the R & D laboratory, which is always under pressure to justify itself to the corporation as a whole.

21. Some industries, by their nature, employ more complex technologies than others. Also, technological opportunity may vary between industries depending on the stage reached in their respective life cycles. Although technological opportunity may have an impact on R & D, etc., which is, in principle, separable from firm size and concentration, a complication arises if, as is likely, technological opportunity also *influences* the latter. This is essentially the point made by Dasgupta and Stiglitz

described earlier. In econometric terms, this makes it doubly important that technological opportunity is explicitly recognised in inter-industry comparison of structure versus invention and innovation. If not, biased estimates of the impact of concentration and size are probable.

22. See, for example, any good industrial economics textbook such as Waterson (1984), Hay and Morris (1980), as well as our Chapter 3. Kamien and Schwartz (1982: 51) provide a brief discussion related to the present context.

23. See Comanor and Scherer (1969), Schmookler (1966) and Bosworth (1980) for discussion of the validity of patent data in this context.

24. So although a high R & D to sales ratio may indicate a research-intensive firm or industry, equally it may reveal that a typical pound spent on R & D adds little to sales.

25. But see Kamien and Schwartz (1982: 58) for discussion of the circumstances when this may be unwarranted.

26. See, for example, Loeb and Lin (1977), Shrieves (1978), Rosenborg (1976), Phillips (1971), Biname and Jacquemin (1973), Defay (1973), Adams (1970), Howe and McFetridge (1976), Link (1978).

27. See also Chapter 2 in this volume.

28. See Ray (1969, 1984) and Nabseth and Ray (1974) for suggestive evidence that this is precisely the case for the UK as compared to its international competitors.

29. See Davies (1979: Ch. 3) for a brief description of this and a sample of other process innovations, and for an evaluation of what seem to be a set of fairly common characteristics possessed by most contemporary new processes.

30. Other examples which establish that diffusion is often a long drawn-out process can be found in Mansfield (1961), Romeo (1975) and many other studies.

31. Griliches investigated the spread of new innovation (hybrid corn) in different states in the USA. Unlike Mansfield, he offers no formal model explaining why the diffusion curve should be logistic (see below). See also Dixon (1980) for a critical update of Griliches' work.

32. In that context eqn [17] tells us that the proportion of people previously unaffected who contract the disease in the time period depends positively on the proportion already infected. The same sort of argument applies to the spread of rumours: the chances that anyone not previously having heard of a rumour will hear of it is larger, the greater is the proportion of the population already having heard, and thus able to pass it on.

33. Equation [20] follows from [18] by cross-multiplying and taking logarithms.

34. See for example Romeo (1975, 1977), Globerman (1975), Swann (1973), Metcalfe (1970) (who uses a slightly different form of S-shaped curve).

35. Rogers (1962) provides a good survey of research areas in which S-shaped diffusion curves have been reported, including the use of steel axes by aboriginal tribes!

36. See Bonus (1973), Cramer (1969) and Aitchison and Brown (1957).

37. This is on the assumption that firm size has a favourable effect on the probability of adoption. But the model is sufficiently general to allow the contrary, in which case the inequality in [21] is reversed. Empirically, however, all his results are consistent with the former.

38. There is considerable evidence to support the lognormal actual size distribution assumption (see Chapter 3). Lognormality for the critical size distribution rests on an application of the multiplicative form of the central limit theorem.

39. Allowing for changes over time in actual firm sizes, Davies shows that there may also be cyclical fluctuations around these underlying trends, corresponding to fluctuations in the growth path of the industry.

40. Bonus models the diffusion of new consumer durables among a population in which consumer income has an analogous role to firm size in Davies's model (both being approximately lognormally distributed).

41. In this model the scale advantage derives from the assumption that the technology has a fixed cost (pr) which is invariant with respect to the scale of the firm: large firms are thus able to spread that cost over a larger output.

42. Davies (1979: Ch. 3) provides a brief introduction and reference to the literature on 'learning by doing'. He also reports some examples from his own sample of innovations.

43. Quirmbach (1986) has shown, however, that non-instantaneous diffusion in Reinganum's model is not the result of strategic behaviour; rather, it is generated by the cost assumptions of the model.

44. It should be stressed that the model of this paper is independent of (indeed inconsistent with) the epidemic model of aggregate diffusion (Davies 1979: 21).

45. The analogy here is with the income–consumption relationship studies in previous work on consumer durables.

46. This is analogous to the view that, in comparing the research activity of large and small firms, one should be concerned with relative as opposed to absolute R & D expenditure.

47. Romeo's work again imitates Mansfield but is seriously flawed by idiosyncratic econometrics (Stoneman (1983: 85–6)). Nabseth and Ray include four essentially descriptive case studies (ibid.: 86).

48. Not only would such an index require a massive act of data collection, but also it would involve insoluble conceptual difficulties. For example, what relative weights should we attach to invention, as opposed to innovation, as opposed to diffusion?

49. Thus we are concerned with only a very small part of the enormous productivity literature. We ignore, for example the macro-economic literature on productivity and growth. (See Stoneman 1983: Chs 12–15 in particular.)

50. See Leibenstein (1966, 1975, 1978) for lengthy discussions of this term, and Stigler (1976) for a critical reaction.

51. Primeaux (1977) conducts an innovative empirical analysis of costs in a sample of municipally owned local electricity utilities which suggests that greater X inefficiency is tolerated in less competitive market structures. This is consistent with Leibenstein's original expectations and advocacy.

52. Since all firms do not, of course, produce the same output, the axes are redefined empirically to measure labour and capital inputs per unit of output. Invariably outputs are proxied by value added, and researchers often measure labour *cost* on the horizontal axis (to capture differences in the quality of labour). Both practices risk systematic measurement error when there is monopoly (or monopsony) power in the product and/or labour markets.

53. Todd also includes a more general discussion of the measure.

54. We should stress that many studies do not make explicit which, if any, production function underlies their productivity measures. Here we employ the Cobb–Douglas merely because it allows us to formalise our criticisms very simply. Alternative forms of production function would change the detail, but not the substance, of the ensuing discussion.

55. See Stoneman (1983: Ch. 1) for an excellent definitional survey of technical progress in the production function context.

56. In terms of regression analysis, in which the level or rate of growth of productivity is the dependent variable, this requires the inclusion of capital intensity or its rate of growth as an explanatory variable. Failure to do this is likely to lead to biased

estimates of the effects of concentration on technical change, since capital intensity and concentration are interrelated (see Chapter 3).

57. In effect TFP is labour productivity growth corrected for the growth in capital intensity. This can be seen by re-writing [29] as:

$$\text{TFP} = (\dot{X}/L)/(X/L) - \alpha(\dot{K}/L)/(K/L)\}$$

58. Consider, for example, the relationship between concentration and productivity. In addition to any behavioural influence of concentration on productivity, there is a variety of reasons why the relationship may run in the opposite direction as well. This would be true if, say, rapid productivity growth feeds through lower prices to an increased market size, possibly attracting entry or allowing large firms to build larger plants and to enjoy scale economies, thus consolidating their dominant position. Similarly, exposure to foreign competition may influence productivity, but, equally, high growth or productivity will increase competitiveness and thus benefit trade performance.

59. Phillips in particular presented a confusing, and confused, story. He also found a positive correlation between concentration and the growth of capital intensity. He argued that the latter could also be identified with rapid technical progress and claimed that this too suggested concentrated industries are more technically progressive. This reasoning is hardly acceptable: increasing capital intensity may reflect technical progress, but equally it may merely reflect movements along a given isoquant. Such movements would, of course, generate increasing labour productivity *without* technical progress.

60. By this we mean that they appear to have followed a strategy of large-scale experimentation with different combinations of their explanatory variables in order to maximise R^2. As a result their preferred equations involve elements of double-counting, as well as arbitrary inconsistencies between producer and consumer good sub-samples. Moreover, they include as a key explanatory variable, the growth of output. Not only is this tautologically related to productivity growth, but also it points strongly to a simultaneous model.

61. Even if this is a rather flattering description of US industry, converting the dependent variable in this way should remove much of the inter-industry variation due to innate technological differences. For instance, while labour productivity will inevitably be higher in oil refining than in clothing, *ceteris paribus*, given the nature of the technologies involved, there is less reason for supposing that this will mean higher comparative productivity in UK oil refining as opposed to UK clothing. Note that this is conceptually equivalent to Spence's research design described earlier.

62. From an inspection of residuals, however, Caves (1980: 172) does appear to have identified a tendency for the variability of comparative productivity to be greater among the most concentrated industries. Thus, while there is no systematic tendency for more concentrated industries to perform better or worse on average, they are more prone to deviate substantially from that average.

63. The role of plant size was examined extensively, if rather descriptively, in three very much earlier works on UK–US productivity: Rostas (1948), Frankel (1957) and Paige and Bombach (1959). Their results are somewhat problematic (see Caves (1980: 157), but, on balance, suggest no real advantage in the UK context from larger plants.

64. Another international study which finds no significant influence for concentration is by Hart and Clarke (1980: 86–90). They use data from Scherer *et al.* (1975: tables 3.9,

3.12 and A3.7), on labour productivity in 8 industries in 6 countries. On the basis of multiple regressions including concentration and plant size as explanatory variables, and using dummy variables to control for other inter-country and inter-industry differences, they conclude 'there is no association between concentration and labour productivity when the relationship is properly specified' (ibid.: 90).

References

Adams, W. J. (1970) Firm size and research activity: France and the United States, *Quarterly Journal of Economics*, **84**, 386–409.

Aitchison, J. and **Brown, J. A. C.** (1957) *The Lognormal Distribution*, Cambridge University Press: Cambridge.

Allen, B. T. (1969) Concentration and economic progress: note, *American Economic Review*, **59**, 600–4.

Arrow, K. J. (1962) Economic welfare and the allocation of resources for invention, in National Bureau of Economic Research, *The Rate and Direction of Inventive Activity: Economic and Social Factors*, Princeton University Press: Princeton, N.J.

Barzel, Y. (1968) Optimal timing of innovations, *Review of Economics and Statistics*, **50**, 348–55.

Biname, J. P. and **Jacquemin, A.** (1973) Structures industrielles des regions belges et grandes entreprises, *Reserches Economiques de Louvain*, **39**, 437–58.

Blaug, M. (1963) A survey of the theory of process innovations, *Economica*, **30**, 13–32.

Bonus, H. (1973) Quasi-Engel curves, diffusion and the ownership of major consumer durables, *Journal of Political Economy*, **81**, 655–77.

Bosworth, D. (1980) *Statistics of Technology (Invention and Innovation)*, Review no. 28, Reviews of UK Statistical Sources, Heinemann: London.

Buxton, A. J. (1975) The process of technical change in U.K. manufacturing, *Applied Economics*, **7**, 53–71.

Carlsson, B. (1972) The measurement of efficiency in production: an application to Swedish manufacturing industries, *Swedish Journal of Economics*, **74**, 468–85.

Carter, C. and **Williams, B.** (1959) *Investment in Innovation*, Oxford University Press: Oxford.

Caves, R. E. (1980) Productivity differences among industries, in Caves, R. E. and Krause, L. B. (eds), *Britain's Economic Performance*, Brookings Institution: Washington, pp. 135–92.

Caves, R. E., Porter, M. E., and **Spence, A. M.,** with **Scott, J. T.** (1980) *Competition in the Open Economy*, Harvard University Press: Cambridge, Mass.

Clarke, R. (1985) *Industrial Economics*, Basil Blackwell: Oxford.

Comanor, W. S. (1965) Research and technical change in the pharmaceutical industry, *Review of Economics and Statistics*, **47**, 182–90.

Comanor, W. S. (1967) Market structure, product differentiation and industrial research, *Quarterly Journal of Economics*, **81**, 639–57.

Comanor, W. S. and **Scherer, F. M.** (1969) Patent statistics as a measure of technical change, *Journal of Political Economy*, **77**, 392–8.

Cramer, J. S. (1969) *Empirical Econometrics*, North Holland: Amsterdam.

Dasgupta, P. and **Stiglitz, J.** (1980a) Industrial structure and the nature of innovative activity, *Economic Journal*, **90**, 266–93.

Dasgupta, P. and **Stiglitz, J.** (1980b) Uncertainty, industrial structure and the speed of R & D, *Bell Journal of Economics*, **11**, 1–28.

David, P. A. (1969) *A Contribution to the Theory of Diffusion*, Stanford Centre for Research in Economic Growth, Memo. No. 71: Stanford.

Davies, S. W. (1979) *Diffusion of Process Innovations*, Cambridge University Press: Cambridge.

Davies, S. W. and Caves, R. E. (1987) *Britain's Productivity Lag*, Cambridge University Press: Cambridge.

Defay, J. (1973) *Reserche et croissance economique*, 3, S.P.P.S., Brussels.

Demsetz, H. (1969) Information and efficiency: another viewpoint, *Journal of Law and Economics*, **12**, 1–22.

Demsetz, H. (1973) Industry structure, market rivalry and public policy, *Journal of Law and Economics*, **16**, 1–9.

Dixon, R. (1980) Hybird corn re-visited, *Econometrica*, **48**, 1451–62.

Enos, J. L. (1962) Invention and innovation in the petroleum refining industry, in Nelson, R. R. (ed.), *The Rate and Direction of Inventive Activity: Economic and Social Factors*, Princeton University Press: Princeton, N.J.

Farber, S. (1981) Buyer market structure and R & D effort: a simultaneous equation model, *Review of Economics and Statistics*, **63**, 336–45.

Farrell, M. L. (1957) The measurement of productive efficiency, *Journal of the Royal Statistical Society*, series A, **120**(III), 253–6.

Finney, D. (1957) *Probit Analysis, a Statistical Treatment of the Sigmoid Response Curve*, Cambridge University Press: Cambridge.

Finet, P. (1975) Determinants de la recherche-development industrielle en Belgique, *Recherches Economiques de Louvain*, **41**, 51–61.

Frankel, M. (1957) *British and American Productivity*, Bureau of Economic and Business Research, University of Illinois, Bulletin 81, University of Illinois Press: Urbana.

Freeman, C. (1971) The role of small firms in innovation in the United Kingdom since 1945, Committee of Inquiry on Small Firms, *Research Report no.6*: London.

Freeman, C. (1974) *The Economics of Industrial Innovation*, Penguin: Harmondsworth.

Freeman, C. and Young, A. (1965) *The R & D Effort in Western Europe, North America and the Soviet Union*, O.E.C.D.: Paris.

Gisser, M. (1982) Welfare implications of oligopoly in U.S. Food manufacturing, *American Journal of Agricultural Economics*, **64**, 616–24.

Gisser, M. (1984) Price leadership and dynamic aspects of oligopoly in U.S. manufacturing, *Journal of Political Economy*, **92**, 1035–48.

Globerman, S. (1973) Market structure and R & D in Canadian manufacturing industries, *Quarterly Review of Economics and Business*, **13**, 59–67.

Globerman, S. (1975) Technological diffusion in the Canadian Tool and Die industry, *Review of Economics and Statistics*, **57**, 428–34.

Grabowski, H. G. (1968) The determinants of industrial R & D: a study of the chemical, drug and petroleum industries, *Journal of Political Economy*, **76**, 292–306.

Grilliches, Z. (1957) Hybrid corn: an exploration of the economics of technological change, *Econometrica*, **25**, 501–22.

Hakonson, S. (1974) Special presses in paper making, in Nabseth, L. and Ray, G. F. (q.v.), Ch. 4.

Hamberg, D. (1966) *R & D: Essays on the Economics of Research and Development*, Random House: New York.

Hart, P. E. (1978) Farrell-efficiency, profitability and market structure, University of Reading Discussion Paper, Series A, **107**. University of Reading.

Hart, P. E. and Clarke, R. (1980), *Concentration in British Industry. 1935–75*. Cambridge University Press: Cambridge.

Hart, P. E. and Prais, S. J. (1956) The analysis of business concentration: a statistical approach, *Journal of the Royal Statistical Society*, series A, **119**, 150–91.

Hay, D. A. and **Morris, D. J.** (1980) *Industrial Economics: Theory and Evidence*, Oxford University Press: Oxford.

Howe, J. D. and **McFetridge, D. G.** (1976) The determinants of R & D expenditure, *Canadian Journal of Economics*, **9**, 57–71.

Hughes, K. (1986) *Exports and Technology*, Cambridge University Press: Cambridge.

Jewkes, J., Sawers, D. and **Stillerman, R.** (1969) *The Sources of Invention*, (2nd edn), Norton: New York.

Johannison, B. and **Lindstrom, C.** (1971) Firm size and inventive activity, *Swedish Journal of Economics*, **73**, 427–42.

Kami, T. (1979) The activity of the firm under technological rivalry, Mimeo, Northwestern University.

Kamien, M. I. and **Schwartz, N. L.** (1970) Market structure, elasticity of demand and the incentive to invent, *Journal of Law and Economics*, **13** 241–52.

Kamien, M. I. and **Schwartz, N. L.** (1982) *Market Structure and Innovation*, Cambridge University Press: Cambridge.

Kelley, K. H. (1979) *The Economics of Risky Innovation*, Ph.D. dissertation, SUNY at Stony Brook.

Kendrick, J. W. and **Grossman, E. S.** (1980) *Productivity in the United States: Trends and Cycles*, Johns Hopkins University Press: Baltimore.

Lee, T. and **Wilde, L.** (1980) Market structure and innovation: a reformulation, *Quarterly Journal of Economics*, **94**, 429–36.

Leech, D. and **Stoneman, P.** (1976) An application of random coefficient regression: the case of R & D expenditure and market structure, *Warwick Economic Research Papers no. 91*, July.

Leibenstein, H. (1966) Allocative efficiency vs X-efficiency, *American Economic Review*, **56**, 392–415.

Leibenstein, H. (1975) Aspects of the x-efficiency theory of the firm, *Bell Journal of Economics*, **6**, 580–606.

Leibenstein, H. (1978) On the basic proposition of x-efficiency theory, *American Economic Review, Papers and Proceedings*, **68**, 238–42.

Levin, R. C. (1978) Technical change, barriers to entry and market structure, *Economica*, **45**, 347–61.

Link, A. N. (1978) Rates of induced technology from investment in R & D, *Southern Economic Journal*, **45**, 370–9.

Loeb, P. D. and **Lin, V.** (1977) Research and development in the pharmaceutical industry, *Journal of Industrial Economics*, **26**, 45–51.

Loury, G. C. (1979) Market structure and innovation, *Quarterly Journal of Economics*, **93**, 395–410.

Lustgarten, S. (1979) Gains and losses from concentration: a comment, *Journal of Law and Economics*, **22**, 183–90.

McLean, I. W. and **Round, D. K.** (1978) Research and product innovation in Australian manufacturing industries, *Journal of Industrial Economics*, **27**, 1–12.

Mansfield, E. (1961) Technical change and the rate of innovation, *Econometrica*, **29**, 741–66.

Mansfield, E. (1963) The speed of response of firms to new techniques, *Quarterly Journal of Economics*, **77**, 290–311.

Mansfield, E. (1968) *Industrial Research and Technological Innovation*, Norton: London.

Mansfield, E. *et al.* (1971) *Research and Innovation in the Modern Corporation*, Norton: New York.

Metcalfe, J. S. (1970) Diffusion of innovations in the Lancashire textile industry, *Manchester School* **38**, 145–62.

Mueller, W. F. (1962) The origins of the basic inventions underlying Du Pont's major product and process innovations, 1920–50, in Nelson, R. R. (ed.), *The Rate and Direction of Inventive Activity: Economic and Social Factors*, Princeton University Press: Princeton, N.J.

Nabseth, L. and **Ray, G. F.** (1974) *The Diffusion of New Industrial Processes: An International Study*, Cambridge University Press: Cambridge.

Needham, D. (1975) Market structure and firms' R & D behaviour, *Journal of Industrial Economics*, **23**, 241–55.

Nelson, R. R. and **Winter, S. G.** (1978) Forces generating and limiting competition under Schumpeterian competition, *Bell Journal of Economics*, **9**, 524–48.

Nelson, R. R. and **Winter, S. G.** (1982) *An Evolutionary Theory of Economic Change*, Harvard University Press: Cambridge, Mass.

Ng, Y. K. (1971) Competition, monopoly and the incentive to invent, *Australian Economic Papers*, **10**, 45–9.

Paige, D. and **Bombach, G.** (1959) *A Comparison of National Output and Productivity in the United Kingdom and the United States*, O.E.C.D.: Paris.

Pavitt, K. and **Wald, S.** (1971) *The Conditions for Success in Technological Innovation*, O.E.C.D.: Paris.

Pavitt, K., Robson, M. and **Townsend, J.** (1987) The size distribution of innovating firms in the U.K.: 1945–83, *Journal of Industrial Economics*, **35**, 297–316.

Peck, M. J. (1962) Inventions in the post-war American aluminium industry. In Nelson, R. R., (ed.), *The Rate and Direction of Inventive Activity: Economic and Social Factors*, Princeton University Press: Princeton, N.J.

Peltzman, S. (1977) The gains and losses from industrial concentration, *Journal of Law and Economics*, **22**, 209–11.

Philips, L. (1971) Research, Ch. 5 in *Effects of Industrial Concentration: A Cross-section Analysis for the Common Market*, North Holland: Amsterdam.

Phillips, A. (1956) Concentration, scale and technological change in selected manufacturing industries, 1899–1939, *Journal of Industrial Economics*, **4**, 179–93.

Phillips, A. (1971) *Technology and Market Structure: A Study of the Aircraft Industry*, Heath Lexington Books: Lexington, Mass.

Primeaux, W. J. (1977) An assessment of x-efficiency gained through competition, *Review of Economics and Statistics*, **59**, 105–8.

Quirmbach, H. C. (1986) The diffusion of new technology and the market for an innovation, *Rand Journal of Economics*, **17**, 33–47.

Ray, G. F. (1969) The diffusion of new technology, *National Institute Economic Review*, **48**, 40–83.

Ray, G. F. (1984) *The Diffusion of Mature Technologies*, Cambridge University Press: Cambridge.

Reinganum, J. F. (1979) *Dynamic Games with R & D Rivalry*, Ph.D. dissertation, Northwestern University

Reinganum, J. F. (1981) Market structure and the diffusion of new technology, *Bell Journal of Economics*, **12**, 618–24.

Reinganum, J. F. (1982) A dynamic game of R & D: patent protection and competitive behaviour, *Econometrica*, **50**, 671–88.

Reinganum, J. F. (1984) Practical implications of game theoretic models of R & D, *American Economic Review, Papers and Proceedings*, **74**, 61–6.

Rogers, E. M. (1962) *The Diffusion of Innovations*, Free Press: New York.

Romeo, A. A. (1975) Interindustry and interfirm differences in the rate of diffusion of an innovation, *Review of Economics and Statistics*, **57**, 311–19.

Romeo, A. A. (1977) The rate of imitation of a capital embodied process innovation, *Economica*, **44**, 63–9.

Rosenborg, N. (1976) On technological expectations, *Economic Journal,* **86**, 523–35.

Rostas, L. (1948) *Comparative Productivity in British and American Industry*, National Institute of Economic and Social Research, Occasional Paper no. 13, Cambridge University Press: Cambridge.

Salter, W. (1960) *Productivity and Technical Change*, Cambridge University Press: Cambridge.

Saunders, R. (1980) The determinants of productivity in Canadian manufacturing industries, *Journal of Industrial Economics*, **29**, 167–84.

Scherer, F. M. (1965a) Size of firm, oligopoly and research: a comment, *Canadian Journal of Economics*, **31**, 256–66.

Scherer, F. M. (1965b) Firm size, market structure, opportunity, and the output of patented inventions, *American Economic Review*, **55**, 1097–125.

Scherer, F. M. (1967a) Market structure and the employment of scientists and engineers, *American Economic Review*, **57**, 524–31.

Scherer, F. M. (1967b) Research and development allocation under rivalry, *Quarterly Journal of Economics*, **71**, 359–94.

Scherer, F. M. (1970) *Industrial Market Structure and Economic Performance*, Rand McNally: Chicago.

Scherer, F. M., Beckstein, A., Kaufer, E. and Murphy, R. D. (1975) *The Economics of Multi-plant Operations*, Harvard University Press: Cambridge, Mass.

Schmookler, J. (1966) *Invention and Economic Growth*, Harvard University Press: Cambridge, Mass.

Schott, K. (1981) *Industrial Innovation in the United Kingdom, Canada and the United States*, British North America Committee: London.

Schumpeter, J. A. (1934) *The Theory of Economic Development*, Harvard University Press: Cambridge, Mass.

Schumpeter, J. A. (1939) *Business Cycles*, McGraw-Hill: New York.

Schumpeter, J. A. (1942) *Capitalism, Socialism and Democracy*, Unwin: London.

Shrieves, R. E. (1976) Firm size and innovation: further evidence, *Industrial Organisation Review*, **4**, 26–33.

Shrieves, R. E. (1978) Market Structure and innovation: a new perspective, *Journal of Industrial Economics*, **26**, 329–47.

Smith, R. (1974) Shuttleless looms in weaving, in Nabseth and Ray (q.v.).

Smyth, D. J., Samuels, J. M., and Tzoannos, J. (1972) Patents, profitability, liquidity and firm size, *Applied Economics*, **4**, 77–86.

Stigler, G. J. (1956) Industrial organisation and economic progress, in White, L. D. (ed.), *The State of the Social Sciences*, University of Chicago Press: Chicago, pp. 269–82.

Stigler, G. J. (1976) The existence of x-efficiency, *American Economic Review*, **66**, 213–6.

Stoneman, P. (1981) Intrafirm diffusion, Bayesian learning and profitability, *Economic Journal*, **91**, 375–88.

Stoneman, P. (1983) *The Economic Analysis of Technological Change*, Oxford University Press: Oxford.

Stoneman, P. and Ireland, N. (1983) The role of supply factors in the diffusion of new process technology, *Economic Journal*, supplement, **93**, 66–78.

Stoneman, P. and Leech, D. (1980) Product innovation, process innovation and the R & D/market structure relationship, Paper presented at the EARIE conference, Basle.

Swann, P. L. (1973) The international diffusion of an innovation, *Journal of Industrial Economics*, **22**, 61–9.

Todd, D. (1985) Productive performance in West German manufacturing industry 1970–80: a Farrell frontier characterisation, *Journal of Industrial Economics*, **33**, 295–316.

Waterson, M. (1982) The incentive to invent when a new input is involved, *Economica*, **49**, 435–45.

Waterson, M. (1984) *Economic Theory of the Industry*, Cambridge University Press: Cambridge.

Weiss, L. W. (1971) Quantitative studies of industrial organisation, in Intriligator, M. D. (ed.), *Frontiers of Quantitative Economics*, North Holland: Amsterdam.

Williamson, O.E. (1965) Innovation and market structure, *Journal of Political Economy*, **73**, 67–73.

Wragg, R. and **Robertson, J.** (1978) *Post-War Trends in Employment, Productivity, Output, Labour Costs and Prices by Industry in the U.K.*, Department of Employment, Research Paper no. 3, HMSO: London.

Index